THE RISE OF
THE ENGLISH SHIPPING INDUSTRY

THE RISE OF THE ENGLISH SHIPPING INDUSTRY

In the Seventeenth and Eighteenth Centuries

BY

RALPH DAVIS

Some men of noble stock were made: some
glory in the murder-blade:
Some praise a Science or an Art, but I
like honourable Trade!

J. E. FLECKER

DAVID & CHARLES : NEWTON ABBOT

ISBN 0 7153 5462 0

© R. Davis 1962

First published 1962
Second Impression 1972

Reproduced and Printed in Great Britain by
Redwood Press Limited, Trowbridge & London
for David & Charles (Publishers) Limited
Newton Abbot   Devon

INTRODUCTION

NINE years after the first publication of this book, it is pleasant to record that later works touching on some of the areas it covered have on the whole confirmed or supplemented, rather than overturned the conclusions that I came to. The most noteworthy new work, because closest to the central interests I had in writing the book, is that on the costs of sea transport, begun independently by Douglass North and issuing in a series of articles by him and his collaborator, Gary Walton.[1] They attempt to quantify the decline in shipping costs with some precision, and come to conclusions similar to my own in attributing it in large degree to improved trading organisation and to greater safety from plunderers at sea; though I think they underestimate the part played by technical improvement in ships. W. Salisbury has thrown much new light on the problem of measurement of ships' tonnage, in a series of articles in the *Mariners Mirror* (XXII-XXIV, 1966-68)[2] though I still hold the view that measured tonnage was a concept of only very limited importance to the operator of ships. David Syrett's *Shipping and the American War, 1775-83* (London, 1970) is a very thorough examination of government employment of merchant shipping in wartime, and reinforces my view that this practice was of considerable value to the ship-owner in enabling him to opt out of some wartime risks. A new series of volumes on the history of English ports, the first of which, Francis Hyde's *Liverpool and the Mersey* (Newton Abbot, 1971) appeared recently, promises to fill in this part of the background against which the shipping industry worked.

In this book I elected to deal with the English shipping industry as a service industry that carried goods and people by sea. I therefore ignored the fishery, which is an extractive industry that happens to be carried on at sea. Coastal shipping, on the other hand, was omitted because it was already covered very adequately

---

[1] Notably, D. C. North 'Sources of Productivity Change in Ocean Shipping 1600-1850 *Journal of Political Economy* XXVI, 1968, G. M. Walton 'Sources of Productivity Change in American Colonial Shipping 1665-1775' (*Ec.H.R.*XX, 1967); 'A Measure of Productivity Change in American Colonial Shipping' (*Ec.H.R.*XXI, 1968); G. M. Walton, 'Obstacles to Technical Diffusion in Ocean Shipping, 1675-1775 (*Explorations in Economic History* VIII, 1970).

[2] See also, J. J. McCusker 'Colonial Tonnage Measurement' (*Journal of Economic History* XXVII, 1967).

by two well-known works, J. U. Nef's *Rise of the British Coal Industry* (London, 1932) and T. 'S. Willan's *The English Coasting Trade, 1600-1750* (Manchester 1938). And so, notwithstanding the fact that at different times during the period covered by this book between a quarter and a half of the tonnage of English-owned ships was engaged in either fishing or coasting, this book is about ships in overseas trade.

In a very long and kind review of the original edition,[1] G. V. Scammell drew attention to the fact that the technical history of the merchant ship and of the industry that built it, still remains a largely unexplored field. There has been virtually no advance on this side of the subject in the last decade, though mention should be made of Howard Chapelle's *The Search for Speed under Sail, 1700-1855* (London, 1968) which just touches on the later period of this book. There is much material, some of it mentioned in these pages, from which such a history could be written. Ship design was not one of those technologies that stood still over the centuries before the Industrial Revolution. The changes introduced by the Dutch in the sixteenth and seventeenth centuries, and by English, French and Americans in the eighteenth century, were of real economic importance, having a significant influence on costs, and playing their part in bringing to the forefront the shipping industries of particular countries. It is a subject that I hope will not be too long neglected.

I have taken the opportunity in this new edition to correct a few minor factual errors that have been brought to my notice.

October, 1971   RALPH DAVIS

[1] *English Historical Review*, LXXIX (1964) pp. 555-561.

PREFACE

Books on ships and the sea crowd the shelves of our libraries in endless variety, and scores of new ones appear every year to feed an appetite for the subject which appears insatiable. Naturally enough, the majority of them look to the more romantic or exciting aspects; to stirring adventures, wartime heroism, the hazards of exploration and the picturesque exploits of individuals. All the same, it is surprising that hardly anyone has ever attempted to examine the practical functioning of the shipping industry before modern times, and the material reasons for its growth. Most ships, after all, exist to carry on trade; the principal function of the navy has been to protect traders; and the people who kept the whole complex of trade in motion were anxious to see certainty and routine rather than speculation and excitement in the operation of their ships. Shipowners in sailing ship days, no less than in the era of diesel engines, were in the business for profit. Even Sir Francis Drake owed a good deal of popularity to the good dividends he paid! I hope this book will help all who are interested in ships, from whatever point of view, to see their own special interests against the background of the regular, year-round functioning of a great industry; one from which, like any other, men expected to earn their livings.

My second aim has been to cast a little more light into two centuries of our economic history. The prime question of modern economic history is that of the causation of the Industrial Revolution in England. We are still very far from answering it, and the solution will only come when we can apply our economic ideas to a much wider range of information about the preceding century or two than we have at present. It is my belief that one particularly fruitful field of study may be that of the development of overseas trade and its influences throughout the economy. In examining an industry which was ancillary to trade I hope I have contributed to this wider study, providing another foothold for those who will eventually advance to an explanation of how, in late eighteenth-century England, there came about an industrial explosion that has transformed the world.

I owe a debt to many institutions and individuals for their help.

First I should mention those that gave much needed financial assistance in the early stages of the work; the University of London (through its Central Research Fund) and the Houblon-Norman Fund. Then I must thank the many institutions which gave me access to their records, and the officials who were unfailingly helpful and courteous. Most of my work was done in the British Museum and the Public Record Office, and the Libraries of the Universities of London and Hull and of the London School of Economics, and in the Bodleian Library. The Guildhall Library, London, and the City of London Record Office, the Liverpool Public Library and the Essex County Record Office provided much valuable material. And I am grateful to the Chairman of Lloyd's for giving me access to the Bowrey and other MSS. owned by the Corporation; to the Institute of Chartered Shipbrokers for the use of the Aylward MSS.; and to H.M. Board of Customs and Excise for permission to use the Liverpool Plantation Registers.

The individuals who at one time or another have given advice and assistance are too many to list. I must, however, acknowledge my special debt to three of them, whose criticisms have effected great improvements in the book; to Mr. Robert Craig and Professor F. J. Fisher, both of whom read nearly all the book, and to my wife who read it all — many, many times.

March 1962.   R.D.

CONTENTS

LIST OF ILLUSTRATIONS

ABBREVIATIONS

Add.MSS.	Additional Manuscripts
Adm.	Admiralty
APC	Acts of the Privy Council
BM	British Museum
BT	Board of Trade
CO	Colonial Office
CSPAWI	Calendar of State Papers, Colonial (America and West Indies).
CSPD	Calendar of State Papers, Domestic
CSPV	Calendar of State Papers, Venetian
Econ. Hist. Rev.	Economic History Review
HCA	High Court of Admiralty
HMC	Historical Manuscripts Commission
PRO	Public Record Office
SP	State Papers
T	Treasury
TRHS	Transactions of the Royal Historical Society

Unless otherwise indicated, manuscripts cited
are in the Public Record Office.

I

The Widening of Horizons, 1560-1689

Popular interest in the maritime exploits of the first Elizabethans never fades. The story of the defeat of the Spanish Armada is gratifying not only to English patriotism but to all who welcome the humbling of the arrogant, defiance of the oppressor, the defeat of the great menace by the small, brave victim. The story is a true one, but as its by-product it has produced a myth; the myth of a nation of seafaring Englishmen confronting a Spain of landlubbers, a Spanish fleet manned by soldiers and the conscripted occupants of the country's jails. The truth is that Spain in 1588 controlled a merchant fleet which, if it was rivalled at all in Europe, was rivalled only by the Dutch; a fleet manned from the coasts of Biscay and Leon and from the newly-acquired Kingdom of Portugal, which had been for centuries the homes of a hardy race of seamen.[1] The English by contrast, so far from being at that time the heirs to generations of seagoers, were newcomers to ocean trade and shipping.

In 1560, when an anxious government first investigated in detail the resources available for the defence of Elizabeth I's realm, the English owned, perhaps, some 50,000 tons of merchant shipping of every kind;[2] in 1572 the total had hardly grown, and it included only fourteen ships of two hundred tons or more.[3] At this time the Dutch were creating the greatest of European shipping industries; in the year 1562 the Dutch ships entering the Baltic to fetch timber and corn and hemp numbered 1192, the English 51.[4]

---

[1] A. P. Usher, 'Spanish Ships and Shipping in the 16th and 17th Centuries', in *Facts and Factors in Economic History* (Cambridge, Mass., 1932), p. 192.

[2] SP 12–11–27 lists ships over 100 tons; the total is close to that of 1572, when the total tonnage of English shipping was recorded as some 50,000 tons. The lists quoted here and on the following pages, for years between 1560 and 1629, were evidently compiled with care, and there is no reason to doubt their substantial accuracy. Omissions due to the failure of some officials to send in returns, can usually be filled without too much danger of error. The tonnage appears to be tons burden, the only figure readily available, for all ships, to shipowners and officials.

[3] SP 12–22.

[4] N. E. Bang, *Tabeller over Skibsfart og Varetransport Gennem Oresund, 1497–1660* (Copenhagen, 1906).

Dutch seamen coasted all along the edges of Europe from the Skaw to the Straits of Gibraltar, and to Norway and England, with southern wine and salt, Baltic goods and herring of their own catching. In the Mediterranean the tartanes of Marseilles, the argosies of Venice, Ragusa and Genoa, the galleys of Barcelona, Seville and Cadiz carried to and fro not merely precious cargoes but also vast tonnages of corn, salt and flax. The Spaniards and Portuguese had their fleets of great ships for the passage of the Atlantic and the Indian Oceans to far-distant possessions. In 1560 England ranked low among the maritime states; though her navy was a real force, her merchant fleet was by European standards an insignificant one. It stood far behind that of the Dutch, who were beginning to mutter against their Spanish masters;[1] far behind the combined tonnage of Spain and Portugal; behind Hamburg and perhaps even the declining Hanse city of Lubeck; probably behind France; behind Venice or even Ragusa and Genoa. A meagre coastal traffic, a fishery of moderate scale, a trickle of carrying traffic with the Low Countries, Spain, Portugal, France and the Baltic; this was the maritime basis which Elizabeth I inherited.[2]

If the Spanish Armada had come at the beginning of Elizabeth's reign instead of in the latter part of it (and the Spaniards, Portuguese, Italians, and Germans who contributed ships and crews could have mustered a strong force at any time during this period) it would have attacked an England deficient not merely in naval strength, but even more in the supporting merchant ships and in the crews to man either. The basis on which England established itself in 1588 as the first naval power of Europe was created only during the previous two decades. The mid-sixteenth century may well mark the nadir of English merchant shipping; the seventies certainly saw the beginning of great expansion both in quantity and in kind.[3]

[1] The territories which make up present-day Holland and Belgium were at this time still united as the Spanish Netherlands, but the shipping industry was heavily concentrated in the northern part which was soon to achieve independence of Spain.

[2] Those readers who are familiar with the history of English trade are here reminded that the *volume*, not the *value*, of trade determines the employment of shipping. The point is elaborated in Chapter IX, below.

[3] H. D. Burwash, *English Merchant Shipping, 1460–1540* (Toronto, 1947) pp. 145–64 shows that in the early part of the sixteenth century there had been some expansion of shipping in London and south-western ports, but this was not maintained. G. V. Scammell has recently produced evidence of some growth in the east coast ports in mid-century ('English Merchant Shipping at the end of the Middle Ages; some East Coast evidence', *Econ. Hist. Rev.*, 2nd ser., Vol. XIII, 1961, pp. 327–42).

What were the services which the mid-century shipping industry had to perform? It transported round the English coasts a volume of goods which cannot be guessed at, but which we know had hardly been affected yet by the expansion of coal shipment. It met the requirements of the fisheries, which, employing many vessels in the North Sea and off the coast of Iceland, were also beginning to attract numbers of ships from Devon and Cornwall to the Newfoundland Banks. Foreign trade presented a depressing picture to the shipping industry; though trade was prospering, it was heavily concentrated on nearby ports of the continent from which, as Burleigh wrote, 'One hoye will bryng as much in one yere as 10 merchantes shippes war wont to bryng from the other places in two yeres.'[1] In this as in many other respects the overwhelming weight of the great commercial city of Antwerp was felt; a vast engine through which the streams of trade of northwest Europe were pumped with great and ever-increasing efficiency, draining life from those byways which sought to provide direct sea links between lesser commercial centres.

About the middle of the century, however, new developments set in motion an expansion, which was long to continue, in two branches of English shipping. The first of these was the fisheries; the second, the coal trade. It is difficult to gauge the importance of the fisheries in mid-century, but they were thought to be at a low ebb, and there was much legislation to stimulate them;[2] indeed, Elizabethan legislation on shipping appears almost as a by-product of this concern with fisheries. Favoured by legislation and the demands of a fast-growing population, the fishery in European waters underwent a considerable expansion; by 1614 the East Anglian ports employed over a hundred vessels in the Iceland fishery, besides a great number of smaller craft fishing the North Sea.[3] Even more important, perhaps, was the development of interest in the cod fisheries of the Newfoundland Banks by merchants and seamen in the south-western ports. From this time until the Civil War the number of ships putting out from the small harbours of Devon, Cornwall and Dorset was continually

[1] R. H. Tawney and E. Power (eds.), *Tudor Economic Documents* (1924), Vol. II, p. 125.

[2] The most important measure was 5 Eliz., c. 5 (1563) which sought to increase consumption of fish by declaring Wednesday, in addition to Friday, a day on which fish must be eaten.

[3] Tobias Gentleman, 'England's Way to Win Wealth' (1614) and 'The Trades Increase' (1615), both in *Harleian Miscellany*, Vol. III, p. 403; Vol. IV, p. 222.

growing.[1] The experience of ocean voyaging to Newfoundland, in which so many seamen were trained, must have been invaluable to Hawkins and others in Devon who developed larger ideas of trade and privateering on the African coast and in the Caribbean.

Moreover, many ships, large and small, came to be employed in carrying fish to Spain and the Mediterranean. During the first three decades of the seventeenth century Yarmouth was permitted by the crown to export much of its red herring in foreign ships, but this privilege, constantly attacked by the shipping interest, was abandoned when war stopped the Dutch ships coming. It was on this branch of the carrying trade that Monson wrote in the thirties:

> 'True it is that there is no commodity in the world of so great bulk and small value, or that can set so many ships of burden to work. As for example: a mean merchant may freight his ship of 250 tons with fish that will not cost above £1,600, that forty merchants cannot do of richer and better commodities.'[2]

The second development, the growth of the east coast coal trade, has been exhaustively discussed by Professor J. U. Nef.[3] This too began a little before the middle of the sixteenth century, ran on with great vigour until the Civil War, and then began to slacken its pace.

Newcastle Coal Shipments (000 tons)

1549-50	35·3
1597-8	140·7
1633-4	409·3
1697-8	560·2[4]

The main impulses to the expansion of the total tonnage of English shipping during the whole of the century preceding the Civil War came from these two trades; a writer in 1615 declared that two-thirds of English seamen were employed in the coal trade and the fisheries.[5] One oceanic and one coastal, each was able to absorb and train large numbers of raw landsmen, and turn them into seamen fit to take part in sea affairs in any part of the world.

[1] H. A. Innis *The Cod Fisheries* (Toronto, 1954), Ch. III.
[2] M. Oppenheim (ed.), *The Naval Works of Sir William Monson* (Navy Records Society, 1913), Vol. V, p. 235. He estimates (p. 271) that this cargo worth £1,600 will earn £1,250 in freight to Venice.
[3] J. U. Nef, *The Rise of the British Coal Industry* (1932).
[4] ibid., App. D.
[5] 'The Trades Increase' (1615), *Harleian Miscellany*, Vol. IV, pp. 212–31.

But, important though these occupations were, both of them, at this time, used small ships; they did not contribute to the building up of a fleet of large merchantmen except so far as fishing helped to make up outward cargoes. The creation of such a fleet, from the seventies onward, was due to a number of quite different factors. One was the decline of the Low Countries into war against their Spanish masters, proceeding through local uprisings from 1566 to the general revolt of 1572, the sack of Antwerp by mutinous Spanish troops in 1576, and the closing of the Scheldt in 1585 which obliterated Antwerp as a centre for seaborne trade. For twenty years the goods which Englishmen had been accustomed to bring across the narrow seas from the great entrepôt on the Scheldt and from Amsterdam had to be fetched from other places. True, the old trans-European routes from the Baltic and the Mediterranean to ports of the Rhine delta were re-established as war receded — particularly after 1590 — but by that time the English had firmly established themselves in the Mediterranean,[1] and privateering was bringing in a great variety of the goods of Southern Europe, India and America.[2] The Dutch shipping based on Amsterdam, which for a few years when Holland and Zealand were struggling for life disappeared from the Baltic trade, returned in great strength during the nineties; but the English had meanwhile established themselves in the gap which the Dutch had left, making firm trading arrangements with the port of Elbing, and they maintained a Baltic foothold.

From 1570 onward, a number of influences were strengthening the direct English connections with the Mediterranean. In part, English ships were simply exploiting the opportunites offered by the development under the Dukes of Tuscany of their port of Leghorn, which was within easy reach of Cadiz and Malaga, places long frequented by Englishmen. The Turco-Venetian war over Cyprus, 1570–3, weakened the hold of Venice on seaborne traffic throughout the Mediterranean, and provided the immediate occasion for this English penetration.[3] Once English ships had begun to navigate Mediterranean waters they soon extended their

[1] R. Davis, 'England and the Mediterranean, 1570–1670' (F. J. Fisher (ed.), *Studies in the Economic History of Tudor and Stuart England* (1961)).
[2] K. R. Andrews, 'The Economic Aspects of Elizabethan Privateering' (unpublished London Ph.D. thesis, 1951), Ch. VI.
[3] F. Braudel and R. Romano, *Navires et Marchandises à l'entrée du port de Livourne 1547–1611* (Paris, 1951), pp. 49–51.

sphere, to the Adriatic and Venice at the end of the seventies, to Turkey in the early eighties. By this time, the war in the Nether-lands was making its effects felt there as well; English ships trading into the eastern Mediterranean were bringing home goods which had once come in some quantity through Antwerp.

Finally, the growing alignment of English opinion with the Protestant (Dutch and Huguenot) cause in Europe was by the end of the seventies wiping out all respect for Spanish claims and rights in the New World. Trading expeditions to the Caribbean, degenerating quickly into privateering, become commonplace. The absorption of the Kingdom of Portugal by the Spanish crown in 1580 resolved any remaining scruples about trade on the African coastline, and at much longer range removed the political obstacles to an assault on the Portuguese monopolies of the Indian Ocean and the Spice Islands. These were all events favouring the expansion of English shipping; there had been favourable events before, but now an England which had enjoyed nearly a century of firm government and growing wealth under the Tudors possessed the economic resources to take advantage of them.

The characteristic of all these foreign trades which the English newly entered, or entered on a new scale, after 1570, was that they involved long journeys; instead of Amsterdam — Elbing; instead of Antwerp — Leghorn, Smyrna and the Gulf of Guinea. The most important of the new trades flowering in the eighties — Mediterranean and African — provided immensely valuable homeward cargoes of silk, spices, gold and ivory, to be carried through waters which were dangerous in peace and war. Large ships were used in the Italian trade from its inception, because of the relative safety they offered; and when the Levant trade was developed in the eighties ships were built for it, in considerable numbers, of a size and fighting capacity formerly unknown among English merchantmen. The Levant Company's *Merchant Royal* and *Edward Bonaventure*, which fought in the Armada campaign, were fully comparable with the Queen's warships of medium rank; they had no counterparts at all in the merchant fleet of 1560 or indeed of 1577.

Surveys made in 1577 and 1582 reveal that the merchant fleet was at last beginning to grow:[1]

[1] 1560: SP 12–11–27. The totals recorded are 6 ships of over 200 tons and a further 71 ships of 100–199 tons. Bristol and Somersetshire are excluded, and

English Merchant Shipping, 1561–82

	Total tonnage	Number of ships 100-199 tons	200 tons and over[1]
1560		over 71	6
1572	50,000	72	14
1577		120	15
1582	67,000	155	18

This expansion was not checked by the outbreak of open war with Spain in 1587. Though the Mediterranean trade languished at times of particular danger, and when the Queen's service called for the great ships, on the whole its growth continued and even accelerated through the nineties. Moreover the large Levant ships, if cut off from their regular occupation, could make their way as privateers, and their successes encouraged the building of yet more ships for this purpose, usually by merchants concerned in the Levant and African trades.[2] Mediterranean trade and privateering, at times going hand in hand, maintained an increasing number of large ships. There was a boom in the construction of large ships in the nineties;[3] and the ending of the war with Spain in 1604,

might well have had a few ships of over 100 tons.

1572: SP 12–22.

1577: SP 12–96–267 and SP 12–111–30. Total tonnage cannot be given, as details of tonnage of ships under 100 tons are not recorded. Welsh ports are excluded; it is unlikely that they owned any ships of 100 tons or upwards.

1582: SP 12–156–45. This is an almost complete survey, giving a total of 65,032 tons. Welsh ports are not included, and the figure is increased to 67,000 tons to allow for these.

[1] The tonnage of ships given in this book is, unless otherwise stated, tons burden, deadweight tonnage, carrying capacity – nearly synonymous terms. This was the figure that interested the shipowner — as it does his present-day counterpart — and it was used in all commercial contracts for hire of ships, and until 1773 in government records of merchant shipping. Measured tonnage — the tonnage measured by rules which the shipwrights had developed — was used only as a basis for the shipwright's selling price, and in government contracts. In ships of conventional English build during most of the seventeenth century, carrying capacity was usually about three-quarters of measured tonnage; in the Dutch flyboats and in many of the English-built ships of the eighteenth century the proportion was much higher. An act of 1773 encouraged the use of measured tonnage in official records (13 George III, c. 74) and after compulsory registration of ships was instituted in 1786 (26 George III, c. 60) all official statistics are in terms of measured tonnage, and are not strictly comparable with earlier ones. Measurement rules and their basis are discussed in *Encyclopedia Britannica*, 3rd ed. (1797), Vol. XVII, pp. 415–18; W. Vogel, *Die Grundlagen der Schiffahrtsstatistik* (Berlin, 1911), pp. 1–6; A. Van Driel, *Tonnage Measurement, a Historical and Critical Essay* (The Hague, 1925); R. Stewart-Brown, *Liverpool Ships of the Eighteenth Century* (Liverpool, 1932), pp. 136–40; W. Salisbury, *Mariners' Mirror*, Vol. XLV, 1959, pp. 83–4.

[2] K. R. Andrews, op. cit., pp. 58–9, 196–7.

[3] Information on shipbuilding in this period is from the records of government bounties paid for building ships of over 100 tons (see p. 305 below) in CSPD 1591–1603, *passim*, and SP 38–7/10 and 39–1/10 (Docket Books), *passim*.

B

arousing expectations of greatly expanded trade, led to a sharp new post-war shipbuilding boom, perhaps even to some over-production; 'Our navie of merchant shipps (of the best especially) greatly decaying through the little employment that is for them.'[1]

The shipowner's view of English trade was therefore very different, in the first decade of the seventeenth century, from what it had been thirty or forty years before. Most of the more valuable exports still made a short journey across the North Sea — a little longer now, to Stade or Middelberg instead of Antwerp — and France was still an important customer and supplier. Trade with Spain and Portugal had revived, however, and was growing fast. The Mediterranean was full of English ships, trading to Leghorn and Naples, to Venice and the Greek Islands, to Turkey and Egypt, and carrying goods between those places; the English fisheries supplied an important part of their outward cargoes. Four East India fleets had been sent out between 1600 and 1607, despite Portuguese opposition in the Indian Ocean and the emerging threat of trouble with the Dutch. If Dutch pressure was being felt in the Baltic, English ships were still there in some numbers. At home, the east coast coal trade had trebled in volume in thirty years. The Iceland fishery seemed flourishing; across the Atlantic went over two hundred ships for the Newfoundland fishery, which had employed only thirty in 1574.[2] Nearly every branch of the shipping industry — long- and short-distance, large- and small-ship — was advancing rapidly; and a few days before Christmas, 1606 the *Susan Constant*, *Godspeed* and *Discovery* sailed from London to begin the American colonisation which was ultimately to be the greatest expansive force of all.

Progress was slowing, however, and may even have come briefly to a halt in 1614–16. For with the return of peace between Holland and Spain, in 1609, the Dutch were able to devote their full attention again to maritime and commercial expansion; and anti-Dutch feeling, the child of jealousy, began to appear in England.

<hr/>

[1] SP 14–10–38 (20th November 1604). The Venetian ambassador noted, 'Now that the peace with Spain is thought to be an accomplished fact, everyone is trying to sell their big ships' (CSPV, 30th June 1604, p. 236). But big ships were at this very date being built in large numbers, as the records of bounties show.
[2] H. A. Innis, op. cit., pp. 31, 69.

It was disputes over East India trade, whaling and fisheries that caused most of the bitterness in Anglo-Dutch relations during the first half of the seventeenth century.[1] In the growing body of diatribes against the Dutch, grievances over shipping took only a small place. Nevertheless the shipping industry was beginning to feel itself endangered by Dutch recovery; the years 1615–17 saw a number of measures initiated by the Privy Council in response to merchants' and shipowners' complaints, to aid English shipping,[2] and the well-known pamphlet *The Trade's Increase*, which laments the loss of much carrying trade to the Dutch, was written in 1615. But the complaints of the times must be treated with the greatest caution. Dutch advantages were specially powerful in the North European trades, yet even in these the impact of Dutch competition on England's share was small before the Civil War. The Dutch controlled twenty or thirty times as much Baltic trade as England did; but they had done so for a century or more. Between 1604 and 1624 about one hundred English ships entered the Baltic every year — double the number sent there in the 1560's. Each year after the Dutch made peace with Spain in 1609, a few more Dutch ships sailed from England to the Baltic, but they still averaged only thirty-four a year — one third of the English total — during the ensuing twelve years, and their numbers fell away to nothing as the Dutch again became heavily engaged in war in the twenties. From 1631 until after the Peace of Westphalia in 1648, Dutch ships rarely traded between England and the Baltic, whilst English ships continued to sail for Elbing and Danzig in almost unchanging numbers except during the years 1624–30 when England was herself at war.[3]

If there was temporary stagnation in branches of English shipping activity about 1614–16 it was quickly overcome. After the Privy Council's intervention in 1615–17, wrote Sir William Monson,

'The mariners and owners of ships began building shipping again, and finding profit to be gained by them, and because the pirates and Turks of Algiers and Tunis were many and strong by sea, able to overcome all small ships, they built ships of greater burthen, viz. three, four, and five hundred tons each. . . . Insomuch, that within

---

[1] G. Edmundson, *Anglo-Dutch Rivalry during the First Half of the Seventeenth Century* (Oxford, 1911).
[2] See pp. 302–3 below.   [3] N. E. Bang, op. cit.

seven years after, the state, finding so many great ships built, thought fit to save the five shillings on every ton.'[1]

Certainly there were important developments in the twenties and thirties. Mediterranean trade, both with Italy and with the Ottoman Empire, was growing very fast in spite of the depredations of Moorish corsairs. The East India trade, after hanging in the doldrums for a decade, found new life after 1615–17, and was checked again only when Charles I's meddling in the thirties impaired the Company's relations with Indian rulers. The fast-growing trade with the new American colonies, including the West Indian islands settled between 1622 and 1632, was ceasing to be of negligible proportions. The Newfoundland fishery from Devon, Cornwall and Dorset continued its remarkable upsurge; reaching a peak in the thirties when over 300 ships — possibly as many as 500 — sailed each year from England.[2] The east coast coal shipments trebled again between 1600 and the mid-thirties.[3]

A survey of shipping made in 1629 shows a remarkable expansion since the previous survey, forty-seven years earlier, although its date, it may be noted, was in February of that year, 'towards the end of the Warres, when Shipping was at its lowest'.[4]

English Merchant Shipping, 1582–1629[5]

	Total tonnage	Number of ships 100–199 tons	200 tons and over
1582	67,000	155	18
1629	115,000	more than 178	more than 145

This growth took place despite interruptions by the brief check of 1604–5, some general depression in 1614–16, and war with Spain

---

[1] *The Naval Works of Sir William Monson*, ed. M. Oppenheim (Navy Records Soc., 1913), Vol. III, p. 432. The 'Five shillings on every ton' is the government bounty for large ships (see p. 305, below).

[2] H. A. Innis, op. cit., pp. 69–70.   [3] J. U. Nef, op. cit., App. D.

[4] SP 16–282–136.

[5] 1629: SP 16–132–19; SP 16–137; SP 16–138–11 and 60; SP 16–155–31. This list is far from complete; it excludes the whole of England north of the Humber and Dee, North Devon and Somerset, Sussex and Wales. The total tonnage listed is 93,110. To this I have added 15,000 for Newcastle and Hull, which had 10,138 in 1582 (the London list for 1629 includes a long list of 'Newcastle colliers'); 2000 for Lancashire, 3000 for North Devon and Somerset and 2000 for all others. There were probably a few ships of over 100 tons in these places, and possibly one or two of over 200 tons.

Professor L. A. Harper, in *The English Navigation Laws* (New York, 1939), pp. 338–9, attempts an estimate of tonnage of shipping in 1609–15. It is based on two contemporary analyses of shipping employed in various trades (BM Lansdowne MSS. 142–304 306; *The Trades Increase*), which may not be

and France, 1624–30. Even the extent of unemployment of ships in the downswings indicates the growing scale of the industry. A petition of Trinity House about 1630, for example, declares,

> 'There is now in the River of Thames not less than six thousand tonnes in goodly great shipps from 200 tonns to 500 the like merchants shipps for the service of his Majestie never were in this Kingdome. All lying dead without hope of any present employment.'[1]

The years after the survey of 1629 saw a post-war building boom followed by slump, and then several years of steady advance culminating in the sharp boom of 1636–7.[2] It may be supposed that when the Civil War broke out the industry disposed of much more than twice the tonnage it had had in the year before the Armada came.

From the onset of the Civil War a statistical darkness falls. The Privy Council ceased its enquiries, and no further survey of English shipping was made until 1702. The upheaval involved failure to maintain routine records, and the disappearance of most of those that were kept. The indications are that when the First Civil War came to an end in 1646 there was a very sharp revival of trade, checked to some extent in 1649 by general European hostility after the execution of Charles I, the growth of anti-English privateering, and then the First Dutch War of 1652–4; and that a burst of renewed prosperity after the ending of that war was quenched by the war with Spain from 1655–60, in which the shipping industry suffered particularly. The fortunes of the industry during these two decades fluctuated all the way between excellent and very bad.

Almost worse than England's involvement in war was the spectacle of the Dutch enjoying an unwonted period of peace after 1648. Dutch maritime competition had nearly vanished in the twenties, and for a quarter of a century the English shipowner could feel that, whatever his own troubles, the Dutch were not in a

altogether independent, which present great difficulties of interpretation, and which are under some suspicion as being propagandist. I should hesitate to base an estimate on these two sources; and Professor Harper's method — applying to ships in each trade the average tons of ships in that trade entering London during the war year 1602 — seems likely to exaggerate the total tonnage.

[1] SP 16–257–29.

[2] The certificates given by Trinity House in connection with the issue of ordnance to ships, from 1625–38, provide some guide to the fluctuations in shipbuilding. There is a list of these certificates at the end of each year of the *Calendars of State Papers, Domestic*.

position to take advantage of them. After 1648, however, all was changed; the Dutch were at peace, and the English royal ordinances of 1615–17 and later years which had given some protection to English shipping had no authority now royalty itself had been dispensed with. In every year of the later forties, foreign ships sharply increased their share of English trade with the Baltic; between 1649 and 1651 the number of English ships sailing to the Baltic fell by half, their proportion of all sailings from England to the Baltic from two-thirds to one-third. The Dutch were the chief gainers.[1] At Leghorn, the principal centre for English ships in the Mediterranean, they were outnumbered by the Dutch for a few years round 1650. In the American colonies dozens of Dutch ships laded tobacco cargoes for Europe.[2] Though these alarming intrusions were to some extent made possible by the domestic upheaval in England, they served to arouse a sudden recognition of Dutch predominance at sea, and led directly to the Navigation Ordinances of 1650 and 1651[3] and to the First Dutch War. For the rest of the century, the old grievances against the Dutch were hardly voiced, but Dutch skill in commerce, and above all in shipbuilding and shipping management, maintained a hostility which was compounded of envy and fear.

The problem of Dutch competition was solved by two things; protection and war. The Navigation Ordinance of 1651 (and the Navigation Acts that succeeded it) forbade, with some exceptions, participation by foreign ships in certain English and colonial trades. The First Dutch War had the effect of reconstituting the English merchant fleet, providing it with ships which could compete with Dutch and Scandinavians. The number of ships taken from the Dutch between 1652 and 1654 was enormous — the lowest contemporary estimate is 1,000 ships — and English losses were very much smaller. The tonnage of prizes taken may well have approached that of the whole existing English merchant fleet. Even more important, it changed the character of that fleet. The great defect of the English shipbuilders was that they built ships for strength, manoeuvrability and defensibility; qualities needed in some trades, but not in those using the greatest total tonnage of shipping; qualities that were paid for in expensively built and

---

[1] N. E. Bang, op. cit.
[2] G. L. Beer, *Origins of the British Colonial System, 1578–1660* (New York, 1922), Ch. XI.
[3] See p. 306, below.

expensively operated ships.[1] The Dutch had a more varied repertoire, and produced great numbers of cheap vessels, handled by small crews, which were perfectly suited to all work in Northern waters. English shipowners had bought some of these in the twenties and thirties; they now acquired a great number, cheaply, by purchase from the privateers and men-of-war captains who had captured them. The war turned the English merchant fleet into a well-balanced one, with its defensible ships supplemented by an adequate number of bulk-cargo carriers. For a quarter of a century after this Dutch War ended in 1654, war and purchase maintained the proportion of foreign- (mainly Dutch-) built tonnage in the English merchant fleet at a very high level, probably never far below a half. The English shipping industry had left behind it for ever its old one-sided character; the moans and imprecations against English shipwrights which fill the commercial literature of the third quarter of the century are concerned principally to show the disasters which will occur, inevitably, when the acquisition of foreign ships ceases and the industry has to revert to the use of uneconomic English-built ships. The cry was one of foreboding rather than despair — a foreboding which would have been fully justified had not English provincial shipbuilders, far removed from the haunts of pamphleteers, been quietly evolving new ship types.

The English shipping industry was to suffer a severe blow, however, before its bright prospects could be realised. This was Cromwell's Spanish War of 1655–60. Spain was well situated for preying on English shipping of all kinds; the ports of Spain itself were bases for attacks on Mediterranean and transatlantic shipping, mainly large defensible ships, while the Spanish Netherlands provided refuges for a flock of small privateers (known as Capers) which preyed on English North Sea and coastal traffic in which the cheap bulk-cargo carrier played a large part. Both types of ship, therefore, were lost in great numbers, and English merchant shipping emerged from the war in 1660 at a very low ebb.

Twenty years had then passed since a long period of peace and normality had been experienced; most of the pre-Civil War ships had been lost or worn out, as had many of the prizes of the First Dutch War; shipbuilding, as in all wars, had suffered continuous checks. Samuel Lambe wrote in 1657, 'I cannot hear, for about

[1] This is fully discussed in Chapter III below.

these ten years past, that a trading ship of about 400 tons hath been built in England, and those few that have been built within that time, seldom so big as 200 tons;'[1] while a petition of Thames shipowners and masters in 1660 declared that 'many considerable merchant ships have been broken up, and few are now built for want of employment'.[2] The losses of the Spanish War were thought by contemporaries to have equalled in numbers the gains of the Dutch War; and when, in 1660, the new government of Charles II extended protection to English shipping by means of a new Navigation Act, the industry was hardly able to meet the demands of peace, and the early complaints of Virginia and West India planters that they could not get their crops shifted without calling in foreign ships may well have been justified.

The immediate response to the re-expansion of trade which followed the return of peace, and the imposition of legal restrictions on the employment of foreign-owned ships, was large-scale purchase of ships abroad, particularly in Holland.[3] The Court of Admiralty records for the years 1660–3 contain an unprecedented number of cases dealing with ships bought abroad. A new act of parliament limiting the use of foreign-*built* ships (other than prizes) as well as foreign-*owned* ships, from 1st October 1662, was primarily a response to fears that such heavy purchasing would open the way to ownership frauds that might let foreigners in again; it brought the practice almost to a standstill. The sixties, therefore, saw the beginning of a sharp recovery in English shipbuilding, though it was to be checked by two more Dutch wars. A petition of 1669 stated, 'that at present there are more ships a-building in the Kingdome than at any time for Forty Years past.'[4] The Second Dutch War, 1664–7, produced many prizes; some foreign purchases were allowed to handle the demand for imported timber after the Great Fire of London of 1666;[5] the Third Dutch War brought more prizes, and in the immediately succeeding years there were many fraudulent transfers of ships to English nationality.[6] After this war ended the English shipbuilding industry was very active for several years.

[1] *Seasonable Observations Humbly offered to His Highness the Lord Protector* (1657), p. 4.
[2] *HMC VII (House of Lords MSS. 1660)*, p. 141.
[3] A writer in 1660 declared that four foreign ships were being bought to every English ship built (S.E., *The Touchstone of Money and Commerce*, p. 20).
[4] CO 388–1–350.   [5] SP 29–259–50.
[6] The *CSPD* of 1675 and 1676 are full of discussion of these frauds.

From 1660 until 1689, therefore, the total tonnage of English shipping was growing fast, wartime checks to new building being more than counterbalanced by wartime captures. It is not easy to estimate the size of the shipping industry at this period, but the following figures indicate the course of change:

English merchant shipping, 1629–1702[1]

	Total tonnage (000 tons)
1629	115
1686	340
1702	323

The 1629 figures, as we have seen, come from a survey made near the end of a long and unprofitable war, in which, if losses were not great, prizes were few and the interruption of trade discouraged new building. The tonnage in 1624, before the war, was almost certainly higher; and the ten years that followed the war saw expanding trade and substantial shipbuilding. The figures at the pre-Civil War peak and at the time of Charles II's Restoration can only be guessed at; a guess of 150 thousand tons for 1640 and 200 thousand tons for 1660 would probably not seriously distort the relation between the two years.

Any increase during the period 1640–60 may seem surprising after all that has been said of the difficulties of those years. Yet expansion had been continuing quietly in some directions when not immediately under the pressure of war. The coastal coal trade had continued its progress; the colonial trades, of only moderate significance before 1642, had already emerged in 1660 as among the greatest of English trades; the Baltic and Norway trades had shown some increase. The new forces of growth which would transform the shipping industry in the post-Restoration decades were too strong to be completely stifled even under the pressure of the hardships of 1642–60; and they had indeed received one tremendous impulse — the vast haul of prizes in the First Dutch War.

What were the demands which so greatly enlarged the shipping industry between the Restoration in 1660 and the Revolution in

SP 29–383–60 is a counterfeit grant of freedom for the *Rose and Crown* dated 10th July 1676.

[1] The tonnage statistics from 1686 onward are discussed in Appendix A, pp. 395–406, below.

1688? The expansion of coastal trade and fisheries, which had supplied so much of the stimulus to the growth of total tonnage up to 1640, was at last slowing down. The breakneck advance of the coastal coal trade was being replaced, around mid-century, by a more moderate rate of growth. The Newfoundland fishery, so far as it was carried on from England, had reached its peak just before the Civil War; thereafter the actual fishing was increasingly the work of the permanent colonists of Newfoundland or New England, most English ships coming simply to buy the fish and take it to its Continental markets.[1] The Iceland fishery, said to employ nearly a quarter of all English seamen in 1615,[2] was contracting in the middle decades of the century;[3] while the Spitzbergen whaling, which had been carried on in the thirties in the face of intense Dutch competition, was almost extinguished by 1660. At the Restoration, coastal shipping and fisheries probably occupied well over half the total tonnage of English shipping; in the next thirty years they made little progress. The great expansion during this period took place among vessels for foreign trade. This may explain the common expression, at the end of the century, of the view that English shipping doubled between 1660 and 1688.[4] This was an exaggeration, but one with a significant basis. It was the spectacular side of the shipping industry that progressed most rapidly in this period; the growth was in the number of large ships, and above all of London ships bound for Norway, the Mediterranean, Virginia, the West and East Indies, rather than in coasters and colliers, cross-Channel traders of the south coast or fishing vessels of Cornwall or East Anglia. The frequenter of the Thames waterside may well have observed, over these twenty-eight years, a continuous increase, even a doubling, in the numbers of the big ocean-going vessels and the timber traders which towered above their fellows in the river. These would catch his eye and provide a basis for the impressions and reports which would give their own colour to the contemporary 'statistics' of the industry.

The basis of the expansion is found in the specially rapid growth of two kinds of trade making large demands for shipping

---

[1] H. A. Innis, op. cit., pp. 97–111.   [2] 'The Trades Increase', op. cit., p. 222.
[3] E. R. Cooper, 'The Dunwich Iceland Ships', *Mariners Mirror*, Vol. XXV, 1939, pp. 170–2; F. Brewster, *New Essays on Trade* (1702), p. 7; *Victoria County History, Suffolk*, Vol. II, pp. 218–19, 228–9, 238; J. R. McCulloch (ed.), *Early Tracts on Commerce* (1856), p. 409.
[4] See, for example, C. Davenant, *Works* (ed. C. Whitworth, 1771), Vol. I, p. 363.

— the long transatlantic haul of substantial cargoes of tobacco and sugar, and the transport over a shorter distance of the immense timber cargoes of Norway and the Baltic. Four-fifths of the increase in English foreign-going shipping during the years 1663–86 was attributable to these trades, whose rate of expansion is comparable with that of the South European and Mediterranean trades in the early decades of the century, or of the coal trade over the years 1560–1640.[1]

Tonnage of shipping required to
serve overseas trades (000 tons)[2]

	1663	1686	1771-3
Northern Europe	13	28	74
Nearby Europe and British Isles[3]	39	41	92
Southern Europe and Mediterranean	30	39	27
America and West Indies	36	70	153
East India	8	12	29

Despite the interruptions of war, the bulk trades with Northern Europe and with the colonies in America had grown to very great dimensions during the two decades 1640–60. The value of London imports doubled between 1634 and 1669; within this general advance, imports from Norway and the Baltic, and from America and the West Indies, more than quadrupled, while those from Southern Europe rose by less than half.[4] The colonial trades continued to grow (with wartime checks) into the eighteenth century, though the pace of increase was slowed; in the Northern trades there are some indications that a peak (in volume) was reached in the 1680's, and was not surpassed until the ravages of the great war which embraced the Scandinavian states had been repaired, and Russia had entered fully into Western commerce, in the second quarter of the eighteenth century. These were decades when London was not merely enjoying its share of the

[1] This trade expansion is discussed in R. Davis, 'English Foreign Trade, 1660–1700', *Econ. Hist. Rev.* 2nd ser., Vol. VII, 1954, pp. 150–66.
[2] The figures for 1663 and 1686 are compiled on the basis described in Appendix A, pp. 397–8, below. These are not the actual tonnages of ships engaged in these trades, but a rather smaller total; see p. 399, below. The relations between different trades at different periods, which this table is intended to illustrate, should be quite accurately depicted.
[3] 'British Isles' outside England and Wales.
[4] The trade figures are taken from A. E. Millard, 'The Import Trade of London, 1600–1640' (unpublished London Ph.D. thesis, 1956), Vol. III, and BM Add. MSS. 36785. Though not strictly comparable, they are adequate to give this approximate view of change.

country's growing activity, but engrossing an increasing part of it. The lion's share of the new colonial trades came to London because it had a large prosperous population able to set an example in consumption of the semi-luxuries of America; as they cheapened in the course of the seventeenth century and came into more general use London provided a smaller proportion of the market, and this change was ultimately reflected in some fall in its share of the import of sugar, tobacco, rice, ginger, etc. But in London, too, had been found most of the resources of capital with which the overseas plantations had been built and which financed the trade in their products; the advantage that London enjoyed merely from being early established as the centre of colonial trade was one not quickly or easily overthrown, and up to 1689 it was more than maintained.

Number of ships clearing London:[1]

for	1664	1686
North America	43	114
West Indies	45	133
Norway	26	111
Baltic	22	65

The growth of the Northern trades was a seventeenth-century phenomenon, greatly accelerated after the Restoration. Two special reasons for this acceleration may be disposed of before the causes of long-term growth are considered. The Great Fire of London in 1666 called for a tremendous increase in London timber imports to rebuild the city — their value increased by 150 per cent between 1663 and 1669[2] and certain relaxations were made in the Navigation Acts to enable this vastly increased traffic to be handled.[3] Though London was (except for its churches) rebuilt very rapidly,[4] the boom in Northern trade continued unchecked until the outbreak of the Third Dutch War in 1672; and England's withdrawal from this war in 1674 marked the beginning of a four-year period during which England was the only important maritime neutral in a still warring Europe. She enormously expanded her trade in Northern waters; 'whilst the French, Dutch, Spaniards, Swedes and Danes were at war we

---

[1] Figures from the London Port Books (E. 190).
[2] BM Add. MSS. 36785.   [3] See p 14, above.
[4] T. F. Reddaway, *The Rebuilding of London after the Great Fire* (1949), Ch. IX.

with our shipping were the sole carriers of them all'.[1] Most of
England's wartime business was lost when the general peace came
in 1678, but the small share in Baltic traffic that was retained
represented a trebling of pre-war activity.[2]

Long-term developments were causing a steady expansion of
the Northern trades. Large-scale import of timber appears to have
begun only during the seventeenth century. The growing shortage
and increasing cost of the principal English timbers, oak and elm,
was met by increasing imports, largely of softwoods — fir, spruce
and pine. The oak-timbered building, often with its laths and
boards of oak, was giving way to the brick-built house with deal
joists and boarding. Merchant shipbuilders were gradually driven
to accept the use of foreign timber; Norway or Baltic fir or spruce
became accepted in the larger centres for boards and planking,
Baltic oak for frames was widely adopted, and Norwegian masts,
and later masts imported from Riga, became general. Naval
demands for certain kinds of foreign timber grew rapidly as the
Commonwealth's creation of a large permanent fleet transformed
the whole scale of naval building; after a pause in the sixties there
was particularly heavy use of imported materials in the naval
shipbuilding and repair programmes of 1677–9 and 1686–7. Both
merchant shipping and the navy drew heavily on the Baltic for
other materials — hemp, flax, pitch and tar, rosin and turpentine;
in fact, 'naval stores' in a broad sense were notoriously the
foundation of English trade with the Northern countries. Finally,
the small import of Spanish iron which had long been a feature of
English trade was supplemented after mid-century by the growth
of a great iron import from Sweden, as the English demand for
iron goods of every kind outstripped the capacity of the English
iron-smelters to produce at competitive prices.

To a significant extent, therefore, the English shipping industry
was pulling itself up by its own boot-straps. A ship built entirely
of foreign materials — foreign timber, iron, pitch and tar, hemp —
would call for the transport services of as many as two or three
ships of its own size to carry the materials,[3] and the annual extent

---

[1] Bodleian Library, Oxford. Rawlinson MSS. A.171–278.
[2] N. E. Bang, op. cit.
[3] Displacement tonnage — the actual weight of the materials in a ship —
was far more than its tons burden or carrying capacity (W. Sutherland, *The
Shipbuilder's Assistant*, 1711, pp. 86–8). Most of the weight was in timber,
which required, because of its low density and inconvenient shapes, carriage in

of repairs and replacements was substantial. Moreover, shipbuilding had to provide not only for the maintenance and replacement but also for the growth of the merchant fleet; in peacetime between 1660 and 1689 at an average rate of two or three per cent per annum. A merchant fleet built, maintained and expanded at this rate entirely out of imported supplies would require to import (without allowing for naval demands) nearly a hundred tons of 'naval stores' for every two hundred tons of goods which it brought in for other purposes. Of course much of the material used in shipbuilding — most of the timber, which was the principal item — was in fact home produced, and a large share of the remainder was imported in foreign ships; yet it is worth underlining the fact that the expansion of English shipping engaged in the Northern trades, which in this period contributed so much to overall growth of the shipping industry, was to an important extent due to the demands of the industry itself.[1]

The growth in 'independent' demands of trade, therefore, came from the increased use of imported timber in house-building and of imported iron for all purposes as home demand outstripped supply; and from the enormous widening of the consumption of certain colonial goods — above all sugar and tobacco — as the cheapening of their production in the colonies overseas turned them into conventional necessities of life, within the reach of the mass of the population.

The rapid expansion of 1660–89 in foreign trade and shipping comes between two periods of slower progress — the war decades of 1640–60, the new war decades of 1689–1713 and their long-drawn-out aftermath. This situation has its reflection in the economic literature of the period; from *The Advocate* in 1651 until Sir Francis Brewster's *New Essays on Trade* in 1702, books and pamphlets on commercial subjects commonly devoted much of their space to the problems of the shipping industry; it is in the decades of most rapid growth that most of the complaints and expressions of alarm as to its future can be heard. Before 1651, the attention of the majority of economic writers was given to fisheries and balance of trade questions; after 1700 the discussion of trade in general took a smaller place in published works, which tended

ships of greater tonnage than its own weight warranted. See also R. G. Albion, *Forests and Sea Power* (Cambridge, Mass., 1926), Ch. III.

[1] F. Brewster estimated that a 200-ton ship used 50 tons of imported materials in its building (*Essays on Trade*, 1695, p. 104).

to concentrate on particular controversial problems — the relations between West Indian and American colonies, excise versus customs duties — and shipping questions almost dropped out of view until the question of competition from a newly independent America emerged in the eighties.[1]

[1] There is not, I think, a work in which problems of the shipping industry take an important place, between F. Brewster's *New Essays on Trade* (1702) and Lord Sheffield's *Observations on the Commerce of the American States* (1783).

II

Consolidation, 1689-1775

The year 1689 marks a turning-point, not only in the growth of the shipping industry, but also in general commercial development. This is not merely because it saw the outbreak of a costly war which was savagely fought, with a brief interruption, for nearly a quarter of a century. Long-term influences were also at work to restrict the expansion of English commerce, and these combined with new situations created by war and its aftermath to slow down the rate of development of the shipping industry. Probably no more than fifty thousand tons were added between 1689 and 1739 — a rate of increase of $\frac{1}{5}$ per cent per annum (compound); between 1572 and 1689 the addition had been nearly three hundred thousand tons, and though the period was more than twice as long this represents an annual increase of $1\frac{1}{4}$ per cent, fully maintained right up to 1689. Though wars had caused sharp setbacks there had been no long periods of stagnation, and in decades of peace the industry had bounded forward. By contrast, the size of the English merchant fleet stood still for over twenty years during the wars of William III and Anne, and made only limited progress during the ensuing twenty-five years of peace.[1]

The reason why the shipping industry had grown rapidly during most of the seventeenth century was that a number of new branches of commercial activity were in early stages of development. The Mediterranean, colonial and Far Eastern trades had all been created out of nothing, and the Newfoundland fishery and the coal and timber trades from negligible beginnings, since 1560. All had extended to great size in the course of the sixteenth and seventeenth centuries, and in that first stage of development achieved rates of growth that could not be indefinitely maintained. By 1700, having matured, found and fully exploited their markets and spent the initial impetus of growth,

[1] The sources of the statistics from 1686 to 1788 are discussed in Appendix A, below.

they were employers of much the greater part of English shipping tonnage. The export trade which paid for these imports was also slackening its growth. The seventeenth-century expansion of imports had depended on the earnings of the developing export of woollen goods and of the new re-export of colonial sugar and tobacco and Indian textiles. The woollen industry had received an infusion of new life with the introduction of new varieties of light cloths in the third quarter of the sixteenth century, and the effect of this stimulus had been to carry it out of stagnation into a whole century of new growth.[1] Before 1689, however, many of the markets for English woollens were becoming saturated or being infiltrated by French or German products, and this drive had lost most of its force. As to re-exports, these had sprung from virtually nothing before the Civil War to enormous proportions — nearly a third of all exports (by value) at the end of the century.[2] While sugar and tobacco found their European market still growing in the eighteenth century (if less rapidly than before) England's share in this market fell heavily. Colonial sugar was driven from continental Europe in the 1720's by the products of the French West Indies, and most of the expansion in tobacco re-export went, after 1707, through Scottish ports and enriched the Scottish economy.

English exports and re-exports together had trebled or quadrupled in value in the half-century between 1638 and 1688; between 1688 and 1738 they probably advanced by little more than fifty per cent.[3] New commodities for re-export emerged in the eighteenth century — rice, tea and coffee; but they were insufficient to restore its former vigour to the expansion of exports as a whole. This reinvigoration had to come from new developments in manufacturing industry; and here new forces were indeed at work. The slow growth of exports began to accelerate in the early thirties, was checked by war from 1739 to 1748 and pushed sharply forward again when the war was over. Many new branches of

[1] F. J. Fisher, 'London's Export Trade in the Early Seventeenth Century,' *Econ. Hist. Rev.*, 2nd ser., Vol. III (1950), pp. 151–61.
[2] R. Davis, 'English Foreign Trade 1660–1700', *Econ. Hist. Rev.*, 2nd ser., Vol. VII (1954), pp. 150–66.
[3] Some economic historians suggest that there was a pause in English economic progress as a whole between about 1720 and 1740. This view may be correct, though it stands in need of detailed investigation. The discussion of foreign trade above must not, however, be taken as necessarily giving it support. In some directions, it might be argued, England was becoming more self-sufficient, developing home industries at the expense of overseas trade.

c

industry entered the period of characteristically violent initial growth in export markets. The metal industry, whose products had been little sold abroad before 1700, was becoming a great exporter to America, leaping ahead to account for a significant part of English exports by mid-century. The West Riding worsted industry, which had been quietly expanding its home market over a very long period, began for reasons which its historians do not make clear to achieve a soaring export trade in the mid-eighteenth century. A whole range of minor industries began to pour their products into overseas — mainly American — markets; cordage, hats, leather, linens, silks, none of them in very great quantity, but together making up a large total. Indeed, the chief new feature of the export trade in the middle decades of the eighteenth century is the rapid development of exports of these non-woollen manufactured goods for the first time in English history. All these things together, along with the new rice, tea and coffee re-export, and a rising surplus of English grain for export, lifted trade out of the swamp in which it had been wallowing during the first three decades of the new century. There was a corresponding expansion of imports; and as these changes gathered momentum towards mid-century the way was clear for another general leap forward after the peace of 1748.

The long interval, from 1689 to 1748, between two phases of rapid expansion of the shipping industry, must now be examined more closely. Of the preceding century it is almost sufficient to say that trade and shipping were rapidly expanding in total because each individual trade and its shipping requirements was expanding. After 1689 trade and shipping made slower progress because several important branches were actually decaying, some others were for various reasons in the doldrums, and others again, full of promise for the future, were not yet big enough to tip the overall balance decisively towards rapid advance. The effect of these changes of fortune was further complicated by the uneven effects of wars and their aftermaths.

Between 1689 and 1713, only the years 1698 to 1701 were free of war, and in the last of these the fear of its renewal was already growing. Moreover, England's enemies were no longer the Dutch, safely penned to the east of the Straits of Dover and more inclined to use their marine resources for fleet actions than for commerce raiding. The enemy was now France, with Channel, Biscay and Mediterranean coastlines, a foothold in the North Sea at Dunkirk,[1] and a readiness, after the final failure of its bid for naval supremacy in 1692, to back privateering to the hilt. During the first three years of the war (until the Battle of La Hogue in May 1692) the French battle fleet was able to contest the command of the Channel itself, and two years later large forces had to be sent to the Mediterranean to make it safe for English shipping. Privateers made the Channel, outside the fortified harbours, a place of great danger to unescorted English craft, and losses there were high; and in the West Indies, too, French privateers were very active. In relation to its total size, the English merchant fleet lost as much as it had done in the disastrous Spanish War of 1655–60, though this time the losses were partly counterbalanced by captures. In the war of 1702–13, though convoy and cruisers were better organised, losses were little smaller.[2]

The heterogeneous merchant fleet which emerged from the wars in 1713, with ships of English, French, Dutch, American and many other builds, was probably no larger than that which entered war in 1689. Some statistics are available for 1702:[3]

English Merchant Shipping, 1686–1702

	Total tonnage
1686	340,000
1702	323,000

These statistics are subject to much possible error, but the impression of decline has some support in the statistics of entries and clearances in foreign trade. It is fairly safe to say, at least, that the advance of Charles II's reign was reversed by war and at best hardly recovered on the eve of the renewed outbreak of war in 1702. This view is not without contemporary expression:

'It is a certain Truth and Merchants know it full well (whatever the unthinking Vulgar may imagine to the contrary) that Ships are now but of little Value, notwithstanding the number of Merchants Ships are much less than they were before the War.'[4]

The war of 1702–13 saw further losses hardly counterbalanced by gains.

---

[1] Spanish until 1658, Dunkirk was temporarily in English hands, 1658–62, and was then sold to France.
[2] See pp. 316–17, below.   [3] See pp. 401–03, below.
[4] *A Brief History of Trade in England* (1702), p. 2.

At the end of the seventeenth century the collection of statistics of a new type began; statistics of the entries and clearances of shipping engaged in foreign trade, rather than of ships owned in England. The tables below reproduce figures collected from a number of sources.

Entries and Clearances, 1686–1779
(000 tons)

	Entries			Clearances		
	Total	Eng.	For.	Total	Eng.	For.
1686	466	399	67	361	331	30
1692-3	177	70	107	181	89	92
1693-4	201	95	106	143	74	69
1696				175	92	83
1697				245	144	101
1699-1701				338	294	44
1700-2				318	274	44
1709				290	244	46
1710				311	244	67
1711				324	266	58
1712				356	327	29
1713				438	412	26
1714				479	445	34
1715				426	406	20
1716	349			456	439	17
1717	347			429	414	15
1718	369	354	15	445	428	17
1723	393			420	393	27
1726-8	421			457	433	24
1730		422				
1737		404				
1744		269				
1751	480	421	59	694	648	46
1758	413	283	130	526	427	99
1765	693	568	125	758	690	68
1772	780	652	128	888	815	73
1779	710	482	228	720	581	139

Sources:

1686: Port Books giving numbers of ships; average tonnage of ships in each trade taken from C.O. 388–9 (1715–17).

1692-3, 1693-4: *HMC House of Lords MSS.*, *1695–7* pp. 419–22.

1696, 1697, 1699–1701, 1700–2, 1709, 1723, 1726–8: G. Chalmers, *Estimate of the Comparative State of Great Britain*, (1782), *passim*.

1710–14: C.O. 388–18.

1715–17: C.O. 390–8.

1718: C.O. 390–5.

1730, 1737, 1744: Outports, BM Add.MSS. 11256; London: Adm. 68–195/197.

1751, 1758, 1765, 1772, 1779: BM Add.MSS. 11256.

Entries for 1716–18, 1723, 1726–8 obtained by deducting recorded clearances from the figures of total entries and clearances in *The Wealth and Commerce of Great Britain Considered* (1728), p. 7.

Tonnage of English-owned Shipping
(ooo tons)[1]

	Total	London	Outports
1572	50		
1582	67		
1629	115		
1686	340	150	190
1702	323	140	183
1716			215
1723			219
1730			235
1737			248
1751	421	119	302
1752	449	131	318
1753	468	132	336
1754	458	120	338
1755	473	131	342
1763	496	139	357
1764	523	135	388
1765	543	134	409
1766	562	133	429
1767	557	139	418
1768	549	123	426
1769	574	128	446
1770	594	150	444
1771	577	133	444
1772	584	133	451
1773	581	136	445
1774	588	133	455
1775	608	143	465
1786	752	186	566
1788	1055	315	740

The old impetus of advance was not fully recovered after the wars. The years 1713–15 saw — as did immediate post-war years throughout the eighteenth century — the shifting of heaped-up surpluses of colonial goods, the movement of great quantities of English goods to colonial and other markets, and a general filling in of stocks of imported goods which had been allowed to run down. After the checking of this post-war boom early in 1715, however, English shipping had great difficulty in making further progress.

[1] See Appendix A, below, for a discussion of the sources, and a caution on making comparisons of the 1716–86 figures with earlier and later ones.

The Jacobite insurrection of 1715 disturbed trade; it was followed by an English dispute, in 1717–19, with the Baltic powers engaged in the Great Northern War; by a brief war with Spain in 1718, and by the commercial dislocation which resulted from the collapse of the South Sea Bubble in 1720. Not until the mid-twenties were some signs of renewed advance to be seen, and even this faltered after a decade and was cut off by another war in 1739.

Apart from temporary setbacks, there were permanent depressive influences left over from the wars. In the first place, there was the Union with Scotland of 1707, entered into, from the English point of view, because Scotland was threatening a renewed separation of crowns which might add it to the list of England's enemies. Union brought Scotland within the English tariff barrier and the circle of the Navigation Acts, and there was a rapid upsurge of Scottish trade with the English North American colonies.[1] By 1730 half the tobacco imported to Britain, and a larger share of the re-export, went through Glasgow and other Scottish ports. Though the English import continued to expand at a fair pace, much of the impetus was taken from the growth of *English* tobacco trade by Scottish participation; nearly twenty thousand tons of shipping was employed in the sixties in taking tobacco to Scotland, which would have been English if Scotland had remained an independent state. The Scots played only a small part in other branches of trade, confining themselves to securing their own needs.

Another lasting effect of war was that legal trade with France, checked by prohibitions between 1678 and 1685, and flourishing vigorously in the last years before the war, 1685–8 (from which period come our pre-war shipping statistics) was almost killed by heavy differential duties on French goods. They were replaced not only by imported wine and salt from Portugal, but also by the products of expanded home industries — silk, linen and paper manufactures, and salt from Cheshire. The apparent fall in the trade is not the true one, for the legal customs entries which provide the ultimate basis for all shipping statistics were partly replaced by a great smuggling business, handling great quantities

[1] A small Scottish trade with the colonies had been carried on illegally from the 1680's onward.

In order to provide consistent figures, entries from and clearances for Scotland have been excluded from the 1686 figures in the table on p. 26.

of wine, brandy and textiles, which grew into a major occupation of the people on the south coast. Entries of English ships from France reported at London fell from 38 thousand tons in 1686 to 6 thousand in 1726, and outport tonnage probably dropped similarly. Making every allowance for smuggling, there was undoubtedly a heavy fall in the shipping employed in Anglo-French trade, only partly counterbalanced by the growth of trade with Portugal.

Two other branches of shipping activity declined, for reasons unconnected with the war; the Turkey trade and the Newfoundland fishery. The English trade with Turkey, precursor of all English long-distance enterprise, was beginning to feel the impact of a new French competition in the 1680's, and after 1713 the French rapidly encroached on its position in the Levant. A continually declining number of fishing vessels went from English ports for the Newfoundland Banks, and even the sack ships which sailed to purchase cod from the Banks fishermen now frequently met in Spanish ports New England ships selling their catches.[1]

The east coast coal trade, even more important to the shipping industry, was in a nearly stagnant state. Its growth, which had proceeded for a hundred and fifty years at a great if decelerating pace, came to a temporary halt at the end of the seventeenth century.[2] The exhaustion of the most accessible seams was causing the pits to move westward, away from the coast, and downward further into the earth, posing costly problems of overland transport and of pumping, which the primitive railway and steam pumping engine were only beginning to solve; London's demand was ceasing to grow as coal prices rose and as population stabilised; whilst the areas in which the rapid growth of industry continued — Yorkshire, Lancashire and the north and west Midlands — were on the whole supplied with coal from local sources or by inland navigations, and made few demands on the coastal colliers. In the second and third decades of the century the north-east coast coal shippers were continually in difficulties, and they declared their troubles dated from the ending of post-war prosperity in 1718.[3] The coal export from Newcastle and Sunderland,

[1] H. A. Innis, *The Cod Fisheries* (Toronto, 1954), pp. 144–67.

[2] J. U. Nef, *The Rise of the British Coal Industry* (1932), App. D.

[3] *House of Commons Journals, 1727–32*, p. 372. See the long discussion of this subject in E. Hughes, *North Country Life in the Eighteenth Century* (Oxford, 1952), pp. 151–66.

and the Whitehaven trade with Ireland, was growing rapidly, but
these were not large in relation to the total commerce that passed
along the principal artery of the coal traffic. Expansion did get
under way again in the thirties, but it was checked by war,
especially when France entered the war against England in
1744.

The old branches of trade with Europe showed little advance in
the two decades after 1715. Spain and Portugal, though they were
taking more English goods, paid increasingly in silver and gold;
the Low Countries and Germany carried on a trade of moderate
and fairly stable volume (if immense value) and Hamburg, Bremen
and Emden were using more of their own ships in trade with
England. Two branches of the export trade to nearby Europe,
however, were growing. Coal export expanded continuously;
though it was small in value, its volume was enormous, exceeded
by that of only one other exported commodity. For above all, this
is the period of English corn export. The small irregular corn
export of the late seventeenth century developed as a regular trade
in the war years, when vast surpluses were sent out to Spain and
Portugal, continued at a high and generally growing level for over
thirty years after the war ended, to achieve a peak in 1750, and then
began to decline, ceasing as a regular feature of English trade in
the mid-seventies. The carriage overseas of some scores of
thousands of tons of corn each year, though most of it went across
the narrow seas to Holland and France, had a real importance to the
English shipping industry.

Baltic trade went through great difficulties after 1689. The
Baltic powers resented the attempts of the Western belligerents to
check each other's trade with them, and in 1693 formed an Armed
Neutrality to resist blockade. The North itself, however, was
drifting towards the war which broke out in 1700 and continued
in one form or another until 1721. During this period the merchant
fleets of the Scandinavian states suffered great losses;[1] the ports of
the East Baltic were from time to time cut off from their hinterland; the Russians in 1709–10 finally conquered a north-east Baltic
coastline, including the ports of Riga and Narva. At times, as in
1717–19, England found herself in open hostility which caused the
breaking off of trade. The long-term effects were important. England

---

[1] A. N. Kiaer, 'Historical Sketch of the Development of Scandinavian
Shipping', *Journal of Political Economy*, Vol. I, 1893, pp. 329–64.

was driven to contemplate the dangers of relying on the Baltic for naval stores on which her life depended, and began to foster their import from the American colonies; masts, pitch and tar in the eighteenth century were largely drawn from the far side of the Atlantic. Russia on the Baltic began a commercial expansion which by mid-century was making the new city of St. Petersburg a main centre of English trade. Even more important in determining the volume of English Baltic trade, perhaps, was the long stagnation of the English shipping industry, as a result of which this trade, after a brief restocking boom in 1720, drifted along at an unchanging level for many years. In the wars, however, the Danish, Norwegian and Swedish shipping industries had been severely damaged. The large share which Scandinavians had had in the carriage of their own products to England disappeared; English ships replaced Danish and Norwegian, which did not begin to regain their old position until England became immersed in the great mid-century wars of 1739–48 and 1757–63.

The trades beyond the oceans were more flourishing. The West India trade burgeoned immediately the war was over; plantations were restored and reinvestment began as the fears of destruction or confiscation disappeared. After 1720, however, the growth of sugar production paused for some years, and a new rapid expansion which in 1728–30 doubled the level of English sugar imports was quickly cut off by the collapse of sugar prices below generally profitable levels; the trade then continued unchanging — at the new high level — until mid-century. American tobacco trade expanded, though mainly, as we have seen, to the benefit of Scottish shipping; but other products were by now beginning to come in great quantity from the mainland colonies — pitch and tar, rice and timber (hardwoods in particular) — and the total volume of American trade with England was therefore growing very fast. The last of the extra-European trades, the East India trade, was rapidly increasing; but it was still the user of only a small proportion of England's total shipping tonnage.

If we consider as a whole the fortunes of the English shipping industry in the thirty-five years which separate the Peace of Utrecht from the Peace of Aix-la-Chapelle in 1748, the conclusion must be that this was a period of only very moderate expansion; indeed that from 1715 to 1728 expansion may have ceased altogether, to be resumed for a few years until European war and other influences slowed it again before the mid-thirties. The expanding branches of the carrying trade were unable to overcome the effect of stagnation in some important trades and the decline or collapse of others.

There is little contemporary comment on this slow growth. This is understandable; there *was* overall growth, not decline. The prophets of ruin in the past had usually spoken in the midst of unexampled progress; in the mid-seventies and the eighties of the previous century the output of new ships from English yards and of depressing literature from the pens of English pamphleteers had reached their peaks simultaneously. Above all, however, the fate of the shipping industry had ceased to be a problem to whose solution writers felt it necessary to turn their attention. It was now obviously established too firmly for Dutch machinations to destroy it and it had long since ceased to be dependent on foreign wars to supply it with ships capable of cheap operation. The pamphleteers turned their attention to other problems. When, towards the end of the eighteenth century, enquiring minds examined the progress of shipping, the only statistics available to them were of clearances from English ports, which showed a marked expansion — an expansion based, of course, on the development of the short-distance coal and corn export trades. Because these trades handled such vast tonnages of goods; because they were growing much faster than almost any other trades; and because they were on the whole short-distance trades in which one ship could make six or eight voyages a year, the statistics of clearances which they influenced considerably exaggerated the development of the industry in this period, and produced from the writers who used them expressions of delight at the progress revealed.[1] While clearances of English ships for foreign parts doubled in tonnage between 1686 and 1751, entries hardly changed (see table on p. 26, above); and the latter reflect more accurately the development of the industry.

Before proceeding to the last stage of this enquiry — the great new expansion of the shipping industry which began around mid-century — something should be said of the progress of the individual ports over two centuries. The table below illustrates regional development.

[1] e.g. G. Chalmers, *An Estimate of the Comparative Strength of Great Britain* (1784), pp. 235–36.

*Percentage of total English tonnage owned
in various regions*[1]

	1582	1702	1788
London	18·7	43·3	29·9
East Anglia	27·1	11·6	7·7
South-east[2]	16·2	8·4	5·3
Total, all south-eastern England	62·0	63·3	42·9
South-west[3]	20·9	17·6	13·9
North-east[4]	15·0	13·1	28·1
North-west[5]	2·1	6·0	15·1
Total, rest of England	38·0	36·7	57·1
TOTAL TONNAGE (000)	67	323	1055

Two things must be borne in mind when examining the shipping owned at individual ports. First, that the coal ports were usually the largest shippers of cargo; and though coal was carried over short distances, the volume of the trade was so vast that it always employed a high proportion of the total tonnage of English shipping. In 1701 four of the ten leading provincial ports (by tonnage owned) were coal ports or ports where ships were owned for use in the coal trade; as were five of the leading ten in 1788. The second is that many of the ships owned in small ports were entirely engaged in the trade between or from greater ones, visiting their home ports rarely.[6] Several of the ports of Essex and Suffolk — Ipswich was chief of them — owned ships engaged in the coal trade between London and Newcastle during the seventeenth century, and the ports' shipping rather than their own trade declined as ownership of colliers passed, in the decades around 1700, to northern ports. Collier ownership in the eighteenth century was based on Whitby and Scarborough, rather than on the actual ports of coal shipment, Newcastle and Sunderland. The home ports of a great many of the ships carrying on London's overseas trade in the early seventeenth century were in the outer reaches of the Thames estuary, and as London owners took control

[1] See Appendix A, below.
[2] South bank of Thames estuary to west border of Hampshire.
[3] Dorset, Devon, Cornwall, Bristol Channel ports, Wales to Cardigan.
[4] Lincolnshire northwards.
[5] Aberystwyth northwards.
[6] The port of ownership is the port which the master declared to the customs authorities as the ship's home port. Always, or nearly always, this was the place where the managing owner was to be found.

of more and more of the vessels engaged in its foreign trade, the importance of these estuarine harbours, as shown by the statistics, declined.

London was by far the greatest of the English seaports, without a serious rival. Until far into the eighteenth century the volume of its foreign and coastal trade at least equalled that of all other ports together. London participated fully in all important new trading developments from the reign of Elizabeth I until the American War of Independence, with the exceptions of long-distance fishery and coal exporting. London pioneered the Mediterranean and East India trades in the last decades of the sixteenth century and for two hundred years ships from the outports were rarely seen in the Mediterranean and were unknown in the Indian Ocean. London opened up the American and West Indian colonies, and for over half a century almost monopolised their trade, throwing a meagre share to Bristol. The western seaports only began to encroach seriously on London's sugar and tobacco trade at the end of the seventeenth century, and right up to American Independence London carried on over half the English trade with the colonies in these two major commodities. London's demand for imported timber and iron, for house- and ship-building, was the first to appear on a large scale in the seventeenth century, and grew faster than that of other ports until the end of the century. Most of the vast shipments of Newcastle coal were destined for London, and London played a considerable part in the corn export which developed after 1700.[1] London's share of the older trades was not, perhaps, fully maintained after the middle of the seventeenth century — certainly the provincial ports were importing more of their wine directly — but London always had a big part in every trade except the Irish. Through most of the seventeenth century London was increasing its share in the total volume of English trade and shipping; then the shift of colonial trade towards the western ports, and of Baltic and Norwegian trade to those of the north-east (both groups serving the rapidly industrialising North and Midlands), and the increasing importance played in the total volume of trade by exported coal and corn, began slowly — very slowly — to nibble at its pre-eminent position. In 1702 London was probably a little past its highest

---

[1] In the peak years of the trade, London was usually second only to Yarmouth as an exporting centre.

relative standing, and during the first half of the eighteenth century London shipping hardly grew while that of Liverpool and some of the coal ports and the East Anglian corn-shipping centres leapt forward. In mid-century London shipping and trade began to grow rapidly; but this was part of a more general expansive movement, and London made no *relative* recovery. London's percentage of the tonnage of ships entering from abroad declined slowly from 59 in 1686 to 54 in 1718 and 49 in 1772.

Thousands of tons of shipping owned in leading English ports.[1]

	1582	1629	1702	1788
London	12·3	35·3	140·0	315·3[2]
Newcastle	6·8		11·0	106·1
Liverpool	·4		8·6	76·1[3]
Sunderland	nil		3·9	53·6
Whitehaven	nil		7·2	52·3
Hull	2·5		7·6	52·1
Whitby	nil		8·3	47·9
Bristol	2·3	6·0	17·3	37·8
Yarmouth	6·8	5·8	9·9	36·3
Scarborough				21·8
Ipswich and Harwich	3·0	4·6	11·2	9·7
Aldeburgh	2·8	·5	1·8	1·0
Southampton	2·9		3·8	7·8
Exeter	1·0		7·1	11·5
Lynn	1·7	2·4	5·7	17·1
Leigh	1·9		nil	nil

In the early seventeenth century East Anglian ports owned great numbers of ships engaged in London's overseas trade and coal

[1] The first ten ports listed are the first ten, in order of size, in 1788; other ports have been included if they were among the ten largest ports in either 1582 or 1702. Sources: 1582 SP 12–156–45; 1629 SP 16–137, SP 138–4, 138–60, 138–11, 270–64, 282–125, 155–31, 132–19; 1702 CO 388–9 (adjusted as explained in Appendix A, below); 1788 Customs 17–10.

The 1788 figures are of measured tonnage, and are not strictly comparable with the others. The error may become considerable in making comparisons between individual ports; e.g. while some ships carried less than their measured tonnage, colliers usually carried far more. At the 1786 registration, for example, Scarborough owned 152 ships of 24,887 tons measure; 'on an accurate calculation, is equal to Thirty-five thousand tons burden' (BT 6–189); at this time East Indiamen were being registered at figures slightly less than their tons burden.

[2] W. Maitland, *History of London* (1756), Vol. II, pp. 1260–2, lists London-owned ships totalling 178,557 tons in 1732.

[3] Liverpool is said to have owned 2·6 thousand tons in 1672 (SP 16–326–142) and about 20 thousand in 1739 (D. MacPherson, *Annals of Commerce* (1805), Vol. III, p. 221).

trade. Ipswich, however, played an important independent part in the Low Countries and Baltic trade at the beginning of the seventeenth century, as well as being the leading port in collier ownership. Its overseas trade disappeared rapidly after mid-century as London, Hull and Newcastle captured its Baltic connections, and by the end of the century it was losing its coal interests and declining fast.[1] Yarmouth, always a place of some importance at the entry of a great inland waterway system into which it brought coal and timber, and from which it drew great supplies of corn, and with a growing herring fishery, fully maintained itself during the seventeenth century, but its time of great prosperity came with the corn export boom of the first two-thirds of the eighteenth century.[2] From the sixties Yarmouth was fast losing ground, but it still ranked at the end of the century as one of England's leading ports. There was no south coast port of major importance as a shipowning centre, though Exeter maintained a valuable trade.

In the south-west was Bristol, for long the second port of England.[3] Despite its considerable Irish trade and its connections with France, Spain and Portugal, Bristol's shipping had declined to small proportions during the sixteenth century. Its revival

Number of ships entering Bristol.[4]

from	1621	1638	1687	1700	1764
America	—	2	28	24 ⎫	137
West Indies	—	2	42	50 ⎭	
Newfoundland	6	3	3	9	6
Mediterranean	—	3	1	—	9
Spain and Portugal	29	36	49	27	48
Norway and Baltic	—	6	17	1	35
France, Flanders, Holland, Germany	25	71	96	10	8
Ireland	82	140	88	83	79

[1] J. U. Nef, op. cit., Vol. I, pp. 25–8; D. Defoe, *A Tour through England and Wales* (Everyman edition), Vol. I, pp. 40–6.
[2] Other East Anglian ports — above all Lynn, Wells and Ipswich — prospered from corn export; they declined more sharply than Yarmouth because their other interests were much narrower.
[3] On Bristol, see P. V. McGrath, *Merchants and Merchandise in Seventeenth Century Bristol* (Bristol Record Society, 1955); and W. E. Minchinton 'Bristol: Metropolis of the West in the Eighteenth Century', *TRHS*, 5th ser., Vol. IV, pp. 69–90.
[4] Sources: 1621 and 1638 P. V. McGrath, op. cit.; 1687 Port Books: 1700 BM Add. MSS. 9764–116; 1764 R. Brooke, *Liverpool 1775–1800* (1853), p. 505.

came with the opening up of English colonies in the New World; although Bristol secured only a small share of the trade, this was sufficient to transform the port in scale and character.

Before the end of the seventeenth century the transatlantic trades employing large ships on long voyages were responsible for four-fifths of the shipping tonnage owned at Bristol, though in numbers of ships the nearby trades kept a majority. Bristol entered the slave trade soon after 1700 and quickly became heavily engaged in it, taking a lead in opposing the attempt to reintroduce the Royal Africa Company's monopoly in 1713. In the thirties, however, Bristol's expansion began to slow down as the growth of the sugar trade came temporarily to an end; and after the Seven Years' War the town failed to take a full share in general recovery. The development of the port of Liverpool, and of river and later canal connections between the Midlands and the Mersey, were beginning to deprive Bristol of some of the advantages which it had gained from being the port of the Severn Valley.

The smaller south-western ports were losing ground long before Bristol, and in the eighteenth century their shipping activities showed serious decline. The first cause of this was the gradual abandonment of the Newfoundland fishery which had been a major industry for a whole range of Devon, Cornwall and Dorset harbour towns and villages; from several hundred vessels engaged before the Civil War the numbers had come down to a few dozen at the end of the seventeenth century. The share in the import of American tobacco and its re-export to Europe which had been secured in early days by merchants in such ports as Barnstaple, Bideford, Exeter and Plymouth was lost at the end of the century to the larger ports, Bristol and Liverpool.[1] Finally, the beginnings of decline in the Devonshire cloth industry in the second quarter of the eighteenth century took away employment from the droves of small craft which had carried Irish wool to Ilfracombe, Minehead, Barnstaple and other North Devon harbours.

Bristol's failure to keep its share of growing transatlantic traffic is to some extent associated, of course, with the tempestuous ascent of Liverpool, the eighteenth century's success story.[2] A fishing village which before 1660 was capturing some of Chester's trade

[1] Possibly because the financial burdens associated with enormous increases in tobacco duty became too great for these small-town merchants to carry.
[2] There are many histories of Liverpool; C. Northcote Parkinson, *The Rise of the Port of Liverpool* (Liverpool, 1952), is the most useful.

with Ireland as the problems of maintaining the River Dee channels became insoluble, Liverpool began to develop an interest in transatlantic trade at the end of the sixties, but as late as 1688 it was still simply one of the more promising minor ports of England, probably about equal, in tonnage of ships it owned, to Whitehaven and Whitby.[1] The wars of 1689–1713 and later gave it great opportunities, for its outlets were remote from the main haunts of French privateers. Moreover, it had a rapidly developing immediate hinterland, and this was being widened to Bristol's detriment, by transport improvement in the Midlands.[2] Lancashire had a rapidly growing demand for colonial goods, and could supply some of the cheap linens and cottons widely used in the slave trade, the West Indian islands and the southern colonies of the American mainland. Liverpool's shipping received a further massive stimulus around 1700 from the development on a vast scale of the rock-salt deposits of Cheshire, exported via Liverpool to Ireland and later to the Baltic, Germany and Flanders.[3]

Number of ships entering Liverpool[4]

from	1687	1764
America	13 ⎫	188
West Indies	8 ⎭	
Africa	—	7
Mediterranean	—	4
Spain and Portugal	4	16
Norway and Baltic	6	66
Holland, France and Flanders	11	17
Ireland and Isle of Man	131	464

The great coal ports were in the north of England.[5] Newcastle's coastal and foreign shipments were on a scale so vast that in terms

[1] SP 16–326–142; *HMC House of Lords MSS. 1689–90*, p. 168; W. Camden, *Brittania* (1695 ed.), p. 766. As early as 1686, however, Bristol had remarked on 'the shifting of the Plantation Trades, of late years, to the northern ports, Chester, Liverpool, Workington and Whitehaven' (CSPAWI 1685–8, No. 638).

[2] See, for example, the petitions from the wide range of midland towns, extending as far as Derby and Lichfield, which in 1720 declared they obtained their colonial goods through Liverpool, and wanted the improved facilities which the new River Weaver navigation would bring (*House of Commons Journals*), *1718–22*, p. 278.

[3] T. C. Barker, 'Lancashire Coal, Cheshire Salt and the Rise of Liverpool', *Trans. Lancs. & Cheshire Hist. Soc.*, Vol. CIII, 1951, pp. 83–101.

[4] Sources: 1687 Port Books; 1764 R. Brooke, op. cit., p. 505.

[5] Nef, op. cit., App. D.

of cargo handled and tonnage of ships employed it was always the leading provincial port. Sunderland, though it grew much faster and overtook Newcastle as a coal exporter in the eighteenth century, never approached Newcastle's volume of home trade. Even greater as a centre of coal export was Whitehaven, but its coastal shipments were negligible.[1] Both Newcastle and Whitehaven had a limited participation in other trades — Newcastle with the Baltic and Holland, Whitehaven with North America.

Hull was falling out of the ranks of the leading ports in the early seventeenth century. Around mid-century, however, it began a modest expansion, based on the growing demand for Swedish iron in the Sheffield and Birmingham districts, and for imported timber throughout the great river basins which it served. This trade grew steadily, the pace quickening in the 1730's; and from the middle of the eighteenth century the insatiable demands of northern and midland industry in the first stage of their industrial revolution set Hull out on a period of growth comparable to Liverpool's; by 1772 it had reached equality with Bristol in the volume of its overseas trade. This trade was heavily concentrated on the Baltic — by this time, above all, on Russian ports — but like all the major ports Hull developed other interests, including a modest participation in the American tobacco trade.[2]

Number of ships entering Hull[3]

from	1687	1728	1772
America	1	1	15
Mediterranean	—	—	4
Spain and Portugal	—	13	14
Holland, Germany, France and Flanders	44	80	72
Norway and Baltic	109	125	181

The first signs of a new quickening of the pace of change, appearing in the thirties, were cut off by war; they burgeoned the more rapidly, therefore, when in 1748 peace returned after nine

[1] See J. E. Williams, 'Whitehaven in the Eighteenth Century', *Econ. Hist. Rev.*, 2nd ser., Vol. VIII, 1956, pp. 393–404.
[2] There is no adequate history of Hull in print; but two unpublished Ph.D. theses cover the field well; W. J. Davies, 'The Town and Trade of Hull, 1600–1700' (Cardiff, 1937), and G. Jackson, 'The Economic Development of Hull in the Eighteenth Century' (Hull, 1960).
[3] Sources: 1687 Port Books; 1728 and 1772 G. Jackson, op. cit., p. 184.

D

years. From 1748 until the American Revolution there is a rapid and almost continuing expansion of the shipping industry — not checked even by the Seven Years' War except during its first two unfortunate years. Though many branches of trade, overseas and coastal, were growing, the advance was most marked in the three most distant ones — to America, the West Indies, and the Far East — and in the trade to the Russian extremity of the Baltic.

The American mainland colonies had by now grown far beyond the role of sub-tropical dependencies with a northern fringe of independent-minded subsistence farmers. With a population approaching two million in mid-century, a number of towns large by any English provincial standard, a substantial merchant fleet engaged in inter-colonial and even transatlantic traffic and a prosperous and educated merchant and professional class, they had begun to burst some of the bonds of economic as of political tutelage. They were rapidly becoming England's greatest customers for a wide variety of new products, and the northern colonies paid for their needs largely from the proceeds of their own trading in the West Indies and from the activity of their shipping and shipbuilding industries. To the very end of the colonial period, however, the great staples which filled the ships that sailed from America to England were the products of the southern colonies — of sub-tropical plantation and forest economy. While the north grew more competitive as it grew richer, the south remained firmly bound, economically, to the British market. The tie was in part an artificial one. The leading southern export in value and volume continued to be tobacco; four-fifths of this was re-exported to Europe, and when the Revolution broke North America out of the circle of the Navigation Acts this re-export trade was replaced by a direct traffic between Virginia and Maryland and their continental markets. Long before this, however, tobacco had ceased to be almost the sole commodity of Anglo-American trade. It occupied over two-thirds of the hold space in ships bound to England in 1700; less than a third in 1753; probably no more than a fifth twenty years later, though the absolute magnitude of tobacco shipments was growing almost continuously. The bulk cargoes that supplemented it in quantities that grew enormously in the first half of the century, were rice, pitch and tar from the Carolinas and Georgia. From the middle of the century timber was coming in great amounts (masts from New Hampshire and Canada and hardwoods from the south) and in the sixties and seventies corn from Virginia and Pennsylvania made up many cargoes. The import of all these (except the last) had been accelerating even before 1739; after 1748 it leaped forward; checked by the American political 'Non-Importation' movement in 1769, it more than recovered in the last years before the Revolution.

West Indian sugar imports had jumped to much higher levels than any known before, in the years 1728–30, and had then subsided into a prolonged stability; they began a new expansion during the Seven Years' War and doubled in the twenty years before 1775, from forty to eighty thousand tons a year. Moreover, they were by mid-century being increasingly supplemented by a new bulk import — timber; the mahogany and other tropical hardwoods which were coming into favour for furnishing English dining-rooms. Attached to English markets even more firmly than the southern colonies of mainland America, the West Indies devoted themselves to production, and left trade and shipping to English merchants.

In the same two decades before the American Revolution the tonnage of ships coming in from the East India Company's territories also doubled. They carried a great variety of goods, and it is hard to pinpoint particular commodities as providing the basis for expansion. Undoubtedly, however, the rapidly expanding branch of the trade at this time was with China, the principal moderately-priced commodity handled was China tea, and with the tea came great quantities of silks and porcelain.

The most rapid development in this period from 1748 to 1775, therefore, was in the most distant trades — the American, West Indian and East Indian trades with England, which between them perhaps demanded the services of some 150 thousand tons of shipping in 1748 and almost double that tonnage in 1775.[1] The American and West Indian trades had long been among the leading employers of shipping; when they were small their growth, though rapid, had made little impact on the total size of the merchant fleet, but by the eighteenth century they used a sub-stantial proportion of its total tonnage, and every further burst of expansion caused a significant increase in the total. Their moderate

[1] A small but increasing part of the shipping in colonial trades was American.

expansion in the twenties and thirties had done much to prevent actual decline in the total size of the shipping industry; their rapid expansion after mid-century was the major cause of the rapid growth of the whole industry, for by this time nearly half of all English shipping was engaged in the transatlantic traffic. Similarly the development of the East India trade led it to make a significant proportional contribution to overall expansion in the mid-eighteenth century, as it had not done since its early days.

These trades were causing a new acceleration in the growth of the shipping industry and this growth meant demand for larger imports of Baltic hemp, flax and timber. Moreover, the enlarged American trade required an enormous expansion in the export of iron goods — the axes, hoes, plough-shares and above all nails which were needed to extend the frontier of civilisation. The prosperity of English iron manufacturing, which was a leading feature of the eighteenth-century economy, was largely based on American markets; and it required rapidly growing supplies of iron from Sweden or Russia to supply the workshops. The Baltic and Norwegian trades, therefore, which were the branches of European trade whose growth in this period nearly matched that of transatlantic trade, were largely dependent on the growth of American trade; and to an important extent, indeed, on the growth of the merchant shipping industry which the latter demanded. Whilst the Norwegians and Danes had by this time recovered a very substantial share in the carriage of goods to England from their own territories, trade with the Russian ports of Riga, Petersburg and Helsingfors and (outside the Baltic) Archangel was carried on almost entirely by English ships.

We are approaching the modern world; the world of machinery, of the mass movement of raw materials for the machines and of foodstuffs for their tenders. The first slight twitches of the expansive process which was to produce it had been felt by the shipping industry in the thirties; the snows were loosening, and in mid-century the avalanche of economic change began to move — slowly enough, in retrospect, but at a pace which even in the fifties and sixties began to produce cries of wonder from those who were being carried away by it. Twice the English shipping industry had met demands which called for greatly accelerated growth — in the sixty years after 1580, in the three decades after

1660. After each of these expansive periods, wars and their aftermath had caused a pause. Now, after 1739, wars were to come thick and fast; there was war in forty-three of the next seventy-six years. As before, wars were destructive of shipping and halted the growth of the industry; but now the pace of growth was to become so fast in peace years that the overall advance was rapid in spite of war; the size of the industry was doubled again in the forty years after 1748, and redoubled before sinking into the stagnation which followed the Napoleonic wars. The whole framework within which the shipping industry operated was now changing as, with population and industry at last growing fast, England was transformed into the workshop of the world, and in consequence demanded, in immeasurably greater quantities than ever before, the foods and the raw materials to sustain and give employment to her toiling millions.

III

Ships and Shipbuilders in the Seventeenth Century

The sixteenth century saw great technical changes in the ships of Northern Europe; changes which have a well-documented history.[1] Broadly speaking, they were of two kinds. First was the transition from the one-masted to the three-masted ship, giving scope for a variety of sails with particular functions; the merchant ship rig which was then developed consisted of spritsail, foresail and foretopsail, mainsail and maintopsail, and a lateen mizen. It was modified by a series of small steps over the next century. The second change, associated with the first, was the lengthening of the ship in relation to its beam; a change which might or might not (according to the ship's intended use) be accompanied by a refinement of the lines of bow and stern to give greater speed and manoeuvrability. The ship of 1450 rarely had a keel more than twice as long as the beam; in ships of 1600 a ratio of three to one was becoming common.[2] The new masting and sail plan is found in quite small English ships at least as far back as the 1530's,[3] but the full development from 'round ship' to 'long ship' is later, dating for warships from the 1570's; even as late as 1600 nearly half the royal ships had a proportion of keel length to beam of less than two and three-quarters.[4]

This technical revolution was still working itself out at the time of the appearance — or rather reappearance — of the large merchant ship in English ownership. If the accounts of sixteenth century commerce can be believed, Englishmen had almost

[1] See, for example, C. Singer, E. J. Holmyard, A. R. Hall and T. I. Williams (eds.), *A History of Technology* (Oxford, 1957), Vol. II, pp. 585–8; Vol. III, pp. 474–8. R. Morton Nance, 'The Ship of the Renaissance', *Mariner's Mirror*, Vol. XLI, 1955, pp. 180–92, 281–9; M. Lewis, *The Navy of Britain* (1948), pp. 70–84; G. S. Laird Clowes, *Sailing Ships, their History and Development* (1932), pp. 52–71; R. and R. C. Anderson, *The Sailing Ship* (1926), pp. 116–39. H. D. Burwash, *English Merchant Shipping, 1460–1540* (Toronto, 1947), pp. 82–144, gives an account of early English ship types.
[2] The length of the keel was not, of course, the overall length of the ship; in the types now being considered the latter was usually a third or more greater.
[3] Clowes, op. cit., p. 65 and Pl. IX.
[4] M. Oppenheim, *A History of the Administration of the Royal Navy and of Merchant Shipping in Relation to the Navy, from 1509 to 1660* (1896), p. 124.

abandoned the use of large ships in the middle of the century, when the strangling of direct English connections with the Mediterranean and the Baltic, and the quarrels with Spain, intensified the concentration of English trade on nearby Antwerp and the ports of France.

The large vessels that gradually wore out or were lost and not replaced were 'round ships'; then, quite suddenly, in the last quarter of the century, when the 'long ship' was being developed, the need for large ships was revived. A direct trade to Italy had been recommenced about 1570; it was extended a decade later to the eastern end of the Mediterranean; by 1590 nearly twenty ships were going every year to Turkey, Venice and the Greek islands. Meanwhile, oceanic privateering on a large scale was beginning to replace the isolated ventures of the sixties. These operations called for heavily armed ships of the largest kind — 'defensible ships' — and their requirements set the pattern of building of all ships of more than the most moderate size. The foundation of the English East India trade after 1600 strengthened the need for heavily armed ships, and even after war with Spain was ended, they were still in demand to stand up to the corsairs based on the Moorish ports, who plundered the small and weak during thirty years of depredation in the Mediterranean and on the Atlantic coasts of Europe. Moreover, the least patriotic of Englishmen would not be allowed to forget, during and for many years after the long struggle with Spain, that the Armada had been defeated only with the help of dozens of large merchant ships built to fight, and that such an emergency might well occur again; not until the end of the seventeenth century did the warship become differentiated so radically from the large merchantman that the latter ceased to be of value in the line of battle.

During more than half a century of continuing expansion before the Civil War, therefore, English shipwrights who were concerned in the building of ships of any size[1] were committed to the substantially built, heavily-masted and well-gunned ship for mercantile purposes as for privateering and the navy. English ships sailed triumphantly in waters from which Spanish and Italian shipping had been driven by corsairs, and foreign owners sought to buy English-built merchantmen.

[1] Small vessels of a few score tons could be built by almost any well-trained carpenter in a coastal town.

The complicated nomenclature of sailing ship types which is familiar today was developed late in the eighteenth century. Though some special names were used much earlier — ketch, brig, hoy, pink — they rarely fit the careful definitions of modern times, and the most useful grouping of ships, as they existed about 1640, can be made by taking size as the principal criterion. First, there was a tiny group of very large ships[1] of 350 tons and upwards. The largest of all merchant ships built before the end of the eighteenth century, the *Trade's Increase* of nearly a thousand tons burden which the East India Company had had built in 1609, was an object-lesson rather than an example. A ship 'for beauty, burthen, strength and sufficiency surpassing all merchant ships whatsoever', she had been lost at Bantam on her first voyage in 1610; and whatever was lost with her, the realisation that in a vessel of this size it could have been a hundred thousand pounds worth of cargo deterred the Company from building more like her. There were, however, ships of six to seven hundred tons in the forties. All this group of ships of over three hundred and fifty tons was engaged normally in the East India or the Levant trade. Many of them followed the short-lived fashion of the larger warships of the time in having a fourth mast, the bonaventure mizen; the rest were three masted. They were two- or occasionally three-decked, heavily gunned and strongly manned, and they constituted the navy's chief reserve of fighting ships in wartime. Most of the individual ships can be identified; there were about thirty of them in 1640. (There had been one, of doubtful value, in 1582.) In their general structure and masting, however, they were little different from other ships, down to fifty or sixty tons — the ships which served the Iberian peninsula and the French wine trade and carried on much of the trade in the North Sea. Almost all these, large and small, were three-masted ships, the main and foremast square-rigged, with lateen mizen; most carried guns in numbers proportioned to their size. Variation in type, as distinct from variation in size, only became important in ships of less than fifty tons or so. Among these, the smallest vessels, there was a variety of two-masted rigs — the most popular were the vessels then called ketches — and of one-masted hoys and doggers, shallops

[1] Today, ships as small as the giants of the early seventeenth century are hardly to be found outside the coastal and short-sea trades. Most of the Central Electricity Authority's colliers which come up the Thames to the power stations are larger than any ship built before the nineteenth century.

and clinker-built boats. These traded with France, Ireland, Holland and Flanders, and round the English coast; almost all of them carried a few guns. Some foreign-built ships, perhaps of the flyboat type, had come into English ownership as prizes in the French and Spanish war of 1624–30 or by purchase, but there is no evidence that the number was large.[1] The English merchant fleet was, on the whole, English-built.

Quite early in the century the unsuitability of English-built ships to some trades was being made apparent. The export trade in coal, for example, was nearly all carried on, in the decades around 1600, in foreigners' ships. 'Hither even to the mine's mouth come all our Neighbour Country nations with their Shippes continually, employeing their owne Shipping and Marriners.'[2] There was no obvious reason for English employment of defensible ships in the coal trade, which was never endangered except in time of war; yet as larger ships began to come into its employ some, at least, conformed quite closely to the warship type,[3] and were, in fact, used for naval purposes during the Spanish War of the mid-twenties.[4] Even the imposition of discriminatory duties against foreign ships lading coal, in 1620, had little effect.[5] 'The Flemings have eaten us out, by reason that they carry halfe as cheape againe as we can, in regarde that their fashioned shippes saile with so few men. Whereupon our marchants do usually lade the Flemings and lett our owne lye still.'[6]

The 'Flemings' — that is, the Dutch — had indeed reacted to the technical changes of the sixteenth century in a way sharply contrasting with the English. True, they built warships, privateers,

---

[1] On Bristol purchases, see J. Latimer, *Annals of Bristol in the Seventeenth Century* (Bristol, 1900), p. 129.

[2] 'The Trades Increase' (1615), *Harleian Miscellany*, Vol. IV, pp. 212–31.

[3] See, for example, SP 13–180–77.

[4] Four large Newcastle colliers were used as convoys for the Iceland fishing fleet in 1627 (APC Jan.–Aug. 1627, p. 2) and later constituted part of the Channel squadron (ibid. p. 63).

[5] Professor Nef's view that this measure was effective (*The Rise of the British Coal Industry* (1932), Vol. II, p. 25) is not borne out by the figures he quotes; these show that foreign participation was as great as ever in 1633. Miss Bertha Hall shows the position in her (unpublished) London Ph.D. thesis, 'The Trade of Newcastle and the North-East Ports' (1934), p. 68.
Ships clearing from Newcastle for foreign ports:
             1616   69 English,   489 foreign
             1633   116 English,   432 foreign.
The change had come by 1661, but it was due to other factors, discussed below, which operated after mid-century.

[6] SP 14–9 (1626).

ships for the Mediterranean trade, which (with modifications for
the conditions of navigation among their native shoals) were much
the same as the English; but their shipbuilding techniques were
not dominated by these needs; they built very different ships as
well. Far back in the sixteenth century, Amsterdam had grasped
from the weakening hands of the Hanseatic towns the great bulk
trades of Northern Europe — the carriage of corn and timber
southward, of salt and fish northward. Dutch carrying interests
were reinforced by enormous herring, cod and whale fisheries.
They traded in waters which had been dominated by the old-
fashioned Hanseatic hulk;[1] waters which by the sixteenth century
had become fairly free from piracy and which were rarely penetrated by the Moorish corsairs. They traded in goods whose value
was small in relation to their bulk, goods which could be risked
at sea in large shiploads, and whose price was markedly influenced
by transport costs. Most Dutch shipping, before the Revolt of the
Netherlands, was engaged in the fisheries or in the Northern
trades, and in carrying bulk cargoes of French and Portuguese
salt and wine to the north. It was pointless to build for these
purposes ships which were fast and defensible if — as was the
case — this type of building was expensive and the operating
costs per ton were high. Alongside the warship types, therefore,
the Dutch evolved their own special form of the 'long ship'; the
bulk cargo-carrier known as the *fluit* (*anglice* flyboat).[2] Its
'invention' is traditionally ascribed to 1595, but it was, of course,
the outcome of a long process of experiment and modification,[3]
and from it branched out in the course of the seventeenth century
a whole range of types for particular kinds of cargo.[4]

[1] Hulk, like argosy, is in origin the name of a ship type; an old-style 'round'
cargo-carrier, often of enormous tonnage, with three masts. A fleet of Hanseatic
hulks formed part of the Spanish Armada; they can hardly have added to its
fighting capacity.
[2] The latter term will be used in this book.
[3] There is a useful account of the flyboat's development in B. Hagedorn,
Die Entwicklung der wichtigsten Schiffstypen bis ins. 19 Jahrhundert (Berlin, 1914),
pp. 102–16. The writer shows how it differed from earlier vessels, but does not
make any useful comparisons with contemporary English ships.
[4] I have some misgivings about the account given here of the contrasting
development of English and Dutch ships. Other English trades than those to
the Levant began to grow fast in the second half of the sixteenth century —
the Newfoundland fishery from the 1550's, the coal trade which at least trebled
between 1550 and 1600, the Baltic trade which was seriously penetrated in the
seventies, during the most critical stage of the Dutch struggle for independence.
Between them, these trades must at the beginning of the seventeenth century
have used more than half the total tonnage of English merchant ships; and they

The secret of the flyboat's cheap operation was in the smallness of its crew in relation to its carrying capacity. Just what features enabled the flyboat to sail with little more than half the crew carried by comparable English ships in similar conditions is a nice technical question that has not been systematically discussed either by contemporaries or by modern historians of sailing ships. However, it seems evident that both in hull design and in masting the flyboat differed markedly from the English 'defensible ship'. Though the keel was exceptionally long,[1] her builders eschewed the fine lines which created awkwardly placed and awkwardly shaped sections in the interior; the bottom was relatively flat, the rake was small, and the bows were bluff. George Waymouth wrote, about 1610,[2] 'The ships in the Low Countries are built longer according to their bredth and depth, than our Ships are. They bee built with broader and longer bottoms proportionable to their length, than our Ships bee.' In relation to their main dimensions, therefore, the Dutch ships had an unusually high volume of accessible cargo space; they 'measure little and stow much'.[3] This was not important in every trade; the ship carrying iron, for example, would be weighed down to her minimum safe freeboard long before the hold was filled. But in the numerous important trades which were concerned with commodities lighter than water or very little heavier — in modern terms, with a high stowage factor — hold space rather than weight determined what a ship could carry. Secondly, being little concerned with speed, they carried a relatively small area of sail — and sail area was the chief determinant of the size of the crew of any given ship. Sir

---

were beginning to use fairly large ships. Nevertheless, the undoubted concentration of English shipbuilders in the seventeenth century on ships which were small-scale warships seems to me most easily explicable by the circumstances, explained above, which set the pattern of building large ships for distant trades and privateering, and the acceptance of that pattern by anybody else who wanted a large ship. By 1604, even the Merchant Adventurers trading across the North Sea claimed to be using many large ships which had taken part in naval actions alongside the Queen's own ships (SP 13–8–58). Professor Violet Barbour's 'Dutch and English Merchant Shipping in the Seventeenth Century', *Econ. Hist. Rev.*, Vol. II, 1930, pp. 261–90, is a valuable discussion of the subject.

[1] The keel might be as much as four times as long as the breadth. See, for example, the dimensions of 27 captured Dutch flyboats in use by the English navy as victuallers, in J. R. Tanner (ed.), *Calendar of Pepysian Manuscripts*, (Navy Record Society, 1903–22), Vol. I, pp. 286–8.

[2] BM Harleian MSS. 309–68.

[3] SP 29–326–60 (1672). In modern shipbuilding language, they had a high block coefficient.

William Petty, in the 1670's, writes of 'The Hollanders under-
masting and sailing such of their Shipping, as carry cheap and
gross Goods, and whose sale doth not depend much upon Season'
and he goes on to work out the cost advantages of this practice.[1]

Designed primarily as a slow cargo carrier, the flyboat had other
lesser advantages. It was lightly built, chiefly because its cargo
was not of great value but also because it did not need to provide
the strength and stability of a gun-platform; while the absence of
guns saved a little cargo space and tonnage, as well as a gunner's
wages.

The creation of the flyboat to meet the needs of trade in North
European waters, and the proliferation of special types which the
vast scale of that trade made possible, gave Dutch merchant
shipping the basis for its grip on much of the carrying trade of
Europe in the seventeenth century; and this, in its turn, made it
easier to build and operate ships economically. The impact of
Dutch competition with England was blunted in the twenties and
thirties by administrative measures against the use of Dutch-
owned ships, by some English acquisitions of ships built in
Holland, and above all by Dutch involvement in war; it reappeared
in an intensified form after 1648, shattering all complacency among
English shipowners. A belated but widespread recognition was
then accorded to the advantages of the Dutch flyboat and its
sisters, and the old satisfaction with English shipbuilding and
English ships broke down. The advantages of Dutch ships in
cheapness of operation and building, and handiness for the
carriage of bulk cargoes were widely remarked upon. The first of
the long line of envious pamphleteers, *The Advocate* (1651) wrote,
'Few Merchant Ships among the Hollanders were Ships of much
Defence, unless those going to India; and so they were neither
at so great a charge of Guns in building them, nor did carrie a
proportion of men or victual (in setting them out) near, or answer-
able to English shipping of the same Burthen.' He had many
successors in the next three decades.

Under the fire of criticism, English shipbuilders were slow to
react and adopt new methods. They had no reason to. The
upsurge of opinion against the Dutch, in precipitating a series of
wars, solved for some decades the problem of supplying cheaply-

[1] 'Political Arithmetic', in C. H. Hull (ed.), *The Economic Writings of Sir
William Petty* (1899), p. 261.

run ships to the English shipping industry. For while it need not be supposed that war was actually started for the purpose of stealing Dutch ships, the capture of a large fleet of prizes was in fact one of its dramatic and important effects. The number of prizes was very great in the First Dutch War, and there were substantial hauls in the Second and Third. The following are estimates of the number of prizes taken in wars of the seventeenth century:

First Dutch War, 1652-4	1,000-1,700[1]
War with Spain, 1655-60	400[2]
Second Dutch War, 1664-7	522[3]
Third Dutch War, 1672-4	500[4]
French War, 1689-97	1,279[5]

There was, in fact, a kind of large-scale exchange of merchant ships in these wars, from which England gained in numbers and tonnage in the Dutch Wars, and lost in the others.[6] But England secured, in the Dutch Wars, substantial advantages from the exchange which brought her large numbers of Dutch bulk carriers.

A few figures will illustrate the effect of this exchange. Among the passes issued in 1662-4 for protection against Moorish corsairs, 180 out of 590 were for foreign-built ships,[7] although

[1] Shaftesbury Papers in the PRO (GD 29-2).
[2] There is no contemporary estimate of prizes taken in the Spanish or the Third Dutch War. Prize cases dealt with in the Court of Admiralty totalled 256 in the Spanish War, 358 in the Second and 344 in the Third Dutch War. (PRO Indexes 9009, 9010, 9011.) The numbers dealt with by the Court are known from other sources (see nn. 3 and 5, below) to be far below the true total of prizes in the seventeenth century. The implication that the number of prizes taken in the last two Dutch wars was about equal, is not contradicted by contemporaries; but they considered that very few prizes had been taken in the Spanish War. In November 1692 Pepys wrote that England had taken five times as many prizes from the Dutch in three wars as had been taken up to that date in the French War. (J. R. Tanner (ed.), *Samuel Pepys Naval Minutes* (Navy Record Society, 1925), p. 270.) Up to the end of 1692 about 470 French prizes had been taken (SP 30-774); on Pepys's calculations, then, some 2,000 to 2,500 prizes in all were taken from the Dutch. The prizes of 1652-4 and 1672-4 are estimated on the basis of these two pieces of evidence, and the known number taken in the Second Dutch War. See also W. Laird Clowes, *History of the Royal Navy* (1897-1903), Vol. II, p. 155; *A Brief History of the Trade of England* (1702), p. 26; R. Coke, *A Discourse of Trade* (1670), p. 27.
[3] BM Egerton MSS., 861.
[4] See n. 3, above.
[5] SP 30-774. This total excludes 17 warships. The tonnage of the merchant ships captured totalled about 140 thousand.
[6] English losses in the war of 1624-30 were probably over 300 ships; in the Spanish War of 1655-60, between 1000 and 1800; in the three Dutch wars together no more than 500; in the war of 1689-97 perhaps as many as 4000. See pp. 315-16, below.
[7] Adm. 7/630.

passes were never applied for in the Northern trades, which had most use for such ships. The figure is astonishingly high;[1] it would have been higher five years later, immediately after the Second Dutch War. Moreover, the foreign-built ships were on the average larger then the English-built, so that the proportion of foreign tonnage was higher still. It is probably true to say that between 1654 and 1675 foreign-built ships were never less than a third of the total tonnage in English ownership, and that at the latter date they accounted for something like half of it. The problem of securing a properly balanced English merchant fleet had reached a solution; but it was a solution which could only be temporary, and one which posed a challenge.[2] It was temporary, because Dutch wars could not be expected to recur into the indefinite future; indeed, for fifteen years after 1674 England was at peace with all the world. The passes issued in the mid-eighties already show a striking change. Though issued to ships in a slightly wider range of trades than those of 1662–4, they now included a far smaller proportion of foreign-built ships; in 1686–7, 131 were foreign-built out of a total of 1,532.[3] The influence of more than a decade of peace was being felt.[4]

However, shipowners and merchants now had many years' experience of the value of the flyboat, and would no longer be satisfied with the continuous supply of 'defensible ships' turned out by the English shipwrights. The flood of complaint at English

[1] 140 of these 190 ships were Dutch-built.

[2] Several pieces of evidence support this conclusion; in particular the lists of 'ships made free' between 1668 and 1676 (Rawlinson MSS. A 295–87; SP 29–383–149/151, 384–149/153, 383–63). See also the Bristol Port Book of 1670, one of the few Port Books which give the tonnage and build of ships; of English owned vessels of over 100 tons entering during the year, 15 were English- and 26 foreign-built.

V. Barbour, op. cit., pp. 289–90 estimates that a third or a fourth of English tonnage was foreign-built in 1678, basing this on her estimate that there were some 1,200 foreign-built ships in English hands. Her figures depend on Sir John Shaw's lists of 'ships made free' which on the one hand appear to exclude the prizes of the Third Dutch War, but on the other include a number of fraudulent grants of freedom to foreign-owned ships which were seeking a refuge in a temporary neutrality while the European war continued, without English participation, from 1674 to 1678. Professor Barbour has told me in conversation that she would now be inclined to make an upward revision of her estimate.

[3] Adm. 7–75/76.

[4] If purchases of foreign-built ships after 1676 (when the easy granting of freedoms for them was stopped) were few, simple arithmetic applied to any plausible assumptions about ship losses and the volume of English shipbuilding will show that the proportion of foreign-built tonnage could not have been more than one-fifth by 1688; almost certainly it was much less.

SHIPPING IN THE THAMES AT WAPPING, EARLY EIGHTEENTH CENTURY

by John Hood

JAMES II RECEIVING THE MATHEMATICAL SCHOLARS OF CHRIST'S HOSPITAL

shipbuilding methods was at its strongest in the sixties, seventies and early eighties — after the English shipowners had acquired this experience — and they were already observing how dependent they appeared to be on the continuance of a more or less accidental foreign supply, since the shipwrights appeared unwilling to change their ways. Sir Josiah Child wrote in 1669 that the English would have been wholly beaten out of the bulk trades

'had we been necessitated to build English ships, and not been recruited at moderate prices by flyboats (being ships proper for this Trade) taken in the late Dutch War. . . . The Act of Navigation is now of seventeen or eighteen years' standing, yet in all these years not one English ship has been built for this Trade.'[1]

'No English ship hath been built for the timber trade since the Rump first made the Act of Navigation,' wrote one of Sir Joseph Williamson's correspondents in 1670,[2] and the timber merchant Thomas Papillon confirmed that 'the English neither have, nor ever have had, ships suitable for the timber trade, those hitherto used having been chiefly foreign prizes'.[3]

Between the outbreak of the First Dutch War in 1652, and the passing of the era of foreign acquisitions in the late seventies, therefore, the English shipbuilders had little incentive to build ships in imitation of, or to compete with, the flyboats. Williamson commented in 1670 that if no such ships had been built in England for seventeen years, the obvious conclusion was that no demand existed for their building.[4] But shipowners foresaw with some dread the day when this fortuitous supply would have worn out. After 1662 the Navigation Acts prevented a solution through the *purchase* of foreign-built ships; though under various pretexts some purchase abroad did continue for another fourteen years, it almost came to an end after 1676.

Yet, while the foreign-built component of the English merchant fleet diminished steadily in the eighties and nineties, and there was still wide-spread hostility to the Dutch, the agitation about Dutch maritime superiority failed to reappear in any strength. Once the way had been shown, through the use of Dutch prizes, to cheaper

[1] *A New Discourse of Trade* (1669), p. 127.
[2] SP 29 281a–252.
[3] A. F. W. Papillon, *Memoirs of Thomas Papillon* (1887), p. 69.
[4] SP 29–258–85. See other expressions of the same view at this time in CO 388–1–345, 388–1–350.

shipment, there could be no voluntary return to the use of expensive defensible ships. If we observe, therefore, that by 1700 complaints were no longer made about the failure of English shipwrights to produce ships for great stowage and cheap operation; if we note that in the contemporary literature the impossibility of competing with Dutch and Scandinavian ships in this field was no longer axiomatic;[1] then the implication is clear. Some section of the English shipbuilding industry had begun to respond to the stimulus of new demands, and to produce ships which could compete with the Dutch.

Before following this development into the next century, a view must be taken of the industry which built ships in England, up to 1700.

The English master shipwrights were practical men, working by rule of thumb, basing themselves firmly on long experience and generally contemptuous of theoreticians and innovators; or, to put it less politely, they built ships 'onely by uncertayn traditionall Precepts, and by Deceiving Ayme of theyre Eye'.[2] There were few textbooks of the shipbuilder's art before the late eighteenth century, and such as there were came from the pens of men who made no mark in the practice of shipbuilding.[3] The shipwrights of London and a few other places were organised in guilds[4] and arranged some systematic training through apprenticeship; inevitably, this perpetuated traditional ways. On the other hand, the

---

[1] In 1698 Davenant said English ships were built on the Humber and Trent as cheaply as Dutch (*The Political and Commercial Works* (ed. C. Whitworth, 1771), Vol. I, p. 427). The English agent in Hamburg in 1692 wrote of Lubeck-built ships being one-third cheaper than either English- or Dutch-built. (BM Add.MSS. 37663; Rycaut-Nottingham, 15th November 1692.)

[2] George Waymouth, 1610 (BM Harleian MSS. 309–68).

[3] Dr R. C. Anderson lists the traceable works on shipbuilding in English and other Western European languages in 'Early Books on Shipbuilding and Rigging', *Mariners' Mirror*, Vol. X, 1924, pp. 53–64, and '18th Century Books on Shipbuilding and Rigging', *Mariners' Mirror*, Vol. XXXIII, 1947, pp. 218–25.

Mr A. G. Vacoe describes in the *Mariners' Mirror*, Vol. XXXIII (1947), p. 55, a conversation he had with a shipwright who was building wooden schooners of 100–250 tons at Tripoli in 1942. 'I asked one old man who was laying out the frames of a vessel what designs he worked from. He said he had none; he was working by eye. As for the design, he got that "out of my father's head".'

[4] These old shipwrights' guilds spent much of the seventeenth century in a struggle — ultimately successful — with a new organisation chartered by James I in 1612 with the intention of embodying all the shipwrights of England and Wales. There is a brief account of the London shipwrights guild by E. A. Ebblewhite in *Brassey's Naval and Shipping Annual, 1925*, pp. 302–14.

shipbuilding business did not usually run to dynasties (despite the ever-active Petts); though son might follow father, as did a Castle, a Graves, a Johnson, the grandsons adopted different callings.

Small vessels, up to a few score tons, could be and were built in any sheltered waters, and by any competent carpenter, and only intensive study by local historians can reveal much of this side of the industry. The building of larger ships by the professional master shipwrights, who usually disposed of permanent slipways and in a few cases of graving docks, was an industry which has left some traces behind. In the early seventeenth century, it is clear, it was heavily concentrated on the Thames (at Shadwell, Rotherhithe, Blackwall) and in the estuarine creeks of East Anglia. A record, incomplete but probably not seriously misleading, of large ships built between 1626 and 1637, gives the following places of building:[1]

London	52 ships of	11,625 measured tons
Ipswich	35	8,180
Other East Anglian ports	48	10,505
All other ports	24	4,220

Few of the builders are recorded as building as much as a ship every year; the largest — John and Matthew Graves of Limehouse, Robert Tranckmere of Shoreham and Zephaniah and John Foord of Ipswich — each built 12–15 ships, of something over 3,000 tons, in these twelve years. Even allowing for the large part that repair work played in the shipwright's activities, it is plain that merchant shipbuilding was not then or later in the century a trade in which great capital could be put to use or large fortunes made.

The history of the industry during and after the Civil War is much more obscure. Most of the old names disappear, though in London William Castle, a beginner in the thirties, was being followed by his son Robert in the sixties, and a Greaves and a Taylor may have succeeded their fathers. At the head of the new names, competing with the Castles, was Henry Johnson (a former apprentice of Peter Pett) who had taken over the East India Company's Blackwall Yard in 1654. Yet even Johnson, the Castles, and their leading rivals James Buckoll and Richard Boys, could turn out only a large East Indiaman or a pair of ships of

---

[1] Trinity House Certificates, listed at the end of each year of the *Calendars of State Papers, Domestic.*

E

moderate size apiece each year. Their businesses were not on a large scale. They employed no great capital. Ships were almost invariably built to order, on terms precisely laid down by contract, for individual purchasers' requirements varied enormously in detail, and a shipwright risked more by building speculatively than he suffered from waiting for orders to come in.[1] Payment was always made by instalments as the work proceeded, so little working capital was required. Johnson owned the yard he used, but many builders leased them, and their permanent equipment consisted of no more than a few heavy timbers.[2] None of the London builders can have regularly employed a hundred men in peacetime, and of them all only Johnson, who had much wider interests in shipowning and East India trade, made a substantial fortune. Pepys questioned, 'What shipwrights, new or old, have ever raised estates by this trade, as particularly the Petts; and if any, whether in the merchants' service or the King's, where the greatest artists have always been; and reckon up instances of the poor families of the best;'[3] and he considered that Sir William Batten's daughter disgraced her family by marrying the younger William Castle.[4]

One thing is plain in this period; the falling away of East Anglian shipbuilding. Though Ipswich, Woodbridge and other harbours had built ships of every kind, their mainstay had been the supplying of the coastal coal trade, and their products could not compete with the flood of prize ships so eminently suited to this trade. As Defoe wrote,[5] the decline of Ipswich was due to 'those Dutch vessels which cost nothing but their caption, were bought cheap, carried great burthens, and the Ipswich building fell off for want of price'. The preamble to the *Act to Encourage the Building of Shipps in England* in 1685 declares that

'For some years past and more especially since the laying of a duty upon Coals brought into the River of Thames[6] there hath been

---

[1] A typical shipbuilding contract is reproduced in Sir Richard Temple (ed.), *The Papers of Thomas Bowrey* (Hakluyt Society, 1925), pp. 129–36. There is an unusually long and detailed draft contract in W. Sutherland, *Britain's Glory, or Shipbuilding Unveiled* (1717), pp. 75–96.

[2] The total value of all stocks of timber, metalwork and yard equipment in Johnson's shipyard at Blackwall in 1686 was only £868 (BM Add.MSS. 22183–94).

[3] *Naval Minutes*, op. cit., p. 163.   [4] *Diary*, 5th July 1663.

[5] *A Tour through England and Wales* (Everyman edition), Vol. I, p. 41.

[6] In 1667. Professor Nef's statistics show that, contrary to the implication of this preamble, coal shipments along the east coast rose markedly between

observed a more than ordinary decay in building Shipps in England and particularly in Newcastle Hull Yarmouth Ipswich Aldborough Dunwich Walberswick Woodbridge and Harwich where many Stoute Shipps were formerly built for the Coal and other Trades. . . . but by the Discouragement that Trade hath ever since laine under occasioned chiefly by the Freedom which Forreigne Shipps and Vessels bought and brought into the Kingdome have enjoyed equall to that of English built Shipps the Merchants Owners and other have not been able to build as formerly which hath caused many of our English Shipwrights Calkers and Seamen to seek their Imployments abroad whereby the Building-Trade is not onely wholly lost in severall of the aforementioned places and in others very much decayed . . .'.

In London, which had always specialised in strongly-built armed ships, the expansion of Levant, East India and West Indies trade brought prosperity to shipbuilding, unhampered by the foreign competition. But the north-east provides the key to new developments in shipbuilding. Checked, like East Anglia, by the vast inflow of prize-ships, the north-east coast shipbuilders were stimulated by them to new expansion — new in kind as well as in quantity.

1667 and 1685 (op. cit., App. D). It was not the tax on coal that ruined East Anglian shipbuilders.

IV

Ships and Shipbuilders in the Eighteenth Century

In the days of sail the cost of sea transport was principally the cost of paying and feeding a crew. During the seventeenth century the Dutch had led the way, as we have seen, in operating with ships that needed small crews in relation to the cargo they carried, and the English had followed their example, when they could, by using captured Dutch-built ships. In the eighteenth century, however, English shipbuilders made their own way towards operational efficiency. The clearest way of measuring their success is by looking at the gradually decreasing ratio of crew to tonnage; that is, to use the somewhat artificial concept of 'tons served per man'. The picture can be drawn with some accuracy from 1726 onward, when this sort of evidence can be extracted from the records of 'Seamen's Sixpences'[1] but to point the contrast it is as well first to glance back briefly at the manning position in the previous century, so far as this is possible.

It is clear that in the early decades of the seventeenth century, ships going southward from England — to Spain and Portugal, the Biscay coast of France, the Mediterranean and the East Indies — were very heavily manned. These vessels had to defend themselves against the corsairs who were ready to prey without limit on English shipping in the Mediterranean and off the Atlantic coast of Europe, until naval expeditions began to curb their eagerness. The guns which ships carried might well have to be used, and it was a good thing to carry a crew which could at least man a single broadside. But as the dangers declined, so crews were reduced gradually towards levels determined by the requirements of serving the ship; curiously enough, the number of guns carried was little if at all reduced, though they could no longer be fully manned. In the thirties, the English ships going to Cadiz and

---

[1] The payments at the rate of sixpence a month made by merchant seamen for the upkeep of Greenwich Hospital (see R. Davis, 'Seamen's Sixpences; An Index of Commercial Activity 1697–1828', *Economica*, n.s. XXIII, 1956, pp. 328–43). Details of tonnage and crews of all ships entering London are in the Ledgers of the Receiver of Sixpences from 1725 (Adm. 68–194/218).

Malaga for wine and fruit carried crews averaging one man to 6·7 tons; [1] in 1686–7 the corresponding figure is 7·7 tons. [2] This is the only trade for which the very early data are plentiful, but it certainly reflects the experience of all other trades which took ships into water swept by the corsairs. The small changes indicated — representing the reduction of the crew of a 150-ton ship by two or three men — were unrelated to technical improvement; such trades continued to be operated with 'defensible ships' though with crews less adequate to defence. Both the government and the Levant Company tried to limit the temptation put in the way of the corsairs, by ensuring that ships engaged in the most valuable branch of Mediteranean trade were manned adequately for defence; an act of 1662 required that ships over 200 tons entering the Mediterranean should carry at least 16 guns and 32 men, on pain of paying extra customs duties, [3] while the Levant Company ordered in 1688 that ships in its service should carry at least fifteen men per hundred tons. [4] Both efforts were quite ineffective, because such levels of manning were more appropriate to the twenties and thirties than to the time of Charles II. [5]

In most trades, a slow improvement in manning evidenced itself between the last years of Charles II and the thirties and forties of the next century; figures which are available for the trades with Spain and Portugal, Virginia and Maryland, and the West Indies (apart from Jamaica), [6] show that rather smaller crews were carried in 1726 and 1736 than half a century earlier:

London Ships: tons served per man

for	1686	1726	1736
Spain, Portugal	7·9	9·1	9·8
Virginia, Maryland	9·8	10·8	11·0
West Indies (except Jamaica)	9·3	9·8	10·4
Jamaica	8·7	8·6	9·7[7]

[1] Data from charter parties in HCA records.
[2] From passes, Adm. 7–75/6.   [3] 2 and 3 Charles II, c. 12.
[4] A. C. Wood, *History of the Levant Company* (Oxford, 1935), p. 211.
[5] Statistics of manning in the Mediterranean trade are bedevilled for nearly a century by masters' habits of declaring their crews as 32 men; it is easy though time-wasting, to find out, for example, that the 200-ton ship of about 1730 normally carried 18 or 19 men into the Mediterranean.
[6] Ships going to Jamaica were exceptionally heavily manned in 1726 and 1736 because of the quarrels with Spain over Caribbean smuggling, in which Jamaica was specially concerned.
[7] 1686 from passes (Adm. 7–75/76); 1726 and 1736 from Seamen's Sixpences Adm. 68–194 and 196).

In the English Channel and the Spanish and Portuguese trades economic conditions favoured the use of small ships whose manning per ton was necessarily heavier than that of bigger vessels;[1] improvement might have occurred if the southern countries had possessed competing merchant fleets. The transatlantic trades were sheltered by the Navigation Acts from foreign competition, and did not follow up the possibilities which had been suggested in the seventeenth century by their tentative use of Dutch flyboats.

On the other hand, the North Sea and Baltic trades, even quite early in the seventeenth century, present a quite different picture. They were exposed to the competition, first of the Dutch carriers and later of the efficient native shipping of Scandinavia. Moreover, though the Moorish corsairs did occasionally appear in the Straits of Dover and perhaps, in the early twenties, in the mouth of the Thames, their regular beat did not extend far into the English Channel, and ships which would not go west of the Straits of Dover had no need to be equipped for encounters with them. The *Endeavour* of Shields, of 140 tons, carried only nine men (one to 15·5 tons) on a series of coastal and Norway voyages in 1632–3,[2] while the collier *Edward and Sara* in 1650 needed only thirteen men to serve her 280 tons (one to 21·5 tons).[3] During the wars of the sixties and seventies colliers were expected to surrender for naval service men in excess of a ratio of one to 20 tons.[4] The Dutch themselves hardly managed with less in their own flyboats; but it is impossible to say how representative these two English examples are.

When the first substantial body of statistics is available for use, in 1726,[5] a level of one man to about twenty tons is found to be characteristic of almost the whole of London's vast traffic to Norway and Gottenberg — a traffic which accounted for nearly a quarter of the tonnage of ships entering London. The ratio of 20·3 tons per man found in 1726 was not improved upon in the next half century. Ships similarly manned were finding their way into the Baltic trades to Sweden, Danzig and the newly acquired Russian ports of the North Baltic. These trades did not yet employ

---

[1] The average size of ships in Spanish trade fell sharply in the third quarter of the seventeenth century.
[2] HCA 30–635.   [3] HCA 30–638.
[4] J. U. Nef, *The Rise of the British Coal Industry* (1932), Vol. I, p. 391.
[5] See p. 59, n. 7, above.

a great total tonnage, and many quite small ships, whose size inevitably meant heavier manning per ton, were still engaged in them, so that the average in those trades was only 13–14 tons per man. However, all the larger vessels entering the Baltic achieved the high manning ratios of around twenty tons per man. The coastal coal trade, too, was using ships manned at much the same levels as˙the Norway and large Baltic traders.[1]

This means that in the northern trades and in the coal trade, from the time of the first Dutch flyboat prizes in the 1650's, if not earlier, there must have been a continuous supply of cheaply operated ships; that when the last Dutch prizes taken in 1674 had worn out or been lost, there was already an alternative source of supply of the same sort of vessel. Some further prizes, it is true, were taken in the later French wars, but not enough of them were of the flyboat type to replenish virtually the whole northern fleet. The conclusion is inescapable that by the last decades of the seventeenth century English shipwrights had started to build their own version of the cheaply operated ship, and that they were turning it out in large numbers during the long period of peace whose centre is 1726.

This conclusion raises an important question about the ship-building industry. In the early seventeenth century the Northern trades had used ships built in East Anglia, as well as a few from Newcastle and adjacent ports. All the East Anglian building centres were overwhelmed by the torrent of Dutch prizes, and never recovered. Ipswich, Woodbridge, and the rest, with their large and old-established yards, still cherishing occasional contracts for East Indiamen, Levant traders and even warships, were too slow to adapt themselves to the new requirements of the coal and timber trades. Who, then, met these new requirements?

There is no direct evidence about shipbuilding in the critical period, from about 1680 to 1720, when the flyboats were wearing out and the English were compelled to build their own coal, timber and flax carriers. Four things are certain, however; that shipbuilding on the north-east coast was of small importance during most of the seventeenth century; that by the early eighteenth century considerable numbers of ships were being built somewhere

[1] See T. S. Willan, *The English Coasting Trade* (Manchester, 1938), p. 16. The considerable number of north-east coast colliers whose masters paid their Seamen's Sixpences in London in the second quarter of the eighteenth century show manning ratios of twenty tons per man or more.

in England for great stowage and cheap operation; that by the middle of the eighteenth century Whitby and Scarborough ships had a special reputation for just such qualities; and that, when the registration of ships began in 1787, the north-east coast from Newcastle down to Hull was by far the largest seat of the ship-building industry, and had obviously been so for a very long time. I take this as indicating — in the absence of positive evidence — that the north-east coast was the place where sprang to life, in the decades around 1700, the new industry with the future in its hands, the building of English ships which could adequately replace the vanishing Dutch flyboats. John Cremer went to Leghorn in 1715 in 'a North Country Cat about 300 tons or more. An old Vessel noe body could tell her age' with a crew of fifteen. This was the kind of ship which, forty years earlier, writers said was not built in England.[1]

Enormous opportunities were open to shipbuilders who could fulfil this need, and it is not surprising that the opportunities should have been seen most clearly in the region which had particular use for such ships. Unhampered by the strong traditions and the more varied opportunities of the East Anglian builders, favoured by the longer survival of the woodlands of the Trent and Ouse valleys,[2] with nearby iron manufacturers to supply their needs, the local builders of modest keels and coasters turned to bigger subjects and were justified by huge success. Possibly they were reinforced by immigration from East Anglia; there are indications of a squabble over Ipswich shipwrights at Newcastle.[3] It may be significant that Ambrose Crowley's great ironworks, which in London was particularly concerned with ships' fittings, moved to Sunderland in 1682, taking many of its craftsmen with it.[4]

The chief places of building were Whitby, Newcastle and the banks of the Tyne down to South Shields, Scarborough, Stockton and Sunderland. Whitby, much the most important during the middle decades of the eighteenth century, had always had a small shipbuilding industry; a few ships of over a hundred tons were

---

[1] J. C. Cremer, *Ramblin' Jack* (ed. R. R. Bellamy, 1936), p. 71. Two pinks of 200–300 tons were launched at Stockton in 1677; one of them 'the largest vessel that ever came nigh Stockton' (SP 29–391–59). Ships described as pinks were very often of the new, flyboat-type, construction.
[2] R. Fisher, *Hearts of Oak* (1763), pp. 38–9.
[3] Rawlinson MSS. A.177–167.
[4] E. Lipson, *Economic History of England* (1948), Vol. II, pp. 178–9. Crowley's bills continually appear among ships' papers in the late seventeenth century.

built there in the early seventeenth century.[1] Yet it was eclipsed at that time not only by the industry of the south but even by that of nearby Tyneside. It was primarily a fishing village, owning a handful of ships. Certainly it was growing fast towards the end of the century; both Blome's *Britannia* (1673) and the 1695 edition of Camden's *Britannia* describe it as owning a large number of ships[2] and in 1710 there were said to be 120, of sizes ranging up to 350 tons.[3] At this time it was the sixth shipowning port of England, outdistanced only by London, Bristol, Newcastle, Yarmouth and probably Scarborough.[4] The growth of shipping is not proof of the growth of shipbuilding, but in this case the two are likely to have gone together. When, in 1702, parliament provided for substantial improvement of the piers, they were to be paid for in part by a toll on all coal laden in Tyne ports (except in Yarmouth ships);[5] this was the first of a series of such measures, among which the act of 1726 was particularly important in making possible the building of very large ships in Whitby harbour.[6] The improvement in the harbour was no doubt essential to further growth; but the demand for it, and the acceptance of a general levy on almost all coal shipping, is surely indicative of the growing importance of Whitby to the coal trade. By 1733 Whitby owned 120 ships 'and most of them are the largest that are employed in the coal trade',[7] and in 1738, when the Newcastle hostmen had grievances about the irregular loading of coal ships, they made them to the shipowners of Whitby and Scarborough.[8] The Thameside public house, 'The Prospect of Whitby', is traditionally so named because it looked out on a stretch of the Thames up which the collier fleets passed to the City. Though the tradition may be implausible — it is more likely the house was established by some retired master of the *Prospect*, of Whitby — it shows clearly the connection in the public mind between Whitby and the

[1] *CSPD, 1625-6*, p. 532; *1626-7*, p. 500.
[2] Blome said there were 100 ships; this at a time when the port of Hull, if the Mayor can be believed, possessed only 44 (SP 29-325-127). Camden's editor says there were sixty ships of 80 tons or more; this would be sufficient to put it in the front rank of English seaports.
[3] *The Case of the Town and Port of Whitby* (1710).
[4] BM Add.MSS. 11255.
[5] 1 Anne, C.19.
[6] *House of Commons Journals, 1745-50*, p. 910.
[7] *House of Commons Journals, 1732-7*, p. 388.
[8] F. W. Dendy (ed.), *Extracts from the Records of the Company of Hostmen of Newcastle-upon-Tyne* (Surtees Society, 1901), Vol. CV, pp. 196-7.

Tyne-London coal trade. Nor was it the coal trade alone that Whitby served. In 1751, more than half the English ships entering London from Norway, and one in five of those entering from the Baltic, were Whitby-owned, and these were generally large ships of 300-500 tons.[1] By this time, a very rapid expansion of Whitby ownership was taking place, though as a trading port Whitby remained insignificant.[2]

There is little record of early Whitby shipbuilding; indeed, the historian of Whitby dates the building of large ships from 1730.[3] Thirteen years earlier, however, Jarvis Coates had built the *William & Jane* of 237 tons, and there is no reason to suppose that this was the first ship of such a size; Coates had been in business since 1697.[4] The first dry dock was built in 1734, and in mid-century there were many builders at work; Benjamin Coates, Robert Barry, Thomas Fishburn, the Dock Company's Partners, and William Coulson, who had come from Scarborough fifteen or twenty years before. At Fishburns' yard a 369-ton collier barque, the *Earl of Pembroke*, was built; this was the vessel selected in 1768 by the Board of Admiralty for an expedition to the South Seas; renamed *Endeavour*, it was commanded by Lieutenant James Cook, who sailed up the east coast of Australia and claimed it for the British crown.[5]

Scarborough was of less importance, though for a time it was the leading collier-owning port of England. It appears to have grown in stature during much the same period as Whitby. Two 100-ton ketches for the navy were built there in 1691 — the only naval ships built north of Hull before the middle of the eighteenth century.[6] As at Whitby, the remodelling of the harbour (in 1733) was financed in part by the collection of tolls on coal loaded at north-eastern ports (except in Yarmouth ships).[7] There was far less space for shipbuilding than the great sheltered river mouth of Whitby provided, and the industry never approached Whitby's in size. Nevertheless, it was a substantial one. The local historian[8]

[1] Adm. 68-199.
[2] See the figures in Add.MSS. 11255.
[3] G. Young, *A History of Whitby* (Whitby, 1813), pp. 548-54.
[4] R. Weatherill, *The Ancient Port of Whitby and its Shipping* (1908), pp. 25-30.
[5] J. C. Beaglehole (ed.), *The Journals of Captain James Cook* (Hakluyt Society, 1955), pp. cxxiii-cxxviii.
[6] BM Add.MSS. 9324.
[7] 5 George II, c. 11.
[8] A. S. Rowntree, *The History of Scarborough* (1931), pp. 187-92.

records a handful of seventeeth-century shipbuilders; the Tindalls, who were still building in the nineteenth century, had records dating back to 1691 and claimed that the family business was operating much earlier. By the middle of the eighteenth century Scarborough building was probably passing from its highest level.

Sunderland had a very rapid rise, both as a coal-shipping and a shipbuilding port, after measures were taken to improve the depth of the harbour in 1717;[1] Newcastle (or South Shields) and Stockton also built considerable numbers of colliers.

There is some reason to suppose that the ships being built in these places around 1700 resembled the Dutch flyboats, though the evidence is exiguous. In the late seventeenth century the term 'pink' was sometimes used almost as a synonym for 'flyboat' — as when the Council of Trade in 1672 directed that encouragement should be given to 'the Building of Pinkes, Flutes and other great Ships, for the more convenient carryage of Masts, Timber and other Bulky Commodityes'.[2] Now a pink was simply a pink-sterned ship, and a pink stern was one, very narrow at the top and broadening below, whose description tallies quite closely with the typical flyboat stern. Not all pinks were flyboats, for there were many small pink-sterned craft, but it may well be that the eighteenth-century vessels described as pinks included many of the flyboat type. There are large numbers described as pinks in the ships' passes from the 1680's onward until the middle of the next century.[3] Ships belonging to the north-east coast ports were not heavily represented in the trades for which passes were needed; it is noteworthy, though, that in 1732–3 nearly two-thirds of the three-masted ships belonging to the north-east ports which did obtain passes were described as pinks; the corresponding proportion for London was one-sixth, and for the west coast ports one-sixteenth.

If this is so — and it is admittedly conjectural — the main technical development in English shipbuilding of the early eighteenth century was the adoption, for appropriate purposes, of

[1] There is some information on shipbuilding in Sunderland, South Shields and Stockton in the *Victoria County History, Durham*, Vol. II, pp. 303–8. Though Newcastle was always a shipbuilding centre, there is virtually no information about it before the later eighteenth century. Much of the shipbuilding credited to it in the statistics was carried on at South Shields.
[2] C. M. Andrews, *British Committees, Commissions and Councils of Trade and Plantations, 1622–75* (Baltimore, 1908), p. 128.
[3] One- and two-masted vessels were given type names descriptive of their rig.

the hull forms used earlier by the Dutch, which made possible a high carrying capacity in relation to the ship's main measurements. This is the explanation of the small crews of English ships in the Northern trades, where great stowage was particularly important.

Another new source of supply for the English shipowner was in the colonies of the American mainland, and especially in New England.[1] Ships built there ranked, for all the purposes of the Navigation Acts, as English-built, and English owners could acquire them without any disabilities. All along the northern part of the New England seaboard, shipbuilding timber grew close to the shore, pitch and tar were easily obtainable; iron was beginning to be worked in America late in the seventeenth century. The English government tried from time to time to encourage the export of shipbuilding materials from the colonies to England, but they had little success except with tar and pitch.[2] The cheaper kinds of timber could not bear the cost of shipment across the Atlantic, but if it were turned into ships on the spot these could carry their own cargoes eastward. Shipbuilding was begun on a small scale in the earliest settlements; it grew rapidly and after the Restoration was supplying all North America's own needs, for coastal craft, West Indies schooners and the fisheries, and was turning out many ships for the trade of New England with Europe.

Sir Josiah Child saw and dreaded these possibilities. 'There is nothing more prejudicial and in prospect more dangerous to any Mother Kingdom', he wrote, 'than the Encrease of Shipping in her Plantations, Colonies and Provinces.'[3] He died just too soon to read the persuasive advocacy of extensive colonial shipbuilding by the author of *Considerations on the East India Trade* in 1701,[4] who proposed to use the cheap timber, pitch and tar, with negro slaves to do the work and Dutch mass-production methods. 'This were a surer way, and less odious to our Neighbours, than any Act of Navigation, for only English bottoms to be employed.'

Ships built in New England nevertheless played only a small part in English traffic during the seventeenth century. By 1686

---

[1] There is a useful summary of the history of American shipbuilding, with references to the literature, in J. G. B. Hutchins, *The American Maritime Industries and Public Policy, 1789–1914* (Cambridge, Mass., 1941), pp. 144–57.
[2] See R. G. Albion, *Forests and Sea Power* (Cambridge, Mass., 1926), pp. 238–45.
[3] *A New Discourse of Trade* (4th ed., 1740), p. 223.
[4] J. R. McCulloch (ed.), *Early Tracts on Commerce* (1856), p. 619.

half the vessels trading between New England and Old England were American-owned and presumably American-built; but outside this particular trade American-built ships were rarely employed in English affairs.[1] Some ships were bought in America by English merchants even before the English Civil War, but as late as 1668 such purchases were still, apparently, regarded as a little unusual.[2] Wars, which hampered English imports from Norway and the Baltic, assisted the New England shipbuilding industry, and by 1689 the industry was sufficiently large and well-established to take advantage of English demand in the wars which filled most of the next twenty-four years. From the nineties until the Peace of Utrecht references to English purchases in the colonies are abundant. With the ending of the war, these English purchases dropped for a time to a lower level; but English-owned colonial-built ships were being used in some numbers in all the trades with the North American colonies, and to a small extent to the West Indies. On the whole, they were quite small ships; the great bulk-cargo carriers were not American products, and the advantages of American-built ships were not in cheap operation — at this time they were manned on the same levels as English-built ships — but in cheap building.

Nevertheless, the Thames shipwrights complained in 1724 that

'By the great number of ships and other vessels lately built, now building and still likely to increase to be built, in New England and other parts of America, the trade of the petitioners is much decayed ... great numbers of those able shipwrights, brought up and employed by Petitioners, for want of work to maintain their families, have been necessitated to withdraw themselves from their native country into America and other foreign parts.'[3]

On this the Council of Trade reported that 'We have good reason to believe, the number of shipwrights in Great Britain is diminished one half since 1710. This diminution is chiefly owing to the great numbers of ships built annually in your Majesty's plantations, but particularly in New England'.[4] Currency manipulation and

---

[1] Adm. 7-75/76.
[2] SP 29-242-64. See also S. E., *The Touchstone of Money and Commerce* (1660).
[3] CO 5-869, p. 67.
[4] CO 915-430. The year 1710 was a serious one for London shipbuilders because it saw the end of naval contracts to private yards, which were not resumed until 1741.

consequent inflation in Massachusetts and Rhode Island soon afterwards gave the American industry a setback;[1] but apart from this interval in the thirties American supply showed an upward trend in the first three-quarters of the eighteenth century, with great temporary expansion in each war. Perhaps by 1730 one English ship in every six was American-built, and by 1760 one in four.[2] In the late sixties, however, the pace of American ship-building quickened, and for a few years large ships as well as small poured out of the yards for English owners. Richard Champion stated in 1774 that nearly a third of British owned ships were American built (2,342 out of 7,694).[3]

Purchase from America came to an end when independence thrust the new nation beyond the pale of the English Navigation laws. 'A very important advantage [of the American War] was the recovery of the valuable trade of shipbuilding, which had in great measure been, very impolitically, sacrificed to the zeal for promoting the prosperity of the colonies.'[4]

In the eighteenth century, as in the seventeenth, wars yielded a harvest of foreign prizes. The numbers, in the sixty years to the end of the Seven Years War, were much the same as in the previous sixty years, but of course in 1739-48 and 1756-63 they were added to a merchant fleet far larger than it had been.

1702-13	2,203[5]
1739-48	1,499[6]
1756-63	1,855[7]

These ships were of all kinds; English ships recaptured; German, Dutch or Scandinavian vessels seized for infringement of the blockades; a handful were Spanish or Portuguese; the majority were French. While no doubt many were Dutch-built there was

[1] Peter Faneuil wrote in 1736, 'It is much cheaper to buy Vessells in the River of Thames than to have them built here for the present' (W. B. Weeden, *Economic and Social History of New England, 1620-1789* (Boston, 1789), p. 484).

[2] These approximate figures may be deduced from passes, assuming that very few American ships were employed in the Baltic and North Sea trades.

[3] *Considerations on the Present Situation of Great Britain and the United States of North America* (1784), pp. 14-15. Chalmers's figures for the same date show 2,311 out of 6,219 as American-built, but these are based on Lloyd's Register of Shipping, and are incomplete and probably selective (*Opinions on American Independence* (1784), p. 99).

[4] D. Macpherson, *Annals of Commerce* (1805), Vol. IV, p. 10.

[5] SP 30-774.

[6] HCA Index to HCA 32-94/160 (warships are excluded from all these figures). The HCA records probably represent total prizes accurately after the exposure of scandals in the war of 1702-13.

[7] HCA Index to HCA 32-161/259.

not in these wars an accession of ships, largely of a single type, radically changing the make-up of the English merchant fleet, such as the Dutch Wars of the seventeenth century had provided. The eighteenth-century wars contributed a well-balanced addition to total English shipping, leaving the English shipyards, on their side, the task of meeting a demand for a variety of types.

Nevertheless, the effect of the capture of prizes must have been to depress English shipbuilding. The physical loss of English ships was probably on a smaller scale. After 1692 France abandoned attempts to dominate the seas, to give permanent protection in wartime to her long-distance trade, while turning from naval actions to commerce-raiding. English blockade in wartime became fairly effective, compelling France to look to neutrals to supply her, and the French mercantile marine languished. The vast numbers of English ships captured by the privateers were not wanted, therefore; they would have been so many more to rot at anchor in the mouth of the Garonne or the Seine. English ships bound homeward with bulk cargoes of the kinds badly needed in France would be taken into French ports, but many of the others were ransomed. In such a case, any specially valuable portable cargo was trans-shipped from the captured vessel, a hostage (usually the chief mate) was taken into the privateer; the master was required to sign a form[1] undertaking to pay a specified sum of money on his arrival in port (perhaps no more than a quarter or a fifth of the value of the ship and cargo); and the ship was released, with a protection valid for twenty-four hours against other French privateers. It is impossible, for this reason, to estimate how many English ships were physically taken into French possession; the figures quoted for captures include a large number that were ransomed.[2]

[1] The fact that these forms were printed (in French on the front and in English on the reverse) with special headings for each of the French admiralty jurisdictions, indicates that great numbers were used. One in the HCA dated 1712 is numbered 4246, from the admiralty of Dunkirk (HCA 15–29; *Hope*). The practice of ransom was not a new one, but it had been less widely used in the past.

[2] Purchase abroad was not unknown in the eighteenth century. For a few years, indeed, foreign-built ships occasionally obtained the freedom of English-built by means of private acts of parliament; but this practice was ended after petitions in 1709 against 'the excessive number of bills brought in for naturalising foreign-built ships' (*House of Commons Journals, 1708–11*, pp. 148, 150, 151). Failing such naturalisation, these vessels were restricted by the Navigation Acts to a very narrow range of uses; but there was nothing to stop the owner of a ship built in Sweden, for example, employing her in trade with that country. His difficulty was that he had practically no alternative trades to fall back on.

Thus the old shipbuilding industry of London and the East Anglian ports was threatened from three sides. It is not surprising that it languished, faced as it was by the competition of the new yards of the north-east coast which were almost monopolising the building of bulk-cargo carriers, and with that of American builders who could provide ships for the transatlantic and southern trades at lower costs, as well as being periodically overwhelmed by the influx of scores of thousands of tons of prize ships of every variety. London shipbuilders remained important, because they kept the monopoly of building East Indiamen, and ships for the Levant trade and some of the larger West Indiamen continued to be produced on the Thames. All round the coast small local shipbuilders or carpenters continued to supply local needs for small ships, and in a few ports ships of some size were constructed. But the construction of large ships — except the very largest — had shifted decisively to the north-east coast, and in the late sixties and seventies, to a lesser extent to America. Accurate statistics are available only from 1787, when registration began, and the situation had by then changed markedly from that which had obtained a decade earlier, both because a substitute had had to be found for American shipbuilding and because commerce had grown. Nevertheless, some of these statistics are worth reproducing.

Tonnage of ships built in England, 1790–1 (two years)

	Tonnage built	Number of ships built	Number of ships over 200 tons
London	16,372	119	25
East Anglia	7,787	136	2
South Coast	15,740	341	7
Bristol Channel and Wales	8,240	145	10
North-west Coast	14,945	166	18
North-east Coast	40,926	249	88
TOTAL	104,010	1,156	150[1]

In the last two or three decades before American independence, these various suppliers of ships to English owners developed their techniques in ways which made possible marked reduction in the size of ships' crews. The following table illustrates the change:

[1] R. Stewart-Brown, *Liverpool Ships of the Eighteenth Century* (Liverpool, 1932). The largest individual shipbuilding ports, after London, were Newcastle (12,444 tons), Whitby (11,945), Hull (8,193), Liverpool (6,710), Yarmouth (4,302), Sunderland (3,951), Whitehaven (3,630), Bristol (3,071).

Average tons per man, British ships entering London[1]

from	1686	1726	1751	1766
Hamburg and Bremen		10·1	12·2	14·3
Holland		8·8	10·8	11·8
France		8·4	10·6	10·9
Spain and Portugal	7·9	9·1	11·5	12·6
Norway		20·3	21·6	20·0
Riga and Petersburg		13·5	18·1	19·4
Jamaica	8·7	8·6	11·4	14·4
Other W. Indies	9·3	9·8	10·5	13·5
Virginia and Maryland	9·8	10·8	13·0	15·6

Translated into more concrete terms, this means that the 120-ton ship coming home from Cadiz, for example, which in the 1630's would have carried 18 or 19 men and in the 1680's 15 or 16, dropped one or two more in the next half century and then came sharply down to a crew of 9 after 1760. The 200-ton Virginia trader, during most of the seventeenth and the early eighteenth century, carried 20 or 21 men; by 1766 the normal crew would be more like 13.

This drastic reduction in crew size in the middle decades of the eighteenth century bespeaks a technical advance of some magnitude. For obvious reasons, it did not affect warships, whose superior size and self-importance, matched by superior documentation, has caused them to monopolise the attention of writers on the history of ships. No expert on ship design has ever examined in any detail the ordinary merchant ship of the seventeenth and eighteenth centuries, and, apart from East Indiamen, only the types that developed at the very end of the 1790's are at all well known. The evidence of such a development in merchant ship design is, therefore, indirect. It is none the less conclusive.

The tables used here are constructed entirely from the records of Seamen's Sixpences[2] (whose general accuracy has been discussed elsewhere) or, for the year 1686, from the Registers of Passes. Suspicion about any eighteenth-century statistics is, no doubt, well justified, but the internal consistency of the data that can be built up from these particular records must convince anyone who works on them of their general validity. Moreover, long before I discovered the records of Seamen's Sixpences, this particular fact about the rapid decline in size of crews had been impressed on me by the abundant and incontrovertible

[1] Adm. 68–194/203.   [2] Adm. 68–194 *et seq.*

F

evidence in Court of Admiralty cases, mostly concerned with crews' wage claims. To take examples from slightly different cases, the owners of the Newcastle collier *Hunter,* of 300 tons, declared in 1759 that she 'had on board in the Service of the said Ship eleven Mariners officers included which was and is a full and sufficient Complement or Number of Hands to navigate the said Ship or any other Ship of the like Burthen and Rigging in the like Voyage'.[1] Similarly the *Betsey & Sally* of 170 tons was said in 1766 to be navigated to Portugal by a crew of nine 'which was and is a full and sufficient complement or number of Hands to navigate her or any other Ship of the like Burthen and Rigging in the like Voyage'.[2] Both these ships were involved in collisions, and the owners were anxious to show that their crews were large enough for proper handling. The suggestion that these were adequate crews for such ships would have been laughed out of the court a hundred, or even fifty years earlier. Again, the manning scales which were taken for granted by officials and writers in the late eighteenth century were ludicrously small by comparison with those found a hundred years earlier. George Chalmers, writing in 1790 on the alleged shipping tonnage of 1688, goes on to 'allow them to have been navigated at the rate of 12 mariners to every 200 tons';[3] nobody in 1688 would have allowed such a thing, except in reference to the largest colliers and timber carriers.

Two things were happening. First, ships were being built, of almost every size, which could be manned by crews much smaller than those needed by the ships they replaced — except in the Norway trade, where a satisfactory manning level had been reached a century or more earlier. Second, the relative efficiency of the large ship was being increased, for the reduction in crew size (per ton) in large ships was, in and after mid-century, considerably greater than in small ones.

The size of ships was held down not by technical obstacles but by market possibilities; the larger the ship, the greater the risks of under-lading or of delay in securing a full lading. These risks were reduced, in each trade, as the demand for tonnage in particular ports grew towards a point where any single ship's contribution to meeting that demand was insignificant; the Russian and Jamaica trades, that saw the most rapid growth in the middle

[1] HCA 15-53.   [2] HCA 15-57.
[3] *Estimate of the Comparative Strength of Great Britain* (1794), p. 57.

decades of the eighteenth century, saw also the most rapid transition to the use of very large ships. The advantages of size in reducing running costs per ton had to be balanced against the increase in the risk of under-utilisation, and the growth of most trades was gradually lowering that risk.

Towards the middle of the century, however, a new factor appeared. Until the 1730's or 1740's the economies of size, except in trades which carried goods with peculiar stowage requirements, such as timber, were quite small; the larger ship was in many trades operated at a cost hardly less per ton than a smaller one. (Below a certain minimum size, it is true, costs did rise sharply.)[1] Quite suddenly, the margin of efficiency of the large ship over the smaller began to increase rapidly. In the sixties the wage and victualling costs per ton of a large ship might be only two-thirds those of a ship half the size. Risks of under-utilisation had to be large to outweigh such economies.[2]

By 1766, standards of manning of London ships in all the European trades had nearly reached those attained long before in ships going to Norway; the differences in average manning in that year revealed by the table on page 71 simply reflect the use of smaller ships in the trades outside Norway and the Baltic. In the transatlantic trades crews were much larger, but manning had nearly been assimilated to the standards of the Virginia traders, long the most efficient. East India ships were alone in maintaining very heavy manning.

Average tons per man, in ships of various sizes[3]

Trade	Tons: 300 and over	200-299	150-199	100-149	50-99	under 50
Hamburg and Bremen		18·9	15·7	13·3	11·4	
Holland			16·5	13·1	10·6	8·1
France				14·8	10·9	6·9
Spain and Portugal		16·5	14·5	12·4	10·4	7·0
Norway	21·9	19·0	17·0			
Riga and Petersburg	21·9	17·5	15·1	13·3	11·4	
Jamaica	16·0	14·8	12·2	10·5		
Other West Indies	15·8	14·5	13·5	11·0	7·9	
Virginia and Maryland	18·7	16·6	13·3	12·5		

[1] This was about 50 tons in European (other than timber) trades, and 100 tons in transatlantic trade.

[2] The larger ship cost a little more per ton to build and repair, but the difference this made to operating costs was trivial.

[3] Adm. 68–203; Ships entering London.

It is to be hoped that nautical archaeologists will one day investigate these matters; in the meantime, we can only make tentative suggestions about the nature of the changes which led to the improved efficiency indicated by the declining crew size.

In the first place, the changes in hull design, introduced long before for the Norway and coal trades, were spreading to ships in other trades. It is significant that by mid-century the shipbuilders of Whitby were getting orders not only for timber-carriers and colliers, but also for ships for the West India and other distant trades. It is not without importance, too, that the vessels chosen for James Cook's voyages of exploration were Whitby-built colliers. No two services could be more different than the coastal coal trade and the long ocean voyages for which the *Earl of Pembroke*, collier, renamed *Endeavour* was engaged; if Whitby ships were suitable for such purposes they could be used in any trade where speed was not of the first importance.

The rule for measuring ships' tonnage, used by shipbuilders, by the Navy when hiring merchant ships, and by the Liverpool dock authorities, always produced a figure different from the tons burden which interested the merchant shipowner.[1] The variation differed from ship to ship, but measurement was thought in the seventeenth century to produce, on the average, an excess of about 30 per cent over tons burden. Late in the eighteenth century this difference had almost disappeared, taking the English merchant fleet as a whole, and for ships in many trades it had been reversed, tons burden exceeding measured tons. That is to say, late in the eighteenth century ships (particularly the larger ships) were carrying much more, in relation to their main dimensions, than they had done a century earlier. To do this, they were probably following the Dutch flyboats and the English colliers in the abandonment of fine lines, and coming closer to the shape of the oblong box which will — at its own pace — carry more than anything else contained within the same dimensions. 'In time of war', said Captain Stevens in 1748, 'ships are built sharp, and in time of peace, full . . . most ships are now built in such a manner as to take the Ground loaded', i.e. full-built, flat-bottomed.[2] 'Flat floors for stowing and carrying great burthens, or sharp floors for sailing fast,' wrote William Hutchinson towards the end of the century.[3]

[1] See p. 7, above.   [2] *House of Commons Journals, 1745–50*, pp. 761–65.
[3] *A Treatise of Naval Architecture* (1794), p. 19. See the drawings of an

It is possible to write much more positively about rig, for this has left ample evidence behind.[1] The great step forward in late medieval times — the introduction of the lateen mizen to the square-rigged ships of Northern Europe — had resulted, by the early sixteenth century, in a common rig of spritsail, foresail and foretopsail, mainsail and maintopsail, and lateen mizen. This rig, which has been supposed almost universal in ordinary merchant ships as late as the early eighteenth century[2] was in fact being modified at least as early as 1600 in merchant ships of quite moderate size, and by 1700 was hardly ever to be found. After 1600 many of the larger merchant ships carried a third (topgallant) sail on the mainmast; fore-topgallant sails were coming into use soon after, but were uncommon before the fifties. Both these sails were used increasingly, until by the 1720's all but the smallest three-masted ships carried at least one of them, and ships of quite moderate size had both. Staysails, too, were in use here and there early in the seventeenth century; they came quite rapidly into general use in the second half of the century, and were increased in numbers, so that a typical ship of the years around 1750 would carry two (usually maintop- and fore-staysail) and many carried three. The mizen-topsail, again, was well-known before 1650 and spreading very fast into general use; by the eighties most ships had one. Throughout the seventeenth century the spritsail was very often supplemented by the spritsail-topsail; after the advent of the jib in the 1720's there was a period when these three sails were available for use simultaneously, but the jib gradually drove out its two rivals. Studding sails were known before the seventeenth century and very slowly spread into quite wide use, but many ships did not use them even in the middle of the next century. The growing practice of reefing sails is reflected in the disappearance of bonnets, carried by most ships of the 1650's but almost unknown after 1700.

English West Indiaman in F. H. Chapman, *Architectura Navalis Mercatoria* (Stockholm, 1768), Pl. 52.

[1] A ship arrested by order of the High Court of Admiralty might ultimately be sold, or might be released on a money security being given. In either case the ship was appraised, and a complete inventory of everything removable was made. The many hundreds of appraisements and inventories which are in the court records (HCA–4) make it possible to trace in great detail the developments in equipment — including sails — for ships of every size, from the sixteenth century to the nineteenth.

[2] G. S. Laird Clowes, *Sailing Ships, their History and Development* (1932), p. 89.

There was, then, a steady growth in the complexity of three-masted rig. The *Robert Bonaventure*, 150 tons, carried in 1644 a mainsail, maintopsail, foresail, foretop-sail, mizen and mizen topsail, spritsail and spritsail-topsail, and one staysail. The *William & Mary*, a ship of the same size just a century later, had all these except the spritsail-topsail; she had two staysails (main-topsail- and foretopsail-staysails) and was embellished additionally with main- and fore-topgallantsails and a jib.[1] These two ships were quite typical of their respective epochs.

The gain from this gradual multiplication of sails was an improved capacity for sailing close to the wind; since every voyage down the English Channel was likely to encounter the prevailing south-westerlies this was specially important to English shipping — though not so markedly as to make any clear impact on the rather vague records of average voyage times. Faster and safer voyages were made possible. In addition, the breaking up of the total sail area into smaller units should have made it possible to handle ships with slightly smaller crews.

To these gradual and continuous developments in rig was added, from the second quarter of the eighteenth century, a new element in the adoption of two-masted rigs for larger ships. Nobody would have considered, in 1644, replacing the *Robert Bonaventure* of 150 tons by a two-masted vessel; the owners of the *William & Mary* in 1745 would find it difficult to decide between the two-masted and three-masted alternatives available to them. It has long been known that the large brig and snow had come into widespread use before the end of the eighteenth century; it is now possible to date their advent fairly precisely. Two sources point to the same conclusions. The Court of Admiralty appraisements show that, between 1680 and 1720, the dividing line between the normally two-masted and the normally three-masted ship came at 50–60 tons burden; that is to say, almost all ships other than coasters (outside the coal trade) and those engaged in traffic across the English Channel and the Irish Sea were three-masted.[2] Change began to come in after the ending of the long war with France in 1713; by the early thirties the dividing-line between the two- and three-masted ship was at 80–90 tons,

---

[1] HCA 15–5; HCA 15–43.
[2] There is no significant difference in this respect between English-built ships and foreign-built ships in English ownership (Rawlinson MSS. A.295–87 — a list of foreign ships made free, 1674–6).

and was rising rapidly to well above 100 tons in the forties and 140–150 tons in the sixties. The evidence from ships' passes issued by the Admiralty[1] leads to the same conclusion, though it must be remembered that passes were used mainly by ships trading outside the English Channel, the North Sea and the Baltic. They show that in 1686–7 there was only a handful of two-masted ships of more than 40–50 tons; in the eighteenth century the dividing lines are as shown in the following table:

Port of ownership	1733-4	1753-4	1773-4
London	100-120	130-150	140-160
Bristol, Liverpool, Whitehaven	70-80	100-120	100-120
North-east ports	(a)	160-180	200-220

(a) Too few ships from these ports were engaged in trades needing passes, for any satisfactory estimate to be made.

The appraisements, of unquestionable accuracy, may be thought to be too few to support their conclusions adequately. The passes may be suspected of inaccuracies though they yield very large samples. But the two sets of evidence lead to an identical conclusion which can hardly be doubted — that the two-masted ship (generally, in eighteenth century, described as brig or snow) began to go up the scale of size at some date well on into the eighteenth century, the change reaching its fastest rate in the middle decades. The passes suggest — though this conclusion is less certain — that the north-east coast was the leader in this as in other shipping developments, and that plantation-built ships were, as yet, in no way in advance of English-built.

In the eighteenth century the word 'snow' begins to appear in every casual aside in naval histories or in the accounts of ports or of voyages. The *Oxford English Dictionary* gives the first printing of the word as applied to an English ship as 1722. The Whitby collier brigs are among the earliest merchant ships to have attracted the attention of the nautical archaeologists; who has heard of them before the eighteenth century? These two ships, the brig and the snow, may be called the typical ships of the middle decades of the eighteenth century. They were almost identical and both were used for all purposes, but the snow was more commonly the ocean voyager while the brig could be found most often in home waters, and particularly those of the North

[1] Adm. 7–75 *et seq.*

Sea. One of their best-known characteristics was the small crew they required.

With the growth in the number of different types of rig, the practice of classifying ships by rig began to appear late in the eighteenth century. The names did not correspond with modern usage; 'brig' for example was simply an abbreviation of 'brigantine' and the two terms were sometimes used interchangeably for the same ship. In considering the composition of the English merchant fleet on the eve of the American Revolution, size is still a more useful means of classification than rig; the build of hulls might be more useful still, but reliable information on this escapes us.

In 1774, all the larger ships — that is all ships over 300 tons and nearly all over 200 — were three-masted. A distinction was beginning to emerge, however, between the 'ship-rigged' vessel with square sails on every mast (though of course the mizen carried a lateen sail or a spanker as well) and the 'bark' (barque)[1] with no square sail on the mizen mast. After mid-century, the maximum size of merchant ships began to increase again, as it had not done since the last decade of the seventeenth century. East Indiamen, which had been vessels of 500–700 tons during much of the eighteenth century,[2] passed the 700-ton level again in 1764 with the *Speke*, and in 1769 the *Prince, Princess Royal* and *Bessborough* of 860–870 tons for the first time exceeded the size of the *King William* of 1690.[3] In the Baltic trade, the typical 300–350 ton trader of the previous half-century was being replaced in the sixties by ships of 400–500 tons, and a few giants of 600 and even 700 tons were appearing in the North Russian timber trade. Outside the East India, Baltic and Russian trades the very large ship was rare, but on transatlantic routes vessels of 300–400 tons were frequently to be met. The large, strongly built, well furnished and handsomely decorated East Indiamen, and the largest West India traders, were Thames-built ships, costly to build and costly to run; the large Baltic traders were turned out of the yards of Whitby, Newcastle and Scarborough, and their function was cheap operation to carry cheap cargoes.

[1] This term, again, was not consistently applied; see W. Falconer, *A Universal Dictionary of the Marine* (1769), under BARK.
[2] See p. 262, below, on ambiguities in East India tonnage.
[3] The 1690 figure for the *King William* is probably of tons burden; the other figures for East Indiamen are measured tonnage, which at these dates was probably slightly more than tons burden.

London had owned about 30 ships of 350 tons or more in 1640. By 1689 the number had more than doubled, to almost 70, nearly half of them in the East India trade; in the next half-century, while the merchant fleet continued to grow, the number of ships of this size was not augmented.[1] Between the end of the 1730's and 1774, however, the number of these large London ships doubled again to about 150, and the registration figures of 1788 show 200 ships of 360 tons or more belonging to London.[2] There were probably less than half-a-dozen ships of this size belonging to the outports at any time in the seventeenth or early eighteenth century; their numbers began to go up in the 1730's as the larger timber-carriers passed this size and a handful of the largest Bristol and Liverpool ships attained it. In 1788 there were 110 ships of 360 tons or more belonging to the outports, half of them to ports of the north-east coast.[3]

All these large vessels were ship-rigged. In the next range of size, from 200–350 tons, this can no longer be said. Ships of this size were still the mainstay of the transatlantic trades — many of them, in 1774, were American-built — and made up a majority of the Baltic and Norway traders and of east coast colliers. Some of the larger ships bringing goods from Spain and the Mediterranean were also within this range of size. Many of the east coast colliers were barques, and this rig may have been extended to some vessels in other trades.

Nearly all ships, however, were much smaller than 200 tons, even as late as 1788. The registration of that year enumerated 9,355 ships owned in English ports; 7,756 of them — five ships out of every six — were of less than 200 tons. The proportion would have been appreciably higher two decades earlier. In this range, where most ships were to be found, the two-masted ship now predominated. There were collier brigs — few colliers of less than 200 tons were three-masted — and brigs and snows carried on most of the trade with Southern Europe, Germany and Holland, and much of the transatlantic traffic. The colliers and some of the other craft trading in the North Sea were built on the north-east coast; a high proportion of the remaining tonnage must, in 1774, have been American-built.

[1] W. Maitland, *History of London* (1756), pp. 1259–62, lists 68 ships of 350 tons and over belonging to London in 1732.
[2] Customs 17–10.
[3] ibid.

At the very bottom, the vast numbers of small craft of 20, 30, 40 or 50 tons which carried on much of the coasting trade, which plied across the Channel and to Ireland, and were well-known in Amsterdam and Hamburg, included along with brigs and ketches a variety of one-masted craft — hoys, doggers, bilanders, sloops and a handful of schooners. They were the products of the small building yards still to be found in all ports of the English coastline.

In numbers, in build of hull, in rig, in size, English merchant ships had seen great change in the two centuries between the dates of the Elizabethan surveys and the beginnings of detailed registration of ships. The first portents of even greater changes, which would transform the shipping industry, were just visible to the most far-seeing; Fitch's steamboats were on the Delaware in 1785, Wilkinson's iron boat on the Severn two years later. Before their promise was realised, however, the operation of wooden sailing ships was to have another three-quarters of a century of expansion, on a scale as yet unprecedented.

V

The Shipowners

The London directories of the eighteenth century leave their readers in no doubt that the city was a great seaport. These small volumes list an abundance of craftsmen and dealers whose occupations depended on the sea, and who served the owners of ships — ropemakers and anchorsmiths, blockmakers and sailmakers, ship-chandlers, ship-insurers, shipwrights, ship-brokers, even ships' husbands. Yet one absentee will be noticed; the shipowner himself.[1] Until the eighteenth century was very far advanced, shipowning was no man's trade; instead, it was a minor function of people whose most important interests and investments lay elsewhere. Most shipowners were merchants, most merchants were at some time shipowners, but shipowning claimed only a small proportion of each man's capital, and received a correspondingly small share of his time and attention. Only when the Industrial Revolution was changing the scale of English commerce did shipowning become an occupation in its own right; the London shipowner, so described in the directory, does not appear until 1815.[2]

The merchant-cum-shipowner was in no way unusual in the diversity of his occupations. Seventeenth-century business was not altogether ripe for intense specialisation, and as late as 1780 the division of labour was seen more in industry than in commerce. The merchant of the seventeenth or eighteenth century might describe himself, for example, as 'Turkey merchant' or 'Russia merchant', yet be ready to take part in a wide range of business affairs beyond his special field; bargains in Baltic flax, Maryland tobacco, Scottish linen or Dutch madder could all attract him. Among such possible side interests, none was more commonly followed then shipowning. If we lift our eyebrows at the sight of Richard Thompson & Co., bankers owning 'parts of East India

[1] The first directory is *Kent's London Directory* of 1728. It is not suggested that the term 'shipowner' was not in use; but it was very rarely used in circumstances in which an individual's principal occupation had to be identified.
[2] Shipowners appear in the first Hull directory, in 1790; there are none in the eighteenth-century directories of Bristol, Liverpool or Newcastle.

81

shipping' we should notice that this was but one of 'several advantageous and profitable trades' into which they put the money deposited by their customers; they invested in the silk, wine and Russia trades, in lead mining in Wales and linen manufacture in Ireland, and indeed 'omitted nothing within the compass of our ingenuity'. Ingenuity was, perhaps, stretched further than was discreet in a banking firm, contributing to the ruin which came to Thompsons' in 1675; but the indiscretion consisted in carrying over, into the business of Thompsons' the bankers, the habits which had made Thompsons' the merchants so successful.[1]

Nevertheless, to most people who took part in business enterprise there was a profound difference between investment in trading operations and investment in shipping. Before the days of the limited liability company there were two normal forms of business organisation. On the one hand there was the sole trader; on the other the partnership in which the partners were sufficiently few for all to be actively engaged. The joint stock company was uncommon in English business except during a period of some thirty years before the 'Bubble Act' of 1720, and the large unincorporated partnership was developing only slowly, painfully, with uncertain legality and for a narrow range of purposes, in the eighteenth century. The character of the normal shipowning group, however, was entirely different from that of the ordinary partnerships of its day; it was a large partnership, often of ten or twelve, sometimes of more than twenty members, with affairs managed on behalf of them all by one or two partners or even, in some cases, by a ship's master who was not a partner. In this dissociation of ownership from management — and indeed from any activity to safeguard the capital invested beyond the most cursory and formalised supervision — shipowning was, and had been for many centuries, an important exception to general commercial practice in England.

Property in a ship was divided into equal parts or shares. These parts were usually, though by no means invariably, divisors of four — eighths, sixteenths, thirty-seconds, occasionally sixty-fourths;[2] a pattern of ownership which was international[3] and of

[1] *The Case of Richard Thompson & Company* (1678).

[2] Ordinary partnerships often had a similar arrangement of ownership in divisors of four, but this was to facilitate irregular sharing; it was not associated with large numbers of partners.

[3] The pattern of ownership of parts is discussed in great detail, for ships

very great antiquity; indications of it can be found in the Laws of Oleron, dating back to the twelfth century.[1] The Merchant Shipping Act of 1854 settled the sixty-fourth as the invariable unit of ownership of British ships, which it still is. The smallest ships — especially coasters outside the coal trade — frequently had single owners or were divided into only two, three or four parts, but few ships of more than a hundred tons had such small owning groups; the spreading of ownership in these larger vessels is typified in the *Arcana Galley* of 250 tons, with 21 owners in 1689, or the collier *Lambton Anne*, of 200 tons, which in 1719 had 17 owners.[2] The shares were usually distributed fairly evenly; a particular owner might hold one, two or three thirty-seconds, but the very large individual holding, standing out from a ruck of small holdings, was as uncommon as the ship with a single owner. Sir Henry Johnson, an exceptionally large investor in shipping, owned parts of thirty-eight ships (nearly all East Indiamen) in 1686; in only one of them was his share more than one-eighth, although his total holdings amounted to eighty-eight thirty-seconds.[3] Seventy years later, Richard Lascelles was a shareholder in twenty-one ships; his total holdings were thirty-two sixteenths.[4] Effective control was usually left in the hands of the man who had initiated the buying of that particular vessel and had offered shares in it to his friends and acquaintances. For every ship was a separate venture, whose originator laid off all but a small remnant of his commitment in the way a professional bookmaker hedges his bets. Among merchants engaged in foreign trade, in particular, there was a criss-cross pattern of shareholding in a great number of ships. Every ship had a different list of owners, sometimes hardly less fortuitous a group of people than the buyers of tickets in a lottery, and with as little conscious identity or continuity. Thomas Bowrey, whose papers provide a

owned at Lubeck, in E. Baasch, 'Zur Statistik des Schiffspartenwesens', *Vierteljahrschrift fur Sozial- und Wirtschaftgeschichte*, 1919, pp. 211–34. See also A. E. Christensen, *Dutch Trade to the Baltic about 1600* (Copenhagen, 1941), Ch. III, and J. Schreiner, *Nederland og Norge* (Oslo, 1933), pp. 26–33.
[1] *The Black Book of the Admiralty* (ed. Sir Travers Twiss, 1871), Vol. I, pp. 89–132. See also R. C. Jarvis, 'Fractional Shareholding in British Merchant Ships with Special Reference to the 64th', *Mariners' Mirror*, Vol. XIV, 1939, pp. 301–19.
[2] HCA 30–635; HCA 24–124; HCA 15–35.
[3] BM Add.MSS. 22184–151.
[4] R. B. Sheridan, 'The Sugar Trade of the British West Indies, 1660–1756' (unpublished London Ph.D. thesis, 1951), p. 76.

rare opportunity for viewing affairs from the centre of a web of shipping partnerships, had a quite different set of part-owners for each of the ships whose affairs he managed,[1] and in this he was undoubtedly typical of his time.

Why did shipowning partnerships take this characteristic form, so far removed from the practice of other trades? Why could people be found who were willing to invest, in this industry, in enterprises which they did not manage; and on the other hand why were men who had arranged the purchase and intended to handle the commercial operation of a ship willing to share ownership and profits, and even some degree of potential control, with outsiders?

It is convenient to answer the second question first; and to do so by examining initially the problem of the mariners, active or retired, who organised many shipowning partnerships, and then that of the merchants who organised the great majority of them.

The advance from chief mate to master of a ship effected for the individual concerned a transformation in status and a trebling of income, and opened the way to much greater prizes. It took the lucky individual firmly into the middle class, and offered him the possibility of saving for old age or of turning into a merchant; it put a fortunate few on the road to real wealth, aldermancy and knighthood. Such a prize was not always awarded, in the seventeenth or the eighteenth century, simply for merit; influence with the owners of capital, or capital at the mariner's own command, pushed its owner ahead much more certainly and rapidly. For many a man who had made some progress in his career at sea, the purchase of a ship was seen as a way to secure the valuable perquisites of command; but it was a way likely to require the bringing in of outside capital to supplement his own limited savings. Mortgage was an unsatisfactory expedient; in the shipping industry it took the form of the bottomry bond which, while providing for cancellation of the debt if the ship were lost, required in return a very high interest rate, commonly 36 per cent.[2] It was often used by ships' masters to raise small sums, but to

---

[1] Bowrey MSS. in the Guildhall Library, London, and the Library of the Corporation of Lloyd's.

[2] Sir Dudley North in 1691 suggested that 36 per cent was a regular rate for bottomry and that 'The Trade of setting out Ships, runs very much upon this course' ('Discourses upon Trade' in J. R. McCulloch (ed.), *Early Tracts on Commerce* (1856), p. 521). The rate did in fact vary, and could be very much higher in emergency, but his figure is a fair average.

William Lem
B·R·O·K·E·R,

Sells Ships or parts of Ships by Publick
or private Sale. Lets Ships to Freight,
Enters & Clears Ships at the Custom House:
Makes Insurances on Ships & Merchandize.

Attends at his Office in Exchange Alley, LONDON
From 9 in the Morning, till 8 in the Evening.
Orders left at his House in Lime Street,
or at his OFFICE,
will be punctually comply'd with.

I. Kirk Sc.   St. Pauls

LXXXV

A SHIPBROKER'S TRADE CARD, LATE EIGHTEENTH CENTURY

A DANISH TIMBER BARK, AND SMALLER ENGLISH SHIPS, IN A NORTHERN
TIMBER PORT, 1736
by Samuel Scott

attempt to finance a ship mainly in this way was to invite disaster. Thomas Fortescue of the *Jacob* tried it in 1660; he raised £900 in loans on bottomry when he was buying and fitting out the ship; she was arrested for debt a year later and was then valued at £850, so it is unlikely that he put up much money of his own.[1] It was far better to canvass relatives, friends, business acquaintances, prospective suppliers of ship's stores and former shipmates, to get part-owners who would bear some of the burden. The prospective master, or his father or brother, is found at the centre of many shipowning partnerships, supplementing his own resources by drawing in those of his friends.

The ship's master could have no better investment than the ship he commanded, if he were confident of his own abilities, and when the way was open masters constantly strove to increase their holdings — like Henry Denton, whose father 'kept asses and by mere dint of starving himself, saved as much as bought his son a share in a ship . . . and by the success of the share has risen to be a principal owner'.[2] Samuel Pinder of Whitby had acquired at the time of his death in 1703 $\frac{6}{16}$, $\frac{1}{3}$ and $\frac{1}{64}$ of his ship; he had obviously bought parts as they became available. He also owned $\frac{1}{32}$ part in each of eight other ships.[3] Richard Haddock increased his holding in his ship the *Supply* in six successive voyages from $\frac{1}{16}$ to $\frac{4}{16}$; in his next command, the *Bantam*, he held $\frac{6}{16}$.[4] The Courts of Directors of the East India Company and the Levant Company were constantly recruited from former masters of ships in the companies' employ, who had settled ashore on the profits of their commands and increased their fortunes by investment in shipping and by trade.

The active mariner had a strong incentive to put his money into a ship, because this was the simplest way towards securing all the perquisites of a ship's master. The retired mariner, who had settled ashore with a small or moderate fortune, might feel he could best use his resources by turning his maritime experience to account in organising and managing shipping partnerships; Samuel Standidge of Hull, long after he settled ashore in the 1750's and became one of the richest merchants in the city, was content to describe himself as 'Master and Mariner'; his chief interest was

[1] HCA 15-8. The ship realised only £615 when she was sold.
[2] *Strother's Journal* (Hull, 1912), pp. 41–2.
[3] G. Young, *A History of Whitby* (1817), p. 563.
[4] BM Egerton MSS., 2523–2524.

always in shipping.[1] Thomas Bowrey was for some twenty years occupied, ultimately as a master, in East India shipping. Coming ashore in London in 1689 with a few thousand pounds, he bought a little house property and financed a china shop, but the greater part of his fortune was invested in a small group of ships which he managed. Around 1700 these were engaged in the temporarily free East India trade. He was part-owner of the *Rising Sun*, *Mary Galley*, *Macclesfield*, *Trumball Galley*, *Horsham*, *Prosperous* and *Rochester*, and managed the affairs of several of them. He organised groups to charter other ships for the East India trade, one of which, the *Worcester*, was involved in a disastrous affair that played a part in bringing about the Union of England and Scotland.[2] The net result of the operations which his surviving books record was heavy loss, but he evidently had more successful ventures, for his wife inherited a useful estate when he died in 1713. Though he put most of his fortune into shipping, he employed in it even greater sums provided by his acquaintances; his own funds would hardly have sufficed to set out one ship in the particularly costly trade in which his experience lay.[3]

One motive for the taking of partners by the managers of ships, then, was to secure some of the capital they needed. This may have influenced shipowners of every kind, but it was particularly important to the master-owner. Yet this is not a sufficient explanation for the formation of ownership groups, particularly of that very large number which owed the first impulse to a merchant. The large ship of the early seventeenth century, outside the Levant and Indian Ocean trades, was of some 200 tons; its setting out cost no more than £2000. Its counterpart in George II's day, of 300–400 tons, cost no more than £5000. Merchants' capital resources were not so small that it was always imperative to divide ownership of such vessels into sixteen or thirty-two parts. Outward bound with cloth, or coming home with wine from Portugal or sugar from Barbados, a ship would often carry consignments, for each of several merchants, worth nearly as much as

---

[1] G. Jackson, 'The Economic Development of Hull in the Eighteenth Century' (unpublished Hull Ph.D. thesis, 1960), p. 287.
[2] R. C. Temple, *The Tragedy of the Worcester* (1930).
[3] Bowrey's shipping papers are divided between the Guildhall Library, London, and the Library of Lloyd's; other papers are in the Library of the Commonwealth Relations Office and in the Birmingham City Library. Sir Richard Temple has published, as *The Papers of Thomas Bowrey* (Hakluyt Society, 1925), a selection of business papers relating to the *Mary Galley*.

the ship itself. Even the finance of the great East Indiamen[1] was well within the capacity of the individual magnates who in fact owned only small shares in them. The *Charles the Second* of 800 tons was almost the largest merchant ship built in the seventeenth century; she cost £15,680 to build and equip for her first voyage in 1683.[2] The *Grantham*, a full-sized East Indiaman of her day, sixty years later (though of only 567 tons) cost £12,000.[3] These were not large sums to the Childs, the Riders or the Heathcotes, whose fortunes might be measured in hundreds of thousands of pounds.

The practice of selling parts is in fact most often associated with the all-important problem of risk.[4] Losses of ships by storm, bad navigation, piracy and privateers, fire and runaway crews, were high even when England was at peace with all Europe; in the second quarter of the nineteenth century, the average loss of ship by these accidents and mishaps was four or five per cent per annum.[5] A hundred years before this losses were probably no smaller; and in earlier centuries, when Moorish corsairs were among the normal hazards the seagoer faced, and even European piracy had not been completely wiped out, the shipowner ran much heavier risks. The individual investor in shipping could reduce the likelihood of total loss by spreading his investment over several ships — owning one-eighth of eight ships rather than eight-eighths of one. The chances of partial loss were, of course increased; but partial loss was not ruinous. This system of division into shares was the original means adopted to spread the risks of shipowning; it was very much older than the practice of insurance in North European countries. As late as the seventeenth century, when the insurance of goods carried by sea was becoming a regular merchant routine, the ships that bore them were, more often than not, uninsured. Though little is known about early marine insurance in England, it seems likely that the somewhat reluctantly developed habit of insuring ships received a marked

[1] After the mid-seventeenth century the East India Company operated almost entirely with ships it hired.
[2] HCA 15–129.
[3] L. S. Sutherland, *A London Merchant* (Oxford, 1933), p. 120; and Essex County Record Office, Chelmsford, D/DFr. T.77.
[4] See A. E. Christensen, op. cit., p. 106. There is an extensive discussion in V. Barbour, 'Marine Risks and Insurance in the Seventeenth Century', *Journal of Economic and Business History*, Vol. I, 1929, pp. 561–70.
[5] W. S. Lindsay, *History of Merchant Shipping and Ancient Commerce* (1876), Vol. III, pp. 467–9.

G

fillip in the wars of William III and Anne and that, encouraged by the tighter organisation of private insurers associated with Lloyd's Coffee House, and by the creation of two strong insurance corporations in 1718[1] shipowners began to insure as a matter of course in the early decades of the eighteenth century.

Even then, however, insurance was not a complete answer to the owners' problems. Insurance could not be secured automatically; in the argument in 1717 on the setting up of the insurance corporations, their supporters argued that 'at some seasons of the year, especially in the winter, it is very difficult to get insurances made from the Baltick or from the West Indies, and for large sums of money it is at all times very difficult'.[2] The tricks and evasions of insurers and their propensity for going bankrupt under the strain of wartime losses were notorious,[3] while marine policies until the 1730's always provided that the insured should bear a proportion of the loss. Not until about 1720 was marine insurance sufficiently well developed to provide a reasonable alternative to the method of risk-spreading by the division of ownership into small parts.

There were, in fact, significant new developments in ownership structure during the eighteenth century. Until about 1700, the division of ownership was being more and more widely extended; the sixteenth was replacing the eighth, the thirty-second was replacing the sixteenth; lists of owners grew longer. This may be no more than adaptation to the slowly-rising average tonnage of ships; but subdivision reached its maximum in the decades before 1700 although the size of ships continued to increase. In the early decades of the eighteenth century a tendency can be discerned towards decline in the average number of owners of a ship.[4] Moreover, the existence of a single majority holding associated with a number of small holdings became a little more common, and ships of some size were, more often than before, owned by individuals and by small groups of two or three people engaged in permanent trading partnership. These were as yet only tendencies,

---

[1] The Royal Exchange Assurance and the London Assurance.
[2] CO 388–19.
[3] V. Barbour, op. cit., pp. 582–7.
[4] E. Baasch, op. cit., indicates that in the eighteenth century the average number of owners of a ship of any given size, which had been rising, declined quite sharply. Though Lubeck shipping operated under very different conditions from English, it was probably influenced by the development of insurance in the same way and at much the same time.

and the extent of the change may easily be over-estimated. So far as they do exist, however, these tendencies may be associated with the growing use of insurance, which made it less necessary for the shipping entrepreneur to spread his risks and to share his profits with sleeping partners. In the preceding century the organiser of the shipowning group is usually recognisable only because he was the part-owner whose name appeared on such formal documents as charter-parties, or by the evidence of his activities presented in the Admiralty Court. Though the term 'ship's husband' had been used, it had not been very generally applied, and there had rarely been a special remuneration for work done and time devoted to the ship's affairs. The managing partner in the group had shared the profits *pro rata* with all the others; if he had any special gain, it was in the advantage he derived from having a ship under his control — and this, we shall see, was not always very substantial. His motive for sharing with the sleeping partners had been to spread risks, and when, through the development of insurance, this motive lost some of its strength, the ship's husband began to expect some special reward for his activity, over and above his bare share of the profits. As the eighteenth century proceeded he more and more frequently drew some small commission or lump sum payment from the returns of the voyage; he became a more clearly defined figure, to whom the title 'ship's husband' was habitually accorded, and a few ships' husbands specialised in ship management to such an extent as to use that title to describe their main occupation.[1] In *Kent's London Directory* for 1780, John Dixon, Charles Foulis and Messrs. Lashbrook and Rohissen are described as ships' husbands, and William Hutchinson, Robert Taylor and Messrs. Hubbart and Donovan as ships' agents.

The first tentative steps towards concentration of ownership and professionalisation of management were to lead, in time and in their different ways, to the separation and specialisation of merchant and shipowner. But this came in the nineteenth century. In the meantime, shareholding in ships provided outlets into which the typical merchant fed some of his capital, and many merchants who engaged in trade by sea found it convenient to organise the buying of one or two ships, spreading wide the owning partnerships but keeping the management in their own

[1] Though there is no reason to suppose that it was the *sole* occupation of any of them.

hands. Why were they prepared to undertake management, before the day when managers or ships' husbands drew any special remuneration for their labours?

In the commercial community of the seventeenth and eighteenth centuries, a community that did business in both hemispheres before the days of radio and telegraph, a community in which commercial information, advertisement and specialised services were only beginning to be organised for general use, one of the greatest assets of any merchant was his connections. The most important connections, of course, were with his agents and factors in various ports at home and overseas, but almost as valuable were contacts with his fellow merchants at home and with reliable — and themselves well-connected — master mariners. Shipping offered the merchant a further opportunity to exploit these connections, while using capital most of which was put up and risked by other people. He was encouraged to embark on shipping enterprises in the hope that in spite of the fierce competition of the freight market his friends would do him favours; that in spite of the risks, his information would be slightly more reliable than the next man's; that if some critical emergency should arise in a distant land beyond his knowledge or direct control, the weight of his influence would ensure that his ship was assisted or favourably dealt with. These may well have been illusions; if favours were received, favours were expected in return, and the mercantile community was in effect bound together in a network of back-scratching. They were optimistic and stimulating illusions, nevertheless, and the kind that led to action; sometimes, too, the gains could be genuine.

If his trading connections tempted a merchant into buying a ship, it was not usually for his own cargoes. As a trader, the merchant was an individual seeking to have his goods carried at the lowest price; as a shipowner he was acting for a group of partners who were entitled to expect that he would seek out the highest freights — and his interest, as a shipowner, coincided with theirs. Moreover, outside a handful of trades the individual merchant rarely had whole shiploads of goods to be moved over a single route, and if he traded in valuable goods he would hesitate to risk the loss of a substantial consignment of them in a single ship.

Generally speaking, when integration does not by itself produce cost reductions, the gains from integration are likely to be least when the market for the goods and services integrated is highly competitive; and the freight market in London and in many of the chief harbours which English ships visited was competitive. Before the seventeenth century opened, there was a well-established market for shipping services with physical centres at such places as the Royal Exchange in London and the Tolsey at Bristol. To these centres the merchant could resort, in peacetime, with every expectation of finding a ship which would carry his few tons of goods at the right time, or a ship that he could charter for a round voyage to bring home a cargo of bulky colonial produce on behalf of himself and business associates. At the principal harbours of shipment abroad his agents could in normal years confidently expect that cargo space would be offered at the right season. In such circumstances it was a disadvantage to be tied closely to the use of a particular ship which he operated on behalf of a wide partnership.

Two important trades, however, stand out as exceptions to this general rule, sharply differentiated from all others; two trades where the shipowning group and the trading group coincided, the ships carrying cargoes entirely owned by the shipowning partnership, shipping and trading intertwined in a single common venture. They were oddly contrasted — the coastal coal trade, and the slave trade between England, Africa and America; one coastal and, for all its size, almost parochial, the other transoceanic; one handling a virtually indestructible commodity, the other a fragile cargo that was literally perishable; one using the oldest and leakiest ships afloat, the other calling for strong and well-found vessels. True, they both handled bulk cargoes, which were more easily managed as entities than as separate lots with separate owners. In both cases, transport costs accounted for a high proportion of the commodity's price as landed at its destination — at least half in the case of coal unladen at London, nearly half in the case of the slave herded on to the wharf at Kingston, Jamaica. Yet there were other bulk trades — timber, for instance — in which transport and commerce were not amalgamated in this way, and the circumstances of coal and slave traffic must have special explanations.

The seaborne trade in coal was organised by people whose interests and connections were in origin maritime rather than commercial. Usually the master bought coal on behalf of his

owners at Newcastle or Sunderland,[1] sold on their account at
London, and paid the costs of the ship's voyage out of the proceeds.[2] The master, who was nearly always a part-owner, was the
central figure in arranging shipment and sale. Behind him was the
owning group of ten, fifteen or more persons, and these owners
were in East Coast ports, but not in London. Ipswich was,
according to Defoe, 'the greatest town in England for large colliers
or coal ships, employed between Newcastle and London'[3] until the
last quarter of the seventeenth century; the minor ports of
Aldborough, Wivenhoe, Woodbridge and Malden were associated
with it in this trade. Because coal shipment was in the aggregate
a very large business, requiring a great amount of capital, it is not
surprising to find that ownership went outside the normal ring of
merchants and embraced not only mariners but also shopkeepers,
innholders, craftsmen — anyone with a few pounds to invest, even
the gentry of the East Anglian countryside. At Ipswich as late as
1720 'the greater part of the inhabitants of that town are either
owners of Parts of Ships, or masters of Ships, chiefly employed
in the Coal Trade, or in the Fishery'.[4] The reason for the original
settlement of collier owning in these ports is hard to determine.
It is probably connected with the unwillingness of London
merchants to take any large part in the finance of coastal shipping
(a characteristic which was still marked in the eighteenth century);[5]
the nearby East Anglian ports, at the time when the coal trade
began its rapid expansion, contained fishing and trading communities oriented towards the sea, and had a well-established shipbuilding industry based on local timber supplies.

Towards the end of the seventeenth century the hold of these
towns on the Newcastle coal trade began to weaken. Defoe says
that they were supplanted by Yarmouth and London, whose
merchants bought great numbers of Dutch prizes in the three
Dutch wars, cheap and capacious vessels which they 'thrust into

---

[1] Chartering ships to carry coal was not unknown on the east coast, but it
was uncommon.
[2] This account of the east coast coal trade applies equally to Whitehaven's
coal trade with Ireland.
[3] D. Defoe, *A Tour through England and Wales* (Everyman edition), Vol. I,
p. 40.
[4] *House of Commons Journals, 1718–21*, p. 364.
[5] The compiler of the returns of shipping after 1751 says 'No coasters belong
to this port' [London] (BM Add.MSS. 11256–50). This was not altogether
true then and London certainly owned coasters earlier in the century; but most
coasters trading to and from London were owned elsewhere.

the coal trade to the decay of Ipswich'.[1] This view must be treated with caution, for the supply of Dutch prizes was only temporary.[2] The eighteenth-century rivals and supplanters of Ipswich were in fact ships of the north-east coast, built and owned in Whitby, Newcastle and Scarborough. This geographical shift of the coal-carrying interest may be accounted for by the development of the shipbuilding industry of the area and its creation of new types of craft specially suited to the coal trade.[3] Moreover coal merchants in the northern towns, keelmen, coal producers and royalty owners were starting to take an interest in coal ships; in the early eighteenth century such great coal families as the Liddells and Claverings[4] and the Lambtons[5] appear as shipowners. The violent upsurge of coal production, which had been proceeding for a century, was slowing down; profits which would once have been devoted to further colliery development spilled over into shipowning, as an outside investment not requiring detailed supervision.

The initiators of the owning groups in north-eastern ports were most commonly ships' masters, active or retired, who gathered in as co-owners others of their own kind as well as the merchants of their locality and the coal interests. Even so, these Scarborough and Whitby owning groups found themselves, like their East Anglian predecessors, very much in the hands of the ships' masters who handled the business. Ships were built for the coal trade and masters appointed, as Richard Hamby of Aldborough was in 1660, 'to the onelie effect and purpose that he should for the said owners and to their use exercise and use the said ship in the Newcastle coal trade . . . and as wind should serve should come with the said ship to Aldborough'.[6] Thereafter the masters went their own way, and, so long as they obeyed the general direction to use the ships in this trade without too many diversions, managed ship and business as they thought fit. 'Several of the Masters go

---

[1] op. cit., p. 41.

[2] Dutch prizes ceased to become available after 1674, and new legislation in 1685 (1 James II, c. 18) made it impossible for prize ships coming into English hands after that date to enter profitably into the coal trade. London never owned many colliers, and Yarmouth claimed, in 1705, only a very small fraction of east coast coal shipping (*House of Commons Journals, 1702–4*, p. 511).

[3] See pp. 61–6, above.

[4] E. Hughes, *North Country Life in the Eighteenth Century* (Durham, 1952), pp. 201–2. The Liddells, for example, had parts of twelve ships in 1716.

[5] HCA 15–35 (*Lambton Anne*).

[6] HCA 13–129; *Content*.

to sea for many years, and never account with their Owners, and there is no compelling them, but by a tedious suit in Chancery,' complained an owner in 1730.[1] The independence of the masters of these ships was so great, and was thought to be so excessive, as to provoke an attempt in 1731 to curtail it by statute:[2]

'Whereas the Masters of Ships employed in the Coal Trade are for the most part invested both with the Grand Bill of Sale and Possession of such Ship or Ships as he or they are Masters of, by which means many Ill-disposed Masters, although they hold but small Parts in their own Right, refuse to obey the Directions of their Owners, or to render an Account when thereunto required. . . . Every Master of a Ship or Vessel using the Coal Trade shall be subject to the Direction of the Owner or Owners of the Major Part of his Ship or Vessel, and shall keep, and once a Year render to such Owner or Owners, if required, a true, plain and just Account in writing of the Produce and Expense of every respective Voyage he or they shall make within such Year in such Ship or Vessel.'

Here, then, is a trade in which seafaring folk connected with such shipbuilding towns as Ipswich and Whitby took over a merchanting function; one needing little capital beyond the cost of the ship, for the voyage was short and coal was a cheap commodity sold in London for ready cash; one in which, at both ends of the voyage, there were agents ready to deal with anybody who appeared, so that the special kinds of business connections which merchants can establish were not needed. Coal shipment presents an example of the amalgamation of trading with transport, the coalescence of merchant and shipowning profits, distributed by master to owners as 'dividend' on the ship's voyage. It was, however, an amalgamation which arose, not through merchants reaching out to control shipowning, but on the contrary, through the maritime interest which organised the shipowning groups absorbing the trading function.

In the slave trade we again find the group of proprietors of the ship owning, at the same time, the cargo carried. For a long period (from 1673 to 1702) after it first became important, this trade was the monopoly of a chartered company. There was some free trade earlier in the seventeenth century, however — around 1660 there was for a time no company organisation. Moreover,

---

[1] *House of Commons Journals, 1727–32*, p. 516.
[2] 3 Geo. II, c. 26. This appears to have added nothing to the legal obligations of the master; it was simply a statutory reaffirmation of them.

interlopers continually infringed the Royal Africa Company's monopoly, and other traders sent their ships further afield, to Madagascar, in the hope of circumventing the monopoly legally. In all these fields, the ships which come to notice carried cargoes solely for the benefit of the ships' owning groups.[1] After 1702, as the centres of the slave trade began to move away from London to Bristol and Liverpool, the organisation retained this character. Not only were transport costs in this, as in the coal trade, all-important in determining profitable selling prices; but the value of the cargo delivered depended, to a much greater extent than in any other trade, on the speed and care with which the master accomplished his voyage to the West Indies. The closest possible relationship was desirable between the master and the owners of the cargo, and it was achieved by uniting the shipowning with the trading group.[2] However, the master was not in this trade the tyrannical ruler of his owners. Large capital was needed to finance the long voyages and the victualling of the slaves, as well as the purchase of trade goods. The buying of the trade goods in England, and the sale of the sugar, cotton, rice or pimento which the ship finally brought home, required merchant skills; in the West Indies, and sometimes even on the Guinea Coast itself, the master was under orders to take instructions from his owners' resident agents. In this trade, merchants organised and directed the shipowning partnership.

In no other trade, before the very end of the eighteenth century, were shipowning partnerships normally organised so as to associate the shipowners with the cargoes carried. There were trades, however, in which the managing owner of ships organised shipping partnerships to provide the vessels he needed to carry his own' goods. Foremost among these was the import of timber from southern Norway and the Baltic, and later from New England. The great London timber merchants drew widely on London business circles to take shares in their ships, but these part-owners had no participation in the ships' cargoes. This was another traffic in which transport costs bulked very large in the final cost

---

[1] Early traders: *Constant Ruth*, 1652 (HCA 15–6); *Ethiopian*, 1660 (HCA 24–114); *Charles*, 1661 (HCA 13–74). Interlopers: *Dorothy*, 1681 (HCA 24–121); *Philadelphia*, 1687 (HCA 24–124). Madagascar traders: *Daniel & Thomas*, 1689 (HCA 24–123); *Happy Return*, 1689 (HCA 24–123).

[2] The Royal Africa Company itself usually chartered ships, and secured the owners' and masters' interest by agreeing to pay freight per head of slaves *delivered alive*. It is hard to see why this kind of arrangement was not adopted by independent slave traders.

of the commodity — a third or more of delivered prices in east coast ports. 'The Lumber Trade', wrote Brewster in 1695, 'is more profitable to the Ship and Men than to the Merchant.'[1] The cargoes were cheap in relation to their bulk, and were normally moved in whole shiploads for a single merchant; in its total volume the timber trade was the largest of foreign trades, and it usually employed ships which were not fit for the carriage of any other goods except coal.

Sir William Warren, the greatest of the timber merchants of Charles II's time[2] was also one of the largest shipowners. Random gleanings from the Admiralty Court records reveal fourteen ships in which he was a part-owner during the 1660's and 1670's, and these can only represent a fraction of his holdings; moreover, his parts were usually large — eighths, quarters, even halves. Though he did not confine himself to the Norway and Baltic timber trade,[3] this was his principal business, and most of the ships he employed in it were under his own management. Nevertheless, his business retained some flexibility; the fleet he controlled had to be augmented by chartering when his trade was exceptionally active, as in 1665 when, to handle very large government contracts for masts, he hired twenty-eight ships for Gottenberg and twelve for New England.[4] Warren's rivals — Charles and John Shorter, Edward Dering, William Wood — also managed considerable fleets of ships in which they were part-owners, and used them for their own trade. Timber, however, was not a homogenous commodity with a ready-made market. The merchants were the key figures in the trade, and the ship's master was firmly under their control; he was simply the navigator, obeying his principal's factors in the Scandinavian and Russian ports and the managing owner himself in England.

Again, in the colonial trades, and particularly in West Indian sugar, a novel situation in the eighteenth century induced some merchants to organise shipowning groups to provide ships for

---

[1] *Essays on Trade and Navigation* (1695), p. 89.

[2] He was a friend and helper of the young Samuel Pepys, and turned to Pepys for support in 1688 when casualties to ships and a fire in his timber yard brought him into financial difficulty. There are many references to Warren in Pepys' Diary.

[3] His varied enterprises included the shipping of munitions to the Moors at Sallee, and taking supplies to the English garrison at Tangier to support their defence against the Moors.

[4] *HMC Lindsey MSS.*, *Supp.*, pp. 117–23.

their own purposes. In London and Bristol, a small group of
factors competed vigorously for the opportunities to sell the
sugar cargoes of the island planters; each factor had his established
connections, but transfer of a planter's affairs from one factor to
another was not uncommon, and was in fact encouraged from
time to time by the setting up of a returned planter as a factor in
England. A guarantee of shipment of the crop early in the season
could attach planters more firmly to their factor; and since the
large factor was assured of heavy cargoes (whose risks in transit he
did not have to bear) from his wide circle of planter clients, he was
often ready to provide ships managed, and in part owned, by
himself. If, by tying his ships to serve his clients' interests before
any others, he sometimes suffered as a shipowner, he could on
the other hand look to the added certainty given to his earnings of
commission.[1] Again, however, this was not a necessary development; the same guarantee of prompt shipment was provided by
many other factors who simply chartered ships for early arrival
in the West Indies.

All this adds up to a formidable total of instances in which
managing owners organised shipping groups for the fulfilment
of their own transport requirements. The list could be extended.
Merchants in the eighteenth-century iron trade (another trade
with cargoes of low value) were big employers of ships which they
managed.[2] Many ships sailed every summer to load, for the
account of their owners, the products of the Newfoundland
fishery; they sold the cod-fish in Portuguese or Spanish ports and
loaded for home with wine or raisins, partly for the owners'
account and partly on freight. In the minor ports of southern and
western England owning groups were frequently very small and
the sole owner was quite common; in these places the amalgamation of shipowning with trading was quite commonly found.
Thomas Benson of Northam (near Bideford), Member of Parliament and in 1753 absconding bankrupt, was in his early days a
ropemaker and merchant, who extended his interests into the
Newfoundland fisheries and the Virginia tobacco trade; he
managed several ships which were occupied in these trades and
was sole owner of at least two — the *Peter* and *Placentia* — and
almost certainly of others.[3]

[1] R. Pares, *A West India Fortune* (1950), pp. 208–11; see pp. 272–3, below.
[2] G. Jackson, op. cit., p. 283.   [3] E. 134, 31 George II, Easter 1.

When all the exceptions have been made, however, it is probably true that before the American War of Independence most ships carried most of their cargo for non-owners who chartered ships or hired cargo space in them. When new trades were opened up, it might be necessary for the traders to use their own ships until the risks of the voyage had been assessed; thereafter they reverted to hire, the Virginia traders within a decade, the Levant traders within a few years of the first establishment of their business. The East India Company, engaged in operations over great distances, with the added dangers of armed conflict whenever a foreign ship from Europe was sighted in the Indian Ocean, bought its first ships, built others on the Thames and in Ireland and eventually established its own building and repair yards at Deptford and Blackwall. As its trade became conventionalised, however, it became possible to hire ships at reasonable charges; from 1629 onwards the shipowning function was being hived off, first to the shipowning community in general and ultimately to a narrower group which found profit in this special function and was widely recognised and resented as 'the East India shipping interest'. Blackwall Yard was sold in 1654; it continued to build ships for the East India trade, but they were no longer owned by the Company.[1] Even the Royal African Company, engaged in a field in which private traders found it advantageous to own the ships which they operated, carried on most of its transatlantic traffic in hired ships,[2] changing this policy only after its monopoly was broken and for a few years an attempt was made to compete on even terms with the private traders.[3] The Hudson's Bay Company, it is true, retained its own handful of ships, for no amount of habit and usage could do away with the great danger of its voyages. The South Sea Company owned some of the ships with which it traded to South America; but its active life was a short one in which its operations were always beset by political as well as maritime hazards.

The typical managing owner, in fact, was one who sent his ship (if she were not on charter) to the places he himself traded with, not primarily to carry his own cargoes but because these were the places where he had factors and agents who would secure cargoes

---

[1] R. Wigram and H. Green, *Chronicles of Blackwall Yard* (1881).
[2] K. G. Davies, *The Royal African Company* (1957), pp. 196–7.
[3] Africa Company shipping papers, T.70–1225 and T.70–26/27.

for the ship from other merchants. Naturally he would, when it was otherwise convenient, put his own goods in this ship rather than another, to help the success of her voyage. The papers of William Norris of Liverpool give a clear picture of a shipowner behaving in this way.[1] He sent the ships he managed to the places, usually in America, where he had agents, and they loaded his own cargoes and such others as they could secure. The ship *Mersey* came into the river in 1702 with only some twenty tons of owners' goods aboard, 'and filled up with freight at £5–£6 per ton'. The *William Galley* arrived in the Mersey the following year with a substantial cargo of sugar, indigo and logwood for himself and his brother, and 'some little freight aboard, not much'. In 1693 he was hiring ships to carry his goods from Virginia; in 1695 he sent a ship to Cadiz laden entirely with his own goods. His use of ships depended in fact on the state of the freight market. The *Charity* was considered in 1693 for a voyage to the West Indies to trade on Norris's account, but in the prevailing conditions, he wrote, 'I saw there was no profitable means to get her abroad only to Norway which freight would not countervaile here above 30/- per cent for deales so advised to lie by or take sail coastwise.' Richard Haddock of London left behind him records which similarly illustrate these practices.[2] He spent the peace years of the 1660's as a master of merchant ships, the *Supply* and *Bantam*, which made regular voyages to Italy, and in the lists of part-owners of these ships we find a few of the names which are recorded elsewhere as their freighters. Haddock's commands were, in today's parlance, cargo-liners, and they were probably put into the Italian trade because their principal owners were concerned in it. But the part-owners provided only a small part of the cargoes carried, while on the other hand the great merchants among them must have made use of many other ships for their traffic.

On the whole, then, it was trade that gave its assistance to shipowning, rather than vice versa; the merchant entered the potentially profitable business of shipowning because he had connections which were likely to enhance these potentialities, not because he needed a ship to carry his goods. This was the typical situation; the many exceptions have been noticed.

[1] Norris MSS., Liverpool Public Library.
[2] BM Egerton MSS., 252/24.

What of the passive investors who owned the majority of the parts; who were they, and what attracted them to this form of investment?

It is extraordinarily difficult to obtain a broad view of the structure of ownership in the shipping industry before registration began in 1786. Few complete lists of owners survive;[1] incomplete lists are biased towards the active owners — that is, they usually overstate the merchant interest. The following table, prepared from complete or almost complete sets of Bills of Sale for fifty-three ships, gives some indication of typical occupations of late seventeenth-century shipowners:

Merchants, aldermen, freemen of London Companies	174
Miscellaneous tradesmen	25
Tradesmen connected with shipping and victualling[2]	26
Shipwrights	8
Gentlemen, esquires, baronet	24
Widows, spinster	12
Yeomen	1
Mariners (a) masters of the ships concerned	40
(b) others	28
	338[3]

In London, shipowning was almost confined to merchants (including those who had adopted more exalted titles as aldermen or gentlemen) and their widows, seamen, and tradesmen who had special connections with shipping as suppliers of stores, victuals or the ships themselves. In the provinces, however, the active owners had to look to a much wider range of persons to raise their necessary capital; 'Almost all the shopkeepers and inland traders in seaport towns, and even in the waterside part of London itself, are necessarily brought in to be owners of ships,' wrote Defoe in 1725.[4] The casual way in which the provincial shopkeeper could drift into and out of shipowning is exemplified by William Stout of Lancaster, who set up in business in 1687.[5] In 1698, he writes,

[1] The Liverpool Plantation Registers of the mid-eighteenth century, at the Customs House Library in London, give complete lists of owners of ships, but not their occupations.
[2] Ship-chandlers, sailmakers, anchorsmiths, ropemakers, bakers, coopers, butchers, salters, woodmongers, wharfingers.
[3] There are a very few (not more than ten) other part-owners of these ships, of whom nothing is known.
[4] The Complete English Tradesman, p. xi.
[5] The Diary of William Stout (1851), pp. 48–63, 95.

'I being at this time much out of business, I was persuaded by
some neighbours to stand a sixth part share in a new ship of 80
tons, now building near Warton.' He held his share of this vessel,
the *Employment*, for four years, until she was wrecked; he consistently lost money on her operations and abandoned seagoing
ventures for some years. In 1719, however, these memories had
faded, and he 'was persuaded by Thomas Backhouse, an attorney,
who owed me about £40, to take for it part of a new ship in
payment, as it cost him'. Stout, however, distrusted the master
of the ship, and sold his part (at a loss of £10) before the ship
sailed, and 'she was lost the first voyage after, by the carelessness
and negligence of the master, to the total loss of the owners'.
Stout once tried his luck to oblige a business acquaintance, and
once took a roundabout way to collect a debt; these are common
reasons why people became shipowners. The ship-chandlers and
shipbuilders who were always represented in high proportions
among the owners were trying sometimes to secure business,
sometimes to recover the price of work already done. Thomas
Coalthurst approached William Johnson in 1707 with the proposition that the latter should take a quarter share in the ship
Coalthurst was buying elsewhere

> 'and as an inducement to [Johnson] to purchase take and hold part of
> the said Ship . . . and as an inducement to become concerned therein
> the said Thomas Coalthurst proposed that your Orator exercising
> the trade of shipwright should have the benefit of doeing all the
> Shipwright's business that was wanting to fitt the said Shipp out for
> a Voyage to sea.'[1]

William Hall in 1662 contracted to buy a new ship from Richard
Boys, shipwright; he had to borrow money to pay the instalments
due to Boys on signing the contract and launching, and finding
himself short of money for the final payment he induced Boys to
become part-owner for one-sixteenth in order to reduce his debt.[2]

To large numbers of part-owners, however, shares in ships were
simply investments from which they hoped profits would accrue
with very little attention. We must return, therefore, to a question
which has been posed earlier; why were people willing in this
industry to invest in enterprises whose management was in other
hands, when such passive investment in private business was so

---

[1] *Johnson v. Coalthurst*, C.6–357–85.
[2] *Joseph & Hellin*, HCA 15–8, 13–75.

rare elsewhere? The answer is that passive investment — if it could be made with tolerable safety — was a desirable thing, and shipping was one of the few outlets, and indeed almost the only *profit-sharing* outlet[1] to which it could be directed with some degree of safety. This seems paradoxical, when we contemplate the perils of the sea, storm, shipwreck, piracy, fire, barratry and all the rest; but ashore the dangers to the incautious investor's property were even greater.

The investor in a part of a ship had in practice, though not in legal theory, a safeguard which limited his liabilities. He invested in a tangible piece of property, which remained little changed apart from gradual wear and tear. He normally paid the fitting-out costs before she sailed. The only substantial liability to be incurred by the ship in her voyages was the wages of the crew, and if the ship were lost the law did not require that wages be paid, even to surviving crew.[2] If she were not lost, some freight would be earned, and even if the gross earnings of a voyage were small, it was rarely that the unpaid balance of wages exceeded the value of the ship. Thus, while the part-owner of a ship certainly had, in law, an ultimate responsibility for its debts, it was most unlikely that he would be heavily called upon to meet them. He might well lose all or most of his initial investment (as one may in a modern limited company); but he was not in practice in the same situation as the investor in the ordinary profit-sharing partnership of the time, who could easily be totally ruined by being called on to meet large debts of a partnership in which he had invested a small part of his fortune.

Moreover, the shipowning partnership circumvented the great practical difficulties which, under English law, faced attempts to set up and operate large unincorporated partnerships. Not only were all members of an ordinary partnership liable to the extent of their whole individual estates, if need be, for the debts of the partnership, so that the prudent man avoided partnership except when he intended to take a close and continuous interest in the

---

[1] Compare the struggle to compel the East India Company to issue more capital, and so spread the ranks of the profit-sharers in this comparatively safe investment, in the 1670's and 1680's. K. G. Davies, 'Joint Stock Investment in the Late Seventeenth Century', *Econ. Hist. Rev.*, 2nd ser., Vol. IV, 1951–2, pp. 290–2; W. R. Scott, *The Constitution and Finance of English, Scottish and Irish Joint Stock Companies to 1720* (Cambridge, 1912), Vol. II, pp. 150–1.

[2] C. Molloy, *De Jure Maritimo et Navali* (1676), p. 222, 'Freight is the mother of wages'.

management of its affairs. They could only withdraw from partnership with very great difficulty and at the risk of ruining the remaining partners by leaving them short of capital. The death or bankruptcy of a partner, too, required the withdrawal of his capital at whatever inconvenience or loss to the other partners. A new partner could not be introduced without the unanimous consent of the other partners, and on terms they agreed to; it was impossible for a partner simply to sell his share and thrust the purchaser into the partnership. The difficulties and dangers of changing the structure of the partnership while it was a going concern were further reasons for confining membership to a small circle, well acquainted with each other's affairs and modes of behaviour. Finally, the large partnership faced practical inconveniences when it became entangled with the law; all its members had to be joined in formal legal processes such as the conveyance of property, and in lawsuits whether as plaintiffs or defendants. Although in the eighteenth century methods of getting round some of these legal difficulties were evolved[1] they were complicated and unsuitable for small business.[2]

The legal status of the shipowning partnership was quite different. Because it was an institution of very great antiquity, it was regulated by the special body of law which governed maritime affairs, administered in the High Court of Admiralty. Admiralty law centred not on the person but on the ship, and the effect was to create — for practical purposes, though the lawyer may dislike the use of the term — a corporation centred on each ship. Shares in a ship were freely transferable by simple execution of a bill of sale, without reference to other part-owners; the ship could be sued and even arrested for debt or tort; a single part-owner could sue on behalf of the ship; a majority of the owners could (subject to some not very important safeguards) direct the ship's affairs even against the will of the other part-owners. An apologist for the Court of Admiralty wrote in 1690:

[1] See A. B. Dubois, *The English Business Company after the Bubble Act* (New York, 1938), especially pp. 217–22 for the obstacles remaining to the large partnership when the legal position had been tidied up as much as was possible.
[2] On the legal position of partnership see W. S. Holdsworth, *History of English Law*, Vol. VIII (1925), pp. 217–18, 242–3. There is no adequate history of partnership law, and so far as I can ascertain there has been no attempt by lawyers to compare the situation of the shipping partnership and the ordinary mercantile partnership. One of the earliest works on partnership law, W. Watson, *A Treatise on the Law of Partnership* (1794), discusses the law as it affects both kinds of partnership, but in an unsatisfactory way.

H

'By the sea-laws, the ship is liable to the builders, amenders and victuallers thereof, but by the common law, the person that made the agreement, who often is an insolvent master, or part-owner, and sometimes set up for that very end, is only liable, so that if the builder, repairer or victualler should be constrained to sue at common law, they would not only lose their chief security, but would also be forced to bring each man his separate action; whereas they might all be joined in one action in the admiralty. Besides, the ship or vessel being proceeded against in the admiralty, every part-owner is liable for his share; whereas if the master, or part-owners, that made the contract, be sued at the common law, if he be solvent, will be constrained to pay the whole; and yet, many times, cannot recover the respective shares of partowners; at least, without beginning another suit in chancery.

If a part-owner refuses to contribute to the setting out of a ship, the admiralty court uses to take bail of those that would set the ship forth, to return her within a competent time, or else to pay the other part-owner, that refuses, to contribute for his part, according to an appraisement then made. And if this practice of the admiralty should be interrupted, it would be in the power of any one cross part-owner to keep the ship by the walls.'[1]

Thus the degree of limited liability which in fact existed, together with the liquidity given by the legal simplicity of transfer and the existence of an extensive market for shares in ships in major ports, made parts of ships attractive as investments to people both inside and outside the world of commerce. Executors and legatees did not hurry to get rid of shares which came into their possession. An extreme example of dead hands maintaining their grip is provided by the *St Patrick*, seven of whose eleven owners in 1745 were executors of the estates of gentlemen in London or the West Indies.[2]

The duties of owners once the ship was built and her master appointed were not heavy; they are set out quite adequately by the statement of Robert Browne, owner of one quarter of the *Hope* in 1661, that he 'hath sett the same forth in several voyages[3] and hath payed and contributed his quarter part of the charges of setting her forth, and hath received his quarter parte of the profit

---

[1] 'Reasons for settling Admiralty Jurisdiction', 1690 (printed in the *Harleian Miscellany*, Vol. VIII, pp. 371–82).
[2] HCA 15–44.
[3] This simply means that he did not raise objection to her being sent on her voyages.

thereof, from Thomas Frost the master of her'.[1] They could be
stirred or goaded into activity by prolonged dissatisfaction. The
Old Falcon was employed for years before 1621 in the Newcastle
coal trade 'by meanes of the overruling procurement of Cuthbert
Gray' (a Newcastle coal merchant who owned one-eighth and was
obviously the managing owner); whatever its conveniences to
Gray this employment was damaging to the ship and unprofitable
to the rest of the owners 'who thereupon concluded that the shipp
should goe no more to Newcastle, but be repayred and made fitt
for other imployments'.[2] This was a revolt against the managing
owner. A ship's master was deposed by the esquire and three
gentlemen, the widow and baker, spinster and vintner of Colchester, who were the 'major part of the owners' of the *Abigail* in
1679, protesting against the master for not rendering accounts to
them. They had left the whole management of the affairs of the
ship to him, and exercised their entrepreneurial function simply
by appointing a new manager when the old one became unsatisfactory.[3] The part-owner might be driven to obstructiveness by
his grievances, as was Sir Fisher Tench, gent., who in 1724 wrote
to the managing owner of the *Content* in the following terms:

> Sir
> There was a person from you called upon me with the Ship's
> Accounts. I think he told me there was about a Ballance of Forty
> Pounds to fit her out again. I shall not give my consent to send
> her abroad any more, nor will I part with my share at any Publick
> Sale. I will rather content myself with the Losse, than be further
> ill-treated.
>
> > Your humble servt.
> > Fish. Tench[4]

The part-owners were entertained to feasts in the ship — on
her first setting out, on the presentation of periodical accounts,
sometimes at the commencement of a long voyage; asked why he
thought Christopher Boone was a part-owner of the *Great
Alexander* in 1659 one of the ship's officers replied, 'the reason for
his belief is that the said Mr Boone together with other of the said

[1] HCA 24–116.
[2] *Gold v. Gray:* C.2 (James I) G 8/23.
[3] HCA 15–10.
[4] HCA 15–34. Fruitless opposition. The owners sought and obtained from
the Court of Admiralty authorisation to send the ship out without Tench's
consent.

ship's owners a little before the said ship went on her voyage . . . came on board her and there had a feast and was entertained as an owner.'[1] Such occasions might give part-owners the only opportunities of becoming acquainted with one another; indeed, part of the strength of the managing owner's or the master's position was that very often he was the only person who knew who all the owners were, especially after parts had changed hands a few times. Dissatisfied part-owners bringing actions in Chancery against husband or master normally asked the court to require the production of a list of owners and where they were to be found. Abraham Coleman in 1705, for example, complained that the husband of the *Providence* 'does so order that matter that your Orator shall never know who are the severall persons concerned in the said Shipp or where they live, so that your Orator for want of proper particulars shall never be able to bring his cause to hearing'.[2]

Peter du Cane, who described himself as a merchant but derived most of his income from land- and fund-holding, may serve to typify the eighteenth-century passive investor in shipping.[3] Du Cane's fortune had been made by his grandfather in financial operations in William III's wars; Peter had large investments in East India stock (he was a director of the Company in 1750-1) but he engaged in trade in a small way during most of his life, and (unprofitably) in marine insurance in 1740-1. He owned $\frac{1}{16}$ of the *Asia* from some date before 1735 until she was sold in 1740; $\frac{1}{16}$ of the *Tagus* from 1738 until 1752; $\frac{1}{32}$ of a Scarborough collier, the *Anne & Mary*, from 1735 until 1762. All these were long-term investments, and they did not yield very good returns; only when the *Anne & Mary's* master had failed to pay a dividend or render an account for seven years did Du Cane rouse himself to write a chiding letter:

London, 20 Jan. 1757

Capt. Francis Goland
   at Scarborough
I am surprised by lookeing back to my books to find I have received no Dividend on the Ship since June 1750. Surely in almost seven years she must have made some Dividends though none have been brought to me. I wrote you on this subject about 2 years ago, to

---

[1] HCA 13-74.   [2] *Coleman v. Shawler*, 1705, C.6 345-38.
[3] Du Cane MSS., Essex County Record Office, Chelmsford.

which I don't remember to have rec'd any answer. If I don't hear immediately something to my satisfaction, you must excuse me if I make an enquiry in a way I would rather be prevented doing. I must desire you to send me a list of all the owners, with the places of their abode.

I am, etc.

He had his share of unfortunate ventures; the *Ducane*, presumably so named because he was owner of a whole quarter part in her, was lost soon after she first went to sea in 1736, and the *Queen of Hungary* privateer, in which he took a share in 1744, captured only one small prize during her career, and was written off as valueless five years later.

No part-owner could avoid risk of loss; investors from outside the business world were perhaps less willing than others to accept philosophically the failure of some of their enterprises. The writer of the *London Spy* (1698) presents a not implausible picture of the dispirited shipowner who hears with joy of the loss of the ship in which he held a quarter share:

'Tis the best news thou couldst have brought me, for if the old bitch of a *Betty* had survived the dangers of the sea much longer, I believe she and the master together would have brought me to the parish. . . . No more long bills for refitting, no master's long accounts for damage sustained by storm. No, no, if ever they hook the old fool again to make ducks and drakes of his money in salt water, I'll give 'em leave to draw a rope through his guts and tie him to a cable to make a buoy on. . . . The Merchants are a pack of sharpers, masters of ships arrant knaves, a vessel but a doubtful confidant, and the sea a mere lottery.'[1]

To the risks of loss through incompetent, unfortunate or fraudulent management must be added those of fraud in the sale of parts. There was nothing to prevent the reckless or unscrupulous from selling twenty or thirty sixteenth parts in a single ship, and the courts were many times faced with disputes between pretending part-owners arising from such practices. More often than not the trouble arose from excessive hopefulness rather than deliberate fraud. John Stowe, for example, bought a small vessel named the *Joseph & Benjamin* in November 1668. He mortgaged half of her to George and Domingo Francia on 10th November, sold $\frac{9}{16}$ to various people between 1st and 7th December, mortgaged another $\frac{1}{4}$ on 7th December, sold another $\frac{2}{16}$; mortgaged the

[1] E. Ward, *The London Spy* (1698; ed. R. Straus, 1924), p. 378.

last unmortgaged quarter on 19th December and then sold a further $\frac{2}{16}$. When he failed to meet his obligations to repay the first loan[1] the whole financial structure blew up and he was called upon to explain why he had disposed of twenty-nine one-sixteenth parts.[2] Over-mortgaging was a common device of the hard-pressed master seeking to finance his own command. Absolute sales of more parts than the whole were much less common — or perhaps offered less likelihood of redress in court. Mrs Edwards, a properous midwife, for many years invested her surplus earnings without her husband's knowledge, on the advice of one William Judson, in whom she 'had great trust and confidence'; from time to time he 'did buye for her and helpe her to some parte or partes of ships'. But she trusted him too long and he helped her too often, for after she had paid him £350 for a share in the *William & Thomas* in 1671, Judson failed in business, and it then appeared he had issued Bills of Sale 'far beyond the proportion of the whole ship'.[3]

The remedy for this kind of fraud was seen to lie in registration of ownership. In his pamphlet *Trade Revived* (1659) John Bland proposed a Register of Shipping

> 'which will be of great use to Merchants and owners of Ships, and will hinder those Frauds as by Masters of Ships are usually put upon the Owners, making many times, and that too often, seventeen, eighteen and sometimes three-and-twenty sixteenth parts in a Ship, whereby some must be Couzened'.

But the many attempts to secure royal or parliamentary action to this end all came to nothing.[4] A petition was presented to the King in 1663 for 'The Erection of an Office to enrol all Bills of Sale'[5] and there was a similar proposition to parliament in 1678.[6] The matter was pushed vigorously in 1696 and 1697, when attempts were made to introduce into the House of Commons a

---

[1] Mortgage of a ship took the form of a Bill of Sale which contained provision for its automatic cancellation if a certain sum were paid to the mortgagee by a given date; otherwise the sale became absolute.

[2] HCA 15-9.

[3] HCA 13-131.

[4] It was observed that the Dutch derived many advantages from their compulsory registration of title to ships and other property ('Considerations on the East India Trade', 1701, in J. R. McCulloch (ed.), *Early Tracts on Commerce* (1856), p. 611).

[5] *CSPD, 1663-4*, p. 166.

[6] 'Heads for a Discourse to Parliament for encouraging Navigation' (Rawlinson MSS., A 447-1).

bill 'For Registering All Bills of Sale of Ships, and Vessels of Burden in a General Register Book'.[1] In 1736, following a petition from merchants and shipowners, a Committee of the House of Commons thoroughly investigated frauds in the sale of parts, and a bill 'to Establish an Office within the City of London for Registering Bills of Sale of all Merchant Ships . . . together with the Assignments and Alienations of such Bills of Sale of such Ships, or any part or parts thereof' passed its second reading, only to be dropped with the prorogation of the parliament, and the measure was never revived.[2] The fact that the bill fell through at so late a stage seems to indicate that the evils it proposed to remedy, though undoubtedly real, were not widespread. Thereafter the shipowning community apparently reconciled itself to the existing position, for it initiated no further registration projects.

Registration under the Navigation Act of 1696[3] gave no help for the shipowner; it was simply to provide authentication of British build and ownership for the customs officials; the register was not public and was probably not kept up to date with changes in ownership. Its extension in the act of 1786 for the general registration of all ships over fifteen tons, however, did at last bring some limited protection to the investor in shipping. This register was to record the names of owners at the time of first registration of the ship (though not the size of their shares); and it declared that

'When and so often as the Property in any Ship or vessel, belonging to any of His Majesty's Subjects, shall be transferred to any other or others of His Majesty's Subjects, in Whole or Part, the Certificate of the Registry of such Ship or Vessel shall be truly and accurately recited, in Words at Length in the Bill or other Instrument of Sale thereof, and that otherwise such Bill of Sale shall be utterly null and void, to all Intents and Purposes.'[4]

From that time onward, therefore, the new buyer could at least demand that the title to a part he was acquiring should be traced back to this original list of owners.

[1] Petition in the National Maritime Museum, Greenwich, dated 1695; draft Bill in BM Add.MSS. 5540–120 (the papers of John Cary of Bristol); *House of Commons Journals, 1692–7*, pp. 432, 459, 669. See also S. Baxter, *Reasons for bringing in a bill for registering all Bills of Sale of Ships* (1700).
[2] *House of Commons Journals, 1732–7*, pp. 599, 642, 680.
[3] 7 and 8 William III, c.22.
[4] 26 Geo. III, c. 60.

VI

The Merchant Seamen

So far the ship's crew has been something of an abstraction, merely an indicator of technical conditions in ships and on sea routes. It is time now to take a closer look at the men themselves — who they were, how they came to the sea and what rewards it gave them. We may start by considering a few random examples, drawn from various trades and periods, to introduce the typical ranks and skills that combined to form a merchant ship's company.

In the very first years of the seventeenth century, an estimate was made for the crew of a ship of 160 tons to go to Malaga. She was to carry a master and two mates, a boatswain, gunner and carpenter, a surgeon and 18 hands; a crew of 25 in all.[1] The *Abraham* of 200 tons, which made voyages to Barbados in the thirties, carried a master and two mates, a boatswain, gunner and carpenter, but in this vessel the last three each had a mate, and there was a specialist cook and a surgeon besides the deckhands. The number of hands varied between 17 and 19, making a total crew of 28 to 30.[2] Jumping forward another thirty years, we may pick out a very different ship, the foreign-built *Falcon* of 200 tons, trading to the Baltic in 1672. She had only 17 men in all; a master and only one mate, a boatswain, gunner and carpenter, a surgeon and eleven men and boys. Even the gunner might have been omitted in these waters safe from piracy, had not war with the Netherlands just broken out.[3]

The East Indiaman presents a very different picture. Setting out for the far side of the world on a voyage which might well last two years, facing many hazards from disease as well as from weather and the king's enemies, she began her voyage well provided with supplies of all kinds, including men — both seamen and specialists. Take the *Colchester*, of 450 tons, for instance, which sailed at the end of 1703. In addition to the master she had

---

[1] BM Lansdowne MSS., 157–116/118.
[2] HCA 30–636.
[3] HCA 24–117.

five mates and three midshipmen. The boatswain had two mates
or servants, the gunner three and the carpenter four. There were
cook and cooper, each with a mate, besides a steward and a
captain's steward with two assistants, a purser, a caulker and his
mate, a joiner and two tailors. Finally, there was the surgeon with
two mates, and 51 men and boys, of whom a few, a little more
highly paid than the rest, were dignified with the title of quartermaster. A total crew of 89 was carried in this ship.[1]

At the opposite end of the scale, the *Pearl*, of 70 tons, trading
round the North Sea and once to Portugal between 1717 and 1720,
carried only a master and mate and a crew of three, to which an
extra hand was added for the Portugal voyage.[2] The slightly
larger *Mary Galley* of 80 tons made a voyage to Jamaica in 1735
with master and mate, a second mate who doubled the duties with
those of boatswain, and a cook and 7 men and boys to make up a
total of 11.[3] Finally, in the ships of 1766 crews were much
simplified; the Bristol slaver *Juba*, of 300 tons, had a master and
three mates, a carpenter and a cooper, a surgeon and 14 fore-
mastmen and boys; a crew of 21 in all. The third mate probably
acted as boatswain.[4]

This handful of varied examples is far too small to provide an
accurate general picture of the size of crews, which must be looked
for in the kind of evidence quoted in earlier chapters. It does,
however, indicate how crews were constituted. Every crew began
with master and mate; in the 12-ton shallop working across the
Channel between Southampton and Boulogne it might well end
there, this pair making up the whole crew. After the Civil War, as
crews were generally becoming smaller, there were some decades
when it was unusual for a ship of under 200 tons to carry a second
mate. In the course of the eighteenth century the refining of
navigational skills began to require the employment of second
mates again in ships of quite moderate size, in spite of the continuing fall in overall numbers of crew. Third mates were never
carried before 1700 except in Levant and East India ships, but
they, too, appeared a little more frequently during the eighteenth
century. The East Indiamen had fourth, fifth and sometimes
sixth mates, and a few midshipmen. The most senior specialist,
the carpenter, was carried by most ships going far beyond the

[1] Rawlinson MSS., C.966.
[2] HCA 15-36.   [3] HCA 15-39.   [4] HCA 15-56.

confines of the Channel and North Sea. The doctor or surgeon was once to be found in nearly all ships of over 200 tons going far afield, but during the eighteenth century he was hired less frequently for ships in the transatlantic trades and came to be almost confined to those going to the tropics — the African coast or India — and to the Mediterranean. The purser, often found in the middle decades of the seventeenth century in Mediterranean and American traders, had nearly disappeared by 1700; the business and clerical work he had done was absorbed by increasingly literate masters, aided by agents ashore. His rare appearances after 1700 are as a captain's clerk, of very low status.

At a lower level, almost every ship carried a boatswain, combining the duties of a foreman over the crew and of craftsman in those maintenance duties which required specifically seaman's skills. The rigging, the upkeep of which was a complicated and continuous task, the sails (except in the rare ship that carried a sailmaker), the boats, and all kinds of minor fitments, as well as the supervision of the appropriate stores, all came within his orbit. The gunner, rarely omitted in the early seventeenth century from the crew of a ship going westwards or southwards from the Channel, was a fast disappearing figure thereafter. Then and later his status varied enormously, from a seaman paid two or three shillings a month for small extra duties, to a busy full-time craftsman almost on an equality with the carpenter, and with his own specialist crew. Even before 1700, however, he must usually have had other functions than looking after the armament, and by that date he was rarely to be met with except in Levant, East India and the bigger West Indies ships. In the middle of the eighteenth century, gunners were almost unknown except in East Indiamen. The cook, the one specialist almost universally found, 'a most necessary member so long as there will be bellies',[1] came far below these in status, quite often on a level with the able seamen, paid at their rate for a task which, if it was a specialised one, was not to be regarded as a skilled craft.

The usual officers and specialists, then, were the master with one mate or two, boatswain, carpenter and cook; to which were often added in the seventeenth century a surgeon and gunner, and sometimes a purser. There were odd specialists; coopers, carried in many of the larger ships on transatlantic, Mediterranean or

[1] W. Welwod, *An Abridgment of all Sea-Lawes* (1613), p. 21.

Indian voyages; stewards, found not infrequently in ships of all kinds; and such people as sailmakers, smiths, tailors, barbers, joiners, poulterers, trumpeters, armourers, butchers, caulkers, many of whom were mustered in every large East Indiaman, but who were rare birds elsewhere. Moreover, specialists' mates abounded in the larger vessels. The boatswain's mate was usual in large ships; the carpenter often had a mate in ships of quite moderate size, and in the largest would have three or four; doctors' and gunners' mates were quite often to be found before 1700. The East Indiaman, again, might extend to cooks' mates, coopers' mates, caulkers' mates and even trumpeters' mates.

Finally, there was the unspecialised crew before the mast, by no means homogenous but including a substantial majority of able seamen — able to 'hand, reef and steer'. In some ships a few of these were designated quartermasters; nearly always, with or without this title, a handful of the most experienced had a shilling or two a month extra pay. After the able seamen came a tail of ordinary seamen, in wartime some 'landsmen', and lastly the boys, ranging from those about to blossom into ordinary seamen down to the last and latest thirteen-year-old at eight shillings a month. The ship's boy had the distinction of appearing regularly in charter-parties, which specified that a ship would be manned by 'the master, (seventeen) men and a boy'. His unique function was to stay on board as watchman in foreign ports, when the rest of the crew had gone to taste the pleasures of the shore.[1]

Many of the seamen, boys, specialists' mates and even occasionally the specialists themselves or the masters' second mates, were serving apprenticeships to more senior members of the ship's company, to officers in other ships, or to carpenters or surgeons ashore. From the point of view of the ship they were serving in, however, this was irrelevant; they were employed in certain ranks, and treated and paid accordingly — though the apprentice had to hand over the pay he earned to his master.

To the boy or young man who could not anticipate that parental or other influence would provide him with an easy road to command of a ship and whose own qualities were not outstanding, the sea might appear to offer only hardship and danger, the possibility of harsh treatment, and rather precarious material

---

[1] C. Molloy, *De Jure Maritimo et Navali* (4th ed., 1688), p. 219, writes of 'The Ship's Boy, who keeps her continually in harbours'.

rewards. The career of a common seaman was not, therefore, one which the son of the even moderately prosperous tradesman or skilled artisan would be encouraged to enter; recruitment was mainly from the lowest ranks of society, from the children of labourers, farmhands, seamen themselves, and from young men who were dissatisfied with, or could obtain no employment in, the lowest of shore occupations. This recruitment leaves no record. No doubt many men and boys simply walked on board ship and were taken on, appearing in the wage bills at ten or fifteen shillings a month when the able seamen earned twenty-five. The Newcastle coal trade was for a long time an easy place for such learners to make their first essay at life afloat; it was said to be

'If not the only, yet the special Nursery, and School of Seamen. For, as it is the chiefest in Employment for Seamen, so it is the gentlest and most open to Landmen; they never grudging in their smaller Vessels to entertaine some two fresh-men, or learners; whereas, to the Contrary, in the Shippes that voyage to the southward, or otherwise, farre out of the Kingdome, there is no Owner, or Maister, that will ordinarily entertaine any Land-men, be he never so willing, as being bound by the Charter-Partie to the Merchant, as they say, not to carry but sufficient Men, and such as know their Labour. It is by great favour that others slip in, and they very likely'.[1]

It may well be that in the seventeenth century enough men were trained in this, and those subsidiary breeders of seamen, the Newfoundland and Iceland fisheries, to satisfy most needs, for between them they employed more than half the English seamen of the first decades of the century.[2] The coal trade was hardly a 'gentle' one, but it was in the main a summer trade, and the ships were only a few days at sea on each voyage. The fishing vessels had large crews for the work on the fishing grounds, and in the long outward voyage much of the crew was superfluous and might begin to learn seamanship. The growth of these occupations lagged behind that of other trades, however. The Iceland fishery declined sharply during the middle decades of the seventeenth century, while the Newfoundland fishery came increasingly to be carried on by settlers in Newfoundland and Maine. The coal trade was still, in 1671, referred to as 'the greatest nursery of seamen we have in England'; a member of the House of Commons observed

[1] 'The Trades Increase' (1615), *Harleian Miscellany*, Vol. IV, pp. 220–1.
[2] ibid.

that 'In Kings' Ships and Merchants', you must have Seamen; in the Coal Ships Country Fellows, who are made Seamen quickly'.[1] Thirty years later a writer characterised the large body of naval seamen who had originally come in from the coal trade:

> 'If his breeding has been North of Yarmouth, he is distinguished with the title of Collier's nag; and indeed he is a rare horse that will never fail you in bad Weather, being as insensible to Rain, Cold or Thunder as a Cannon-Bullet. He is generally above the common size of other Tars, in Bulk, Strength and Courage, which is mainly owing to his northern Diet, which he thinks on with a heavy Heart every time he sees a good Coal Fire. He is a great Admirer of North-country Beef and Pease-Pudding, yet allows Newcastle Ale and Salmon to be the most Superlative Diet in the Universe.'[2]

But even the coal trade was faltering in its expansion in the early decades of the eighteenth century, and increasing numbers of seamen had to learn their trade in the ordinary course of carrying it out on the oceans.

The intake of seamen was increased by the effects of successive wars. Every war swept a higher proportion of the country's merchant seamen into the king's ships and killed or maimed a great many of them; and pushed to even greater heights the wages of those lucky enough to escape the net. Into the openings so left came old men retired from the sea, foreigners, young boys, and not least large numbers of landsmen attracted by the high wages of wartime seafaring. From William III's time onward, increasing numbers of ships actually describe some members of their wartime crews as 'landsmen'. Their wages were low by comparison with those of the able seamen, but far exceeded the earnings of any labourer — and of a great many skilled men — ashore. The attractions were increased when, in 1704, legislation guaranteed such landsmen afloat freedom from impressment during their first two years at sea.[3] Some of the men who made up this great wartime influx must have found their vocation at sea, and did not or could not abandon it when war ended and the survivors of the regular seamen came back from the king's service. The annual recruitment needed for the maintenance and growth of the merchant service can hardly be guessed at, because, apart from

---

[1] *Debates of the House of Commons, collected by Anchitell Grey* (1769): Colonel Birch on 13th April 1671.
[2] E. Ward, *The Wooden World* (ed. G. R. Callender, 1929), p. 97.
[3] 2 Anne, c. 6.

death and desertion overseas, each of which took a considerable
toll, there was a continuous and probably large draining away of
men who abandoned the sea and settled ashore in their prime.

The seaman and even the officer (except, sometimes, the master)
was hired by the voyage. When the voyage was completed he
might wait ashore until his ship was ready to sail again, but he
was unlikely to do so unless his ship was engaged in coastal or
shortsea trades. Edward Barlow habitually spent many months
ashore, idling or visiting relations and showing off his money,
between voyages. But the day would come when the seaman had
spent all his money and his host's welcome grew cold:

    ' "Why", said the sailor to his landlady in Wapping, "Would you
have the conscience to turn me adrift, now I have spent all my money
aboard you, before I have got another voyage? You are as hasty with
a body to turn him out as a boatswain in a storm." '[1]

In winter, moreover, it might be difficult for him to find a job
at sea at all, because much sea traffic was seasonal, and a large
part of the merchant fleet was laid up during the winter. At Hull,
its historian wrote:

'During the evening of the winter months, the streets are crowded
with boys, intended for the sea-service, who spend their time in open
violation of decency, good order and morality; there are often fifteen
hundred seamen and boys, who arrive from the whale fishery, and
often double that number of unemployed sailors, are left at leisure
to exercise their dissolute manners on the inoffensive passenger in
the public street.'[2]

Every year, in December or January, many seamen were driven
to find themselves other occupations; some, surely, settled down in
them before spring came again. For large numbers of men,
indeed, sailoring was normally a casual employment, into and out
of which they drifted as they found employment harder to come
by on sea or on land.

Taking one year with another, some thousands — almost
certainly a very few thousands — of men and boys had to be
drawn in annually to maintain the service of the merchant shipping.
Sons and nephews of seamen, paying apprentices and paupers,
farmhands attracted by the pay in peace and artisans by the

[1] E. Ward, *The London Spy*, 1698 (ed. R. Straus, 1924), p. 330.
[2] G. Hadley, *History of the Town of Kingston-upon-Hull* (1788), p. 424.

prospects in war; one way or another they came in, learned hard
things in difficult and dangerous ways, mastered them and
became accepted members of the seagoing community, died early
or late, left the service for good reasons or bad, or stayed on to
the end as masters, mates, boatswains or those elderly deckhands
of whom Edward Barlow wrote,

> 'Always in need, and enduring all manner of misery and hardship,
> going with many a hungry belly and wet back, and being always
> called "old dog" and "old rogue" and "son of a whore" and such
> like terms, which is a common use amongst seamen, and that would
> be a great grief for an aged man.'[1]

There was, however, another and quite different source of
recruitment to the sea. To be the master of any but the smallest
ship was a worthwhile and profitable profession, which attracted
a small but continuous flow of youths from much higher levels of
society. These were the sons of minor merchants and prosperous
ship-masters, men with influence and connections in maritime
circles, able to dispose of a few hundred pounds at need to further
a boy's career. The boy going to sea with such a background could
be sure that his early years afloat were only a brief prelude to
command of a ship. He was not always better treated in his first
years than his fellow seamen, but his prospects were very different,
embarking on a career that was likely to bring him to the sort of
modest wealth in which he had grown up in his father's household.

Many, but by no means all, of these boys were apprentices.
Moreover, apprenticeship was often entered into by boys going
to sea without such prospects; not all indentures so much as
provided that the master should instruct the apprentice in 'the
same Art of Navigation which he now useth by the best means
he can'. Many lads were apprenticed to second mates and even
boatswains, who would have been hard put to it to inculcate
such skills. By the early eighteenth century the seven-year
apprenticeship to the sea was something of a rarity; in the enormous apprenticeship records kept by the Inland Revenue after
1709, the mariners with their three-, four- or five-year apprenticeships stand out among long columns of seven-year apprentices
to other trades.[2] Four and five year apprenticeships to seamen
can be found in the seventeenth century, though a longer term

[1] Basil Lubbock (ed.), *Barlow's Journal* (1934), p. 162.
[2] Data from registers of stamp duties on articles of apprenticeship, IR-1.

may have then been rather more common.[1] The conditions of the apprentices varied enormously. Premiums, when they were paid at all, were small — £10 or £20 was quite usual in the eighteenth century. The extremely rare large premiums, such as the 200 guineas paid by Thomas Betton of London, merchant, for binding his son to Whittington Williams for five years in 1724,[2] undoubtedly covered initiation into far more and more profitable mysteries than those of the sea. Looking back from his old age in the mid-nineteenth century to the situation of the prospective officer in the 1780's, Captain R. W. Eastwick wrote,

> 'It was the custom in those days to article a lad for a period of four years to the seafaring profession, however respectable he might be, and boys did not enter on the life in the merchant service as midshipmen, but as common apprentices, very dirty to look at, messing in the fo'castle with the sailors, and being expected to perform all the most menial duties on board.'[3]

The number of navigation apprentices grew as the science became more refined in the course of two centuries, but even towards the end of the eighteenth century Samuel Kelly was not apprenticed when he went to sea (in 1779) although he was recommended to masters so that he received favourable treatment, was taught navigation, and secured early promotion and a command at the age of twenty-three.[4] Always, the key to success was not apprenticeship but connections.

Many apprenticeships were nothing more than introductions to the lower ranks of seafaring. Although they called for small premiums or none, the sacrifice of wages after the first year or two makes them seem, to modern eyes, very doubtful bargains in a trade that was open to entry in easier ways. Thomas Barlow put it plainly when writing of his own apprenticeship which began in 1659:

> 'If I had known as much then as I know since, and what it was to serve apprenticeship seven years at sea, I would have gone and learned as much in two or three voyages as a hired servant, and many do it

[1] Trinity House brethren, under the charter of 1685, could take apprentices only for seven year terms.
[2] IR 1–10.
[3] H. Compton (ed.), *A Master Mariner, being the Life and Adventures of Captain Robert Eastwick* (1891), p. 21.
[4] C. Garstin (ed.), *Samuel Kelly, an Eighteenth Century Seaman* (1925), pp. 19–20, 166.

by the voyage or the year, and them that they go with give them about £3 or £4 the year; than to have served seven years to it and get another man four score pounds and myself little or nothing the better.'[1]

Yet even Barlow admitted that 'though my master did but show me little concerning navigation, yet if I had given my mind to have learned it from another, my master would not have been unwilling to have paid for it'.[2] In other words, it is not easy to draw a sharp distinction between the apprentices who were enrolled to become masters and those who were to remain seamen unless they pulled themselves up by their own great exertions. The distinction was real enough, but it lay ashore, not afloat. By the middle of the eighteenth century, however, apprenticeship generally was becoming less popular, the number of sea apprentices dropped, and voluntary apprenticeship became more often specifically for navigation and directed to the training of officers and future masters. For a time the numbers of those apprenticed simply to the crafts of the seamen were augmented by pauper apprentices under an act of 1704[3] which may have made a considerable contribution to eighteenth-century recruitment. Their condition was miserable, if Colchester apprenticeships of 1704–57 are at all typical;[4] they were bound for long terms — seven, eight, nine years — and, unlike other apprentices to the sea, were entitled to no pay during all this time; the master was obliged to provide two suits of clothes on completion of their service.

What was ordinary apprenticeship worth? It usually carried with it some pay, on a rising scale, commonly £2 or £3 a year if the master provided clothing, and more if he did not. The master maintained his apprentice between ships — though he might set him to work to earn money at tapstering or some other unseamanlike occupation. Robert King of Ipswich was given the high pay of £4 a year in the first two, £5 in the third and £6 in the last year of his apprenticeship 'towards the findeing and provideing himselfe linnen and wollen hose, shoes and other necessaryes the said terme, and keeping himselfe in the winter season . . . the tyme the shipp lye upp'.[5]

[1] Barlow, op. cit., p. 29.   [2] ibid., p. 30.
[3] Boys over ten years of age who had become chargeable on the parish might be apprenticed to shipmasters until they reached the age of twenty-one (2 and 3 Anne, c. 6).
[4] There is a register of Colchester apprenticeships in the library of the National Maritime Museum.
[5] HCA 15–30.

As to training, the apprentice should have learned enough in a couple of years to get employment as an ordinary seaman. Eastwick, after sixteen months at sea 'had gained a practical knowledge of many a seaman's duties, and by the end of it there was scarce an operation on board in which I could not lend a hand if ordered, and I knew every rope in the vessel, and its use, by heart'.[1] Seaman's employment meant seaman's pay — but not for the apprentice's benefit. The pay was his master's whether he had given instruction or not. Barlow was earning nineteen shillings a month, an ordinary seaman's rate, after three years at sea;[2] William Ayre was getting seaman's pay after serving twelve months of his apprenticeship in 1746.[3] Thomas Davis, who was apprenticed for seven years in 1683, was hired out as an able seaman eighteen months later, and after five years at sea was employed as a mate, though still an apprentice whose earnings had all to be handed to his master.[4] Some apprentices acquired surprising skills to put money in their master's pockets; Thomas Jones, indentured to the master of the *Hannah & Elizabeth*, was employed at thirty shillings a month in 1725 as the ship's steward and surgeon.[5] Jones was exceptional; most of these apprentices genuinely earned their pay as trained seamen, and a large number of them were sent off by their masters, after a year or two, to serve in different ships in fresh trades. Indeed, their indentures often required that they gain wider experience than their masters could provide for them; many of the boys apprenticed to the Colchester coasting skippers, for example, were to be sent to sea for two years in a foreign-going ship during the term of their indentures.

The ship's carpenter always served an apprenticeship. He was the most important of the specialists which a ship carried, and the one whose trade was most closely associated with the sea. His training was through an initial apprenticeship to a shipwright ashore, but, though its term was seven years, he was sent to sea as a carpenter's mate after a year or two in the yard, and in fact served most of his time at sea, earning a useful sum for his master. Humphrey Lincoln went as carpenter's mate in an East Indiaman, in 1688, after only seven months of his apprenticeship had gone by, and earned thirty-five shillings a month.[6] John Okill, a Liverpool master shipwright, had no less than fifteen apprentices

[1] Eastwick, op. cit., p. 25.   [2] Barlow, op. cit., p. 555.   [3] HCA 15–44.
[4] HCA 24–124 (*Susannah*).   [5] HCA 15–35.   [6] HCA 24–124.

at sea in 1752, each earning between fifteen and thirty shillings a
month for him![1] The master might be a master-shipwright, that
is a yard owner or foreman, but the majority of apprentices were
indentured to skilled craftsmen employed in the yards, and their
premiums in the eighteenth century were no more than £5, £10 or
occasionally £20. Possibly the premium was low in this rather
well-paid craft because the apprentice could so quickly begin
to earn money for his master. When his time was expired the
carpenter was qualified to work as a shipwright ashore or as a
capenter at sea, and in fact often alternated between the two. He
could make repairs to hull, masts and yards when needed, whether
in dock in England, in a gale at sea, or in some creek of the
Caribbean or the Cape Verde Islands; given the material he could
build a new ship with the help of some unskilled labour. The
caulker who sailed in a few of the largest ships was recruited and
trained in the same way, but most caulkers worked ashore.

No other specialist trade was primarily concerned with the
sea, unless it be the gunner's. The gunner, however, had no
special avenue of entry or training; usually he was a seaman who
had served some years in the navy, but this was common experience. The cook, too, was not a man specially trained for his
job; his qualification was often that, like Long John Silver, he was
a seaman who had been partially incapacitated in some accident.
The other skilled tradesmen — the doctors and coopers, and the
rarer armourers, pursers, butchers, smiths, etc. — were trained
without reference to the sea, and were attracted to it in the small
numbers required, presumably, by family connection, desire to see
the world, or possibly the pay. Few profited so well by their time
at sea as did Robert Wigram, who was apprenticed to a physician
in 1762 and sent to sea as surgeon's mate in an East India ship in
1764; in seven years at sea he 'gained a perfect knowledge of the
trade of India and China' and so 'had great advantages as a
drug merchant' when he settled ashore in 1771; he went on to
become a wealthy merchant, shipbuilder, owner of East India
ships and a peer.

Up to a point, promotion was open to anyone who was not
excessively stupid, who was more sober than most, and who put
aside some of his earlier earnings to make advancement easier.

[1] Okill MSS., Liverpool Public Library.

Drunkenness and wildness characterised the merchant seamen, and the exceptions stood out. Apprenticed or not, well-connected or not, a steady and competent man could expect to become in turn quartermaster and boatswain or gunner. From here to second mate was not, during most of our period, a difficult step, nor did it involve a vast change in status or pay. The second mate, except in East Indiamen, was a rather inferior being, responsible for discipline and working the ship rather than navigation, not infrequently acting in addition as gunner or boatswain. Only the chief mate, apart from the master, needed to be a competent navigator; he would have to take over the ship if the master died at sea, as he was quite likely to do.[1] A man who had not acquired skill in navigation might be appointed second mate — though this became increasingly unlikely during the eighteenth century — but he would never be chief mate unless in a coaster. Here was the true dividing line between the skills of the seaman and the officer.

The extent of the necessary formal training in navigation grew very rapidly after the middle of the seventeenth century. It was still possible in the sixties for illiterates to command ships; Bills of Sale and other documents are met with, occasionally, signed by the master with a cross. A cabin boy wrote for the owners the account of a ship's voyage to the Baltic in 1663 because the master could not write well enough.[2] It was true during much of the seventeenth century, as Monson wrote in the thirties, that

> 'The Principall thing in a pilot or coaster of our coast is to know where he is . . . the skill of a coaster is to know the land as soon as he shall descry it.'[3]

For voyages round the coasts of Europe such knowledge for long remained an adequate qualification, and it was an essential part of the fitness of a master for any voyage. If he did not have this personal knowledge of the coasts he was sailing for, he had to hire a mate who could be 'pilot'; as late as 1686 John Mun was hired as mate and pilot of the *Society* for a Norway voyage: 'the Master had never been the voyage before so that the said John Mun had the sole care and government of the said Ship'.[4] For the voyages in

---

[1] At various dates between 1720 and 1724 the Royal African Company owned 44 ships; during this time 22 masters died in their service. This was, of course, an exceptionally unhealthy trade (T 70-1225).

[2] SP 29-440-87.

[3] M. Oppenheim (ed.), *The Naval Tracts of Sir William Monson* (Navy Record Society 1902-14), Vol. IV, p. 31.

[4] HCA 24-122.

which a ship was likely to be more than three or four days out of sight of land, however, some capacity for scientific navigation was not merely a useful trimming to practical experience, but an absolute necessity. Not that it produced very good results. To quote Monson again:

'There is no certainty in the art of navigation, in our ordinary masters that take charge; for if there were they would not vary so much from one another as usually they do. For proof whereof, let there be four or five masters or pilots in one ship that goes or comes from England to the Terceiras; if they be any time in traverse at sea you shall have some of them thirty leagues before the ship, and others as many leagues behind the ship.'[1]

Both the young administrator Samuel Pepys, and the young merchant Dudley North, were disgusted at the lack of theoretical understanding of the methods they used which was shown by the officers they sailed with: 'the master and mate . . . are a sort of people, who do all by mechanick rule, and understand nothing, or very little, of the nature and reason of the instruments they use.'[2] Pepys returned to the subject in middle age, on his voyage to Tangier, and secured practical demonstrations of the in-accuracy of officers' calculations.[3]

The master's business, in fact, was to arrive somewhere off the coast he wanted, avoiding known shoals, preferably in the morning, and to be able to recognise the precise point where he had made his landfall so that he knew whether he must coast eastward or westward, north or south, to reach the port he was destined for. His chief guides were dead reckoning with compass and log; his *Rutter* or coasting pilot brushed up his own knowledge and reminded him of the navigational dangers on the coast.

But there was more to navigation than this, and, surprisingly, even before the middle of the seventeenth century most masters had some acquaintanceship with scientific navigation, if we may judge from the almost invariable inclusion among their effects of a *Waggoner*[4] — a sort of primitive Nautical Almanac[5] — and of

[1] Monson, op. cit., Vol. IV, p. 395.
[2] Roger North, *Lives of the Norths*, Vol. II, p. 306 (see also Vol. III, p. 91).
[3] E. Chappell (ed.), *The Tangier Papers of Samuel Pepys* (Navy Record Society, 1935), Vol. LXXIII, pp. 126-9.
[4] From L. J. Wagenhaer, *Spiegel der Zeevaerdt* (1584); a collection of charts and data, translated into English in 1588.
[5] The true Nautical Almanac dates from the French *Connoissance des Temps* (1678); the English *Nautical Almanac* was not established until 1767.

cross-staff and quadrant, the primitive forerunners of the sextant.[1] The need for real skill in the use of these, and in mathematical calculation, grew steadily with the expansion of transoceanic commerce. This need brought about a substantial revision of pre-sea training of potential officers, in the decades round 1700, which in turn widened the gap that had to be crossed by those who entered the merchant service as seamen.

Practical use of instruments was no doubt a skill best acquired at sea. Some mathematics were, however, required for the resulting calculations, and until the last third of the seventeenth century there was no grammar school in England which taught mathematics.[2] There was a growing number of private teachers, some of whom combined this work with instrument-making and the publishing of books for mariners, and men with serious pretensions to become good navigators resorted to these; but there was, apparently, no place for the training of the boy of thirteen or fourteen preparing to go to sea. Royal interest in maritime affairs led in 1673 to the foundation of a navigation school at Christ's Hospital, to instruct forty boys in mathematics and navigation. The first fifteen boys had passed through it by 1675 and were examined by Trinity House; the King sought 'the goodwill and assistance of the principal companies of merchants by their inter-position with the masters employed by them' to get good apprenticeships for the boys, and each master was promised a royal grant of a seaman's pay for each apprentice he took.[3] William III contemplated setting up another navigation school in 1702, but apparently nothing came of this.[4] Two other schools where boys could be taught 'such part of the mathematics as are requisite to instruct youth in the Art of Navigation, to fit them for the Sea Service'[5] were founded; Sir Joseph Williamson's Mathematical

[1] Though the quadrant was invented late in the sixteenth century, Joshua Kelly, writing *The Modern Navigator's Complete Tutor* as a textbook for his navigation school in 1724, thought it necessary to explain the use of the more primitive cross-staff as well as the quadrant.
[2] 'I have never heard of any Grammar School in England in which it [i.e. Mathematics] is taught', wrote John Newton in 1670. I owe this quotation, and much of this discussion on training in navigation, to E. G. R. Taylor, *The Mathematical Practitioners of Tudor and Stuart England* (Cambridge, 1954). Her later work, *The Haven Finding Art* (1956), has also proved very useful.
[3] SP 40–82, 42–20. A. Bryant, *Samuel Pepys: The Years of Peril* (Cambridge, 1935) and *Samuel Pepys: The Saviour of the Navy* (Cambridge, 1938) have many references to this school, in which Pepys took a close interest.
[4] *House of Commons Journals, 1702–4*, pp. 254, 470, 475.
[5] Joseph Neale's will, quoted in E. G. R. Taylor, *Mathematical Practitioners*, p. 237.

School at Rochester in 1701,[1] and Neale's Mathematical School in
Fleet Street, London, in 1715.[2] The Royal Hospital School at
Greenwich, effectively established in 1716 for naval orphans —
though its reputation became so high that entry was sought for
many children not so qualified — also taught mathematics and
other subjects for intending seamen;[3] it was said in 1750 to teach
a hundréd boys, who were to be apprenticed to ships' masters or
to the officers of men-of-war.[4]

In the early eighteenth century, therefore, some scores of boys
were being sent to the newly-established schools in and around
London and given some training to prepare them to become ships'
officers. Moreover, the private teachers who gave training in
mathematics and navigation were also growing in numbers. Some
were ex-captains or practical seamen, like Joshua Kelly who had
his school near Wapping New Stairs; some, such as John Sellers,
were instrument makers first and teachers afterwards; increasingly
they branched out from, or became partners in, writing-masters'
practices — the teaching of arithmetic and book-keeping to
budding merchants, as Cutler & Groom of Wapping in 1711
advertised themselves:

'Teachers of Writing, Arithmetick, Merchants Accompts, Geometry,
Algebra, Trigonometry, Navigation, Astronomy, Gunnery, Gauging,
Dialling, Perspective, Measuring; the use of the Globes, and all other
Mathematical Instruments, the Projection of the Sphere, on any
Circle, etc.'[5]

These places took in young men who needed to supplement their
seafaring experience with the science of navigation, and any
seaman who had guarded his money could acquire most of the
skill he required from them. Robert Knox, who went to sea as a
boy, was stranded in Ceylon and kept there for twenty years; on his
return to England in 1680 he attended a mathematical school to
fit himself for the sea again, and immediately afterwards was given

[1] C. Bird, *Sir Joseph Williamson, Kt., the Founder of the Rochester Mathematical School* (Rochester, 1894).
[2] E. G. R. Taylor, *Mathematical Practitioners*, p. 237.
[3] N. MacLeod, 'History of the Royal Hospital School', *Mariners' Mirror*, Vol. XXXV, 1949.
[4] J. J. Cartwright (ed.), *Travels through England of Dr. R. Pococke* (Camden Society, 1888–9), Vol. II, p. 67.
[5] Advertisement pasted in the log book of *Henry*, Daniel Groom master (HCA 15–30). There are similar advertisements in the newspapers of this period.

command of the small East Indiaman *Tonqueen Merchant*.[1] The private teachers had by this time begun to give training to boys as well as to men who had been to sea; as early as 1696 the fourteen-year-old Nathaniel Uring spent six months learning the rudiments of navigation in London before he was sent to sea on a Newcastle voyage,[2] and John Cremer in 1714, waiting for a ship was sent to 'one Mr Atkinson, a Mathematickal School Master on Rotherif wall'.[3]

There were similar teachers in the provincial ports. At Hull the Trinity House was employing a teacher to train a dozen or so boys in navigation early in the eighteenth century; this effort blossomed, rather belatedly, into the Trinity House School in 1786.[4] At Whitby, Charlton's Mathematical School was famous in the mid-eighteenth century; it prepared Francis Gibson for sea in 1763; 'so well had he profited by the instructions of his master that during his first voyage he made a chart of the coast and harbour at Goldsborough in New England'.[5]

With the development of this more formal training in navigation, the good navigating officer became more skilled at his craft and the gap between navigating officer and those below him became wider and more difficult to cross. The seaman's skills changed little while those required of his officers became greater. Nevertheless, opportunities did remain open to those who were determined to learn and to advance themselves.

Advancement from boy or ordinary seaman to chief mate was made by a series of steps, none of which was very high, though the change in status and earnings which the whole series carried with it was considerable. But the step from chief mate to master was one which carried a man into a new place in society; from being a perpetually supervised employee to being the employer's representative working, usually, beyond the range of easy control; from a constantly subordinate position to one afforded a fairly high status by the employer's own need for an agent who could deal on something like equal terms with factors and merchants; from an

[1] *Dictionary of National Biography*; Robert Knox.
[2] *The Voyages and Travels of Capt. Nathaniel Uring* (ed. A. Dewar, 1928), p. 1.
[3] J. Cremer, *Ramblin' Jack* (ed. R. R. Bellamy, 1936), p. 64.
[4] G. Jackson, op. cit., p. 29.
[5] G. Young, *A History of Whitby* (Whitby, 1817), p. 871.

income hardly exceeding a modest salary to one which could legitimately soar far beyond the salary contracted for, and even, in the extreme cases of some eighteenth-century masters of East Indiamen, reach thousands of pounds a voyage. Here the interest and recommendation of owners was all-important. A seaman could serve under ships' masters and earn their golden opinions, but for advancement beyond the status of chief mate not their opinions, but the goodwill and respect of merchants was needed. The master alone was appointed by the owners; in principle by the owners of the majority of the parts in the ship, in fact usually by the managing owner acting alone. For the master was the owners' agent, responsible not only for navigation but also for maintaining their interests, maritime and commercial, while the ship was far removed from their control; able to bind them for debt and render them liable to penalties for his contraventions of the law.[1]

Professional ability by itself, therefore, could not be wholly sufficient to secure a command.

'As the whole care and charge of the ship and goods are committed to the master, it is the prudence of the Owners to be careful who they will admit Commander of their Ship, since their actions submit them to answer the damage, of whatever other Act he shall do in reference to his Imploy . . . they seldom suffer any to go Skipper or Master, but he that hath a share or part in her.'[2]

Most masters were small part-owners; they had interests in the ship's profitability and in the preservation of it as an asset, while the other owners had tangible security from which they might recover losses due to a master's bad faith. To buy a small part — a sixteenth or a thirty-second — was not seriously beyond the means of the prudent man who had served a few years as a mate. Willingness to do this was usually essential to obtaining a command; it was rarely sufficient to ensure one. Only if a seaman could raise the money to buy, not a tiny fraction but a substantial share — a half or more — would such a financial gesture by itself be sufficient to attract co-owners; the monetary tangles into which some masters were led by their attempts to acquire large shares without adequate resources have been touched on in Chapter V.

---

[1] Until 1735 owners were liable without limit for such acts by the master as embezzlement of cargo, even if they were totally innocent parties. From that date, their responsibility was limited by 7 Geo. II c. 15 to the value of the ship and freight — still a serious enough loss.
[2] C. Molloy, op. cit., p. 203.

The surest way to become a ship's master was to be the nephew of a rich merchant, or the son of a minor one with important shipping interests, or of a master of good reputation. Time after time, in the records and the literature of the merchant service, we can observe son succeeding father as master, or commanding the ship which his father owns; or we find the master's name corresponding with names in the list of owners. Yet, of course, the able mate was not without his chances. If the master of his ship retired and was willing to recommend him — or better still turned to ship management himself; or if the master died at sea, he had his opportunity to command. Moreover, the shipping industry was growing fast, an adequate supply of ships' masters had to be found somehow, and many managing owners without nephews or other protégés had to look round and appoint the best man they could find and hope he justified their trust. Indeed, it is evident from the casual nature of the employment of many masters that there was an open market, even if it was a limited one with most of the best plums withdrawn. On the Royal Exchange in 1698, Ned Ward could observe,

> 'That man . . . is the greatest merchant in England, and those fellows that come astern, and now and then come upon his quarter, with their topsails lowered, are commanders of ships who are soliciting for employment.'[1]

Command when it was obtained might well be precarious. The status of masters, their relations with their owners, varied enormously. On the one hand were those who were glad to get any voyage as master, who would attend an owner they knew for weeks on an indefinite promise of employment, or would take a post on indefinite terms and hope that it would turn out all right — and sue the employer when it failed to do so. Henry Wallis waited on Daniel Gates all through the winter of 1684–5, from August until March, for fulfilment of a half-promise of employment, offering in the end to go as mate if need be; 'but Mr Gates did not think the said Henry Wallis fit by reason of his age for that employment'.[2] George Simon had been master of three different ships in foreign trade, but in 1674 had to accept employment as second mate in a collier.[3]

Every contract was made for a single voyage, and many owners employed masters on a voyage-to-voyage basis. This does not

[1] E. Ward, op. cit., p. 71.   [2] HCA 24–122.   [3] HCA 13–131.

mean that they were anxious to keep changing masters, but unless owners were willing to pay half-pay between voyages the master might not be able to sustain himself in the long interval, and was compelled to seek another ship, as the rest of the crew did. Nevertheless, records which report ships' activities over many years[1] show that masters were much more often than not maintained in their commands for several voyages, if not for the whole lifetime of the ship. The well-regarded master, in the trades where ships and cargoes were most valuable — East India and the Levant — could expect permanency of tenure and the provision of a new ship when his own was too old for its trade,[2] and there were no doubt such masters in other trades. The authority of the master corresponded, on the whole, with the permanence of his tenure. The temporary, one-voyage employee was likely to be entrusted with little beyond navigation and the handling of the crew; the owners at home, the supercargo or agent abroad, dealt with commercial affairs. At the other end of the scale, such a man as Richard Haddock, whose papers record his activity in traffic with Italy in the third quarter of the seventeenth century, was the effective manager of the ships he commanded, arranging the voyages, accounting himself to general meetings of owners, and taking advice rather than orders from agents abroad.[3] Nathaniel Uring, at the age of thirty-five, was settling his own arrangements about voyages and cargoes, listening to the advice of his owners' agents in Mediterranean ports but making up his own mind whether he should take it, and finally, when his ship was 'perfectly worn out with age' selling her in Lisbon.[4]

The nature of the commercial functions which a master might have to undertake, and the limitations on his authority, are discussed in Chapter VIII. Though the extent of his commercial functions was tending to grow, the change was not, perhaps, very great between the early seventeenth century and the American War of Independence. The creation of a network of overseas agents for English firms led, quite early in our period, to the abandonment of the practice of merchants travelling with their goods, and more gradually to the disappearance of the supercargo — the merchants' agent travelling with the ship — although

---

[1] For example, the London Seamen's Sixpences records, Adm. 68–194/218.
[2] L. S. Sutherland, *A London Merchant* (Oxford, 1933), pp. 86–107.
[3] BM Egerton MSS., 2521–24.
[4] Uring, op. cit., p. 213.

supercargoes are found occasionally until the nineteenth century; from the point of view of ships' masters, the increasing rarity of such travelling companions more or less balanced the growing likelihood that they would find themselves in ports where owners or freighters had trusted agents.

Whatever care and precautions the owners took, they were not invariably successful in finding commanders who embodied all the desirable virtues with none of the corresponding vices. James Houblon, one of the greatest merchants of his day, took a gloomy view indeed when he wrote in 1685:

> 'A fourth reason for the present discouragement our navigation is under is the great and almost general debauchery and prodigality of Masters of Ships to maintain which both when they are on their voyages and in their families at home they run in debt and render bad and doubtful Accounts to their Owners, waste the Ship's provisions and stores.'[1]

There were, indeed, occasional criminals who ran away with their ships, privately insured and then wrecked them, or sold the cargo and absconded with the proceeds. But the incompetent or the irresponsible could ruin their owners just as effectively as the criminal, and, short of ruin, cause them endless trouble. They came in all varieties, but drunkenness was the vice most widely reported; there were too many masters like Thomas Clarke of the *Constant Elizabeth* (1682) who brought golden opinions but turned out to be

> 'A very careless improvident and riotous person, and also a very angry furious and passionate person, and is very quarrelsome, and he is also very much addicted to excessive drinking of strong drinks, brandy and other liquers . . . the boate belonging to the said Vessell, while in port, hath often wayted upon and for him the said Clarke till Midnight, and sometimes till one or two of the clock in the morning, and was then forced to returne on Board without him, and the said Thomas Clarke did often lye on shore, and neglect the care of the Vessell wherewith he was entrusted.'[2]

There were incompetent masters like Captain Williams of the *Parham*, who took his ship up the Bristol Channel in mistake for

---

[1] A Discourse Touching the Grounds of the Decay of the English Navigation (Bodleian Library, Rawlinson MSS. A 171–278).
[2] HCA 24–121.

the English Channel, when returning from the West Indies in 1731, to whom his owner wrote in unkind terms:

'How in the world you should commit such a blunder can't imagine now in the Summer when it's not bad weather and near 17 hours daylight. Can't remember of any such mistake made by anyone in my life at that time of year.[1] Won't redownd to thy credit or reputation.'[2]

Minor abuses of authority were manifold. Joseph Broad refused to sail the *Mary & Martha* out of Rye when ordered by his owners because he intended to exercise his vote at the pending mayoral election.[3] Edward Hales in 1724 told his friends 'that he would goe to Hull to see his old sweetheart Jenny Spavat or to that effect'; he diverted his voyage and stayed twenty days in Hull, where he had no business, frittering away his owners' funds on such things as 'A Jack and Pendant, which the deponent believes was to be put up when he was to make merry or entertain Company aboard his Ship and was not any necessity for the buying of the same.'[4]

We may believe that such masters did not hold their positions for very long, that they changed from ship to ship as fast as their employers learned that their habits were costly in money or time, and received letters like the one that came to Captain John Combes one January morning in 1721:

Capt. Jno. Combes
Your affairs oblidging you to absentt your self from attending the service of our Ship the Grocer, and att the same time to use us very ungratefully, these putt us under a necessity of dismissing you from our service for it cannot be supposed we can Entertaine a Man who is endeavouring to destroy us. We therefore hereby discharge you from our Service in any kind on board our said Ship the Grocer.

We are your Friends
Jos. Wordsworth Jr. (etc.)[5]

Nevertheless, they were men who had somehow reached the top of the tree; during the tenure of their command they had absolute authority over the mates, the carpenters and boatswains, and the seamen who served in their ships, and could make life tolerable or

[1] Note the implication that it was not unknown for ships to make this error in poor weather.
[2] W. E. Minchinton (ed.), *The Trade of Bristol in the Eighteenth Century* (Bristol Record Society, 1957), p. 111.
[3] HCA 15–35.
[4] HCA 13–88 (*Nathaniel & John*).
[5] HCA 15–36.

unbearable as they wished. The risk of being put under command of such men must have been one of the most potent forces driving capable officers to seek promotion to their own commands.[1]

[1] The Hudson's Bay Company in its early years had endless trouble with incompetent, careless, drunken and dishonest masters. See E. E. Rich, *The Hudson's Bay Company, 1670–1870* (Hudson's Bay Record Society, 1958), Vol. I, pp. 91, 110.

VII

The Pay and Conditions of Merchant Seamen

There were three systems of calculating seamen's wages. The least important was by shares of the ship's earnings, the normal means of remunerating crews of fishing vessels and, in part, those of privateers, for fairly obvious reasons. It was occasionally used as well in small craft plying along the Channel coast, as in the *Ann*, in 1685, whose owners were to have $\frac{9}{27}$ of the proceeds of each voyage, the master $\frac{6}{27}$ and the crew $\frac{4}{27}$ each, i.e. one-third to the owners and two-thirds to the crew.[1] Half a century later a ship's master declared that in coasters on the south coast 'The Master hath two thirds of the clear earnings of such vessels for victualling, manning and wages and the Owners have one third of such earning'.[2] Possibly fishing was interspersed with the ordinary trading voyages of such craft, or at any rate their crews were recruited from men who were often engaged in inshore fishery and used to the share system; it may have been felt, too, that because the master of such a small vessel was close to his crew, had less authority over them, and was himself a less responsible person than the master of a larger ship it was necessary to give every man an incentive to operate the ship efficiently.

The other two systems were of roughly equal importance. Payment of a lump sum for the voyage was usual in all the other short voyages in which English ships engaged; in coastal, cross-Channel and Irish Sea trades and in those round the borders of the North Sea, to Flanders, Holland, Hamburg and Norway and, in the seventeenth century, to the French Biscay ports. There is a sharp division between these and the trades in which monthly wages were paid — those involving the longer voyages to the Baltic,[3] North Russia, Spain, Portugal, the Mediterranean, and beyond Europe to America, Africa and the East. Firmly established

---

[1] HCA 24–122.

[2] E.134, 2 Geo. II, Mich. 27. The system was also in force in the East Coast ship *Two Brothers* of Wisbech in 1734–5 (HCA 15–39).

[3] Though wages for Baltic voyages were occasionally paid on a lump sum basis.

custom determined the kind of wage payment, and masters and crews took it for granted that the custom would be followed when signing on for any voyage.

Lump-sum wages were paid in trades where the voyages were short; the time variations, however large in relation to the average length of voyage, were not likely to be large absolutely, and would usually be ironed out in the course of a year in the average of several voyages. Until well into the eighteenth century a majority of Englishmen in trading ships were employed in trades where lump-sum wages were customary, but they were less litigious than those in the long-distance trades, and have left fewer records behind. The one thing that is clear is that the high degree of stability in peacetime wage levels, which we shall observe in monthly wages between about 1680 and 1775, applied also to lump-sum wages. Throughout this period of a hundred years, the able seaman in the Norway trade from London, Hull or Newcastle was usually, in peacetime, paid £3 5s.; the seaman who voyaged regularly in the Newcastle-London colliers could expect to receive 30–35 shillings a voyage, according to the season.

Wages in the lump-sum trades must always have borne a well understood relationship to wages for more distant voyages; they could be translated approximately by those who received or paid them into earnings per month, and compared with earnings elsewhere. They were not necessarily quite so high; the frequency of seeing the home port and in some of these trades the greater regularity of employment were advantages which may have been paid for. But the movement of monthly wages, and their general level, should indicate approximately the changing fortunes of all seamen, and the relation between their earnings and those of men in other occupations.

Two things must be said by way of preface. There are occasional suggestions that wage rates varied according to the voyage; for example, Adam Smith wrote,

'In time of peace, and in the merchant service, the London price is from a guinea to about twenty-seven shillings the calendar month. . . .'[1]

Certainly there were, during much of the seventeenth century, small differentials between, on the one hand, the unhealthy East

[1] *The Wealth of Nations* (Everyman edition), Vol. I, 98.

India and Africa trades, and on the other those to Spain or Virginia, but the variations were not important — rarely more than a shilling or two a month — and after 1700 they no longer appeared regularly; Smith must have been misled by a knowledge of one or two unusual examples.[1] Secondly, the wages of masters and often of mates were lower in the outports than in London. The wages of the lower ranks showed no significant differences, however, for able seamen formed a homogeneous labour force, well informed as to conditions and pay obtainable at various ports, and were not easily obtained anywhere in Britain on terms differing from the best they could hear of.[2]

The fluctuations of able seamens' wages[3] in the century and three-quarters between 1604 and 1775 are briefly as follows. In the first decade or two after the ending of war with Spain in 1604, the able seamen could expect 17 to 18 shillings a month, rising to 19 to 20 shillings in the thirties,[4] a level at which the rate remained stable until the outbreak of the First Dutch War of 1652–4. Then wages rose to 30 to 38 shillings, falling to 23 to 24 in the brief period of peace and rising to 30 to 38 again in the Spanish War of 1655–60. For a few years after 1660 they were back at the old level of 20 shillings or a little under, but when a second war with the Netherlands became inevitable, late in 1664, wages shot up, and settled at 35 to 38 shillings until the war ended in 1667. They did not, however, return then to the old rates, probably because of the great demand for shipping and seamen to import the timber needed for rebuilding London after the Great Fire; wages remained, until 1671, between 27 and 30 shillings. The war which broke out with the Dutch in 1672 ushered in a long period of unusually high wages, reaching 35 to 40 shillings between 1672 and 1674. Though England then left the war, there was no general peace until 1678, and while English ships were acting as carriers

---

[1] There is the peculiar case of the *Lucretia*, in 1755, whose crew were to get 25 shillings per month, but 'in case of slaving at Senegal to increase the wages to 28/- per month' (HCA 15–55). But the ordinary crew definitely signed on for a slaving voyage to West Africa at that date received no more than 25 shillings.

[2] Possibly an outport differential opened up in the wartime peaks of wages. G. Coade, *A Letter on Trade* (1747), p. 68, says that at London seamen's wages were then 55–60 shillings a month, while at Bristol and Exeter they were only 45–50 shillings.

[3] There are many hundreds of wage records in the High Court of Admiralty. They are more ambiguous, and less plentiful, before the mid-seventeenth century than they become later.

[4] There was presumably a rise in wages during some part of the war of 1624–30, but I have no data to show this.

K

for embattled Europe wages remained at 27 to 28 shillings a month, rising briefly to 30 shillings when it was expected, in 1677–8, that England would re-enter the war. The general peace brought a stabilisation of wage rates, but not at the level of the early sixties; from 1679–88, and thereafter in peacetime for the next century, seamen's wages were 24–25 shillings a month.

In 1679, twenty-seven years had elapsed since a firmly established wage rate had been broken by the onset of the First Dutch War, and in all except five or six years of this period unusual conditions, whether in peace or war, had prevented a return to the old rate. It was not difficult for an entirely new level of wages to establish itself. Contemporaries ascribed the failure to return to the old wage rates after the last abandonment of them in 1664 to the provision of the Navigation Acts that three-quarters of the crew of any ship which was to be treated as English were to be Englishmen, creating something like a monopoly for English seamen.[1] But it is doubtful whether, except in wartime, more than a few hundred foreigners were employed in British ships;[2] thousands more foreign seamen could have been brought into the English Merchant fleet without infringing the Navigation Acts. The rise in wages was due primarily to the very rapid growth of the English merchant fleet between 1660 and 1688 (which the Navigation Acts undoubtedly fostered) and to the increasing naval peacetime establishment; and it was facilitated by the breakdown of the standard in the long disturbed period between 1652 and 1679.

Though peacetime wages were stabilised after 1679, wartime fluctuations grew ever more violent as wartime naval demands became greater. In 1689 wages shot up to 45 shillings a month, and then crept to 50 shillings; in the early nineties 55 shillings was not uncommon and only with the easing of the maritime strain in 1695 did they fall again to 45 shillings. After the interval of peace, 1697–1702, when wages were at 24 to 25 shillings, they rose to 30 shillings in the spring of 1702 and climbed gradually to reach 45 to 50 shillings a month in 1708. In 1712 they promptly fell

---

[1] e.g. R. Coke, *Discourse of Trade* (1670), p. 29; 'Britannia Languens' in J. R. McCulloch (ed.), *Early Tracts on Commerce* (1856), p. 318.
[2] The Registers of Admiralty Passes of the 1680's (Adm. 7-75/76) show the number of foreign seamen carried; most ships declare none at all, though the law would allow them several. It is unusual to find a clearly foreign name in any list of a ship's crew, except in wartime.

to the peacetime level again; rose briefly though perhaps not universally in the short wars of 1718 and 1727 to 30 shillings, but apart from these remained stable for over twenty years, until the mid-thirties. The troubled state of Europe, causing a partial naval mobilisation in England, resulted in a rise to 35 to 40 shillings in 1733–5, but wages fell back to their old level until England went to war in 1739. By 1740 wages had reached 50 shillings a month, and from 1745 to 1748 the usual level was 55 shillings. The rise in wages during this war provoked the only attempt to limit seamen's wages by statute; from 25th March 1741, for a period of one year, they were not to exceed 35 shillings a month.[1] The Act was disregarded, and this provision was not renewed. A brief return of peace brought wages down again, but the expectation of new war caused them to creep up before war broke out in 1756. The beginning of the Seven Years War sent wages up to extraordinary heights, touching 70 shillings a month in the winter of 1757–8 and settling at 60 to 65 shillings until prospects of peace began to appear in 1762. The end of the war saw an immediate fall to 25 shillings, and this rate was generally paid until the outbreak of the American War, though the rumblings of American disturbance in 1769 caused a brief rise to 30 shillings a month.

The stability of peacetime wages over a hundred years in this industry is remarkable. Perhaps it should be said that before 1700 23 shillings was occasionally paid (though, on the other hand, seamen in East India and Africa voyages had their extra shilling or two a month) and that after 1748 25 shillings a month was nearly invariable; by then the 24 shilling rate had become a rarity. That is, the wage level was creeping up very slightly, from an average nearer 24 shillings than 25 in 1680 to an average of almost 25 shillings by the mid-eighteenth century — a rise of perhaps two or three per cent.

It is not necessary to follow in detail the short-term fluctuations of the wages of other members of ships' crews, though they differed from those of the seamen in one important respect, namely, they changed less in wartime. Indeed, they changed only to the extent necessary to keep the wages of specialists and under-officers at slightly higher level than the inflated wages of the seamen, and to keep the mates' wages a little higher still. The masters' pay, which was well clear of any need to make adjustments for such

[1] 14 Geo. II, c. 38.

reasons, never altered between peace and war.[1] The narrowing
of differentials in wartime may be illustrated by comparing two
similar ships in the Africa/West Indies trade, in peace and war.

	Speaker, 1737	*Dragon, 1748*
	shillings per month	
Able Seamen	25	55
Cook	30	55
Gunner	30	55
Boatswain	40	65
Carpenter	60	90
2nd Mate	60	70
1st Mate	80	90
Master	120	120

Before 1650 the pay of the ship's master had become standardised, in all ordinary London foreign-going ships, at 120 shillings
per month, and at this level it remained in peace and war
throughout the period we are considering. It had begun the
seventeenth century at 80 to 90 shillings a month, but in the
transatlantic and Mediterranean voyages which were becoming
frequent in the twenties and thirties this rate was pushed up to
100 to 120 shillings, and the higher rate quickly established itself.
In the outports the master's pay was usually lower; both at
Liverpool and at Bristol the normal rate became fixed at 100
shillings, and at smaller ports a rate as low as 90 shillings can be
encountered in the eighteenth century. Indeed, a historian of
Liverpool ascribes the growth of the port's shipping to the low
wages and short commons of its shipmasters:

'The Liverpool merchants proceeded on a more economical but less
liberal plan, the generality of their captains were at annual salaries,
or if a monthly pay, four pounds thought great wages at that time,[2]
no cabin privileges were permitted, primage was unknown amongst
them, and as to port allowances, not a single shilling was given, while
five shillings a day was the usual pay from Bristol and seven and six
from London. The captains from those ports could, therefore,
occasionally eat on shore, and drink their bottle of Madeira; whereas,
the poor Liverpool skipper was obliged to repair on board to his
piece of salt beef and biscuit, and bowl of new rum punch, sweetened
with brown sugar.'[3]

[1] Except in some of the smaller outport ships whose masters received a low
peacetime rate of pay.
[2] Contemporary wage records show that this is wrong.
[3] Anon., *A General and Descriptive History of Liverpool* (1795), quoted in
Gomer Williams, *History of the Liverpool Privateers* (1897), p. 471. Samuel
Kelly wrote in 1785 of his elderly uncle who 'had sunk a great part of his money

Naturally, lower wages for masters can be found in very small ships when they did pay monthly wages, but it may be said that after about 1650 nearly all ships not paying lump sum wages paid their masters, in the case of a London ship, 120 shillings, or of one belonging to the larger outports, 100 shillings a month. There is a group of regular exceptions at the other end of the scale. The East Indiamen, the Levant traders, and a few of the regular traders to Italy paid £10 a month from the first available datum in 1667 to the end of our period. The masters of the largest London slave ships in the early eighteenth century often had £8 a month.

The pay of mates was not standardised in this way; it varied greatly with the size of the ship, besides undergoing small wartime fluctuations. In most London ships in peacetime, an only mate earned 55 to 65 shillings a month; if there was a second mate the chief had 70 to 80 shillings; in the large ships carrying three or more mates the chief mate regularly earned 100 shillings a month. At the wartime peaks of the 1690's, the late 1740's and the years round 1760 these rates were increased by ten to twenty shillings a month, always, of course, keeping short of the master's wages. In the outports mates earned a little less. The mate's wages, like the master's, had gone up sharply during the first half of the seventeenth century; no more than 40 shillings had been normal just after 1600. The second mate, whose importance varied greatly from ship to ship, could expect between 40 and 60 shillings a month; on these low rates, wartime supplementation to keep him ahead of his inferiors might be considerable.

The carpenter's peacetime wage was almost standardised though its rise to a stable level took longer. In the early seventeenth century the carpenter earned only 30 shillings a month; this rose to 40 shillings in the thirties, and to 40 to 45 shillings in the early sixties. The Second Dutch War saw a leap to 60 shillings, and this the carpenters managed to establish as their peacetime wage rate — with occasional deviations to 55 to 65 shillings — for the next century. The dual pressure of growing demand at sea and the expansion of shipbuilding at home had favoured the carpenters more than any others of the seagoing community; the enormous increase of naval shipbuilding from the levels of the early seventeenth

(gained when captain of a Guineaman out of Liverpool) in shipping and the mines' (C. Garstin, *Samuel Kelly, an Eighteenth Century Seaman* (New York, 1925), p. 132). This does not tally with the story of the poverty of the Liverpool masters.

century, first in the Dutch and then in the French wars, heightened the demand for their services.

Other wages were less standardised, but typical levels, in peacetime and at the peaks of war between 1660 and 1776, were as follows:

	Peace	War
	shillings per month	
Gunner	30–40	50–70
Boatswain	35–40	60–70
Doctor	60	70–80[1]
Purser	40–60	
Cook	25–30	50–60[2]
Carpenter's Mate	35	55–60
Boatswain's Mate	30	50–55

All these wages were normally paid only if and when the voyage was concluded. 'Freight is the mother of wages' was an old-established principle, occasionally challenged in the eighteenth century but on the whole maintaining itself to the end. If the ship completed her voyage she earned — or should have earned — freight; if she were lost or captured, owners and freighters lost, and the mariners should not be the only gainers.[3] Such was the reasoning of the seventeenth century.

Because wages were payable at the end of the voyage, it was important to the seamen that the voyage whose completion would entitle them to the fruits of their labour should be defined with some precision. The crew was nearly always signed on for a specific voyage to and from a certain region. Naturally there were disputes; the agents at ports abroad would sometimes secure ladings for further discharging ports outside the area which the crew had originally contracted for. The crew could usually be persuaded to accept this extension of the voyage by a payment of wages on account. The master of the *William & Jane* was offered at Leghorn in 1689 a voyage to Smyrna; he paid most of the wages earned up to the ship's arrival at Leghorn and 'by and with the consent and agreement of all the Marriners under their hand' proceeded to Smyrna.[4] This situation did, indeed, arise most

[1] The doctor was rising in status in the eighteenth century; before 1689 he commonly earned 50–55 shillings a month in peacetime.
[2] The cook was also going up in the world; many cooks in the seventeenth century earned no more than able seamen.
[3] See, for a good expression of this view, BM Add.MSS. 24107–31 (1695).
[4] HCA 24–124.

often in the Mediterranean, where English ships had an important role in the internal carrying trade, and a practice early developed of including in Mediterranean wage contracts options to the master to make extended voyages. In the *Fortune* (1661) which sailed for a rather indefinite Mediterranean voyage, the crew was to have four months' wages at the end of eight months' service, and a further four months' pay at the end of every four months thereafter.[1] When John Cremer joined his ship in 1716

'The Master, being bound up the Streights, had drawed up a writing for the Ship's Company to sine that they would proceed on the voage, whear was unceartain after our Arival at Leghorn. But the first Mate, an old surly Jack Tar, put all the men in mind to raise their wages theair to 30/- per month when arived at Leghorn, if they went further abroad — as they had now 25/- per month — and to be paid every second delivery port so much sterling for a twelve month certain.'[2]

In 1677 Trinity House, expounding the custom of English navigation in the Mediterranean, declared that in ships on trading voyages from port to port, the masters were to pay at the last discharging port wages due up to that time, minus six months' wages as security for the remainder of the voyage.[3]

For a long time these regular arrangements for payment of wages during the voyage were only made in the Mediterranean trade, but in the twenties and thirties of the eighteenth century they appeared also in the West Indies trade. Payment of wages in the islands had earlier been regarded as a disastrous policy, which invited the crews to desert where new crews could hardly be obtained.[4] As the island labour force became increasingly a slave one, opportunities for unskilled white men without capital disappeared; the islands ceased to be attractive places to desert in, and eventually conditions provided a small reservoir from which crews could actually be recruited. Meanwhile, there appeared a positive inducement to pay crews in the colonial harbours, in the

[1] HCA 13–74.
[2] J. Cremer, *Ramblin' Jack* (ed. R. R. Bellamy, 1936), pp. 74–5. The ship in fact went on to Cagliari for salt, and carried this to Boston, Mass., before returning home.
[3] SP 29–397–37.
[4] See, for example, *CSPCAWI, 1669–72*, No. 645. The danger of a crew deserting if paid in Virginia was indicated in the case of the *Constant* (HCA 24–123); 'there is not any other seamen to be there hired, so the voyage must be overthrown and the ship must there perish' (1690).

shape of debasement of the colonial currencies. Wages paid in Virginia or Jamaica money rather than sterling were a source of profit to the owners, while the crews were glad enough to get some ready money on any terms. Printed wages contracts in use for Liverpool slavers in 1765, for example, provided for half the wages earned on the outward voyage to be paid in America, and only if the local pound was valued at less than half the English pound was an adjustment to be made for this by payment in the relatively good Barbados currency.[1]

Wage payment finally came under legislative regulation with the *Act for the Better Regulation and Government of Seamen in the Merchants' Service* of 1729.[2] This provided that all seamen were to make contracts in writing with the master or owners — they were to 'sign on'. The agreement was to declare the seamen's wages and the voyage for which he was shipped, and would be conclusive evidence on these issues. Wages were to be paid, unless contrary terms appeared in the written agreement, on final discharge or within thirty days of the ship's entry at the Customs House, whichever was earlier. Thereafter all seamen signed or set their marks to some such printed form as the following:

> It is agreed between the Master, Seamen and Mariners of the Ship *John & Hester, Robert Fowler* Master, now bound from the Port of London *for Genoa and Leghorn and back again whereunto the ship shall be bound*
> That in Consideration of the Monthly Wages against each respective Seaman and Mariner's Name set, they severally shall and will Perform the above mention'd Voyage, and the said *Robert Fowler* Master doth hereby Agree with and Hire the said Seamen and Mariners, for the said Voyage, at such Monthly Wages to be paid pursuant to an Act of Parliament made in the Second Year of the Reign of King George the Second, Intituled, An Act for the Better Regulation and Government of Seamen in the Merchants' Service. In Witness whereof they have hereunto severally set their Hands.
> [Here the crew sign, and the date of signing on, his rank and wages are set against each man's name.][3]

---

[1] *Blakeney*, HCA 13–55.
[2] 2 Geo. II, c. 36. The act was to run for five years, but it was renewed from time to time and finally made perpetual by 2 Geo. III, c. 5. As early as 1685 the bye-laws of the London Trinity House had required every master hiring seamen to 'take in writing under the said Seaman's Hand, upon what Condition he is entertained', but I have seen nothing to suggest that this regulation was complied with.
[3] HCA 15–38 (1733). This was a very public form of agreement; every

In various ways, seamen obtained some of their wages in advance. In London, there was an old-established custom that full pay started only from the day of the ship's departure from Gravesend; the crew were entitled only to half pay from the date of signing on until that time, but this half pay was invariably handed over on the day that full pay commenced, so all crews sailing from London had some small amount of money in their pockets. There was, moreover, a growing practice of more regular advances. In the East India trade, at least as early as 1663,[1] seamen received two months' full pay in advance, before the ship sailed; the private traders to India in 1695–1707 were constrained to follow the example of the Company ships.[2] The practice spread in the course of the eighteenth century; in 1729 an Africa trader complained that his crews demanded advances as of right (though he does not say he paid them);[3] in the difficult wartime conditions of 1741 a petition of merchants, owners and masters claimed that they paid a month's advance to every mariner;[4] and after mid-century a large proportion of seamen's pay accounts show an initial advance of two months' pay. The ostensible purpose of these advances was described, at Bristol in 1744:

'It has been always a custom to advance a month's wages to all the men intended to be shipt (except the chief mate) either to discharge the debt contracted to the landlord with whom they lodge or to fitt themselves with clothes and necessarys for the voyage, but since the commencement of the Spanish War the Seamen or rather their landlord when men are scarce insist to have two months' wages advanced.'[5]

The East India shipowners were also prepared to make regular formal provision for allotment from wages — once a rare privilege occasionally granted by owners to ships' officers; East India wage contracts usually permitted one month's wages in every six to be paid to some named person in England. Here too there was a slow imitation of its example.[6]

signatory could read, if he could read, what the pay of other members of the crew was. Later, books of individual contracts came into use.

[1] *Robinson v. Clarke*, 1663 (HCA 13–130).
[2] *Webster v. Winter* (1703), C.6–347–61.
[3] *House of Commons Journals, 1727–32*, p. 253.
[4] *House of Commons Journals, 1737–41*, p. 672.
[5] W. E. Minchinton (ed.), *The Trade of Bristol in the Eighteenth Century* (Bristol Record Society, 1957), p. 153.
[6] The East India Company's ships used wage contracts of a regular form, clearly co-ordinated by all the shipowners, probably with the Company's approbation.

Beyond this, crews of all ships might obtain advances in the course of the voyage from the master, in cash or in goods, and on his own terms. This was no doubt quite generally done, though since the transaction was between master and crew and did not affect the owners, it has left few traces behind. Indeed the False Musters (Navy) Bill of 1690 declared that

> 'In trading voyages it hath been and is accustomed for Captains, Masters, Pursers, Officers and other Seamen on Board their Majesty's Ships as well as Merchant Ships to pay the Seamen by Money or Credit most of their Wages before the said Seamen come home to England, whereby their Families are almost starved for want of Subsistence.'[1]

These advances were made at the master's (or officer's) own risk, and therefore for his profit. The master of the *Royal Duke* in 1761, for example, was charging his crew on the homeward run from Carolina 8d. per lb. for sugar and 11d. for tobacco — commodities which had probably cost him about 3d. and 4d. respectively.[2] But clothes and spirits (rum or brandy) were the usual intruments for chipping away the seaman's wages. Sometimes he was quite evidently being sold goods which he would dispose of at home profitably, but more often his own needs were being supplied from the money which he had earned but not yet been paid.

The seaman's wages when he was paid off, therefore, were reduced by the amount of these various kinds of advances. Moreover, he was after 1696 unique in the English labour force in paying compulsory contributions to a state social security institution — the sixpence a month levy for Greenwich Hospital, which the master had to deduct from all wages. There was a third and much resented deduction, for damage to cargo, or sometimes to the ship's equipment, which could be attributed to the crew — staving of casks through careless loading or stowage being the most common cause. This was occasionally a charge on an individual, but more often a total distributed among the whole crew. Barlow was more than once spurred to eloquence in denouncing this practice:

---

[1] *House of Lords MSS., 1692–3*, p. 230. It was proposed that such advances should be limited to one-third of the pay earned. A South Sea Company charter-party of 1723 provides that no officer is to advance to any sailor, by selling slops or otherwise, more than one-quarter of his wages (BM Add.MSS. 25567).
[2] HCA 15–54.

'The damages arising many other ways, as by many time stormy weather being the chief, for few or no ships go to sea but meet with stormy and blowing weather; and sometimes by old and leaky ships, which are much strained in bad weather, springing leaks that could not be stopped before they are laden, and many times by filling a ship fuller of goods than she could carry, and also goods many times come on board damnified with not being carefully packed up through the negligence of many servants and packers, and when the owners thereof see that there is damage, and fear to lose thereby, then they lay the fault on the poor seamen that sail the ships, and they must stand the damage; whereas they can better lose a pound than a poor seaman a penny, who taketh so much pains for very small gains, which is a thing the unreasonablest that is allowed in England.'[1]

The practice was certainly a general one, for many ships' accounts show such deductions from the wage bill, occasionally amounting to as much as ten per cent of the whole; on the other hand, it must be said that the accounts always show a counter-part in much larger deductions from the freight earned.

The seaman was also supplied, more or less adequately, with his victuals. We must not be misled by accounts of naval victualling in the days when every retired purser was assumed to be a thief grown rich; merchant ships had to acquire their crews voluntarily, and keep them without recourse to the naval penalties for desertion. If salt beef or pork, with biscuit, cheese, beans, dried fish and beer were unappetising diets for long voyages, it may nevertheless be borne in mind that few people on land had a diet which included daily meat in any form, fresh or stinking. Most ships filled up whenever they touched port with fresh meat, vegetables and fruit, in quantities which make it clear that the whole crew shared in them. The cost of victualling ran to some sixteen to seventeen shillings a head per month, rising a little in the eighteenth century; when all allowance is made for the officers' rather meagre extras, something like three shillings a week was spent on food, bought at bulk prices, for the average seaman.[2] The farm labourer on six or seven shillings a week, or even the London craftsman with twelve or fifteen, buying at retail prices,

---

[1] op. cit., Vol. I, p. 90; also pp. 165–6. See also Wm. Hodges, *An Humble Representation of the Seamen's Misery* (c. 1695).
[2] The Liverpool shipwright and shipowner John Okill, in the 1750's, gave his apprentices who went to sea four shillings a week to maintain themselves between voyages. He seems to have had no shortage of apprentices (Okill MSS., Liverpool Public Library).

feeding, housing and clothing a family, could hardly have spent more.

The members of the crew might have other earnings. In the first place, there were certain small payments known as primage and average[1] made by the freighters of a ship which, though payable to the master, were partly for the benefit of the crew. All charter-parties and bills of lading provided for payment of the freight 'with primage and average accustomed' and a writer of 1684 described these payments:

> 'Pay the master Primage and Petitlodmenage, for the use of his Cables, to discharge the Goods, and to the Mariners to charge and discharge them, which said charge is not above 12d. per ton lading. Petty Averidge is another little small Duty which Merchants pay to the Master when they only take Tunnage over and above the Freight, the which is a small Recompense or Gratuity for the Master's care over the Lading.'[2]

Portage was a small reward made after 1676 by the Customs officials to shipmasters, for reporting their cargoes correctly.[3] Of these various payments, average and portage were the perquisites of the master; primage was for division among the crew. It is impossible to make a confident statement on this, but it seems likely that after the big permanent increase in seaman's wages in the 1650's and 1660's masters became increasingly unwilling to divide the primage with the crew, and that in the eighteenth century they always regarded it as their personal gain. As far back as 1678 Trinity House proposed as a reform 'Primage not to be kept from the Seamen by the Master'.[4]

In any event, the amounts were small, amounting in a 200-ton ship to some £5 for primage (at sixpence per ton of cargo, the most common rate) and £4 to £6 of other payments. A good share of the former, and all the latter, would go to the master, making a

[1] There is no connection with the modern use of the term 'average' as meaning the adjustment of the burden of losses at sea.
[2] J. P., *The Merchant's Dayly Companion*, p. 341.
[3] H. Atton and H. Holland, *The King's Customs* (1908–10), Vol. I, p. 104. Portage had two meanings besides the one dealt with here; it was used in the North Sea trades to describe the master's or crew's right to carry a small cargo freight free (F. W. Brooks (ed.)), *The First Order Book of the Hull Trinity House, 1632–65* (Yorkshire Archaeological Society, 1942, Vol. CV, p. xiv) and it was sometimes used in the term 'Portage Bill' meaning Wage Bill.
[4] Rawlinson MSS. A.447–1. See also the agreement made on primage between the Newcastle Merchant Adventurers and Trinity House in 1671 (J. R. Boyle and F. W. Dendy (eds.)), *Extracts from the Records of the Merchant Adventurers of Newcastle-upon-Tyne* (Surtees Society, 1895), XCIII, I, pp. 211–15.

useful addition to his pay if the voyage were short; the crew's share of primage, if they got it, would amount to only a few shillings per head.

The master might occasionally earn a substantial extra payment. Charter parties made abroad usually provided, in addition to the freight money, for a gratuity to the master — 'for the master's cloak' or 'for the master's hat'. In the Baltic trades this was a regular payment, under the name of 'Caplaken', which added quite considerably to the freight. The master of the *Nathaniel & John*, bound from Pillau to London in 1723, was to collect 40s. per last freight for his owners, and 2s. 6d. per last caplaken — which was worth £15 to £20 to him.[1] Again, this was an arrangement between master and freighter with which the owners were not concerned, and which has left few traces; but except when ships were hired abroad such a payment was unusual. Occasionally the master of a ship who was buying and selling cargo on behalf of owners or charterers was paid a small commission, but generally this was regarded as one of the duties covered by his ordinary wages.

Much more widespread was the crew's customary right — its legal standing is very doubtful — to carry some cargo on their own account, possibly in their own quarters but sometimes occupying part of the hold, freight free. The rights varied from trade to trade, but were perhaps most substantial and most firmly established in the East India trade and the African slave trade. The early right in the East India trade was set out in the case of the *Marigold* in 1661:[2]

> 'All though the whole shipp was lett to freight to the said Gouveneur and Company yet the Master and Company have all waies some priviledge of their owne Cabbins and places betweene Deck where they doe not hinder the Freightors' Goods and it is constant Custom for them to carry some Adventures of their owne especially in an East India Voyadge and . . . the said Gouveneur and Company have never sent out or employed any Shippe that the Master and Company have been deprived of the said benefitt and priviledge.'

East India charter parties came to set limits to the cargoes which might be carried by crews, and these regulations became increasingly formalised. In 1674 the crew's participation in the total tonnage of goods homeward was fixed at 5 per cent of the

[1] HCA 15-36; HCA 13-88.   [2] HCA 13-129.

chartered tonnage[1] — a very large allowance in ships of 500–700 tons; in 1772 their freight free allowance was twenty-five tons for the outward and fifteen for the homeward voyage.[2] The master, in fact, secured most of the benefits in this as in other respects. In the *St George* which loaded at Canton in 1748, for example, the captain loaded 55 chests and 150 rolls of China-ware, 117 boxes and tubs of tea, as well as arrack, rhubarb, sticklack, ginger, lacquer-ware and other goods; the chief mate had 5 tubs of tea, the third mate one, and so on down the scale.[3] It was these trading rights that made East India captains wealthy men in the course of four or five voyages; their officers merely secured useful supplements to their wages.

In the Africa trade the masters always, and mates often, claimed rights to carry slaves on their own account freight free. There were constant arguments over the extent of these rights, variant customs being quoted by opposite sides in these disputes, and masters' claims were at times extraordinarily large. In two ships chartered by the companies trading to Africa, in 1667 and 1682 respectively, master and officers had in one case 36 and in the other 39 negroes on their own account.[4] The master of the *Greswold Galley* which went to Guinea and Jamaica in 1703 was specifically allowed to take one negro for himself, freight free; he subsequently claimed that it was the custom of the trade for masters to take two slaves freight free over and above any specifically allowed![5] But the claims made in these cases, which occur continuously from the early days of the trade in mid-seventeenth century right through the eighteenth century, are so varied that it is quite evident there was no fixed custom, but merely a general acknowledgment that the master, and perhaps his mate, had *some* privilege, to carry *some* slaves, freight free. With the steady rise in the value of slaves this privilege became increasingly valuable; the right to carry one slave was worth £25–30 in the mid-eighteenth century. The rest of the crew did not regularly participate in these rights, though there are odd cases in which they clearly took some share

---

[1] E. B. Sainsbury (ed.), *Calendar of Court Minutes of the East India Company, 1677–79* (Oxford, 1938), p. 303.
[2] E. Cotton, *East Indiamen* (1949), p. 32. Cotton has an excellent account of the profits of masters in the East India trade towards the end of the eighteenth century, but this cannot safely be projected very far back into our period.
[3] BM Add.MSS. 18019.
[4] *Hopewell* (HCA 24–121); *Dilligence* (HCA 15–11).
[5] C.6–346–10 (*Harris v. Simpson*, 1706).

in them. The carpenter of the *Blackmore* in 1730 had, in addition to a rather high rate of pay, the privilege of carrying one slave and two parrots to the West Indies, and of bringing one hogshead of sugar and the parrots back to Bristol, freight free.[1] Elsewhere, these rights were less certain and even more variable. In all the American trades — those to North America as well as to the West Indies — it was usual to allow the master some tonnage of goods freight free; two tons in a 200-ton ship was not uncommon. The master was usually charged at a fixed rate, £5 or £6 a head, for any passengers he carried, and was left to make his own arrangements with them to bring himself a profit. Those passengers who indentured themselves to him for the sake of their passage could be sold in America into four years' servitude; the remainder probably paid no more for their fares than the master was charged. In the Mediterranean trade there were similar customary rights, sometimes quite substantial in extent. In 1744 the Levant Company ordered that every shipmaster in its service might carry out on his own account, freight free, goods to the value of £2 per ton of his ship's burden.[2] In all the long distance trades, in fact, there was some more or less firmly established custom which enabled the master, and sometimes his officers, to carry cargo on their own account; a right often disputed as to extent, but rarely as to its existence. Probably this applied to the short distance trades as well. A great many of the masters whose ships brought wine from France and Spain during the seventeenth century had small consignments — a butt or two — for themselves. There was little to prevent a member of the crew from carrying, in his own quarters, a roll or two of damask, a sackful of tobacco, or a box of German toys, so long as he did not, by trying to defraud the Customs, endanger the owners' property. It is said that in Hull ships all seamen were entitled to carry a quantity of goods (fixed by custom) known as a 'furthing'.[3] Clearly there was little scope for crew cargoes in the northern timber, grain and iron trades, and this may account for the appearance of the substantial 'caplaken' in them.[4]

How this affected anyone beyond the officers is not clear, but the probability is that in many trades those members of the crew

[1] HCA 24–136.
[2] SP 110–68 (Levant Company Order Book, October 1744).
[3] F. W. Brooks, op. cit., pp. xiv–xv.   [4] See p. 147, above.

who had a pound or two to invest could find opportunity to earn a few shillings on it; no more than this. Where rights were clearly recognised, as in the East India and the slave trades, the mates might expect to secure some moderate gains. But on the whole, the valuable privileges were privileges of the master — perhaps originally intended to be shared with his crew, though he certainly did not share them for long after the beginning of our period — and for him these privileges could be very valuable. The right of taking two slaves to the West Indies — worth, according to date, between £20 and £70 — of taking two, three or four tons of goods home from America or the Mediterranean without paying freight — worth between £10 and £25 in peacetime; the right to take indentured servants to America, which might yield many scores of pounds; these made substantial additions to the master's earnings (if he had a little capital to lay out) and might well double them. Add the oddments of primage and average and portage, the profits of slopselling, the refunds of out-of-pocket expenditure in foreign ports, and it begins to appear that, at least in voyages beyond Europe, the difference between the earnings of the master and his chief officer was in the proportion, not of the £6 and £4 of their respective wages, but between gross earnings which, leaving aside the East India trade, could easily reach £15 to £20 a month on the one hand, and which would rarely be augmented beyond £5 on the other. Two voyages as a mate convinced Edward Barlow of the necessity to become a master, 'now I understood the way and profit which they had, which none else in the ship had or could expect.'[1] This was the incentive which drove men to dubious financial practices and to self-abasement to secure commands; this was an additional reason why the last step up the ladder of promotion was the hardest and the one in which other factors than merit and efficiency had an important sway. The mate was a superior workman, and paid as such; the master of an ocean-going ship was firmly established as a member of the prosperous middle class.

There were, of course, wide variations in the master's financial prospects. Many a ship's master might envy the small *élite* of East Indiamen's commanders, far above him, each earning his thousands of pounds a voyage, yet look down at the master of the ship in the coastal trades or pounding the North Sea and the Baltic,

[1] Barlow, op. cit., p. 339.

where large extras from private cargoes were not to be earned — though in these the master could be glad of primage which, being paid by the voyage, came in not once but three or four or half a dozen times a year.

Taking everything into account, how did the financial gains of the merchant seaman compare with those of his fellows on land? In the first place, there is one important intangible; the seaman had much better chances of some moderate promotion, which might at least double his pay, than most town artisans or rural labourers. Indeed, even his chances of becoming a master with perseverance and some capacity, were probably greater than any comparable opportunities for people of similar qualities who started with him low in the social scale. There were few avenues from the lowest to the middle ranks of society in England before the twentieth century; this was one of them, in which a long ladder of ranks, the possibility of accumulating a little capital in the higher of them to assist the last step to the highest, and the rapid and almost continuous growth of the industry, were all to the advantage of the able, ambitious and sober man.

On the other side we must remember that the seaman worked a seven-day week at sea, and from his wages he had to provide for whatever interval between voyages would compensate him for this. He came ashore from any long voyage with plenty of money, though if he had a family they would need most of it. For a while he was his own master; but his neighbours who worked ashore were their own masters every Sunday.

The seaman's wage might well be enough to attract the labourer from his plough,[1] the weaver from his loom, the potman from his taps; but to the man who had once been drawn away from the countryside or the small town a wider horizon of opportunity opened itself. He was brought into contact with the life of the great seaports; sooner or later, with that of London, where wages were high. If he were not to abandon the sea, its rewards must be as great as those of the London labourer, which during most of the eighteenth century, and probably for half a century before, could amount to ten or twelve shillings for a full week's employment.[2]

---

[1] Sir Francis Brewster remarked that too great a success in recruiting seamen might cause a 'want of Labouring Men for Rural Employments' (*Essays on Trade and Navigation* (1695), pp. 79–80).

[2] E. Gilboy, *Wages in Eighteenth Century England* (Cambridge, Mass., 1934), pp. 3–50.

L

The seaman's earnings, taking his food into account, did approximate to this. Only in London was a man who had not been apprenticed to a skilled craft likely to earn as much as a seaman.

In spite of this, the industry faced a perennial problem of recruitment. In relation to other employments, seamen probably improved their position sharply during the two middle quarters of the seventeenth century, when their wages rose substantially after the general rise of wage levels had ceased; and it began to go very slowly downhill in the eighteenth century, when their wages were almost stabilised while there was a tendency for wages in other trades to advance.[1] Throughout these two centuries, however, the sea must have had its financial attractions to the unskilled and lowly paid in all the rural districts and the small towns of England. 'The Husbandman of England earns but 4 Shillings per Week, but the Seamen have as Good as 12 Shillings in Wages, Victuals and (as it were) Housing,' wrote Sir William Petty in the early 1670's,[2] when the relative earnings of seamen were at their highest. His view compares extremes, but does not seriously exaggerate them. An able seaman was then earning 7 shillings a week (though his pay was soon to be stabilised at 6) and his victuals were worth another three or more. While it may be said his 'housing' was worth very little, at least it saved him the outlay of a shilling or two in lodging ashore. Petty's husbandman earning 4 shillings a week could probably have been found in the midland counties; even in the counties near London, or on the coast, the agricultural labourer's wages were far below the seaman's earnings; 6 shillings a week in Essex, 8 in Middlesex, 5 in Suffolk, in winter months.[3] All had extra earnings during the height of the summer's activities, but all were poorer than the seaman. This remained true in the eighteenth century, though the gap narrowed.[4]

[1] ibid., passim.
[2] C. H. Hull (ed.), Economic Writings of Sir William Petty (1899), Vol. I, p. 259.
[3] Essex 1661, W. Cunningham, The Growth of English Industry and Commerce (Cambridge, 1907), Vol. III, p. 892; Middlesex 1661, J. E. Thorold Rogers, A History of Agriculture and Prices in England (1887), Vol. VI, p. 697; Suffolk 1682, ibid., Vol. VI, p. 698.
[4] J. Massie estimated that in 1761 the skilled man earned 10s. 6d. to 12s. a week in London, and 7s. 6d. to 9s. in the provinces; the labourer 9s. in London and 8s. in the country. This takes into account some unemployment (J. Massie, Calculations on the Present Taxes Yearly Paid).

At the beginning of the seventeenth century the sea service must have retained, for many people, the glamour and reflected glory of the Armada campaign and the great days of Drake, Hawkins and Frobisher, attracting to itself many people from every rank of society for that reason alone. It soon lost this character, never to recover it, as it took over the humdrum routine of beating out the paths of trade, increasingly protected by the navy. A road to fame still lay through the merchant service during much of the seventeenth century, while the seaman still had a chance of rising to high naval rank — Leake, Lawson, Haddock, Narbrough, admirals all, started as merchant seamen and 'Tarpaulin officers' — but by the reign of Anne this avenue was almost closed. To see the world, to get a good rate of pay, to get a job of some sort at any price, to do what father did — these were the motives of those who went to sea; perhaps some went willy-nilly, drunk or unconscious, as the crimp made up the required crew as best he could.

Out from the lodging houses of Wapping and Shadwell they came tumbling, from the 'Pump & Dolphin', from 'John Spicer's', the 'Four Casks', the 'Starr', from 'Francis Bulfitt's', and the 'Blew Anchor' and the 'Three Marriners', from 'Ann Elliott's', the 'Boatswain & Calls', the 'Noye's Ark',[1] from the arms of wives, mothers, sweethearts or whoever it might be — to what? To October in the North Atlantic; to the long shelterless coast from Flamborough Head to Winterton Ness, to the cheerless Baltic with the first ice forming as the east wind from the plains of Russia blew them home; often in cockleshells which in these times would await a fine day before essaying the Channel crossing. Or to the mangrove swamps of the Niger delta, the Bight of Benin 'where few come out though many go in', to face the yellow fever and malaria and dysentery which would keep them company through the long Atlantic crossing and re-encounter them in new forms when the first lines were thrown to the Jamaica quayside; to Bombay, Calcutta, Madras, Bantam, where the East Indiaman might lose, on occasion, a quarter to a half of her crew.[2] It is hard to imagine the discomforts of the seaman's life at this time; roughly though many lived ashore, the seaman's life was recognised as something exceptional. Dr Johnson, little as he knew about it, said with some truth in 1759,

---

[1] T.1–12 (1690) — a list of lodging houses where seamen were to be found.
[2] Wm. Hodges, *An Humble Representation of the Seamen's Misery* (c. 1695).

'No man will be a sailor who has contrivance enough to get himself into a jail; for being in a ship is being in jail with the chance of being drowned. . . . A man in a jail has more room, better food, and commonly better company.'[1]

Moreover, life on board ship was carried on amid a discipline which grew harsher with the passage of time. It is true we may read of such officers as Captain 'Children' Kennett, who

'generally used Marriners in so kind and tender a manner that when he spoke to or of his Ship's Company he calls them Children in so much the Captains and other Officers at Petersburgh and other places where Captain William Kennett has trades have nicknamed him Children and when any person speaks to him about his Ship's Company, they ask him what is become of his Children.'[2]

But this was said on Kennett's behalf in a case which, primarily concerned with the loss of his ship when he was 'so drunk he could not stand save when holding by the rail' incidentally heard complaints by his crew of his extreme brutality. The courts were full of cases in which seamen complained of excessive beatings, discharge without reason in foreign ports, and arbitrary and savage behaviour of all kinds. Though many grains of salt must be taken with these stories — accusations of brutality were a stock ingredient of wage disputes, and a body of attorneys was said to have sprung up in the late seventeenth century whose speciality was encouraging seamen's legal claims[3] — the prevalent attitudes are made clear by two witnesses. One, a passenger in the *Lyon*, gave evidence on behalf of her master. Supporting the master's claim that a seaman had not been improperly beaten, this passenger assured the court that 'in a few days after such correction he went about his work as before!'[4] The other, John Cremer, writes of the time when as chief mate of a ship, 'one evening being dark, and calling on all Hands in a hurry, the captain being the last, I by mistake, struck him, taking him to be a common fellow; insoemuch I gave him two black eyes that he never forgave me afterward'.[5]

---

[1] G. B. Hill (ed.), *Boswell's Life of Johnson* (1887), Vol. V, p. 137. How the company compared it is hard to say; the ship's crew probably had the better food until the later stages of a long voyage.

[2] *Young Prince*, 1728 (HCA 24–136).

[3] A merchants' petition of 1742, to the House of Commons, which sought to regulate the rise of seamen's wages in wartime, also requested the prevention of vexatious suits in the High Court of Admiralty brought by seamen. *House of Commons Journals, 1737–41*, p. 672.

[4] HCA 15–13.   [5] J. Cremer, op. cit., p. 138.

Of course crews were not easy to handle. We may dismiss the complaints of wealthy merchants sitting comfortably ashore of 'the wretched looseness of the seamen and their often rebellions which hath caused in these late years severall shipps to be both plundered and runn away with'.[1] But there are, again, endless cases of crews, either as a whole or in groups, refusing duty, sometimes for good but often for bad reasons.[2] The Liverpool riots of August 1775, when armed seamen with a wage grievance held the town for three days, show the temper of the men. On the arrival of Greenland whalers in the port, discharging their cargo at the end of the season, a number of owners of ships about to sail apparently tried to reduce sharply the rates of pay they had agreed with the seamen. Trouble began in the slave ship *Derby*, whose rigging was destroyed by the crew, and this example was followed in a number of other ships. Some of the seamen being arrested, a mob of two or three thousand stormed the jail and freed them. After several days of disturbance, during which some merchants negotiated on wages with the sailors' leaders, the seamen, it is said, prepared to attack the Exchange. Whatever their intentions the Riot Act was read, and the garrison which had been put into the Exchange — 'several persons who volunteered for the occasion, some of whom were in a superior rank of life, and others, were engaged by the magistrates and were paid for their exertions' — fired on the crowd. Several seamen being killed, the mob retired, to return with cannon, muskets and cutlasses brought from the ships and bombarded the Exchange — the only time, it is said, when cannon have been used in a civil commotion in England. They were finally dispersed by dragoons from Man-́chester, after holding most of the town completely in their power for several days, during which the only people killed were seamen.[3]

Even drunkeness, the most common and most condoned of offences, could produce great loss and extreme danger; even the officers could cause the master some trouble at times. When, faced with an unruly crew, the master of the *Sisters* tried to ship a new crew at Leghorn, a gunner 'swore that he would fire

[1] Rawlinson MSS. A 171–278 (about 1685).
[2] See the account of the mutiny in the *Ann Dorothy* in 1645, in F. W. Brooks, op. cit., pp. 71–2.
[3] R. Brooke, *Liverpool as it was during the last quarter of the Eighteenth Century, 1775–1800* (1853), pp. 326–47.

them to the Divell or to that effect'.[1] The master of the *St Quentin*
had a busy morning early in 1700, in an Italian port:

'This Morning about 5 a clock I Commanded my Mate to rise he told
me he would not untill he saw his Own Time I hove some Water into
his Cabbin for which he Rose and hit me on the Face with his Fist
and Hand Tore my Shirt and Skin bruised my Face and Nose and
called to Godd to Damm him if he did not knock my Brains out Upon
which I called out for Assistance and Recouvring myself from him
Put him to Flight and he went on to the Boltsprit with a Handspike
and Swore if anyone came near him he would Dash out their Brains
I commanded him in he told me he would not but went up the
Forestay to the Foretopsail Yard and Loosed the Foretopsail the
Reason of which I asked him he told me it was for his Pleasure I bid
him furl it again he told me he would not soe I was forced to leave him
and not being able to stay on the Deck for his Abusefull Language
I went down to my Cabbin. . . . Locking and Bolting my Cabbin Door
and defending myself as well as I could.'[2]

The seafaring life was, moreover, a dangerous one. Most seamen
who left their life stories have some story of wreck, fire or accident,
of which they were the lucky survivors, to relate. If the annual
rate of loss of ships by wreck and burning was as much as four
per cent, and it might well be more,[3] the chances of a seaman
ending his life in such a catastrophe were high; and many a man
fell from the rigging, was washed overboard, or was fatally struck
by falling gear. A record of deaths of master mariners between
1835–48, when conditions can have been little different from those
of a century earlier, showed that nearly a quarter lost their lives
when their ships were sunk, or wrecked, and in addition one in
seven died by violent means, killed by falling masts or drowned.
Less than two-thirds of ships' masters died naturally;[4] and
masters were presumably of higher average age, nearer to natural
death, than their crews.

Finally, what happened to the seaman who grew old, or was
crippled in the service? For most of our period there was little
provision for him, and many writers, from Defoe onwards, pointed
out that this made the seaman reluctant to defend his owners'

[1] HCA 13–88.
[2] HCA 15–19.
[3] W. S. Lindsay, *History of Merchant Shipping and Ancient Commerce* (1876),
Vol. IV, pp. 167–9.
[4] F. G. P. Neison, 'Mortality of Master Mariners', *Journal of the Statistical
Society of London*, Vol. XIII, 1850, p. 197.

property, at the risk of his own life and limb, when attacked by European pirates or privateers.[1] There were a few almshouses established by private charity in the waterfront quarters of seaport towns.[2] The East India Company had some almshouses and paid some pensions and allowances to aged seamen and their widows.[3] Greenwich Hospital, whose upkeep was largely provided for, from the time of its foundation in 1696, by the sixpence a month deducted from the wages of merchant seamen, was exclusively for naval pensioners until 1747, and hardly changed its character even then.[4] Some of the funds created by this collection of sixpences were diverted, after 1747, to the maintenance of almshouses and the pensioning of widows in the leading seaports; they helped to provide the Seamen's Hospitals built at Liverpool, Newcastle, Hull and Bristol.[5] More far-reaching proposals had very little effect. The plan *For Erecting and Endowing for Ever, a plain, neat, cheap, convenient and strong Hospital . . . for the Relief and Support of such Officers and Seamen, as shall be (by Old Age, Loss of Limbs, Sight, Hearing or by Misfortunes in the Merchants Service) rendered unable to get their Livings by Sea or Land* about 1720 received little support.[6] J. Griffin's *Proposals for the Relief . . . of . . . Disabled Seamen in the Merchants' Service* (1746) which carried a long list of promises of support from ships' masters, may have had some influence on the legislation which released some of the Greenwich Hospital sixpences for merchant seamen, and the provincial hospital building which followed. But all these are very late; during most of our period, the maimed or aged seaman had no other resort than the poor law which treated him like any other pauper.

The evils and miseries of life at sea must not be over-stated, or it will be impossible to understand why men in sufficient numbers went to sea at all. Many were lost at sea or by disease,

---

[1] D. Defoe, 'Essay on Projects', in H. Morley, *The Early Life and Chief Early Works of Daniel Defoe* (1889), pp. 83–5.

[2] See, for example, P. V. McGrath, 'Merchant Shipping in the 17th Century; the evidence of the Bristol Deposition Books', *Mariners' Mirror*, Vol. XLI, 1955, p. 37. Trinity House had almshouses, but these were presumably for decayed master mariners (W. H. Mayo, *Trinity House Past and Present* (1905), pp. 71, 73).

[3] See W. Foster, *John Company* (1926), pp. 153–70.

[4] 10 Anne, c. 17, provided for the admission of merchant seamen maimed in the defence of their ships, but this was apparently a dead letter.

[5] R. Troughton, *History of Liverpool* (1810), p. 117; Brooke, op. cit., pp. 66–7; W. Hadley, *History of Kingston-upon-Hull* (1788), p. 756.

[6] BM Pamphlets. 1855, c. 4 (5).

many disabled, some dragged out a miserable old age in the only occupation they knew. On the other hand, as we have seen, they were relatively well paid and their chances of rising in the world considerable; the elderly seaman who had not advanced himself at least to boatswain had probably shown not a few undesirable qualities. Many boys and young men must have spent a few years of their physical prime in seeing new places, experiencing not merely the gales and fogs and chills, but also the wonder of early morning landfalls, the blaze of the Mediterranean in June, the velvet seas of the tropics laced with flying fish, the laughing savages of Genoa and Old Calabar; filled up with experiences to keep them talking for a lifetime, and gone back to the shore to jobs in London, Liverpool, Virginia or Barbados which they would never have dreamed of in their earlier rural and provincial isolation. The sea was a more tyrannical mistress than it is today, and the heart and mind could become satiated with travel and new sights, but every voyage ended, and the seaman who landed with a full pocket and a steady head need never wander more.

VIII

Shipping Management and the Role of the Master

The problems of management of a ship differed in many ways from those of a business on dry land. The owning group was often too large to exercise control efficiently, some of its members incapable of taking part in management and many too occupied with other concerns to give much attention to a particular shipping investment. As we have seen, shipowning was no man's whole business and few men's main business; the owning group had, as it were, some part-time directors and a works manager (the master) but no full time general manager unless the master filled this office too. During long periods the ship was beyond the owners' direct control, even beyond the jurisdiction of the English law; for months at a time there was little that the most agitated of owners could do to secure his interests except take out more insurance. The greatest problem of management, indeed, can be put in a nutshell; to find a paragon to be master, and then devise means to assist him if he really were perfect, rescue him if he turned out a fool, and restrain him if he turned out a scoundrel. This does not mean that managing owners, and the whole owning group, had no function at all beyond the provision of the initial capital; but simply that the exercise of their functions was intermittent, and immense trust had to be placed in a single individual who, though he was usually a part-owner like themselves, was nevertheless primarily an employee. This is one reason why owners so often sought to appoint masters who would be bound by more than mere financial ties; a reason for the frequent employment of sons, brothers, nephews or cousins of the owners or their business associates; for the difficulty which seamen who had nothing to offer but a record of competence and reliability faced when attempting to become masters, unless they could find the money to become major partowners. Nepotism was by no means a wholly discreditable and absurd practice; there were solid reasons for it, but the price had to be paid, of course, in the acceptance in positions of command of men who were in fact of poorer quality than others who were available but outside the family circle.

Some policy decisions required the concurrence of the owners of a majority of the shares in the ship. The appointment of the master was one, the decision whether the ship should be operated at all when times were bad another; sometimes all had a say in determining the general nature of the ship's operations, the branch of trade in which the ship's living was to be sought or whether it was to live normally by chartering. If the ship was well managed, however, decisions requiring a general approval formally expressed might never arise between the time of the creation of the owning group, and the ending of the ship's life. The owners, or many of them, would be called to meet and dine on the ship or in a nearby tavern at the end of every long voyage, or once a year if voyages were short; on this occasion they would be told their dividend, might possibly be asked to sign the ship's account book to signify their acceptance of its accuracy, and could no doubt air grievances and put forward suggestions. One may imagine that this was usually a pleasant social occasion, a celebration rather than an effective contribution to the management of the ship's affairs.

The managing owner or owners, however — the ship's husband or husbands[1] — often had very extensive functions. There were many things to be done in the home port between voyages. The freight of the last voyage had to be collected, and negotiations conducted over the allowances to be made for damaged cargo. The crew had to be paid off. It was necessary to go over the ship carefully to determine her repair needs, major and minor, to make arrangements, if necessary, for graving and re-sheathing, and for replacements of timbers, spars and sails. A new voyage had to be determined on, some thought perhaps given to alternative destinations, charterers had to be found or cargoes sought among fellow-merchants, the ship stored and provisioned for her next outset. In time of war or stress, passes and protections for the crew must be negotiated with the Admiralty; there was a crew to be hired and customs formalities to be completed. Though some of these tasks were left to the master, and it is clearly possible to divide them into commercial and technical functions, there is no hard and fast dividing line between what the managing owner did

[1] See p. 89, above.

and what he left to the master. At one end of the scale was the managing owner of the Norway trader, to whom the master was simply a navigation technician and crew foreman, to be given responsibility only from the moment when the owner went over the side into his wherry as the capstan groaned to haul up the anchor. At the other was the master of many a ship in trade with Italy, who was effectively managing owner himself, carrying out all the commercial functions; to whom the ship's husband was simply the particular owner through whom responsibilities to the owning group were acknowledged, to whom the ship's activities were reported, and from whom approbation, advice and assistance were expected. Between the two extremes there was every gradation from the husband who did almost everything to the husband who did nothing. The exact degree of the master's responsibilities was largely determined by the character of the trade he was engaged, in, but within this customary framework much depended on an owner's willingness to be heavily involved and on the extent of his confidence in the master. Generally speaking, it was in trades where cargoes were not costly and where overseas commercial operations were reduced to a simple routine which did not seriously tax the master's business or social gifts, that he was regarded as merely a sailor and given few responsibilities in his home port. In all the longer distance trades beyond the Atlantic and to Southern Europe and the Mediterranean, the master had to be a person who could be relied on to handle a wide range of business abroad; it was usual to entrust to him many of the decisions — and much of the work — at home. As late as 1663, it is true, Edward Coxere making his third voyage to the Mediterranean as a master

'desired the owners, who were merchants to send a man that understood more of merchandising than I did; though I was brought up a seaman, and was willing to officiate the place of a master, yet was to seek as merchant. The conclusion being so much as the whole cargo to be at my disposing; I found it too heavy for me, though I was encouraged by wages.'[1]

But this was an unusual attitude by that time.

In any event the ship's husband, making his decisions on technical matters concerned with the ship, would naturally lean

[1] E. H. W. Meyerstein (ed.), *The Adventures by Sea of Edward Coxere* (Oxford, 1945), p. 108.

heavily on the master for advice, and the master who was left to perform all or some of the commercial functions in his home port could similarly expect the benefit of his owners' connections and their advice. The connections, however, were more important than the advice, and valuable as they were, it was becoming increasingly possible to supplement or even replace them by the use of professional intermediaries. The ancillaries of shipping management, the specialised meeting places, the brokers and other services were beginning to emerge, and to create possibilities of even greater independence for those masters who had their owners' complete trust.

The business of the seventeenth century was in the main conducted by word of mouth. The mercantile communities of the English seaports — even of London until very late in the century — were small enough to have their meeting places to which all concerned would go at some time in the course of the working day. At London this centre was the Royal Exchange. There, during the three hours a day when it was open, and in the streets behind when it was closed, much of the commercial dealing of London was done, to be formalised later by scriveners and clerks. In such a way Colonel Norwood, who wished to emigrate to Virginia in 1649

> 'Grew acquainted on the Royal Exchange with Captain John Locker, whose bills upon the posts made us know that he was master of a good ship (untruly so called) the *Virginia Merchant*, burden three hundred tons, force thirty guns or more, we were not long in treaty with the captain, but agreed with him for ourselves and servants at six pounds a head to be transported into the James River.'[1]

Samuel Pepys, as his *Diary* tells us, was a great frequenter of the Exchange, both to pick up or spread information and to arrange the commercial business of the navy. Thus on 1st March, 1662, 'To the Exchange, to hire a ship for the Maderas'. Two months later he told the news there of Sir John Lawson's havoc among the Barbary corsairs 'and was much followed by merchants to tell it'. On 23rd November 1663 he was trying to insure ships for Archangel; on 8th December he came there to negotiate the freighting of a ship; and so on. The old Exchange was burnt in the Great Fire of 1666 and was not rebuilt for some years. In the

[1] A. and J. Churchill, *A Collection of Voyages and Travels* (1732), Vol. VI, p. 145.

meantime much of this walking and talking business life of the city had taken itself off to the taverns or to the new-fangled coffee houses; and though the Exchange was rebuilt and became an important meeting place again, it did not quite regain its old status; a writer in 1702 remarks that, 'The Royal Exchange which, twenty years ago, was the principal place in London for Trade, did let quick and at great Rents and Fines; but since then, the Rents are not only considerably fallen, but near one half of the shops are empty . . . and of late Years, near Two thirds of the principal Houses about the Exchange are made into Taverns, Coffee Houses and Ale Houses'.[1]

This decline of the Royal Exchange was hastened by the way in which London's growing commerce created special group interests among the merchants, and helped the creation of new specialised meeting places. The growth of the coffee houses and their specialisation is well known;[2] and the shipping interest had its own particular places of resort. An indication of these is obtained by examining the sites of the auction of ships by the Marshal of the High Court of Admiralty.[3] These sales took place in taverns or coffee houses. For many years after the Restoration they were nearly all held at the house of Major Kelsey, the 'Castle Tavern', situated in Broad Street until 1666 and moved after the Great Fire to Cornhill, nearer the centre of affairs; in 1684 its name was changed, significantly, to 'Ship and Castle'. Until 1686 it had few competitors, though the 'Cardinall's Cap' in Cornhill and the 'Sun Tavern' at Wapping were occasionally used. In 1676 Mr. Haynes's Coffee House in Birchin Lane appeared as a minor rival; this, too, changed its name in the eighties to the 'Marine' Coffee House'. With the sudden disappearance of the 'Ship and Castle' from the record (the last sale there was on 15th November 1688) there was confusion for a few years; then on 28th July 1692 a new name appeared — 'Lloyd's Coffee House', just moved into Lombard Street — and from its first appearance nearly all sales were held there. 'Lloyd's' was for many decades the great centre for all shipping interests, not specially for marine assurance, though cargoes might be sought at the houses devoted to special-ised trades, such as the 'Jamaica' or the 'Virginia Coffee House'.

[1] Anon., *A Brief History of the Trade of England* (1702), pp. 152–3.
[2] E. F. Robinson, *The Early History of Coffee Houses in England* (1893), Ch. VIII.
[3] From notices of auction sales in HCA-4.

To the 'Ship and Castle', 'Lloyd's', the 'Jamaica Coffee House' or such places, therefore, the master might go to seek charterers or freighters, and there he might hang such notices as this one, which, stuck to cardboard and with its string still attached, is preserved in the Court of Admiralty records:

THE FIRST FOR JAMAICA

The Hope, 200 Tunns, 20 Gunns, Joseph Bartholemew.

Ready to take in Goods and Passingers at this House

every day.[1]

At Bristol, ninety years later, Samuel Kelly, master of the brig *Mayflower*, reported, 'When we had delivered our cargo I laid on the berth to load for Liverpool, and as the Welshmen opposed us much it was requisite for me to cruise the city for goods'. He was appointed immediately afterwards to the *John*, loading at Liverpool, a constant trader to Philadelphia and 'according to orders waited on several manufacturers at Birmingham who were in the habit of sending goods to America, to solicit their favours . . . but could not obtain a single package, as the vessel, though only about three years old, was in very bad credit as a slow sailer, always making long passages'.[2]

From the time of the Civil War onward the master could supplement such approaches by advertising in one of the many news sheets which were beginning to appear, whose publishers swiftly learned that advertisements might sustain them for a while when readers would not. The new *City Mercury*, which appeared in 1675 purely as an advertisement sheet for free distribution, declared that it would give

'Notice of all goods, merchandise and ships to be sold, the place where to be seen, and day and hour. Any ships to be let to freight, and the time of their departure, the place of the master's habitation, and where to be spoken with before and after Exchange time.'

Most London newspapers, and the new ones appearing in the provincial ports in the eighteenth century, carried some shipping advertisements such as this one:

---

[1] HCA 15–17 (about 1697).
[2] C. Garstin (ed.), *Samuel Kelly, an Eighteenth Century Seaman* (1925), pp. 166–7.

'Now loading for *Philadelphia*
   The ship SPEEDWELL
John Jones, Master
A new Vessel about 6 months old, burthen 200 tons, will positively
sail in 14 days, having two thirds of her cargo already engaged; for
freight or passage apply to the said master, or
                                   WILLIAM COOKE & CO.'[1]

More important was the appearance of the specialist inter-
mediary dealing with shipping business. The broker was not a
new figure; men who for a commission would bring principals
together for any kind of transaction are to be found in the Middle
Ages, and as late as 1700 most brokers may well have been
unspecialised, putting their connections to any commercial use
that offered. For this was their importance — connections; if the
shipowner left the freighting of his ship or the collection of money
to the master, the master whose own connections supplemented by
advertisement and the haunting of coffee houses produced
inadequate results could call the broker to his aid. The Common
Council of the City of London had noticed this activity in 1674
when it declared that no person was to act as broker 'to make any
manner of bargain or bargains, contract or contracts, in or relating
to the art of trade, of merchandising by exchange, or for letting
of ships to freight or hire, or otherwise howsoever, by any manner
of persons' — unless he had been admitted and sworn as a broker
before the Council.[2] In the last quarter of the seventeenth century
some of these people were describing themselves specifically as
ship-brokers. Not until the end of the century, however, did the
City acknowledge the specialist shipbroker: in 1697

'It is ordered that Mr Attorney General and Mr Recorder be advised
with whether the persons generally called Shipbrokers who are in the
nature of interpreters to masters of ships and assisting them in
receiving their freight and in entering and clearing their ships at the
Customs House are to be deemed brokers within the meaning of the
present Act for restraining the number and ill practice of Brokers and
Stock Jobbers.'[3]

The employment of brokers by ships' masters was by this time
attested with increasing frequency by payments of commission to

[1] *Liverpool General Advertiser*, 24th June 1774.
[2] City of London Record Office, Common Council Journals, 48–31.
[3] City of London Record Office. Ald. Repositories, 101–197.

them, recorded in the ships' accounts. Even so, only a minority seem to have availed themselves of these services, and the functions of the ship broker were not widely understood outside those who made use of them. As late as 1733, for example, 'Mr. John Kemp said that he had been a Husband, a term which signifies a Broker, to several foreign Ships'.[1]

One of the most important decisions the managing owners, or less commonly the owning group or the master, had to make, was whether the ship should be chartered out. This would take many of the operating decisions outside the owners' field of responsibility. Chartering was common, but nearly always it was chartering with a particular voyage in mind, and usually in a ship selected because of owners' or masters' relations with the places it was intended to visit. Though the time charter was a well-known document in the seventeenth century, it was not the true time charter of today, by which ships are hired for a fixed period for undefined purposes, to be used (with some obvious limitations) just as the charterer may later decide. Nearly all time charters were taken up by people with specific voyages in mind; a voyage was in fact always specified in the charter-party, though in early examples the terms were occasionally so vague — 'to any port within or without the Straits' (of Gibraltar) — as to impose no real restriction. The time charter was, in fact, the typical form of the pioneering days of English long-distance shipping, used for the new trades to Russia and the Mediterranean, or later to Virginia and the West Indies, when trading conditions were still uncertain and firm experience of voyage times not yet available; and used much longer for the Mediterranean with its potentialities which the charterer might wish to exploit for a continued port-to-port trade. As the transatlantic trades became conventionalised, the use in them of the time charter died away; it was rarely used for Virginia after 1650 or for the West Indies after 1680. Moreover, a significant change was appearing in the form of the time charter; the responsibility for hiring and paying the crew, which in early charter parties was normally assumed by the charterer[2] was returned to the owners in nearly all time charter-parties after 1660.

---

[1] *House of Commons Journals*, 1732-7, p. 41. Similarly Johnson's *Dictionary* (1755) defines 'Ship-broker' as 'one who procures insurance for ships'.

[2] The master was always the owners' appointee, even when the charter-party prescribed that the charterers should engage the crew.

This again was an indication of a growing capacity among ship-owners to calculate the likely progress of voyages.

The time charter continued to be used, sometimes, for the special circumstances of Mediterranean traffic; elsewhere it was replaced as the typical form by the tonnage charter, which even at the beginning of the seventeenth century was general in the French and Spanish wine trades. It provided for payment to the owners at an agreed rate per ton of goods imported — defined goods, wine, sugar, oil, tobacco, coming from closely defined places. Since it was a condition of the contract that the charterers should lade the ship fully (within a margin of five to ten tons) it secured an almost fixed payment for the voyage. This was the form which after 1660 became typical in all the long and middle-distance trades. It was appropriate to the hire of a ship for the purpose of fetching a particular kind of cargo from a particular place, when the actual cargo was not already known precisely. It usually provided that the charterers could take outward cargo (with no further payment of freight for it), but so long as they did not interfere with the exercise of this right the owners were allowed to do the same, for charterers were not likely to fill the ship on the outward voyage. In order to put some limit on the time the charterers spent in collecting cargo, loading time in foreign ports was limited (though the times were very long) and a daily payment of demurrage for any excess was specified. The lump-sum charter was really little different from the tonnage charter. When the cargo to be lifted was precisely known at the time of chartering — generally when the ship was chartered in the loading port itself — then the freight calculation could be made in advance and the total, rather than the tonnage rate, be incorporated in the charter party. The lump-sum charter was used particularly in the corn trade, where ships were chartered in the loading ports (in England or in the Baltic) for the one-way voyage to the delivery port. It was also sometimes used by very small ships for short round voyages.

When the ship was chartered, the master had a dual respon-sibility. On the one hand, he had to comply in all respects with the charter-party, going to the places specified in it, accepting instructions from the charterers' agents, providing services for unloading and loading if agreed. On the other, he had to watch his owners' interests to see that charter-party conditions were not broken. For practical purposes it may be said that usually the charterers' instructions replaced those of his owners for the conduct of the affairs of the voyage.

Chartered or not, once the ship had passed beyond the confines of the port it became difficult for anyone to control the master's actions. The growing respect for law in Europe, it is true, was by the early seventeenth century closing the safe refuges to which an absconding master might take his ship and sell her. There were no places left in Europe where, in normal times, it was impracticable to set in motion some process of law to recover the ship or punish the absconder. But leaving the criminal master out of the question, the operation of every ship required day to day decisions to be made, some of a navigational but many of a business character which needed the exercise of sound judgment. The distinction between navigational and commercial functions appeared sharply as soon as the ship sailed; while the former were inevitably the master's, the question of who was to perform the latter admitted of more than one answer. Unless the whole route had been precisely planned in advance, and cargoes definitely provided at suitable ports, somebody had to make arrangements for return cargoes, and possibly decide where they should be sought. Cargo taken out from England had to be disposed of. If it was consigned to particular individuals it was simple to unload and hand over to them, and collect the freight; but often the cargo had to be sold — for the owners or the charterers. Money had to be collected and means found to remit it, by bills of exchange, in specie or quite frequently by buying goods with it. All these tasks were very different from the technical job of sailing the ship which was the minimum task for which the master was appointed. To whatever extent they were left to him, it was desirable that the limits of his responsibility, and of his discretion in performing his commercial functions, should be carefully defined in advance. If the ship were chartered, it was the charterers' business to advise and instruct the master, and provided their instructions were within their rights according to charter-party, he was bound to conform; otherwise, his instructions came from the owners.

The master always left England with instructions, often very detailed instructions, in writing. Here is an example:[1]

---

[1] HCA 24 125. Further examples will be found on pp. 172–3, 236–8, 253–5, 270–1, 295–7, below.

London 24th
June 1693.

Mr Edward Mathews
Comander of the *Expedition*
   Loveing friend my desire is you sale with Capt. Nicholas Wills in
the *Providence* to Newfoundland, where arryveing you are to enquire
for Capt. John Templeman Jun. Comander of the *Zant frigott* of
Bristoll to whome I gave orders to buy Thre thousand Kintals of fish
towards the loadeing of your Ship which I hope he hath Effected and
herewith you have my order to Him to loade the said fish on your
Ship and consigne the same to Mr Heneage Fetherstone and Compa.
of Alicante and in case he hath not bought any or not enough to
Loade your Ship then herewith you have my Letter of Credit to buy
your loadeing of fish or what you want thereof which I Desire you to
doe provided you may have it att or under Twenty eight Ryalls pr.
Kintall and Draw the mony on mee or on Mr Philip Andrews of
Plimouth Mr William Hayne of Dartmouth or Mr John Bancks of
Exon and when you are loaden Consigne your fish to Mr Heneage
Fetherstone of Alicante and proceed with the convoy for Alicante and
In default of Convoy with the best Compa. you can gett but doe not
make Consortship with small ships of little force.
In case it hapens that you miss the fish then I desire you not to stay
for the convoy but proceed directly for Alicante where arryving
follow the order of Mr Fetherstone and Co. where you shall land and
where to procead be you loaden or Empty. I would have you load
five to eight Hundred Kintalls of Dry Refuge Fish if to be had at any
Reasonable Termes and if you Cant have fish under 28 Ryalls then
I would have you press the loss.
Pray give me punctuall advice from all parts where you are of what
progress you make for my Government in Insurance faile not herein
and write mee via Bilboa directing your letter to Mr Nicholas
Hutchings and Co. and via Bristoll directing your letter there to
Mr Peter Saunders and write by any ship bound for Barnstable Poole
Weymouth or any part of the West Country. Pray be very punctuall
herein or I shall blame you very much
If you be halfe loaden or thereabouts by then stay for Convoy if any
theare but if you are quite Empty then proceed without staying for
Convoy
You must be very diligent and careful to Inquire Imediately for
Capt Tempelman
Herewith you have alsoe a letter for one Mr Thomas Edwards of
Bristoll a Friend of Mine Whome I am Assured will assyst you in
any thing may offer. You must be watchfull in your voiage to keep

God's worship up and be careful and Diligent. This Mr Edwards I recomend to you is a great Planter and keeps Boates. Inquire for him so soon as you arrive and write him and also to Capt Tempelman and I pray God to send you a safe and good voiage and Remaine

Yr Loveing Friend
Joseph Herne

In case you proceed from Newland without convoy toutch at Malaga for advise about the French and Compa. etc.

In the more distant trades it was usually necessary to leave some flexibility in the instructions, to make possible decisions in the light of the most up-to-date knowledge in ports abroad; to tie a master down too tightly was to invite loss. Yet a vaguely phrased qualifying clause intended to give a master some discretion could very easily be interpreted, if he wished, as authority to disregard the detailed instructions completely and do as he pleased. 'If you are disapoynted in anything above said then you may have liberty to do with our Ship and Goods as you think fitt for our best Advantage' was the appendage to the detailed instructions given to the master of the *Vineyard*.[1] The owner of the *Judith* after setting out full and careful instructions, incautiously ended his letter with the words 'I must laye it all to you and reste' — words which the master interpreted as permission to ignore the rest of the orders, for, as he said in evidence,

'He had sufficient authority from the very words of the said Thomas Teate's second order aforesaid wherein amongst other expressions he useth the expression "I lay or leave it all to you" to sail the said ship to any other port or place beside those to him mentioned if it should seem to him the said Henry's judgment to be most to the advantage of the said ship.'[2]

Apart from the possibility of misinterpreting so completely the scope of his authority, the master nearly always had some alternatives presented to him, and had to decide between them. It was therefore desirable, if possible, to find other ways of exercising some control over the master at a distance — and at the same time, of helping him to carry out his tasks. One method, declining in favour throughout our period, was to send a supercargo with him. The supercargo was not a member of the ship's crew, but a separate employee; a sort of extension of the business house that sent him; he handled the commercial side of the ship's

[1] HCA 24-122.   [2] HCA 24-121.

affairs in port. He was found especially in the newer trades, where firm business connections had not yet been established — for example, in the early West India and Virginia trades — and he survived for a long time in the slave trade, as a specialised haggler with African dealers.[1]

The supercargo often had authority to direct the ship to the ports he considered suitable; in such a case the master was simply the executive agent for taking the ship where the supercargo ordered her; as the master of the *Seaflower*

'was to sail to such ports . . . as he should be directed from time to time . . . it was mutually consented unto and agreed on by and between all the aforesaid owners and Freightors that one John Woodward should be constituted and appointed to be, and should be and go in the said shipp, and for the said voyage, Merchant or Supercargo, and that the said master should observe the orders of the said John Woodward.'

The master's instructions in such a case were short and simple:

Mr John Berron
  You are to saile with our ship Seaflower whereof you go Commander first faire wind, and to observe the orders of John Woodward from tyme to tyme, and doubting but that you will both continue loving Friends. Soe God send you a prosperous voyage and safe returne We remaine

Your loveing Friends[2]

In the *Daniel and Thomas* Captain Cholwell was to have 'command and government of the ship and men' while Samuel Hummffreys was to handle the money and deal in goods, though with Cholwell's advice and approbation.[3] The master of the *John*, bound for Spain in 1673, gave £1,000 bond to the owners 'to perform such duties as the supercargo on board her should direct'.[4] While the owners might trust that they would 'continue loving Friends', such divided authority in fact often led to difficulty and even conflict among men cooped together for many months in a ship, for it was hard to give one a status so superior to the other as to avoid all risk of it. The costliness of supercargoes, the growth of networks of agents abroad and of education and

---

[1] There is an odd case of a master in the Slave trade in 1703 described as 'Master and Commander and also Supercargo'. He was paid on an unusually high rate (*Harris v Simpson*, c. 6–346–10).
[2] HCA 24–115.   [3] HCA 15–11 (1677).   [4] HCA 15–10.

skill among masters, and the liability to friction between masters and supercargoes, all tended to cause the replacement of the supercargo system by others.

Most ships going overseas in the seventeenth century, and nearly all in the eighteenth century, were in fact directed to agents at some of the places they were to call at. The master might not be bound to do as they told him; quite often he was to be given advice and make his own decisions based on it, to accept agents' help rather than orders. Sometimes, too, he would find himself in a port where his owners had no agents. Nevertheless, in the course of time masters were gradually being made more dependent, their actions were being more circumscribed, by agents who were empowered specifically not only to help them but also to give them precise instructions about cargoes and loading ports; even orders to accept instructions from sub-agents in ports to which they were directed unexpectedly. Here for example are the orders given to the master of the *Diligence* in 1728 by her owners' agents in St Kitts — precise and detailed orders clearly issued on the agent's own initiative under a general authority from the principals in England:[1]

St Christopher
October 28, 1728

Captain James Wilson

You are to proceed from here to Sta. Cruiz and there take in all the fustick you can carry for Edward Claxton (or any other person providid he cant load you) for which he'll pay you Twenty-one Shillings per ton Curigeo[2] money, that is three pieces of eight and a half per ton. You'll make all the dispatch possible I don't doubt from Sta. Cruiz as well as for your own sake as the owners since you know how dangerous a place it is to lie long at. Mr Peters has forty barrells of beef on board you for which he'll pay you at Curryso three shillings ye bll. so that I expect the freight from Sta. Cruiz and this beef will furnish you with money enough to fill the sloop.

On your arrival at Curryso do all that you can to dispose of the sloop, if you cant get ready cash for her take good cocoa or good mules. I would not have you sell her for less than she is worth but as you'll be upon the spot and know better than I do what she is worth, I shan't tie you up to any price, if a good offer is made be sure not to refuse it, that is, if anybody will give you forty, thirty-five, thirty, or down to twenty-five mules for her don't refuse it, or a good

---

[1] HCA 15–38.   [2] Curigeo; Curryso = Curaçao.

quantity of cocoa or ready cash, and in case you dispose of her for Mules or Cash, I would have you make all the dispatch you can up here with them, but if for cocoa, send it all to Mr Whipple either by way of Boston or Rhode Island at the first opportunity. If you get a quantity of mules, don't stand for the freight of them up. Two pistoles or three pound is the dearest freight a head for them and if you can't get them up by that means hire a sloop by the day and lay in provisions enough for them that they maybe in good case. Your Bay cargo you may dispose of as well as you can (if the sloop is sold) and what you can't sell bring or send up to me. If you can't sell her, make what dispatch you can for the bay of Honduras and back to Curryso; if yr freight from here and Sta. Cruiz won't fill her, you may take up what you want of any person there and draw on Capt. Whipple for it. Be as frugal as you can and lay out no more than needs must upon her. If you stay at Sta. Cruiz any longer than ten days on Ned Claxton's acct he is to pay you two pistoles a day for each day after, Demurrage. I depend much on your assiduity, and that you'l do everything put in your charge for the owners interest, wherein you'l be sure to find your own. I heartily wish you a prosperous voyage and am

Your friend and humble servt.
Jno. Manning

p.s. Since Mr Peters has ordered his things on shore, you must take in the more fustick at Sta. Cruiz for Mr Claxton, be sur to write me from Curryso whether you proceed to the Bay or not that if you do I may write to London for insurance.

The master, then, was not entirely free from controls, or lacking in assistance, abroad; and if recommendation to agents was lacking, brokers could be found to give help in foreign ports as in England; brokers' fees in foreign ports figure prominently in ships' accounts from the latter part of the seventeenth century. But however firmly he was controlled, much of the success or failure of a voyage necessarily depended on the master. The owners' general conditions about the trade a ship should be put to, their general connections with possible shippers, the capacity of their overseas agents, did much to provide a framework within which profit-making was possible or impossible. But the master's navigational skill, saving days at sea and preventing damage; his capacity to get routine jobs such as watering done quickly at intermediate ports of call abroad and to see that cargo was handled quickly when it was in or alongside the ship; his ability to dispense with an odd man or two for a voyage, saving months' wages; on such things as these the profitability of every voyage to a large extent depended. He had to be entrusted at least with such responsibilities; he might be given wider ones; and even if his part in the management of the commercial side was a small one it was easier for the owners to secure cargoes if their ship's master was personally liked and trusted by the merchants.

This brings us back to the starting point; that the most vital of the management functions of the owners was nearly always the selection of the master. It was a task which, though no doubt in practice often left to one or two owners, required the assent of a majority. Three major decisions; the purchase of the right ship, the determination of what to do with it, the choice of a master; these were the management decisions which, though made only at rare intervals, were primarily responsible for settling the success or failure of the enterprise. In making these decisions, the managing owners and often some other members of the owning group did assume real burdens of management of the highest importance.

IX

Shipping and Trade

So far we have been looking at shipping from the inside; at an industry attracting resources of enterprise, capital and labour to meet its needs. These needs depended, within the given technical framework, on the demands made by trade for the transport of goods, and the nature of these demands now calls for examination. The four chapters that follow discuss the varying demands made by individual branches of trade, and particular ways in which the shipping industry handled them.[1] First, however, some more general problems of the relation between trade and transport must be considered, and the broad pattern of the industry's work set out.

It is essential, at the very beginning, to clear away the notion that the extent of the demand for transport can be judged by the statistics of trade — that is, trade as it is always recorded, valued in pounds, shillings and pence. To the shipowner, the two most important questions to be asked about a commodity have always been 'How far is it to be carried?' and 'How much does it weigh?' (or in some cases the alternative question 'How much hold space will it occupy?'). As to the first of these, it is unnecessary to elaborate on the fact that carrying a thousand tons of goods a year from Newcastle to London created a far smaller demand for shipping than carrying the same tonnage from Jamaica to London; the former task employed one ship of 130 tons making eight voyages a year, but the latter required eight ships of this size because they could each make only a single voyage. Though the factor of distance seems obvious enough when put in this way, a deliberate effort to remember it must be made whenever the size of the English merchant fleet, or of the fleet owned at a particular port, is to be considered as distinct from the annual volume of goods it carried or the tonnage of entries and clearances of ships.

---

[1] The reader who is quite unfamiliar with the pattern of development of English trade may refer to G. D. Ramsay, *English Overseas Trade During the Centuries of Emergence* (1957), and for the eighteenth century to E. B. Schumpeter, *English Overseas Trade Statistics, 1697–1808* (Oxford, 1960).

The other question, or pair of questions, about weight and bulk, raises rather more complications. A ton of coal worth a few shillings and a ton of silk fabrics worth a few thousand pounds are more or less the same to the shipowner; it costs no more to transport the one than the other. In practice, of course, commodities such as these two, lying at the farthest extremes of value, were likely to be handled with differing degrees of care and carried in different sorts of ship. But such differences in the quality of service, where they existed at all, were small and had only very limited effect on freight rates. What really mattered to the shipowner was weight and volume, not value.[1] What created the demand for shipping was mass, not price. Some examples may make this vital point clear. In recent years, some 35–40 per cent of the tonnage of United Kingdom imports has consisted of mineral oils and their products; yet these account for less than 10 per cent of the value of United Kingdom import trade.[2] So, two hundred years ago, roughly half the volume of English imports was made up by timber, and a third of the volume of exports by coal, yet both made only a tiny showing in the trade statistics — timber 3 per cent of imports and coal 2 per cent of exports. The factor of weight, like the factor of distance, seems obvious enough when viewed in isolation, but it is a more awkward one to assess when translating trade figures into demand for shipping. To understand the demand for shipping it is necessary first to ascertain which among the principal commodities of trade were cheap, and which were dear; what goods, though making but a small showing in the trade returns because of low value, were nevertheless important in filling the ships entering and leaving English ports. Thus we must translate the trade *values* of the statistics produced by the Inspectors-General of Customs after 1696 into the trade *volumes* which, with some modifications, indicate the demand for transport services.[3]

The valuations of commodities made by the eighteenth-century Inspector-Generals, though not always completely reliable, give

[1] The one commodity on which freight was paid according to value was bullion. The normal rates in peacetime were, from Portugal and Spain, 1 per cent; from America 2 per cent or 2½ per cent, of value.
[2] Calculated from the *Trade and Navigation Returns*, 1955–9.
[3] There are no comprehensive trade statistics before 1696; but some impressions of the order of size of different branches of trade can be derived from A. M. Millard, 'The Import Trade of London, 1600–1640' (unpublished London Ph.D. thesis, 1957) and from BM Add.MSS. 36785.

a sufficiently clear picture of the cheap and dear commodities of commerce.[1] Here is a list of some of them:[2]

Valuations of commodities, £ per ton

	Imported goods £ per ton		Exported goods £ per ton
Thrown silk	2688	Wrought silk	3920
Raw silk	1904	Woollen cloth	200–1000
Cochineal	1792	Tin	73
Linen cloth	200–1000	Iron goods	55
Coffee	140	Lead	11
Wool (Spanish)	120	Red herrings	11
Linen yarn	98	Pilchards	7
Cotton (Turkish)	65	Wheat	5½
Madder	40	Malt	3½
Flax	35	Coal	less than 1
Pepper	33		
Olive oil (Italian)	28		
Sugar	27		
Wine (Portuguese)	25		
Wine (Spanish)	22		
Currants	21		
Tobacco	21		
Hemp	19		
Rice	15		
Raisins	11		
Iron	10		
Timber (European) about	1		

The reader of this table will not be surprised to learn that silk was imported to a greater total value in the mid-eighteenth century than any other raw material, but that nevertheless its volume was quite small — a few hundred tons in all. When told that much the largest of all importations, by value, was sugar, he will at once realise that the tonnage, too, must have been very great. And he will rightly refuse to judge the importance to shipping of the coal, timber and corn trades by their showing in the trade statistics, which was a small one. As Thomas Tryon wrote in 1669, 'It is the great quantities of Bulksom Commodities that multiplies Ships and Men.'[3]

[1] The valuations, of both exports and imports, are as at ports of loading, and therefore exclude all sea transport costs.

[2] The valuations are those in force in 1754, to be found in Customs 3–54. This record values nearly all the commodities listed above by weight. Three imported and exported commodities valued by other quantities (timber, and woollen and linen cloth) have been given estimated weights for the purpose of the table.

[3] *England's Grandeur*, p. 22.

The complications of weight and bulk, however, are only beginning. Translation into tonnage is not always enough, for tonnage of goods did not invariably correspond with the tonnage of shipping needed to carry them.[1] Take the case of the *Providence* brigantine, which came before the Court of Exchequer in 1714.[2] She was said to be a ship of 150 tons burden, and in fact to have carried 157 tons on a recent voyage to France. At the island of Nevis in 1712 there was a dispute about her cargo, and the independent viewers who were called in to estimate how much she was dead freighted[3] said that she could have loaded, in all, 200 hogsheads of sugar and 80 bags of cotton 'to fill and compleat her full reach and Burthen'. The conventional measures of the time stated that a ton of sugar was four hogsheads, and that a bag of cotton was 200 lb.; on this basis it appears that the 200-ton ship could carry only 58 tons of cargo. Why the discrepancy? In the first place, as we shall see later, the hogshead of sugar had long since departed far from its conventional weight, and at this time it contained, in reality, at least half a ton of sugar. But even if the sugar actually weighed some 110–120 tons, the cotton represented only a further eight tons of weight. The answer is that cotton, as packed at that time, was a very light commodity; a ton of cotton took up three or four times as much space as a ton of sugar — or a ton of water. Though the ship could have borne the weight of thirty or forty tons of cotton, she had not room in her hold for much more than a quarter of that quantity of such a bulky commodity, that is, about eight tons. The freight rate of cotton was adjusted to this fact. The total of the rough calculation corresponds closely with that arrived at (no doubt without conscious calculation at all) by the experienced viewers on the spot.

The invariable measure of a ship's size, from her owners' point of view, was 'tons burden', deadweight tonnage, the number of tons weight which would lade a ship previously empty (except for stores) down to her minimum safe freeboard, or loadline. The majority of goods, even when packed and loaded with all the wastage of space involved in stacking barrels and bales, still weighed as much as or more than the corresponding volume of

[1] In this chapter as elsewhere in the book, 'tonnage' of shipping means tons burden, i.e. weight-carrying capacity.
[2] *Cunningham* v. *Cove*, E.134, Geo. I., Hil. 20.
[3] i.e. to what extent her charterers had failed to provide a full lading.

water; the ship was loaded down to her safe freeboard before the hold was completely full. A few commodities were in a special category as being heavier than the average; but it was, paradoxically, not the heavy goods but the handful of important ones like cotton which were exceptionally light, that caused the most difficulty in the operation of ships. To be precise, there were goods which, when bagged, barrelled, bottled or otherwise packed in the customary way, had specific gravities markedly lower than that of water. These — like the cotton in the *Providence* — would completely fill the ship's hold space long before the ship's weight-carrying capacity had been reached, and the ship's capacity as a carrier then depended not on tonnage but on the cubic measurement of her hold; they had, in modern terms, a high stowage factor.[1] Light goods caused difficulty to the shipowner because of the problems of stability of lightly laden ships; and to the trader because the transport costs per ton had to take into account the excessive space occupied. Cork from Portugal is an extreme example. Imported uncompressed — some 300–400 cubic feet go to a ton — a ton of cork occupies the same space as eight to ten tons of water. A ship with her holds completely filled with cork would ride so high in the water as to appear empty to a boatman alongside. Similarly tobacco in hogsheads in the seventeenth century weighed only half as much as the same volume of water, but it was packed ever more tightly as time went by until just before the American Revolution a hogshead of water and a hogshead of tobacco would have nearly balanced on the scales. West Indian cotton before the invention of powerful bale presses was packed at a density which gave it no more than a third of the weight of water. But far more important than any of these was timber, the bugbear of all volume calculations. The softwoods which made up the greater part of the import from Northern Europe were very much lighter than water, and were not easy to stow without some wastage of space. Moreover, they were cheap, so that the lowering of transport costs was a vital problem to this trade, which always exploited the possibilities of deck cargo and at a very early date was causing shipbuilders to produce vessels of special types suited to its needs.

[1] It may be assumed that ships were so constructed that the hold space was just sufficient to contain enough goods of ordinary weight per cubic foot to weight a ship down to her loadline.

The few exceptionally heavy cargoes presented no serious problems; on the contrary, such goods as lead, iron and copper were often welcome as ballast. When Virginia tobacco in hogsheads and Russian hemp in bales were very light, a few bars of iron squeezed in among the bales or hogsheads would load a ship down satisfactorily without reducing the space available for the main cargo.[1] From Russia, Sweden and America iron was imported at various times (as will be shown below) at very low rates of freight. In 1738 it was said that bar iron from Virginia and Maryland was carried for 10 shillings a ton, while tobacco was paying a rate of £4 to £5.[2] English woollens and Bengal silks were transported in ships whose damp and dirty bottoms were stacked with bars of lead or of Japanese copper, giving stability while occupying space where the valuable textiles could not be stowed without great risk of damage; and these metals, again, were carried at very small charge.

Merchants, shipowners and ships' officers were familiar with the cubic measurements of a ton of all the principal goods of commerce, and their memories could be aided by lists which were generally available.[3] In ports where a variety of cargo was to be had, the mixing of light and heavy goods so as to maximise simultaneously the cubic volume and the tonnage of the goods carried, was one of the nicer arts.

The demand for ship tonnage therefore corresponded with the tonnage of goods to be carried, allowing for the extra storage space required by some light or awkwardly shaped goods, and subject to the adjustments which could be made in some trades by combining cargoes of different kinds. To see clearly where the main work of the shipping industry lay, it is essential to know

[1] 'Lead, tin, pewter, iron and coals were taken on board gratis, or for a very trifle, only to save the charge of ballast' (C. King, *The British Merchant* (1720), Vol. I, p. 354).
[2] *House of Commons Journals, 1737–42*, p. 109; evidence given by John Bannister. Josiah Tucker wrote, in *The Importation of Bar Iron* (1756), pp. 19–20, 'It is impossible to import Iron from North America in any other Shape than as Ballast to other Freights, because if you was to Freight a Ship wholly with Iron, the carriage could not be afforded for less than 25/- or 30/- a Ton, which is such an Expence as the Material could not Bear.' As ballast it went at 6s. to 8s.
[3] East India Company charter-parties specified freight per ton 'according to the usual tonnage of the East India Company and not otherwise', and it issued lists to show the 'usual tonnage' of various goods. Such a list, issued by the Levant Company in 1663, giving the number of hundredweights of different commodities to a ship ton, can be found in SP 110-67.

not what values, but what volumes of various commodities were
coming in and out of English ports; to pay attention not to what
made merchants rich or manufacturers prosperous, but to what
filled the holds of ships and provided their owners' bread and
butter; to look beyond the exotic novelties that were transforming
social life and the technically significant goods that were changing
the economy and to concentrate on the great, commonplace
cargoes — like coal, timber, iron and corn — which by virtue of
sheer bulk constituted the lifeblood of the shipping fleets. An
attempt has been made to calculate from the eighteenth-century
trade statistics the volume of commodities entering and leaving
England in trade with various parts of the world. While complete
accuracy cannot be claimed for the totals, the general picture
presented of the most important commodities and the relative
needs of different regions should not be very seriously in error.[1]
It is true that anyone who looks at the long lists of different items
imported, for example, from Holland, may consider the task of
estimating weights an impossible one and the claim to have
achieved it fraudulent; how can the weights be estimated and
totalled of apparel (suits of); birds, singing (dozens); barbers'
aprons (pairs); beads, crystal (number); bottles, stone (dozens);
dimity (yards); paper, foolscap, fine (reams); and rapecakes
(number)? Fortunately, it is not necessary to try. The weights of
all such miscellanea added together are trivial, and the commodities which were imported into England even to the extent
of a few hundred tons apiece were certainly fewer than fifty in
number. An estimate has been made, for completeness, of the
totals of all the miscellaneous items; it may be far wide of the
mark, but its error cannot make any substantial difference to the
overall totals and their relations.[2] Almost every commodity of

[1] An error is introduced into the original records by the prevalence of
smuggling. The clandestine landing of goods has some importance in the
eighteenth century — many thousands of tons of wine must have been brought
in every year from France. The importance of false entry, with or without the
connivance of customs officials, of goods brought in or exports subject to bounty,
is hard to determine; it may be supposed that few such frauds on a large scale
lasted more than a few years. See T. C. Barker, 'Smuggling in the 18th Century;
the Evidence of the Scottish Tobacco Trade', *Virginia Magazine of History
and Biography*, Vol. LXII, 1954.
[2] It is neither possible nor necessary to include as many as fifty items in the
tables printed here. In collecting the figures to compile them, however, any
commodity which looked as if it might attain import or export totals of more
than five hundred tons was separately recorded. A large component of the
'miscellaneous' total in the table, therefore, is the quite precisely known total
tonnage of these commodities of middling importance.

importance is recorded by weight; the estimates made for two considerable exceptions, woollen and linen cloth, are not, it is hoped, unrealistic. The single major difficulty arises in connection with timber, which was undoubtedly by far the greatest of all imports in volume, and probably exceeded in volume all the other imported goods together. Timber came in a large number of standard categories — in 'hundreds' (meaning 120's) of deals and balks, 'units' of masts (great, medium and small), 'loads' of unspecified 'timber' and so on — and these categories concealed significant variations in size. A hundred of deals contained 120 pieces of wood, and the dimensions of each piece might be as little as 8 ft. × 7 in. × $\frac{1}{2}$ in. or as much as 20 ft. × 11 in. × $3\frac{1}{4}$ in.[1] The largest 'great' masts could contain nearly double the cubic volume of the smallest of the same category, and posed special problems of stowage apart from those of weight and cubic content. There were, however, some conventions in estimating timber volumes and their relation to ship tonnage, and they have been followed here.[2] The results of the calculations made are not inconsistent with the volume of shipping known to have been engaged in the Baltic and Norway trades (allowing for the other commodities which were carried) but it would be unwise to place great confidence in them.[3]

[1] In fact most Norway deals were under 12 ft. long. H. S. K. Kent, 'The Anglo-Norwegian Timber Trade in the Eighteenth Century', *Econ. Hist. Rev.*, 2nd ser., Vol. VIII, 1955–6, p. 63.

[2] H. S. K. Kent, op. cit., p. 72. R. G. Albion, *Forests and Sea Power* (Cambridge, Mass., 1926), p. 9. A hundred of deals is taken to require ship's space equivalent to four 'tons burden', and a load of 'timber' to be the equivalent of $1\frac{1}{2}$ tons. The material on government mast contracts and their shipment in SP 29 suggests that an average requirement of 'tons burden' was 16 for a large, 12 for a medium and perhaps 5 for a small mast. Deals and masts and unclassified 'timber' made up some three-quarters of the value of all 'wood' imports in 1752–4 (though these three categories formed a smaller proportion of imports from some particular countries); and the grand total of timber volume has been completed by adding, for each country, a percentage to the calculated total volume of these three categories equal to the proportion which the value of other classifications of timber bears to their value.

[3] There is a further complication which cannot be allowed for. Recorded 'tons burden' is a shipmaster's estimate of the capacity of his ship, made to a Customs official. How did the master of a ship permanently in timber trade view his 'tons burden'? Did he simply estimate its weight carrying capacity, though this was irrelevant for his particular cargoes? If so, less tonnage was needed, in total, for timber imports, than appears at first sight. For, in the first place, timber ships were designed to have unusually large hold capacity in relation to their 'tons burden'; and secondly, they might carry deck cargoes. Thus the ordinary 400-ton ship could only carry 100 hundreds of deals; the specially built timber ship could take a substantially larger number than this in her holds, and some more on deck.

The grand total of shipping space for imports, arrived at for the average of the years 1752–4 in the table, is 562 thousand tons. This may be compared with the recorded tonnage of ships entering English ports from abroad in the year 1751, which is 480 thousand tons.[1] The correspondence is reasonably close, especially in view of the fact that imports were markedly higher in value, and presumably in volume, in 1752–4 than in 1751.

It will be seen that a handful of commodities created most of the demand for inward shipping tonnage; timber from Norway and the Baltic, sugar from the West Indies, iron from the Baltic, tobacco and (after mid-century) rice and timber from America, wine and brandy from Southern Europe, flax, hemp, pitch and tar mostly from the Baltic. These according to our reckoning, made up over four-fifths of the tonnage of imports; on any conceivable reckoning, at least two-thirds. If the statistics could be taken back a hundred years, to the first decade of the seventeenth century, only one of these commodities — wine — would be found to have anything like its later importance. The quantities of rice, iron, sugar and tobacco imported then were completely negligible; timber imports could be measured in thousands rather than in scores of thousands of tons; flax, hemp, pitch and tar, though not insignificant, came in much smaller quantities. The total of imports in most years between 1600 and 1630 may have been as little as fifty thousand tons, although at particular times, as in 1609 and 1625–6, it was greatly expanded by grain imports from the Baltic.

Only the commodities with the greatest volume have been listed in the table of exports. All other items, including manufactured cloth and metalwares and re-exported sugar and rice, must have made up less than ten per cent of the whole in mid-century, and no more than a quarter even at its beginning.[2] The total of 660 thousand tons which the addition of ten per cent for miscellanea to the total of listed items gives for 1752–4 may be compared with clearances for 1751, recorded as 695 thousand tons. Clearly there is some error here, but again it is not substantial enough to upset the general picture. The bulk-export trades, it will be seen, were confined to Europe, and until the

[1] BM Add.MSS. 11256.
[2] These are very generous estimates; the actual tonnage of the miscellanea was probably less.

Tonnage of shipping required for English imports average of years 1699–1701 and 1752–4 (000 tons)

The upper figure of each pair is 1699–1701, the lower 1752–4

	TOTAL	Fruit	Flax and Hemp	Iron	Dyes	Pitch and Tar	Rice	Sugar	Tobacco	Wine	Timber	Other
Northern Europe	208	—	10	13	—	5	—	—	—	—	178	2
	313	—	17	23	—	1	—	—	—	—	263	9
Nearby Europe	44	—	—	—	1	—	—	—	—	4	10	29
	44	—	1	—	1	—	—	—	—	1	10	31
Southern Europe and Turkey	46	9	—	3	—	—	—	—	—	19	—	15
	39	8	—	1	—	—	—	—	—	13	—	17
West Indies and West Africa	33	—	—	—	4	—	—	23	—	—	—	6
	70	—	—	—	5	—	—	47	—	—	10	8
North America	23	—	—	—	2	—	—	—	15	—	2	4
	88	—	—	3	1	16	11	—	28	—	20	9
East India	5	—	—	—	1	—	—	—	—	—	—	4
	8	—	—	—	1	—	—	—	—	—	—	7
TOTAL	359	9	10	16	8	5	—	23	15	23	190	60
	562	8	18	27	8	17	11	47	28	14	303	81

Tonnage of shipping required for principal exports average of years 1699–1701 and 1752–4 (000 tons)

The upper figure of each pair is 1699–1701, the lower 1752–4

	Coal	Corn	Tobacco	Salt	Fish	Lead
Northern	4	2	1	1	—	1
Europe	21	2	1	1	—	2
Nearby Europe	108	23	6	7	2	6
	293	140	21	18	2	10
Southern Europe	1	4	1	—	8	4
	8	54	—	—	13	2
West Indies	—	2	—	—	—	—
	1	6	—	—	—	—
North America	—	—	—	—	—	—
	5	1	—	—	—	—
East India	—	—	—	—	—	1
	—	—	—	—	—	1
TOTAL	113	31	8	8	10	12
	328	203	22	19	15	15

It has been assumed that the chaldrons of coal recorded in the Customs Ledgers are equivalent to the Newcastle chaldron containing 53 cwt.; Sunderland chaldrons weighed rather more, and west coast chaldrons rather less, but the use of the middle figure introduces no great error (J. U. Nef, *The Rise of the British Coal Industry* (1932), Vol. II, pp. 368–70). Wheat has been estimated at 5½ quarters to the ton of 'tons burden' (*House of Commons Journals, 1737–42*, p. 492).

growth in the eighteenth century of a corn export to the southward, they were confined to nearby Europe including Ireland. Exports, like imports, had changed in character as well as in scale since the early seventeenth century; tobacco, corn and salt had all emerged as substantial exports since that time.

The tables reveal at once an important characteristic of the demand for shipping — its one-way character. The tonnage of English exports to Norway or the Baltic was trivial in relation to the enormous volume of goods coming out of those parts — and was still more trivial in the early seventeenth century before the development of a moderate coal and corn export.[1] Three ships out of every five entering the Baltic from England, both in the

[1] N. E. Bang and K. Korst, *Tabeller over Skibsfart og Varetransport Gennem Oresund, 1661–1783* (Copenhagen, 1930).

1680's and the 1750's, were in ballast — completely empty — though the carriage of a single pack of cloth or hogshead of tobacco was sufficient qualification for the category of 'laden ship'.[1] The sugar, tobacco and dyestuffs from the Caribbean and North America, pepper and saltpetre from India, and in the early part of our period the wine, oil and fruit from Southern Europe, came in heavily laden ships whose owners had been hard put to it to muster partial cargoes for their outward voyages. The following table makes the position clearer; it depends partly on a rather generous estimate of the total volume of exports, but no possible degree of error in the export total can invalidate the general conclusion which emerges. It will be recalled that the greater

Total imports and export by areas (000 tons)

| | 1699–1701 | | 1752–4 | |
	Imports	Exports	Imports	Exports
Northern Europe[2]	208	10	313	30
Nearby Europe	44	180	44	510
Southern Europe	46	25	39	90
West Indies and Africa	33	10	70	10
North America	23	10	88	20
East India	5	neg.	8	neg.

part of the exports of 1752–4 consisted of corn and coal. Corn export, usually negligible before 1700, grew rapidly in the next half-century and in the few years around 1750 attained a peak far above anything seen before or after. To this extent, therefore, the position shown in 1752–4 is an exceptional one, but it was only in the South European trades — those to Spain and Portugal in particular — that corn trade so changed the balance of import and export as to require special notice. Apart from this the picture reveals a substantially unchanging situation, with a heavy excess of export volume (coal, and later corn) from England to the nearby countries of Holland, Germany, Flanders, France and Ireland, and a large excess in the volume of imports from all other parts of Europe and the rest of the world; it can, in fact, be summed up as follows:

[1] A 200-ton ship clearing with no cargo beyond a couple of bales of cloth rates at 200 tons in the shipping statistics; at a few hundredweight in the trade statistics. For reasons of this kind clearances should record a total substantially higher than that of goods carried. This has some bearing on entries as well. The ship which carried outward, or homeward, nothing at all, would not appear in clearances or in entries.

[2] For explanation of these area divisions, see p. 200, below.

Total imports and exports (000 tons)

	1699–1701		1752–4	
	Imports	Exports	Imports	Exports
Holland, Germany, Flanders, France, Ireland	44	180	44	510
All other countries	315	55	518	160

Because of the competition for outward cargo, beyond nearby Europe, outward freights were low — often, in fact, goods were carried outwards for nothing when return cargo was guaranteed. 'Every master here was ready, as is well known, to take on board in England the goods of every English merchant gratis, for the sake of the freight of the back-carriage.'[1] An analogy may be drawn from a very recent time. The English shipping industry in the earlier decades of the twentieth century derived a marked competitive advantage from the fact that it had an outward cargo, coal, which in the days of steamships and steam engines was wanted in vast quantities in all parts of the world. Consequently, English shipowners were able to quote low return freights to Europe.[2] But appearances may deceive. In the seventeenth century the burden of the cost of voyages in ballast or with small cargoes, made habitually and not as exceptions, fell upon trade, and was felt by the shipping industry mainly through any limitation of trade that resulted. In the long run, freights earned had to cover costs. The prices of goods in England were raised appreciably because often one cargo had to bear not only its own carriage costs, but also most of the costs of the outward journey of the ship to fetch it. Only when there was competition from foreign ships which for some reason had two-way cargoes[3] did trade escape this burden.

There were some partial corrections of the unbalance in the volume of trade which are not revealed by the English records of trade. Outward bound ships for the West Indies laded great

---

[1] C. King, op. cit., Vol. I, p. 275. The writer is here referring to the French wine trade; he makes similar remarks on Mediterranean trade in Vol. II, p. 369.

[2] A. Kirkaldy and A. D. Evans, *The History and Economics of Transport* (n.d.), pp. 271–2.

[3] The Dutch had just such an advantage during much of the seventeenth and eighteenth centuries, for they controlled the two-way trade between the Baltic and Southern Europe, exchanging the salt and wine of southern France, Portugal and Spain for Northern timber products and corn. Against this competition English shipping had great difficulty in breaking into the trade of carrying goods out of the Baltic.

quantities of beef, pork, butter and cheese in Ireland. Pipestaves were taken to all South European and West Indian harbours by ships which were to lade wine, oil and sugar in barrels and hogsheads for home; the ships were often diverted to Hamburg or southern Ireland to collect them. Then there were the triangular voyages; to Newfoundland to lade dried cod for sale in Spain from the ships which would then lade wine for home; to West Africa to buy slaves for the West Indies, where in turn the slavers took sugar cargoes for England. These were regular arrangements; individual ships made complicated voyages at times to avoid having empty holds. Yet many of the ships sailing from England did unlade very little cargo at their destinations. It was said in 1739, for example, that the whole of the English export trade to Sweden could be carried in one ship each year.[1] It is true that some colliers made a triangular voyage, going laden to Amsterdam and then continuing in ballast to the Norwegian fiords to lade timber for England; but the Northern trades only approached a little closer to balance when England began to share in the carriage of salt from Southern Europe. As to the colliers and corn ships going across the North Sea to Holland and Germany, many of them secured some return cargo, but the cargoes were rarely full ones. Most cargoes from those places were in fact brought by the regular direct carriers to and fro, which did not dabble in the bulk corn and coal trades, but handled valuable goods whose quick delivery from order was relied upon by merchants anxious to hold no greater stocks than were essential.

Many of the important commodities in English import trade were natural products with seasonal crops of uncertain yield. Sugar, rice, tobacco, flax, hemp, oranges, raisins, oil and wine were all seasonal, and England was at times almost the sole purchaser of the sugar, rice and tobacco in the places from which she drew her supplies.[2] In all these crop trades, in the seventeenth century and to a slightly lesser extent in the eighteenth, traders were anxious to get their ships quickly to the lading ports and be home again with the first of the season's cargoes. Some goods were perishable — oranges, for example. But traders were just as impatient to dispose quickly of cargoes of sugar and tobacco,

[1] CO 388–39, Z. 29.
[2] On the other side, the export of herrings from Yarmouth was highly seasonal, being concentrated in the months of October and November.

where there was no risk of rapid deterioration. The principal reason for this rush for the early market was perhaps the scarcity of mercantile capital and the desire to conserve it — a scarcity felt more acutely in most of the supplying countries abroad than in England, and more acutely in seventeenth-century than in eighteenth-century England. Stocks in England were generally kept at the minimum needed to maintain supply between crops. Immediately before the first shipment of the new crop some shortage was being felt in England, or at least there were some anxieties lest the new crop prove a bad one. The first shipload or two would usually get some of the benefit of scarcity prices, while the late arrivals could look to no benefit from lateness, and in a year of abundant crops might arrive to find the market glutted and everyone confident enough in supplies to be unwilling to undertake further stockholding except at bargain prices. Even more important, most producers overseas depended on the immediate sale of their crops to meet obligations incurred during the year. As a rule neither they nor the local merchants had large reserves of working capital; the producer's response to a period of prosperity was more likely to be an extension of his lands than the saving of money. They could afford stockholding even less than the English merchants; in many cases, indeed, they had to contract for advance payments or incur indebtedness to merchants in other ways in order to carry on at all. The Barbados or York River planter heavily indebted to an English commission agent, the small-scale cultivator of currants on the island of Zante or of olive groves in Apulia, could not afford to hold on to his goods to await the best turn of prices. The burden, and the profit or loss, of such stockholding as could not be avoided was passed on to the international merchant, the English trader, and he in turn spread the burden as quickly as he could manage to sell the goods.

In the eighteenth century growing wealth was beginning to change this situation. In Portugal, prosperous English merchants were before mid-century holding stocks of port for maturing, and shipping it throughout the greater part of the year. The accumulation of planter wealth in Virginia and Maryland was making possible the growth of a well-to-do merchant class, whose activities to some extent evened out the seasonal shipment of tobacco. A striking decline in the seasonality of east coast coal shipments to

London in the second quarter of the eighteenth century[1] was probably due to a similar growth of stockholding capacity among the London coal merchants. Seasonal fluctuations by no means disappeared in these trades, however, and continued to be vigorous elsewhere.

In North European trades a season of shipment was created by the icing of the sea, land and rivers; even Hamburg and Bremen were often closed by ice in midwinter, and seventeenth-century Londoners occasionally saw the Thames completely iced up.[2] Moreover, the slowing down of the tempo of commercial and industrial activity in England in winter, combined with unwillingness to risk ships unnecessarily in winter weather, transmitted some seasonal pattern even to the shipment of mixed cargoes to and from the Low Countries and Germany, though on the other hand corn was shipped in the autumn and early winter.

Seasonality involved only a moderate degree of under-utilisation in the long-distance trades. The sugar, rice and tobacco crops of the Western hemisphere were loaded at the end of long voyages, and except in unusually good years the mustering of cargoes was a long drawn out process. It was difficult for a ship to make two voyages in the season and in practice the voyage out and home, added to loading time and the minimum needed for refit and the collection of some cargo in the home port, rarely took as little as six months and more commonly occupied nine or ten. The great majority of America and West Indies operators regarded one voyage out and home as a proper year's employment of the ship. In the Norway trade and the coastal coal trade the season was so long — normally nine or ten months from the first sailings of the year in March to laying up after the last trip at the end of December — that seasonality was not an important problem to owners. Seasonal shipment was most liable to cause wastage in the middle-distance trades; the Baltic trades with their season curtailed by long winters, the French, Spanish and Portuguese trades with their heavy concentration on wine which shippers were anxious to rush to the market soon after it became available in the late autumn. In the seventeenth century there was some switching between the summer Baltic and the winter wine trades; and later

[1] J. U. Nef, op. cit., Vol. II, p. 389.
[2] Icing was a winter problem in North American ports as well, affecting even the Pennsylvania reaches of the Delaware.

the wastage in Baltic trade was reduced by the development of some carriage of Mediterranean products to the Baltic in English ships. A good deal of seasonal under-utilisation did continue, however; it was taken for granted, absorbed into shipping costs and shipping charges, and created, in a sense, a reserve of shipping which could be drawn out in emergency.

Crops did not merely come seasonally; they also showed year-to-year fluctuations, sometimes accentuated in overseas trade by the inflexibility of internal demand in the producing country. This is most evident in the corn trade. With a production which in the mid-eighteenth century was estimated at some 13–14 million quarters in an average year[1] English arable farmers approximately supplied the home market with its needs. Actual crops, of course, fluctuated very widely around the average, and since home demand only responded grudgingly to price changes, much of this fluctuation was passed on to the overseas trade in corn, which was relatively small. In 1750, the year of maximum export, one million, six hundred thousand quarters of corn of all kinds were sent abroad; the following year just over a million; in 1757 and 1758 the small export was actually exceeded by moderate imports.[2] This marginal export of corn surplus to English needs, a small proportion of the total corn crops even in 1750, was nevertheless in that and neighbouring years nearly as great in tonnage as all other exports together. How it was handled is not clear; neither the history of the trade in corn nor the history of Yarmouth, the principal place of export, has yet been written.[3] The growth of the corn trade during the first half of the eighteenth century, continuous despite violent year-to-year fluctuations, had contributed to the building up of a large fleet of Yarmouth-owned ships;[4] at the peaks of the trade they were supplemented by vessels drawn from the coal and Norway trades. The needs of these trades corresponded quite well with those of corn export, for though the latter began as early as August, it continued through

[1] C. Smith, *Three Tracts on the Corn Trade* (1766), pp. 140–4.
[2] ibid, pp. 107–14.
[3] D. G. Barnes, *A History of the English Corn Laws* (1930), sticks strictly to the subject-matter indicated by the title, and throws very little light on the actual procedures of the trade. He presents (pp. 299–300) tables of exports of wheat and wheat flour from 1697; but these are only a fraction of total corn exports.
[4] This is shown very clearly by the statistics in BM Add.MSS. 11255–6, which also indicate the sharp decline of Yarmouth shipping in the sixties and seventies as corn export fell away.

the winter months when activity in the coal and Norway trades had been greatly reduced. Though most of the export was short-distance, to Holland and France, the demand for ships was very great and fluctuations in this demand must have caused great pressures on the freight market in the autumn and early winter. It was not possible to employ foreign ships to bear some of the burden of peak demand, for corn export attracted a government bounty which was paid only if the corn was despatched in English-owned, English-manned ships.[1]

The American tobacco and West Indies sugar crops were also subject to marked year-to-year variation. These crops were exported almost in their entirety to England and Scotland, so that changes in the size of crop were reflected almost exactly in changes in the demand for shipping tonnage. The ships had to sail from England before the crop yield was known at all accurately. Fluctuations in crops were reflected not so much in the number and tonnage of vessels importing them, as in the difficulties these ships had in getting cargo, measured by half-empty holds and low freights when the crops were poor, and by high freights and quick voyages when they were exceptionally good. The effect of the violent ups and downs of sugar production can be seen in the letters of Sir William Stapleton of Nevis. In 1726 he shipped no sugar for England, for his crop was only sufficient to pay for his local needs of provisions, etc. (No doubt the local merchants and the New Englanders who supplied these sent to England some of the sugar he paid them with.) In 1728 the crop was so large that at the end of the normal loading season in early August he still had one-fifth of it in hand, and all the ships had sailed fully laden.[2] During the eighteenth century the situation was gradually eased by the development of some non-seasonal cargoes—mahogany from Jamaica, pitch and tar from the North American colonies — which were not so costly as to require instant shipment; and in the tobacco trade by some development of stock-holding in the colonies.

In most European trades crop fluctuations were less important to shipping; with short voyages and quick overland communication, reliable information about crops was received in time to adjust

---

[1] 1 William and Mary, c. 12.
[2] E. F. Gay, 'Letters from a Sugar Plantation in Nevis, 1723–32', *Journal of Economic and Business History*, Vol. I, 1929, pp. 149–73.

shipping movements, and alternative cargoes were fairly readily available at the cost of moderate voyages in ballast.

One way in which the shipowner tried to deal with fluctuation in the demand for his services, especially in the transatlantic trades where its effect was most serious, was to induce the overseas producer or merchant to tie himself to the use of a particular ship, year after year. The shipowner could guarantee that even in a good season space would be kept available for his customer — probably space in an early ship — thus relieving the latter of a good deal of uncertainty. For himself, he could hope to be assured of at least part of the cargo he needed even in bad years. If he could persuade his overseas connections actually to own parts of the ship and share its profits and losses, they would be tied to its use, he might expect, even more firmly. Such relationships were on the increase in the crop importing trades during the eighteenth century, yet the free market was never squeezed out even in Jamaica, Barbados or Virginia; and elsewhere it seems always to have predominated in spite of the superficial attractiveness of the firm commitment. For the advantages of these commitments were always more apparent than real; and so far as they were real, tended to benefit the shipper rather than the shipowner. So long as a free market existed it effectively determined, for all ships, the freight rates for the season which prevailed in practice over all prior arrangements and agreements made in London or elsewhere. When ship's master and shipper were face to face, one would demand the ruling price because it was in his favour, and by threatening to abandon the connection, would nearly always get it. As for the producer who was also part-owner, notwithstanding his ambivalent desires for high freights and a profitable ship, for low freights and a profitable crop, the latter was always the preferred alternative, though he would grumble at the resulting poor dividend on the ship. Had the practice of tying ever completely captured a particular trade — that is, had the speculative uncommitted ship ever been forced out — complete inflexibility would have supervened, with some under-laden ships leaving behind some unlifted crops practically every year.

The overall supply of ships, for trade in general, was fairly flexible owing to the various forms of concealed unemployment that were taken for granted in normal times and could be reduced or extended as need arose without painful dislocation. Delays in port were lengthy for good reasons and bad. In many of the harbours where bulk imports were loaded it took a long time to get a full cargo together; the actual loading, which need take no more than a few days, was accompanied by weeks, often months, of haggling and argument and waiting for the general level of freights to settle. Wine, tobacco, raisins, oil, though carried in thousands of tons every year, were shipped by individuals five, ten or twenty tons at a time; those who did have larger amounts to handle preferred not to risk too much in a single ship. At home arrangements had to be made for hiring out the ship, or alternatively the owners had to collect their own goods for outward lading and try to induce others to put goods aboard. In these respects, as in others, the eighteenth century began an improvement; loading times were cut sharply, particularly in South European trades, but they remained very long.

Because there was, for one reason or another, much under-utilisation of capacity, there were important reserves available to deal with specially large crops, whether of sugar or tobacco across the ocean, or of corn in East Anglia. If the West Indian sugar crop was large, ships were quickly loaded at high freights, and a few ships would make two voyages in the year; if it was exceptionally small, loading delays would be unusually prolonged and some ships would be hard put to it to complete the round voyage in the season, though they came home half empty. In the Spanish trade quick loading could mean three voyages in a season instead of two. High freights in European waters would tempt some of the seasonally laid up ships out of hibernation, or cause owners to delay extensive repairs to take advantage of the temporarily good times.

Yet though there was flexibility in the total supply of shipping, obstacles of timidity and conservatism stood in the way of flexibility between trades. The supply for a particular trade was generally expanded and contracted, in the short run,[1] by the more or less intensive use of ships regularly engaged in it, rather than by bringing ships in temporarily from other trades. In good years

[1] Continuing boom in a particular trade was no doubt met partly by buying ships and changing their use, as well as by having new ones built; but the common practice of changing a ship's name when its ownership was changed makes it impossible to gauge from the records how often this happened.

no less than in bad, owners of ships in long distance trade seemed reluctant to fill in short periods of idleness with voyages to nearby ports. In part this was due to the unsuitability of their vessels, in size and build, for most operations in European waters. In part it expressed a reluctance to risk, for a fairly small return, the regularity of the main voyage which was presumably bringing in adequate seasonal profits. And finally, there was sometimes present a rigidity of mind which saw a vessel committed to one function and would not be bothered to fit it to another. All the evidence for the seventeenth and eighteenth centuries points to a growing degree of specialisation, of concentration of each ship on its particular trade; and in the eighteenth century, if not earlier, the great majority of ships in overseas trade made the same voyage year after year for five, ten or fifteen years if peace was maintained; only war changed the routine. Five voyages a year from Hull to Oslofiord and back; two voyages from London to Riga; two or three from London to Portugal; one (or very rarely two) from Bristol to Barbados and home again; these were the nearly unvarying patterns followed. To select one from the hundreds of examples which are available; the *New Elizabeth* of 300 tons sailed on her first voyage to Barbados, as a new ship, in August 1750. Every year except one after that, until 1768, she made the same voyage, sailing in most years in December or January and returning to London between July and October. Even war hardly altered the pattern; her sailing was late in 1758 and 1759, and the 1760 voyage took so long (presumably owing to convoy delays) that she missed her sailing for the following season. This regularity, with the slight check due to war, and this concentration on a single trade, are typical of the great majority of the ships whose voyages from London can be traced over long periods in the eighteenth century.[1] Though it cannot be so firmly established for earlier times, and though regularity was certainly not so great, the impression one receives from all the seventeenth-century material[2] is that then, too, most ships concentrated on particular trades. The generalisation is less true for the short-distance

[1] This view is derived largely from the records of Seamen's Sixpences (Adm. 68–194 *et seq.*). 150 ships were taken from each of the years 1768, 1751 and 1736 and traced backward through the records of their voyages until they disappeared (through using a port other than London, or a change of name) or were described as new ships.

[2] That is, from Admiralty passes and from HCA ships' accounts and other evidence given on utilisation.

trades; though nothing was more regular than the Boulogne or Dunkirk parcels carrier going to and fro once or twice a month, there was a good deal of transfer between coastal traffic of all kinds and the cross-Channel and Dutch trades.

Outside the short-sea and coastal trades the ships that can be found frequently switching from one use to another made up a small minority. There were ships whose owners were prepared to seek cargo wherever opportunities appeared good, and were able to find charterers for all parts of the world; but they were rare. Yet these few ships were the only true equivalents of the modern tramp steamer which is sent to any port where a cargo at adequate rates is offered. An example is the *Pearl* which apparently started life as a collier. She is met with first, in July 1717, completing some unspecified business in the Isle of Wight and sailing from there to Newcastle to take in coal for London. London provided some cargo for Amsterdam; and there the ship was laid up for the winter of 1717–18, from October until March. When spring came she was taken to Newcastle in ballast and returned to Amsterdam with a freight of coal. There was still little cargo available there, but prospects were better at Hamburg, so the *Pearl* was sent there and secured a lading for Viana in Portugal. Laid up for the early part of the winter of 1718–19, she came out to make some coasting voyages up and down the Portuguese coast, finally sailing in June from Oporto to collect a cargo of fish from Newfoundland. This was brought back to Viana, from whence in January 1720 a cargo for London was easily obtainable. At London freight was not easily had; the ship lay idle for four months and then secured a cargo of corn for Portugal. Though her records end there, in December 1720, she was clearly well placed for a homeward wine or fruit cargo.[1]

The division between tramp and liner which is fundamental to the shipping industry of today has very little relevance to the eighteenth or even the seventeenth century. There were these few ships totally uncommitted, whose managing owners or masters accepted the best freight opportunities that presented themselves as each voyage was ending. In the Mediterranean English ships often spent a year or two transporting goods from place to place as offers appeared, but nearly always with an eye to taking oil or currants home when the time was ripe. There were, too, ships

[1] HCA 15–36.

which when disappointed of seasonal cargoes laid themselves open
to offers to fill in time or get home without too much loss; and
such situations almost certainly become more common if we
move backwards through the seventeenth century. But most vessels
had their regular runs and kept to them in good times and
bad, whether directed by owners or charterers, simply because
among their most valuable assets were the masters' and owners'
connections in particular ports overseas. If the owners finally
despaired of their ship's prospects, they were much more
likely to sell her than try to introduce her into a new branch of
trade.

An earlier chapter has shown that these two centuries saw
considerable advances in the design of merchant ships. The effect
was to economise labour, the main cost of sea transport, chiefly
by reduction of crew sizes, though partly by an enhanced
manœuvrability which shortened voyages and made them a little
safer. Costs were also being lowered by other factors; ships built
on the north-cast coast or in America were cheaper than those
from the Thames estuary; improved commercial organisation was
cutting turn-round times, the long cargo-collection delays which
could put months on a voyage; and interest and insurance rates
were falling.[1]

Reduced costs should have had their effect in lowered freight
rates, and it is clear from the studies of individual trades which
follow that they generally did so. One influence the other way
was the rise of seamen's wages which continued through the first
eighty years of the seventeenth century. The strength of this
influence, the narrowness of the sphere in which technical change
was at first allowed free operation, and the long incubation period
of the new shipbuilding centres, kept the general level of freights
steady until the outbreak of war in 1689, though signs of a break
were already appearing; only after peace returned in 1713 did a
new rate structure appear. The freight rates of the 1720's were
in general markedly lower than those of fifty years before, and a
declining tendency showed itself right up to the War of American
Independence. This is not easy to establish as a generalisation.
In the first place, there were exceptions. The North European
trades, under the impact of Dutch competition, achieved their

[1] See pp. 376-8, below.

major technical revolution in shipping during the mid-seventeenth century decades when they were rising to importance. The freight rates in these trades, therefore, were early fixed at a low level, and showed little further change until the beginnings of the development of very large ships towards the end of our period. The monopolists who owned the shipping hired out to the East India Company maintained and probably increased the freights actually earned, though the true freight rates are obscured by the terms under which their ships were hired; reform came only after a parliamentary investigation in 1773. And secondly, variations in the size of measures blur the true movement of freight rates per ton in important cases. In the Virginia and Maryland tobacco trade and in the West Indian sugar trades, changes in the real weight of unit — the nominal ton — on which freight was charged make it difficult to compare freight rates of the seventeenth century with those after 1689. Nevertheless, it is beyond doubt that the cost of carrying a net ton of sugar across the Atlantic was at least a third lower in 1770 than in 1670; the cost of carrying tobacco was even more heavily reduced, though this must be attributed largely to tighter packing rather than the increased efficiency of ships. The South European trades, where these complications do not occur, showed an even greater decline in carrying costs. The reasons for this are varied; they include the greater safety and the consequent reduction of crews as the Moorish corsair menace was gradually overcome in the middle decades of the seventeenth century, and the balancing of inward and outward cargoes through growing corn export in the eighteenth century. Undoubtedly, however, increasing efficiency of ships was a factor here, too, in reducing freight rates.

We shall not go far wrong in saying that, outside the Northern and the East India trades, freight rates, after a long period of near stability, began to tremble very late in the seventeenth century, fell precipitately with the coming of peace in 1713, when the progress of the war years was realised, and declined a good deal further during the next sixty years. This is the peacetime story; in wartime, on the other hand, there is apparent a tendency for the upward swings of rates to become more violent from war to war; certainly the changes during the Dutch wars of the seventeenth century were much less pronounced than those of the French wars from 1689 onward.

NOTE ON CHAPTERS X TO XIII

Nearly every statement in the following chapters depends on statistical analyses of one or more of a few groups of records, or on many individual pieces of evidence from the records of the High Court of Admiralty which appear to point to some general conclusion. To give complete footnote references would be tedious, and of little value. I set out below, therefore, the statistical sources chiefly used for these five chapters. When substantial information has been drawn from some source other than these or the High Court of Admiralty records, it has been footnoted in the ordinary way; as have individual examples. Contemporary descriptions of commercial matters have a very limited value; they are nearly always concerned with trade values, not volume, are usually vague and very often propagandist and demonstrably inaccurate. They are therefore referred to only when their evidence tallies with that from other sources.

The tables on pp. 210–11, 226–7, 243, 256, 266 and 298–9 follow the form, and constitute a further analysis of those on the following two pages.

Statistical Sources:

1. Analyses of all inward and outward Port Books for the year 1686, and of 1687 in cases where the 1686 Port Book is missing, and of many Port Books for the years 1662–4.[1]

2. Records of ships clearing all English ports, with destinations, 1715–17 (CO 390–8). Some use has been made of the similar records for 1710–14 (CO 388–18).

3. Analyses of entries of ships into the Port of London from all parts as recorded by the Receiver-General of Seamen's Sixpences (Adm. 68–194 *et seq.*), for the years 1726, 1736, 1746, 1751, 1766.

4. Trade statistics:
   1663 and 1669 in BM add.MSS. 36785[2]
   1699–1701 in Customs 3–3/5[2]
   1752–4 in Customs 3–56/58

5. Entries and clearances of ships at English ports, 1771–3 by countries (BT 6–185).

---

[1] A much more detailed analysis of the 1686 statistics than is possible here can be found in my London Ph.D. thesis (1955) 'The Organisation and Finance of the English Shipping Industry in the Late Seventeenth Century', pp. 383–426.

[2] Summarised in my article 'English Foreign Trade 1660–1700', *Econ. Hist. Rev.*, Vol. VII, 1954. n.s.

STATISTICAL SUMMARY

Note:

The areas for which statistics are given, and which constitute the basic structure of the following chapters, are:

'Nearby Europe': Holland, France, Germany, Flanders, Ireland, Isle of Man, Channel Isles

'North Europe': Norway, North Russia, Denmark and all Baltic

'Spain and Portugal': Spain, Portugal, Canaries, Madeira, Azores

'Mediterranean': non-Spanish Mediterranean (and in trade figures excluding Mediterranean France)

'East India': all territory east of the Cape of Good Hope

'North America' is self-explanatory

'West Indies': West Indies and the slave coasts of Africa

1. TONNAGE OF ENTRIES AND CLEARANCES (foreign tonnage, included in totals, in brackets) (ooo tons)

	1686		*1715–17 clearances*
	Entries	*Clearances*	
North Europe	141·6 (56·7)	55·2 (19·6)	47·9 (3·3)
Nearby Europe	180·6 (10·0)	187·6 (10·1)	234·5 (12·7)
Spain and Portugal	33·1 (0·6)	24·2 (0·3)	44·1 (1·2)
Mediterranean	25·7 (0·1)	18·8	30·3 (0·2)
East India	5·8	8·4	4·3
West Indies	44·4	34·0	35·7
North America	35·6	33·1	40·3
TOTAL	466·8 (67·4)	361·3 (30·0)	437·1 (17·4)

	1771–3	
	Entries	*Clearances*
North Europe	280·2 (89·7)	89·3 (33·4)
Nearby Europe	218·5 (28·6)	486·7 (24·7)
Spain and Portugal	53·9 (2·6)	29·9 (3·4)
Mediterranean	13·6 (0·1)	29·1 (0·3)
East India	14·1	13·9
West Indies	95·8	104·5
North America	96·9	99·0
TOTAL	773·0 (121·0)	852·4 (61·8)

2. VALUE OF TRADE (£ooo)

	1699–1701		*1771–3*	
	Imports	*Exports*	*Imports*	*Exports*
North Europe	583	335	1502	462
Nearby Europe	1750	3312	2477	6272
Spain and Portugal	834	906	877	1626
Mediterranean	721	802	991	1103
East India	756	136	2096	990
West Indies	765	473	3054	2065
North America	342	378	1454	2518
TOTAL	5751	6342	12451	15036

(Scotland is excluded from all statistics before 1707.)

3. PRINCIPAL OCCUPATIONS OF PORT OF LONDON

	1686 *number of*		1715–17 *clearances only*	
	entries	*clearances*	*number*	*ooo tons*
Northern Europe	412	185	114 (10)	21·3 (1·4)
Nearby Europe	820	465	496 (101)	28·5 (6·3)
Ireland and I.O.M.	41	51	68	4·9
Spain and Portugal	247	182	244 (22)	20·8 (0·6)
Mediterranean	118	79	95 (2)	16·1 (0·2)
East India	15	23	12	4·3
West Indies and Africa	225	161	164	23·8
North America	110	114	130	17·7
TOTAL	1988	1260	1323 (135)	137·4 (8·5)

X

The Nearby and Northern European Trades

Much the greatest market for English goods was found in the ports of the nearby coasts of Europe from Hamburg to the Bay of Biscay and in Ireland, and this same area was the principal supplier of goods to England.[1] At the end of the sixteenth century, indeed, little trade was carried on beyond those parts, and their predominance in English commerce was only gradually eaten away. The import trade was heavily concentrated on London, which took enormous quantities of manufactured goods from Hamburg, Amsterdam, Rotterdam, as well as the greater part of the French wine import so long as this came legally. The provincial ports, however, had a very important role in export, and in all trade with the French Channel ports and Ireland. Much of the miscellaneous trade with France and Flanders was carried on in tiny craft from small harbours of the south coast (with Southampton specialising in the Channel Islands traffic); they dealt with a multitude of minor Continental ports, such as Nieuport, Ostend, Calais, Boulogne, Rouen, Caen, Morlaix, and their total trade, legal and illegal, was substantial. The traffic with Ireland was carried on almost entirely by the west coast ports; on the Irish side it was heavily concentrated on Dublin and Cork, though Belfast began to rise in importance in the eighteenth century.

These trades differ from all others in having an export tonnage far greater than that of imports. During most of our period this was accounted for by the great shipments of coal, cheapest of all commodities, which made a small showing in trade returns but far exceeded in volume all the exports of costly manufactures. Enormous and rapidly growing quantities of coal went from

---

[1] There are no substantial studies of the trades with nearby Europe. C. H. Wilson, *Anglo-Dutch Commerce and Finance in the Eighteenth Century* (Cambridge, 1941) is useful but devotes most of its attention to finance. T. S. Willan, *The English Coasting Trade* (Manchester, 1938), is a comprehensive study of its subject, and J. U. Nef, *The Rise of the British Coal Industry* (1932), gives much attention to shipping matters.

Newcastle and Sunderland to Holland, with smaller but still important amounts to Hamburg, Bremen and Rouen; at the end of the seventeenth century Whitehaven developed an export to Ireland which grew exceptionally fast during the eighteenth century, and Whitehaven's shipments were supplemented by those of South Wales and later of Liverpool.

Coal exports, 000 tons[1]

	Total	*North-east coast*	*Whitehaven and district*	*S. Wales*
1608–9		27	n.a.	—
1685	*c.* 120	77	30–40	7
1733	218	98	*c.* 120	
1752–4	328	168	*c.* 160	

Though the foreign trade in coal was only a fraction of the coastal trade, it made its contribution to the development of the north-east coast as the chief shipowning area outside London, the 'nursery of seamen' and the centre of experiment in the building of bulk cargo carriers around 1700.

Two new bulk cargoes supplemented English exports on a very large scale in the eighteenth century. The first was corn export. Corn had occasionally been exported before 1700, but about that time the traffic became a regular one, its volume rising very fast until mid-century.

Corn exports (000 quarters)[2]

Average of	
1699–1701	119
1709–11	297
1719–21	479
1729–31	269
1739–41	326
1749–51	1258
1759–61	680
1769–71	149

The most important branch — the export of wheat and malt from the eastern counties to Holland — created great prosperity for

[1] J. U. Nef, op. cit., p. 380; J. E. Williams, 'Whitehaven in the Eighteenth Century', *Econ. Hist. Rev.*, 2nd ser., Vol. VIII, 1956, p. 400; BM Add. MSS. 38374–32; Customs 3/33.
[2] C. Smith, *A Collection of Papers Relating to the Corn Trade* (1765) up to 1761; 1769–71 from the London Statistical Society's *Statistical Illustrations . . . of the British Empire* (1827), p. 98.

the East Anglian ports of Lynn, Wells, Blakeney and above all Yarmouth. Smaller, but still substantial quantities went to France, Ireland, Spain and Portugal from the minor ports of the south and south-west, and from London when the accumulated corn surpluses in its warehouses became too great. The other new bulk trade was in Cheshire salt, exported principally from Liverpool; its development just before 1700 was quickly followed by the opening of a huge Irish market, and by mid-century it was beginning to go to Flanders and Germany in large quantities.[1]

There were other substantial export cargoes to North-west Europe, though none of them compared in volume with coal, or with corn and salt in their full development. Hull and Newcastle had an old-established trade in lead; sugar was re-exported, chiefly from London, between about 1660 and 1713 to the whole of Northern and North-western Europe, and after 1713 to Ireland; tobacco was sent to all parts, at first from London but increasingly, in the eighteenth century, from Liverpool and Whitehaven. Even the cloth trade provided several thousand tons of outward cargo for North-west Europe; its value dwarfed that of all other commodities.

Imports from North-west Europe were much smaller in bulk, and few individual commodities were really important to shipping. An immense variety of articles each carried in trivial quantities characterises import trade with this area. The principal imports from Germany and Holland were of linens and metalwares of all kinds, generally of small bulk; the supplementary commerce in such things as Rhenish wine, pipestaves, bricks and tiles, though useful to the shipowner seeking cargo, in no way compared with the export volume. The larger bulk-import trades of the area came from its fringes — wine and salt from the Biscay coast of France, and cattle, meat and dairy produce from Ireland — and both were cut down heavily between 1660 and 1680. The southern (Biscay) coast of France was, economically, part of the South European trading area; it is included here only because of the difficulty of disentangling it, statistically, from the rest of France.[2] It was the most considerable supplier of wine to England, and also sent to the outports great quantities of salt. The prohibition

[1] T. C. Barker, 'Lancashire Coal, Cheshire Salt and the Rise of Liverpool', *Trans. Lancs. & Chesh. Hist. Soc.*, Vol. CIII, 1951, pp. 83–101.
[2] The same trouble arises with the Mediterranean coast of France but trade with this was always negligible.

of all trade with France which first came into force in 1678, and which was succeeded after 1713 by duties which made trade impossible, virtually brought the connection to an end. After this, wine, brandy and fine linens came, illegally, in small vessels from the nearer Channel coast. Ireland sent large quantities of foodstuffs and live cattle to the western ports until the trade in these goods was banned, in the interest of English landowners and farmers, by Acts of Parliament in 1663, 1667 and 1680;[1] it then developed a valuable but less bulky trade in wool (gradually replaced by woollen yarn) and linen yarn, to the Bristol Channel ports and Liverpool. South Irish ports continued to be places of call for English ships crossing the Atlantic, where they bought cheap provisions for their own use and for sale in the plantations overseas.

Shipping served these differing trades in a variety of ways. In the first place, all the ports from the Humber round to the tip of Cornwall employed small ships, most of them under fifty tons, and in the directly cross-Channel trade often of no more than thirty, in regular voyages to Hamburg, Holland, France and Flanders. The Port Books of the Restoration years and of the decade before the American Revolution, and the London Seamen's Sixpences throughout the middle decades of the eighteenth century, show in any year scores of ships each making a regular four or five Hamburg voyages, or a dozen between Southampton and Le Havre or London and Dunkirk, or a voyage every few days between Dover and Calais or Boulogne. The size of the vessels and the character of the traffic were almost unchanging over all this period, and probably far back into the sixteenth century: these craft were simply carriers, taking a varied freight in small parcels from whoever brought it to the quayside. The masters, who were often the sole owners, managed all the ships' affairs. Individual ships were well known in the ports they connected, where there were established places of resort for the masters, and they provided between them so frequent a service that in all the larger ports a shipper could be confident of getting cargo moved within a few days of its becoming available. From an early date, compilers of tradesmen's guides could indicate where vessels for some of the nearby Continental ports might be regularly found; thus *The Carriers' Cosmography* of 1637, which was mainly devoted to listing the overland cartage services, includes the following:

[1] 15 Charles II, c. 7; 18 Charles II, c. 2; 32 Charles II, c. 2.

'Shipping from Scotland is to be found at the Armitage or Hermitage below St. Katherine's. From Dunkirk, at the Custom House Key. From most parts of Holland or Zealand, pinks or shipping may be had at the brewhouses in St. Katherine's'.

Naturally, these ships had their foreign counterparts; most of Bremen's trade with London was carried on in German ships, and there was always a considerable Dutch, Hamburger and French participation in the carriage of goods between their respective ports and England. Though there are complaints about this even after the Restoration,[1] the share of ships belonging to France, Flanders or Holland was from that time onward only a moderate one.[2] In 1771–3 39 per cent of the tonnage of entries from Germany, 27 per cent from Holland and 9 per cent from France and Flanders was of foreign ships. The role of Irish ships in the regular Anglo-Irish trade is hard to determine, since the ships were not easily identified and were not classed as foreign in the statistics. Irish shipping, considerable and fast-growing in the thirty years before 1688, was destroyed during the struggles of 1689–92, and though it made some recovery seems never to have reached its old levels again. In 1698 and in 1722–3, nearly two-thirds of the tonnage of *all* ships trading at Irish ports was English, and the English proportion in Anglo-Irish trade must have been much higher.[3]

A number of larger ships plied between London and Holland and Hamburg. There was, in the first place, the handful of vessels which the Merchant Adventurers' Company chartered twice a year, during most of the seventeenth century, to take their cloths to Hamburg and Middelberg — ships of 150–200 tons, sailing in small fleets — but this regular Company traffic was in decline.[4] Secondly, Hamburg was a supplier of moderate quantities of timber to England; pipestaves were always imported, and after 1721 certain other kinds of German timber.[5] London had a few quite large regular traders which carried such goods in mixed

---

[1] Petition of 1660 in SP–29–440–27; petition of 1664 in SP 29–97–66. PRO 50–24–602 for French shipping about 1670.

[2] Foreign ships predominated only in trade with the Port of Bremen.

[3] F. Brewster, *New Essays on Trade* (1702), p. 106. A. Dobbs, *An Essay on the Trade and Improvement of Ireland* (Dublin, 1729), pp. 14–15.

[4] The Merchant Adventurers apparently abandoned the use of very small vessels during the Anglo-Spanish War of 1587–1604, and never returned to it (SP 14–8–58; June 1604).

[5] This was permitted by 6 Geo. I, c. 15, after being prohibited by the Navigation Acts for over half a century.

cargoes, and foreign ships of the same kind also brought them. A large part of the bulk imports to England, however, came in returning colliers.

In the first half of the seventeenth century nearly all the coal trade with the Continent was carried on by foreign ships. In 1593 seven out of every eight ships clearing Newcastle for a foreign port were foreigners[1] and though the proportion dropped before the Civil War it remained high. The acquisitions of Dutch fly-boats between 1651 and 1674, and the heavy discriminatory duties imposed on foreign colliers in 1660 drove them almost completely from the trade after the Restoration. Thereafter coal was carried to the Continent by English ships, nearly all of them undertaking temporary diversions from the coastal coal trade. The coal they carried was usually owned by the shipowners, though chartering was rather less rare than in the coastal coal traffic. Return cargoes were not easy to find, and many of the ships came home in ballast or very lightly laden; numbers went on to Norway to seek timber freights; a few found timber or similar cargoes in Hamburg itself; the smaller colliers could sometimes snatch parcels of cargo from the regular traders and return home via London. The *Rose* of Boston is perhaps not untypical of the very small coastal collier — she carried only 35 tons — which was ready to switch to Continental trade. Late in 1684 her normal run was carrying coal between Sunderland and London or Boston. In September she crossed over to Rotterdam with coal, earning £25 on the outward and £11 on the homeward voyage. More coastal voyages were followed in July 1685 by another trip to Rotterdam, a coal cargo on the owners' account earning £25, and the homeward freight £12. The following spring she made two Rotterdam voyages from London — that is, not as a collier — and the inward and outward freights balanced at £29 each. Again in the spring of 1687 a Rotterdam coal voyage was interspersed among her coastal travels, producing £14 outward and £13 homeward, and another in March 1688 £25 out and £16 home.[2] The overseas coal trade, however, generally employed much larger ships than the *Rose* — averaging about 100 tons in the decades round 1700, and including many of 200–300 tons — and these would have

---

[1] O. A. Johnsen, 'The Navigation Act of 9 October 1651', *History*, n.s., Vol. XXXIV, 1949, pp. 91–4.
[2] HCA 15–14.

found great difficulty in securing homeward cargoes nearly commensurate with their carrying capacity. Moreover, the continuing growth of the coal export trade (though at a lessening pace after 1700) and the appearance of the corn exporting ships as competitors for return cargoes from Holland, must have greatly worsened the prospects for balanced cargoes.

The coal export trade with Ireland was of much the same character; coal was bought by the shipowners and sent out, and their ships came back, usually in ballast, but some with small quantities of linen or woollen yarn for Liverpool, or of wool or woollen yarn for harbours on the Bristol Channel coast of Devon. The Irish trade from Whitehaven and Workington was the most rapidly growing branch of English coal export during the first half of the eighteenth century, and made Whitehaven, for a time, one of the leading English seaports. It employed some large ships of 150–250 tons, which brought their return cargoes, if there were any, back to Liverpool rather than Whitehaven. The slowing of Whitehaven's growth late in the century coincided with a sharp expansion in the coal export of the Welsh Bristol Channel ports.

Few details are known of the corn export trade which was to reach such large dimensions in the middle decades of the eighteenth century. The conditions on which the corn export bounty was paid prevented the employment of foreign ships. Yarmouth, its principal centre, employed many large ships ranging up to 400–500 tons, and the typical carrier of corn to Rotterdam from this port was about 200 tons. Many of these vessels were colliers, but at the height of the trade in the forties and fifties some were engaged in the corn trade nearly all the year round. The smaller ports — Lynn, Wells, Blakeney — which between them lifted a large proportion of the total tonnage apparently did so by diverting small craft from the coastal trade; for the corn trade had a marked seasonal peak from August to December, which might be prolonged in years of exceptionally high export for another two or three months.

The French wine trade, so long as it was a legal one, employed a large number of ships of all sizes. Many of these were chartered, but chartered or otherwise they were not sent out to lade full wine cargoes for single merchants, but depended at least in part on the master or supercargo picking up extra cargo through his own connections or brokers in Bordeaux, Sherant or Nantes.

While some of the ships were specifically engaged by English merchants to be directed to their factors in France, there was a large speculative element, and numbers of shipmasters went the rounds of the wine-shippers in the French ports during the season to look for parcels of cargo. The trade was unusual in having a seasonal peak in winter; indeed, Roger Coke complained of the trade in 1670 that it was carried on 'in the perillous months for Navigation of September, October, November and December' with great loss to ships and seamen.[1] A certain number of large Baltic traders switched to it in winter, but most of the smaller participants were diverted from more regular cross-Channel traffic and coasting.

Ships entering with wine from France, 1664

January	24
February	2
March	13
April	21
May	9
June	5
July	2
August	—
September	2
October	20
November	13
December	17

The coasting trade, which has been the subject of the monograph by Dr T. S. Willan already noticed, is not dealt with here. But it has an importance for all the nearby trades. Because of its enormous size — the tonnage of coal shipped coastwise from the north-east ports alone exceeded the whole volume of English imports in almost every year of our period — diversions could be made from it to meet special and unexpected peaks in the European trades. This immensely eased the transport problems posed at those peaks. Moreover, much of the coastal shipping was loosely connected with overseas trade; a large proportion of the ships plying the south and west coasts were diverted for occasional voyages when good opportunities offered themselves, to cross-Channel or Irish trade, and the east coast colliers took their turns at the supply of Continental needs as well as those of London.

[1] *Discourse of Trade* (1670), p. 38.

In the Dutch and German trades, and in trade with French Channel-ports and Ireland, there was not the excess of import volume found elsewhere. We should expect, therefore, that inward freight rates would, in these particular trades, have been lower than outward rates. Unfortunately, little can be positively said about these rates. Coal was usually carried in ships whose owners were themselves the coal traders; the corn trade has left few traces behind; most other goods were shipped in small parcels of not easily identifiable or comparable content; and except in the French wine trade chartering was rare. The homeward freight for French wine rose from 27s. to 28s. from Nantes or Bordeaux in the 1630's and 40's[1] to between 35s. and 40s. after the Restoration; no doubt if the trade had continued the rates would ultimately have declined as others did. Charter rates in this trade were slightly higher, the masters taking outward cargoes freight free.

NEARBY EUROPE

1. TONNAGE OF ENTRANCES AND CLEARANCES (000 TONS)

	1686		1715–17	1771–3	
	e	c	c	e	c
Germany	12·7 (3·5)	7·8 (2·7)	22·9 (4·5)	21·8 (8·6)	30·6 (9·1)
Holland	36·8 (2·6)	76·9 (4·1)	106·6 (4·8)	52·0 (14·0)	109·7 (9·8)
France and Flanders	82·5 (3·9)	41·5 (3·3)	17·6 (3·1)	40·3 (3·1)	63·8 (5·7)
Ireland and C.I.	48·6 [13·5]	61·4 [17·3]	87·4 (0·3)	104·4 (2·9)	282·6 (0·1)
Scotland	6·2 (3·2)	2·7 (1·9)			

Note: Irish ships, enclosed in square brackets above, are not included as 'foreign' in the totals in Chapter IX. Scottish ships, and English ships trading to Scotland, are not included in the totals in Chapter IX.

2. VALUE OF TRADE (£000)

	1699–1701 av.		1771–3 av.	
	Imports	Exports	Imports	Exports
Germany	732	779	641	1336
Holland	518	1787	389	1852
Flanders	68	252	107	887
France	100	204	50	241
Ireland and C.I.	332	290	1290	1956
Scotland	97	77	—	—

Note: Scottish trade is not included in the totals in Chapter IX.

[1] The Privy Council attempted to fix the rate in 1616 at 27s. from Sherant and Rochelle and 30s. from Bordeaux (APC 1615–16, p. 612). Sir William Monson says the rate from Bordeaux was 24s. a ton before the war of 1624 (M. Oppenheim (ed.), *The Naval Tracts of Sir William Monson* (Navy Record Society 1902–14), Vol. V., p. 313).

3. CHIEF ENGLISH PORTS ENGAGED IN NEARBY TRADES

	1686 number		1715–17 av. out	
(a) *Continental trade*	in	out	no.	tons
London	820	465	496 (101)	28·5 (6·3)
Newcastle	67	400	266 (26)	27·0 (2·2)
Sunderland	27	248	359 (8)	32·1 (0·3)
Yarmouth	93	82	200	17·0
Hull	44	71	84 (6)	6·2 (0·7)
Wisbech	5	3	121 (20)	5·9 (0·5)
(b) *Irish trade*				
Whitehaven	154	258	474	39·3
Liverpool	130	135	287	9·4
Chester	87	141	144	6·6
Swansea and Neath	1	78	145	5·3
London	41	51	68	4·9
Lancaster	29	49	136	4·3
Bristol	88	63	108	4·3
Minehead	107	26	6	0·2
Barnstaple and Bideford	99	66	77	1·0

4. AVERAGE TONNAGE OF INDIVIDUAL ENGLISH SHIPS

		1686	1715–17 clearances	1726 entries	1766 entries
Germany:	London	136	97	117	129
	outports	90	90		
Holland:	London	80	58	91	82
	outports	70	73		
Flanders:	London	30	31	40	95
	outports	30	33		
France:	London	99	38	43	61
	outports	40	43		
Ireland:	London	60	72	63	65
	outports	44	47		

Legislators, officials, pamphleteers and traders were all concerned, in the third quarter of the seventeenth century, to find
ways of securing for English ships the lion's share of the enormous
traffic between England and the Scandinavian and Baltic harbours.[1]
Yet this important traffic was the growth of very recent decades.

[1] There is a considerable literature in English on the Northern trades, though
only certain aspects of them are dealt with. R. W. K. Hinton, *The Eastland
Trade and the Common Weal* (Cambridge, 1959), deals with the seventeenth
century. D. K. Reading, *The Anglo-Russian Commercial Treaty of 1734* (New
Haven, Conn., 1938), has much information on trading methods, as have two
works on timber trade. R. G. Albion, *Forests and Sea Power* (Cambridge,
Mass., 1926), and P. W. Bamford, *Forests and French Sea Power* (Toronto,
1956). J. J. Oddy, *European Commerce* (1805), is particularly concerned with
the Northern trades. The great source of printed material for Baltic shipping,
however, is N. Bang and K. Korst (eds.), *Tabeller over Skibsfart of Varetransport
Gebbem Oresund* (Copenhagen, 1906–53). I am indebted to Dr S.-E. Åström
for advice on this section.

English demand for timber, iron, flax and hemp, potash, pitch and tar from abroad, which was so vast by 1670, had risen from small proportions at the beginning of the century. The impetus had come from a number of sources; the increased demand for softwoods in house-building, especially after the Great Fire of London in 1666; the great expansion of naval shipbuilding from the time of the Commonwealth onward; the outstripping by the iron-fabricating industries of the capacity of the iron producers in England. In addition, the development of English sea traffic with the Northern countries was a reflection of the growth of the shipping industry itself and its insatiable appetite for shipbuilding materials. After 1651 the exclusion of Dutch carriers from the trade by the Navigation Act gave the task of carrying these goods principally to English shipping, though Norwegian and Swedish vessels took an increasingly important part.[1]

At the beginning of the seventeenth century some pitch and tar, flax and hemp and a little timber (chiefly masts) came into England from North Russia, Norway and the Baltic; corn was brought intermittently from Danzig — occasionally, as in 1609, 1625–6 and in several years of the thirties, in large quantities;[2] and at times Asiatic goods were brought across Russia to Narva or Archangel and shipped to England. The Eastland Company, founded in 1579 to take advantage of the trading privileges granted by the small port of Elbing, was a considerable exporter of cloth, and its principal return cargo was corn. The demand for other goods from the Baltic and Norway was expanding, however, and the importance of the Northern trades to the shipping industry was clearly understood. Already Englishmen appreciated the significance of a trade with vast bulky cargoes of cheap commodities and were alive to the danger of letting it slip wholly into the hands of the Dutch. As early as 1615 the merchants complained that the high freight rates of English ships in this trade compelled them to make use of foreigners, but the Privy Council on this occasion was able to bring shipowners and merchants together and 'so accommodated all those differences, and at so easy rates, as the merchants are well contented withal'.[3] There was, in fact,

---

[1] The act prohibited the import of most goods in foreign vessels other than those of the country of shipment.

[2] N. S. B. Gras, *The Evolution of the English Corn Market* (Cambridge, Mass., 1926), App. B.

[3] APC 1615–16, p. 257.

a rise in the employment of English ships in trade with the Baltic during the four decades before the Civil War, checked only temporarily by trade depression in the early twenties.[1] Before Dutch competition reached large dimensions the Dutch were engulfed in the Thirty Years' War, which from 1625 until 1647 kept their freight rates for Northern voyages more than fifty per cent above the peacetime levels.[2] By the middle of the century regular demand for Norwegian and Baltic products in England was so great that the Northern trades had come to be leading users of English shipping tonnage, and when Dutch competition re-emerged in 1647 it was quickly countered by the Navigation Act of 1651. The expansion of the Northern trades never ceased, though the sources of the chief supplies of timber and iron were shifted, the extent of foreign participation in the carrying traffic underwent great changes, and the overall rate of growth was not constant.

The Northern trades fall into distinct sections; Norway, a timber supplier; Sweden, the great source of iron and, until after 1700, of pitch and tar; the East Baltic coasts with timber, hemp and flax, corn in the early seventeenth century and iron after the 1730's; and the White Sea with potash, hemp, flax and timber.[3]

Norway sent to England very little besides timber — deals and ships' masts and spars. Most of it came from the many small harbours on and around the mouth of Oslofiord; Drammen, Tønsberg, Langesund, Fredrikstad and, in the seventeenth century, the Swedish port of Gothenburg just across the frontier. Little of the timber was paid for by the export of goods from England, though shipments of coal to Norway were growing, and some corn was sent as an export surplus developed in England. The Norway timber trade, concerned chiefly with masts and spars in the early seventeenth century but extended gradually to other kinds of timber, grew to enormous size; for more than half a century it was the source providing a larger *volume* of English

---

[1] N. E. Bang and K. Korst, op. cit.

[2] J. Schreiner, *Nederland og Norge 1625–1650* (Oslo, 1933, pp. 112–61).

[3] Political frontiers around the Baltic underwent great alterations during the seventeenth and eighteenth centuries. Norway was part of the Danish kingdom; and the far south of Sweden was Danish until 1658. Finland, the territories round present-day Leningrad (with the port of Narva) and Estonia were Swedish, and in 1629 Livonia with the great port of Riga was taken by Sweden from the Poles; all this Swedish territory was overrun by Russia in 1704–14 and became part of the Russian Empire. The ports further south, except Prussian Konigsberg and Memel, were under Polish rule or suzerainty.

imports than any other. Late in the seventeenth century it stabilised at or near this high level, when the partial exhaustion of the most accessible woodland made it difficult to expand production further.[1]

All the English ports took some part in this timber trade, for these cargoes which could not bear the costs of unnecessary transshipment had to be carried by sea as nearly as possible to their ultimate destination. While London led the way in this as in other trades, it was closely followed by Hull; there were large imports from Norway into all the other east coast ports of any size — Newcastle, Lynn, Boston, Yarmouth — and the major ports elsewhere, such as Bristol and later Liverpool; lesser shipments went into every port round the English coast. London, however, used much larger ships than the outports; as early as 1660 they were usually over 200 and often around 300 tons, most of them at this time Dutch prizes, though it was still said that old ships useless for other trades found occupation here. In the eighteenth century ships entering London from Norway were almost of a standard size, 300–350 tons, and a large and growing proportion of them were owned in ports of the north-east coast. The outports, however, continued for a long time to use much smaller vessels; even at such busy centres of the trade as Hull and Newcastle the majority of timber traders in 1715–17 were of no more than 100 tons.

Dutch participation, which may have been considerable around 1620, and was certainly very large in the late forties, was checked by the Navigation Acts of 1651 and 1660. Though it was often complained in succeeding decades that the trade was thus thrown into the hands of Scandinavian shipowners, the contemporary statistics indicate that in fact it was shared fairly equally between English and foreign ships. The English possession of cheaply acquired Dutch flyboats gave them a strong competitive position.[2] In 1686 39 per cent of the tonnage of ships entering from Norway

---

[1] P. W. Bamford, op. cit., pp. 136–7. In a declining Norwegian timber trade, England maintained its absolute volume and so increased its share. This seems to explain England's dominant position in the timber trade in the late eighteenth century, suggested by S. Kjaerheim in his article 'Norwegian Timber Exports in the Eighteenth Century', *Scandinavian Economic History Review*, Vol. V, 1957, pp. 188–202.

[2] To meet the suddenly expanded demand for imported timber after the Great Fire of 1666, an Order-in-Council of April 1669 permitted the purchase of 60 more flyboats for the timber trade to supplement the existing fleet of prizes (*CSPD 1668–9*, pp. 290–1).

was foreign; in 1699–1701 just over half the deals imported came
in foreign vessels. The Great Northern War caused heavy destruction in the Norwegian merchant fleet,[1] and by 1715–17 foreign
participation in clearances for Norway had fallen as low as 7 per
cent.[2] Only in the forties did Norwegian shipping begin to recover
its position; by 1771–3 71 per cent of the tonnage of entries from
Norway and Denmark was foreign vessels — a much higher
proportion than in any other trade. The exaggerated view which
contemporaries held of the foreign share in this traffic in the late
seventeenth century may be partly due to the specially large role
played by foreign ships in London trade. Even so, England had
no reasonable complaint if a seafaring nation took a substantial
share in carrying the products of its own land; and in fact in the
later eighteenth century when this share was specially large
complaints were seldom heard.

The London trade in 1660–90 and around 1770 (and probably
in the intervening decades) was handled by a few very large
timber merchants.[3] These, and the merchants in the principal
outports engaged in the trade, maintained very close connections
with factors in Norway — often their own younger brothers or
cousins, or former apprentices — who bought on their behalf and
despatched timber to them on a commission basis. The London
merchants controlled, though they only partly owned, considerable
fleets of ships which they employed for their trade with Norway;
but in the outports a large proportion of the ships used, by
merchants large and small, were chartered. Many were drawn
from the Newcastle coal trade, for there was an important triangular traffic, with coal out of Newcastle or Sunderland to'
Holland, ballast to Norway, and a charter for timber cargo back
to London or a northern port. Ships also came in speculatively to
pick up such cargo as they could, purchasing timber if need be
on their owners' account; sometimes these were vessels which had
failed to get cargoes in the Baltic.[4] Generally, however, ships were

---

[1] A. N. Kiaer, 'Historical Sketch of the Development of Scandinavian
Shipping', *Journal of Political Economy*, Vol. I, 1893, pp. 329–64; Joshua Gee,
The Trade and Navigation of Great Britain Considered (4th ed., 1738), pp. 23–4.

[2] The proportion of entries was probably higher.

[3] On the organisation of the Norway trade see S. Kjaerheim, op. cit., pp.
191–202; R. G. Albion, op. cit., especially Ch. II, IV; H. S. K. Kent, 'The
Anglo-Norwegian Timber Trade in the Eighteenth Century, *Econ. Hist. Rev.*,
2nd ser., Vol. VIII, 1955–6.

[4] See, for example, J. R. Dendy and F. W. Boyle (ed.), *Extracts from the
Records of the Merchant Adventurers of Newcastle-upon-Tyne* (Surtees Society,

directed to their Norwegian loading ports with precise instructions which left their masters small discretion. Whole cargoes were loaded by single factors, usually for single merchants in England who paid for the goods by arranging to meet bills drawn on their Hamburg and Amsterdam agents;[1] there were no odd corners to be filled up by the master's dexterity in worming out small freights from foreign merchants. Leading English traders to Gothenburg in 1675 described themselves as 'seven or eight of the principal traders who actually had freighted many whole ships themselves and also had let many ships to freights'.[2] Outward cargoes were trivial and were handled by the factors, and there was no need to go beyond a very narrow range of ports for timber cargo. The master, therefore, was simply a navigator, with no independent role to play in the commercial operation of the ship.

Entries of ships from Norway and Gothenburg

	London 1686	Hull 1686	London 1736 (English ships only)
January	4	2	—
February	1	—	—
March	1	—	2
April	2	6	2
May	13	11	34
June	9	8	35
July	20	6	18
August	6	8	40
September	21	10	29
October	5	2	14
November	12	5	14
December	6	1	17

The total volume of the trade changed little from year to year. Changes in the level of imports reflected fluctuations in the demands by English merchants rather than in the amount of timber available for shipment, and nothing is heard of ships failing to secure the expected timber cargoes and going elsewhere. It was, however, a seasonal trade (though the season was a very long one) because owners were unwilling to employ their ships

1895, 1899), Vol. II, p. 140. N. E. Bang and K. Korst, op. cit., show English ships occasionally leaving the Baltic in ballast, and Oslofiord would be an obvious place of call for them.

[1] S. Kjaerheim, op. cit., pp. 197–8, shows that by the 1770's the English merchants were actually making long-term contracts and advance payments to the sawmill owners.

[2] HMC Lindsey MSS., p. 138.

in the North Sea in midwinter, and there was some danger of icing in the Norwegian harbours. Large fleets of vessels sailed from the English east coast ports at the end of March or the beginning of April, and plied to and fro across the North Sea until a final homecoming in December.

The voyage from England was short, sometimes taking as little as four days; turn-round in Norwegian harbours was quick — charter-parties usually allowing six to ten laydays — and the round voyage, including unloading in England and preparing to sail again, rarely took more than two months. The regular Norway trader from London or any east coast port made four or occasionally five round voyages a year, lying up in the home port from December to March.[1] There was no alternative occupation to which the larger Norway ships could be directed in winter; the trades which could use such ships had a corresponding winter hibernation.

All trade into the Baltic was governed to some extent by weather conditions. There was danger of icing in the Sound in midwinter, and the winter storms in North Sea and Baltic were severe. The North Baltic ports were completely blocked by ice during much of the winter. In every Baltic trade, therefore, ships sailed from England no earlier than March and tried to be out of the Baltic by November. The cost of being caught by the ice and compelled to winter was several months extra pay and victualling for the whole crew as well as some risk of damage, and masters were naturally inclined to take the most cautious view of the icing prospects.

Sweden was served by two main ports — Stockholm in the Baltic and Gothenburg outside it. Gothenburg, as we have seen, took a large part in the timber trade which was characteristic of the Norwegian harbours further north, but its share in this was rapidly declining by 1700. In the early seventeenth century pitch and tar made up the bulk of Swedish supplies to England, but they were rapidly surpassed in importance by iron; when the pitch and tar trade was lost to America soon after 1700, it was already small in relation to the iron import. Imports of Swedish iron continued to expand rapidly until, in the 1740's,

---

[1] Dr Kent's view (op. cit., p. 71) that six round voyages a year were normal, is not borne out by eighteenth-century evidence. It is apparently derived from the report of a Royal Commission of 1835.

the competition of Russian iron in the English market began to be felt; during most of the eighteenth century iron was the only Swedish product sent to England in any quantity.

The Swedish government, conscious that Europe found its iron, copper, pitch and tar essential and almost irreplaceable, regulated their production, merchanting and shipment in the interest of its own nationals. It was this policy which turned the English government towards the subsidisation of colonial pitch and tar in 1705 (which enabled the colonists very rapidly to capture most of the English market) and it had an important influence on the English attitude towards expansion of trade with Russia.[1]

The English ships engaged in the trade with Sweden were, with the exception of a handful of timber traders, quite small; ships of less than 100 tons came into Stockholm from London as well as the outports, and even in the mid-eighteenth century the average size of the London ships in the trade was only approaching 200 tons. Most of the cargo was of iron, which presented no problems of stowage.[2]

Until late in the seventeenth century most Swedish trade was carried on through the port of London, but the growth of the iron import gave an increasing importance to Hull, since it supplied the Sheffield and Birmingham areas with Swedish iron through the Ouse and Trent river networks; a smaller iron trade developed with Newcastle and other outports. Much of the iron brought to London was carried in Swedish ships, but these were less often seen in other ports. The smaller duties on iron which they paid in Sweden were counterbalanced after 1690 by heavier duties in England on import in foreign ships,[3] and in the eighteenth century, by the lower freights of English ships.[4] Nearly three-quarters of the Swedish iron imported in 1699 came in Swedish ships, but their share fell off sharply during the next few years and never recovered completely. Even so, one-third of the ships entering from Sweden in 1771–3 were foreign — a proportion exceeded only in the Norwegian trade.

A few eighteenth-century iron merchants owned their own ships, and some ships were chartered; but only the largest firms

---

[1] D. K. Reading, op. cit., Ch. IV.   [2] But see pp. 223–4, below.
[3] 2 William and Mary, c. 14. This act imposed an additional duty of 23s. a ton on iron brought in English ships, and 33s. per ton on iron brought in foreign.
[4] CO 388–39.

would take whole shiploads of iron, and all preferred to mix it with whatever other cargo might be available.. Usually, therefore, cargo space in the ships making the Swedish voyage was contracted for in parcels, either by the English merchants before the ships sailed from England, or by their factors in Sweden. Most of the ships engaged were regular carriers for the Swedish trade, their masters well-known to both English merchants and their Swedish factors, and to some extent their success and profitability depended on the goodwill the master acquired; he was therefore a more important person than his fellow in Norway trade.

The South and East Baltic had a varying range of products. There was little English trade with Stettin or the North German ports until Stettin grew in stature as a timber and corn trading centre in the mid-eighteenth century. The first port of real interest to the English was Danzig, the main outlet for the products of Poland and the western Ukraine and the principal grain port of Europe.[1] For England, however, it was more important after 1600 as a supplier of timber, potash and linen goods. Elbing, the old staple town of the Eastland Company, saw few English merchants after 1630, when they began to trade freely at Danzig. Konigsberg and later Memel had much the same commodities to offer as Danzig, with the addition of great quantities of flax. To the north of Memel, all the ports served flax and hemp country, from which vast and continuously increasing quantities were brought to England. The principal hemp port was Riga, the greatest flax supplier was Narva, though St Petersburg was overtaking both in the second quarter of the eighteenth century. Riga and St Petersburg also sent linens and timber (especially Riga masts); and St Petersburg was becoming a leading iron supplier from the 1730's onward.[2]

The East Baltic became, during the eighteenth century, an important market for English cloth; from the shipowners' point of view, however, the lead and tobacco which accompanied it in much greater volume were the more profitable commodities, and bulk trade outward was supplemented in the course of the century by growing exports of coal, salt and malt. Nevertheless, the trade

[1] A useful account of sea traffic at Danzig is W. Vogel, 'Beitrage zur Statistik der deutschen Seeschiffahrt im 17 v. 18 Jahrhundert', *Hansische Geschichtsblätter*, 1932, pp. 78–152 (see especially pp. 104–7).
[2] From Riga northwards the ports were always outlets for the products of Russia, even before they came under Russian political control.

was far from being balanced. Even in terms of value, there was an excess of imports which was met by cash payments at Riga and St Petersburg, supplemented by bills on Amsterdam. As to volume, the total of import cargoes was always far greater than that of exports, and the discrepancy would have grown had it not been for the development of some carrying trade from Southern Europe into the Baltic in English ships, as described below.

In the early seventeenth century the largest calls on shipping were those made spasmodically by the need for corn import to England in years of poor harvests. The corn was brought from Danzig and in smaller quantities from Stettin and Konigsberg, and since English shipping could not usually be found on the spot in adequate quantity, many foreign ships were chartered in the Baltic ports to take grain to England (with no provision for return cargoes). Such English ships as could be made available were chartered and sent out in ballast to load corn.

Entries of ships from Petersburg, Narva, Riga and
Memel, at London

	1686	1766
January	2	10
February	1	4
March	—	3
April	—	—
May	2	—
June	14	5
July	18	38
August	5	19
September	9	5
October	9	30
November	3	22
December	2	18

Apart from this irregular corn trade, which died out almost completely before mid-century, the principal import trades in the seventeenth century were with the ports from Memel northward for timber, hemp and flax. The traffic began to grow very fast at the end of the century, stimulated by the breaking of the English Muscovy Company's monopolistic ring in 1698, the revelation in wartime of the need to shake off dependence upon Sweden for naval stores and iron, the Russian acquisition of a large stretch of the northern and eastern coastline of the Baltic, Peter the Great's encouragement of commerce, and the commercial treaty with Russia in 1734. After this treaty was made, as Russian iron began to come forward in vast quantities, business with the whole East Baltic began to expand at a pace unmatched, for a time, by that with any other area.

The season in the Northern Baltic was very short; ships had to be clear of the Gulf of Finland and the Gulf of Riga in October, and might not be able to re-enter before May. In this short summer it was usual for a ship to make two round voyages from England, sailing early in April for a cargo to be landed in July or early August, and hurriedly clearing again to be back in England for the winter in November or early December. This was possible only with a quick turn-round in both the Baltic and the English ports.

Though there were many regular carriers in these trades their ships were small in the seventeenth century — most of them between 80 and 150 tons, with a handful of larger vessels. Apart from timber (which presumably employed the larger ships) the total volume of cargoes was not very great and the large ship therefore ran considerable risk of being only part-laden. The flocks of small vessels disappeared quite suddenly with the sharp acceleration in the rate of growth of these trades in the mid-eighteenth century; Riga and St Petersburg became in the sixties the resort of many of the largest English ships outside the East India trade — ships of 400–600 tons, which need no longer fear deficiency of cargo.

Tonnage of individual English ships entering
London from north-east Baltic

	over 300	200–299	150–199	100–149	*under* 100
1726	9	—	24	42	25
1766	83	14	2	1	—

Until this late development of very large ships, few were specialised to Baltic trade, and it was common practice to make a winter voyage to the Bay of Biscay to lade French wine.

In the Baltic ports as elsewhere in the North, English merchants were well served by factors closely tied to them, though after the middle of the eighteenth century some of the English factors developed great independent merchant houses in Riga and St Petersburg. The factors arranged for shipments to be ready, and themselves sometimes chartered ships which became available in their ports. Until the full development of the Russian iron trade, the sending of ships to lade goods for their own managing owners was not common. Some ships were chartered, but few merchants or factors could provide full cargoes, and among the smaller vessels were many regular traders which took out mixed English cargoes and brought back parcels of Baltic commodities laded by various factors. The influence of the masters with English merchants and Baltic factors was of some importance to successful operation, though it was tending to diminish; many masters managed their ships with little control from their owners, and had a high status.

Finally, there was the Russian White Sea trade. It had been opened by English merchants in 1553, when Russia had no Baltic outlet. For a while all the varied products of Russia came through Archangel — timber, potash, flax, hemp, wax — and later it handled Persian wares. This English trade was almost destroyed by Dutch competition in the seventeenth century; only a handful of merchants continued to trade there until the end of the Muscovy Company's monopoly in 1698. The trade revived along with the general development of the Russian economy under Peter the Great — despite the new competition of St Petersburg — and in the mid-eighteenth century there was a moderate, though violently fluctuating, iron and timber traffic.[1] Moreover, this was by now being supplemented by the considerable timber trade of the Onega region, which English traders had begun to open up. Only a handful of ships was employed, chartered by the small ring of merchants who specialised in this trade, but they were always very large ones, and the Onega timber trade of the 1760's and after saw ships of 600 and 700 tons.[2]

In the Northern trades as a whole, freight rates were surprisingly stable over a very long period. Sir William Warren claimed that timber freight rates from Gottenberg were 12s. per ship ton in 1664,[3] and receives support from a handful of Admiralty Court cases. Forty years earlier English ships were carrying Norwegian

[1] The seventeenth century White Sea trade is discussed in A. Ohberg, 'Russia and the World Market in the 17th Century', *Scand. Econ. Hist. Rev.*, Vol. III, 1955.
[2] The size of Archangel-built ships surprised Samuel Kelly in 1782. 'Some of these ships are fifteen or sixteen hundred tons burthen, and at that time were allowed to be purchased by British merchants' (C. Garstin, *Samuel Kelly, an Eighteenth Century Seaman* (New York, 1925), p. 63).
[3] HMC Lindsey MSS., pp. 123, 138.

timber for between 9s. and 11s. a ton, and Dutch peacetime rates were probably not lower than this.[1] A hundred years later, Mr Kent assures us, peacetime rates were between 40s. and 50s. a hundred deals, or 10–11s. per ship ton.[2] If the view conveyed by these figures is correct, there was no substantial change in peace-time timber freights from Norway during more than one-and-a-half centuries — between the 1620's and 1790. Data for the main Baltic trades are very scanty, but seem to suggest a similar long-term stability in freight rates for the principal bulk commodity, flax and hemp in bales. A Privy Council decision in 1616 fixed the summer rate for carrying these at 40s. per last (of two tons or a little more),[3] and this rate is encountered right up to 1750, with only small variations except in wartime.

Freight rates for iron from both Sweden and Russia (and, incidentally, from America as well) were peculiar. In many places where there were large cargoes of goods bulky in relation to their weight, there was a demand for heavy goods placed low down in the ship, taking virtually none of the space required for the main cargo, but giving added stability. Iron, as a ballast cargo of this kind, might be carried at an extremely low rate. In 1616, when iron imports from Sweden were small, the Privy Council set the rate of freight at 3s. 9d. per ton — alongside hemp, flax, pitch and tar at 20s.[4] As iron shipments became larger and ultimately dominated Swedish trade, and later and less completely Russian trade as well, the iron traders ceased to be able to exploit a position as shippers of a small quantity of a commodity much coveted as a cargo. When this happened — when large numbers of ships had to be brought to the Baltic for the specific purpose' of fetching iron cargoes — iron had to start paying regular rates, and thereafter only at particular times and places did it tem-porarily enjoy the advantages of being a ballast cargo. In a transitional year in the Russian iron trade, 1752, John Okill paid for two separate consignments of iron from St Petersburg at rates of 5s. and 20s. a ton.[5] In the eighteenth century Swedish iron always had to pay its way fully; Henry Maister in the 1720's paid 26s. per last (of two tons) from Gothenburg and 30s. or 32s. 6d.

---

[1] Schreiner, op. cit., 112–61. His earliest and latest freight rates are little affected by war conditions.
[2] Kent, op. cit., p. 73.   [3] APC 1615–16, pp. 611–14.   [4] ibid.
[5] Okill MSS., Liverpool Public Library. He was paying 50s. a ton for freight of hemp at the same time.

from Stockholm;[1] the rate from Stockholm in English ships in 1737 was said to be 30s. a last.[2]

One of the most important functions of the Dutch shipping industry during the seventeenth and eighteenth centuries was the transportation of bulky cargoes between Northern and Southern Europe — salt, supplemented by wine and tropical goods, from the South; corn, supplemented by timber, potash, flax, hemp and iron from the North.[3] Englishmen looked enviously on this vast traffic, but no English legislation could help them to a share of it, and in open competition they found it difficult to compete. Nevertheless, English ships occasionally took part; as early as 1621 the *William & Thomas* was chartered to go from London to lade corn at Danzig to be carried to Bayonne; when the charterers' agents at Danzig failed to provide the cargo, the master himself secured one for Lisbon.[4] English shipping met and seized its great opportunity, however, in 1674, when for four years England was in the happy position of being the only neutral among the leading maritime powers. Many Admiralty Court cases deal with voyages between the Baltic and Spain or Portugal in those years; passes issued by the Admiralty to protect English ships in the Baltic show that great numbers of them were bringing cargoes, especially salt, from Southern Europe;[5] and the Sound Tables tell the story very clearly:[6]

Ships entering the Baltic from France, Spain, Portugal and the Mediterranean

	English	Dutch
av. 1668–71	7	158
av. 1675–8	128	28
av. 1679–82	47	179

To some extent these figures exaggerate the extent of the transfer of business from Dutch to English hands, for there were many fraudulent sales of Dutch ships to temporary English owners, Admiralty passes were obtained for foreigners, and there

---

[1] Maister MSS., Hull University Library.
[2] CO 388–39. In Swedish ships it was 35s.
[3] A. E. Christensen, *Dutch Trade to the Baltic about 1600* (Copenhagen, 1941), diagrams 20–21.
[4] HCA 13–106 (a bad harvest year in the Mediterranean).
[5] SP 44–49.
[6] N. E. Bang and K. Korst, op. cit.

was misdescription of the ownership of cargoes.[1] Nevertheless, English ships undoubtedly did take a greatly increased share in the North-South carrying trade, and maintained some small part of it even after the coming of general peace with the Treaty of Nijmwegen in 1678. The foothold which was maintained, particularly in the carriage of Portuguese salt to the Baltic, was lost when England was at war, but it was recovered and considerably expanded after 1713.

The importance for England of participating in this trade was that it could provide the cargoes into the Baltic which English ships otherwise had such difficulty in finding. In the eighteenth century coal, malt, and from the 1740's Cheshire salt were going into the Baltic in considerable quantities, yet as late as 1738 more than half of the English ships which went directly from England passed through the Sound in ballast, and many others carried cargoes of trivial volume. But the 253 ships coming direct from England in that year were accompanied by 105 English ships with cargoes from Southern Europe or beyond — from Sicily, the Balearic Islands, Setubal, Lisbon and Cadiz, from the Cape Verde Islands and the south of France, almost all of them carrying cargoes of salt, a few with wine.[2] England's share of Southern traffic with the Baltic was exceptionally good in 1738, but in most peace years up to the Seven Years War it was a substantial one.

Even at this time, however, English ships engaged only in a one-way traffic from Southern Europe. They were not, like many of the Dutch vessels, occupied entirely with a carrying trade between foreign countries, but rather in a mixed trade in which the taking of Baltic cargoes to England was an important component. Possibly the eighteenth-century growth of the traffic was associated with English corn export to Southern Europe; certainly it collapsed in the sixties and seventies with the disappearance of that export. Many ships which sailed from England to Portugal with corn went back to Riga or Petersburg with salt, and came home to England with hemp, flax and iron; for fifty years this was an important three-cornered trade. Very few English ships shared in the export of Baltic corn to the Mediterranean, which gave the Dutch such great employment; a handful took Russian hides to

[1] The State Papers, Domestic, of 1675 and 1676 are full of discussion of these matters.
[2] CO 388–37 (Y. 122).

Leghorn, but most were homeward bound when they laded at the Baltic ports.

One way and another during our period — through the growth of an English trade with the Baltic which was kept out of Dutch hands, and through the development of a modest share in the North-South carrying trade — England slowly drew towards equality with the Dutch in the Baltic, the original and the final stronghold of Dutch maritime supremacy. The Sound Tables again tell the story:

Ships entering the Sound[1]

	Dutch	English
1618	1,794	90
1698	1,028	228
1778	1,161	803

To the Dutch, Baltic trade remained of overwhelming importance to the prosperity of their shipping industry, and its stagnation was disastrous to them. The expanding English Baltic connection, however, was being overtaken and overshadowed by the growth of transoceanic commerce; and it was, to a large extent, itself the by-product of the overall growth of the shipping industry and the large demands this industry made for Baltic products.

NORTHERN EUROPE

1. Tonnage of Entrances and Clearances (000 Tons)

	1686		1715–17	1771–3	
	e	c	c	e	c
Norway	80·8 (34·1)	33·2 (14·1)	30·1 (1·9)	91·3 (64·4)	47·0 (25·0)
Russia	1·3	1·9	6·3	84·7 (0·3)	15·8
Baltic, ex Russia	58·4 (22·1)	20·1 (5·5)	11·5 (1·4)	89·7 (25·0)	19·9 (8·4)
Iceland, Greenland	1·1 (0·5)			14·5	6·6

2. Value of Trade (£000)

	1699–1701		1771–3	
	I	E	I	E
Norway and Denmark	71	42	80	158
'East Country'	176	153	189	90
Sweden	123	62	170	52
Russia	213	78	1045	162
Greenland			18	

[1] N. E. Bang and K. Korst, op. cit. The average tonnage of the ships, both English and Dutch, increased greatly over this period.

3. CHIEF ENGLISH PORTS IN NORTHERN TRADES

	1686		1715–17	
	No. of ships		Ships out	
	in	*out*	*no.*	*tons*
London	412	185	114 (10)	21·3 (1·4)
Hull	109	54	30	2·6
Newcastle	61	4	76 (9)	10·4 (1·2)
Lynn	54	28	18	1·6
Yarmouth	31	8	28	3·9

4. CHIEF PORTS, 1715–17, TRADING TO DIFFERENT COUNTRIES

	Total		Norway		Russia		Other Baltic	
	no.	*tons*						
London	114	21·3	65	14·1	26	4·4	23	2·8
Newcastle	76	10·4	26	2·4	8	1·1	42	6·9
Hull	30	2·6	19	1·5	3	0·3	8	0·8
Yarmouth	28	3·9	26	3·6	1	0·1	1	0·2
Lynn	18	1·6	18	1·6				

5. AVERAGE TONNAGE OF INDIVIDUAL ENGLISH SHIPS

		1686	*1715–17c*	*1726e*	*1766e*	*1771–3e*
Norway	L	201	228	252	268 ⎫	141
	O	n.a.	94		⎭	
Russia	L	213	165	136	265 ⎫	171
	O	—	116		⎭	
Baltic	L	209	126	119	159 ⎫	216
	O	135	136		⎭	

XI

The Southern European and Mediterranean Trades

England had an old-established trade with Spain and Portugal;[1] there were settlements of English merchants at Lisbon and San Lucar (near Cadiz) before the end of the fifteenth century, and despite the political conflicts which repeatedly shook the trade for over a century after the Reformation, economic relations were always renewed and tightened; this political struggle did not, like the later Anglo-French rivalry, cause a prolonged severance of economic ties. The main lines of English import trade with Spain changed little during the seventeenth and eighteenth centuries. Wine was the chief import, already in 1604 coming principally from Malaga rather than from Seville or Cadiz; the quantity increasing during the seventeenth century but eventually stabilised and even declining in the face of competition from French smuggling and the favoured Portuguese product. Olive oil, a vital raw material of the woollen industry, came in great tonnage from southern Spain, but the import began to be supplemented, before the middle of the seventeenth century, by an Italian supply. Fruit (chiefly raisins from Malaga and Alicante, but also including oranges and lemons from Seville) was a large import, growing constantly until after 1713. The products of Spanish America — especially cochineal, indigo and logwood — came in from Cadiz; valuable though these cargoes were, their total tonnage was too small to be of importance to shipping. From the Biscay coast, chiefly from Bilbao, quantities of iron were brought to the western ports, and growing cargoes of wool to Bristol and Exeter.

Portugal had more difficulty in finding cargoes of goods saleable in England.[2] In the early years of the seventeenth century none

[1] Sketches of Spanish and Portuguese trade will be found in J. O. Mac-Lachlan, *War and Trade with Old Spain* (Cambridge, 1940) and V. M. Shillington and A. B. W. Chapman, *Commercial Relations of England and Portugal*. I am indebted to Mr H. W. Taylor for advice on this section.
[2] From 1580 to 1640, Portugal was part of the dominions of the Spanish crown.

of its native products was specially wanted; sugar from Brazil was the trading staple and supplied the English market until, after mid-century, English West Indian sugar began to replace it. There was always a small import of Portuguese fruit — figs, oranges and lemons — and this grew steadily; and a large tonnage of salt went to Bristol and the south-western ports. Port wine import was expanding in the years after 1689, and the customs preference established by the Methuen Treaty of 1704 greatly strengthened its competitive position in the English market. Becoming the chief supplier of legally imported wine, Portugal had at last acquired a firm basis for its trade with England.

These imports from Spain and Portugal, rather precariously maintained, were paid for, and much more than paid for, by almost continuously expanding English exports of woollen textiles; before 1700 the Iberian Peninsula had become England's best market.[1] Lead and tin, though small in value, helped to fill up the outward bound ships, and quantities of colonial goods, especially pepper, went to Spain. From the early years of the eighteenth century, the harbours of Cornwall sent out large numbers of tiny craft laden with salt pilchards, and there was a small coal export from South Wales. Manufactures in some variety — brass- and iron-wares, beaver hats — were despatched in rapidly growing quantities. The excess of export values was increased in a way which played a key role in the supply of shipping for the trade; Newfoundland cod, caught by English and colonial fishermen, was taken in great quantities directly from the fishing grounds to Spain.[2] To all this was added, from the end of the seventeenth century, a rapidly growing export of corn to Spain and Portugal which eventually reached great dimensions, and tipped the balance of volume of total traffic heavily on the side of exports.

The Spanish and Portuguese trades with England saw a spectacular rise in the first half of the seventeenth century, as they came into the first rank of English outlets for woollen goods. Thereafter, while exports continued to grow, both the value and the volume of imports tended to stagnate. Throughout the century

---

[1] The importance of the Spanish and Portuguese markets to England owed much to the development of the colonial possessions, which were supplied with English goods through Seville and Lisbon.

[2] In the official reports sent annually to the English Board of Trade on the Newfoundland fishery, the price being realised for fish was always quoted in Spanish reals (CO 390–6).

after the Restoration there was little change in the total value of the import trade, though within the total Portugal's share rose while Spain's fell.

During the seventeenth century most of this trade was carried on with London, Bristol in second place lagging far behind. Other ports had only a very small share in import trade, though many of them imported some wine directly. This provincial wine trade grew rapidly in the next century, and after 1750 Liverpool and Hull were beginning to rival London and Bristol in their port wine shipments. In the handling of cheap goods the Cornish, Devon and South Wales ports were very active with their import of wool and iron and export of coal and pilchards. The developing corn export of the eighteenth century was carried on partly from the ports of the south and south-west coast, but London took a large share in it.

The chief Spanish port which English ships frequented was Cadiz. It was in a sense a base for the whole Mediterranean trade, a discharging point touched by all ships going to Italy and the Levant, and one from which they often took in extra cargoes for Mediterranean ports. The few ships returning directly from Cadiz to England normally carried olive oil, oranges and lemons or colonial wares. Every ship that called there, whether outward or homeward bound, could expect to take aboard some silver bullion; William Osgodby deposed in 1673 that he had commanded ships trading to Cadiz for twenty years, and

'every such voyage made by him . . . he did receive silver and plate and pieces of eight and gold aboard his said ship lying in the Bay of Cadiz to be transported to England for account of English and other merchants'.[1]

The chief wine port of Spain was Malaga, which was served more by the 'sack ships' from Newfoundland than by ships coming out directly from England. At Malaga, as at Denia, Alicante and Barcelona, raisins made up substantial cargoes. Iron and most of the wool imported came from Galicia, and these commodities were usually shipped at Bilbao. Lisbon for a long time stood far ahead of all other Portuguese trading centres and it was, though to a lesser extent than Cadiz, a base for Mediterranean trade. When wine began to play a significant part in Anglo-Portuguese trade after 1689, Oporto rapidly overhauled Lisbon as the chief

[1] HCA 13–77.

centre of the wine trade, though Lisbon continued to do a more varied business.

From the point of view of shipping, much the most important homeward cargoes were wine, raisins and olive oil. Raisins could be had in Spain in August; the loading period for Spanish wine began in September and reached a peak in the two following months; by February wine and raisins were nearly gone. Olive oil, too, was usually shipped during the winter months.

Number of ships entering London from Southern Spain

	1664 ships with wine, only	1686	1751
January	3	38	15
February	3	12	7
March	9	11	18
April	5	11	10
May	1	7	7
June	2	10	8
July	—	6	2
August	—	16	2
September	—	4	2
October	—	5	1
November	22	14	19
December	23	10	16

Port came rather later, with shipment spread fairly evenly over the winter and spring. This was partly due to the difficulty of getting wine down to the mouth of the Douro during the winter floods; more important, perhaps, when the trade was fully developed in the eighteenth century, was the growth in Portugal of well-capitalised firms of English wine merchants, able to hold stocks on the spot for maturing or for the most favourable market.

Number of ships entering London from Portugal, 1751

January	15
February	10
March	12
April	13
May	15
June	14
July	13
August	13
September	5
October	10
November	8
December	8

In time of peace the volume of traffic was fairly regular, with a long-term tendency for port shipments to increase. Inevitably, there were year to year variations, but as overland communications with England were very rapid, a shortage or surplus of ships for Portugal and Spain need rarely occur and could be rapidly adjusted. Occasionally a vessel which came out directly from England was quite unable to find a cargo to expectation; like the *John*, which, in 1663 unable to get a wine or fruit cargo at Malaga, went off on a round voyage to New England, Barbados and New England again, and ultimately returned to Spain in the following season with a cargo of fish.[1] The trading ships from Newfoundland, however, had to be committed to either the Spanish, the English or the West Indian market before the summer's effect on the vines could be fully estimated, and they might appear in excessive numbers. Even so, ships disappointed of freight at Cadiz or Malaga could often hope to find cargoes if they pushed on into the Mediterranean; the position of Cadiz and its role as information centre for Mediterranean shipping made for great flexibility in local offerings of cargo space.

Late in the seventeenth century, a new and erratic feature entered into these trades, with the beginning of large corn shipments to Spain and Portugal. By the second decade of the eighteenth century the volume of these shipments not only exceeded that of all other exports put together but usually outtopped the tonnage of all imports from Spain and Portugal; the volume balance of the trade was reversed. All corn trades were subject to great fluctuation and this one more than most. The ships used were usually chartered, and chartered for the outward voyage only, coming into the owners' hands again when they had discharged the grain cargo at the overseas port. Though the shipping could spread out through the Mediterranean to find homeward cargoes, it must have created great difficulties in the freight market in Spain and Portugal, particularly in the spring and early summer when the bulk of the corn was delivered. In the early days of this corn export, the *Dorothy* of Poole was chartered to take 637 quarters of wheat to Cadiz. Arrived there, the master discharged, received his freight and remitted it home; unable to secure a homeward cargo, he sailed for the Cape Verde Islands. Here he took in a full lading of 180 tons of salt, which he

[1] HCA 15–8.

carried across the Atlantic and sold in the island of Nevis. Thence the ship went in ballast to Maryland, where a cargo of tobacco on freight for London was secured, and she arrived home fifteen months after sailing on the short Cadiz voyage.[1]

Large shipments of corn were made up from the southern English ports, but most went out from London and a great part of the corn export trade was financed, as one might expect, by those with the best Iberian connections, the wine merchants.[2]

The ships which carried cargoes to and from this corner of Europe were drawn into the traffic in a variety of ways. The quite distinct north Spain trade was served in the main by a numerous group of tiny trading and fishing vessels (averaging only 30 to 40 tons even in the latter part of our period) which carried pilchards and occasionally cod from Devon and Cornish ports. From the latter part of the seventeenth century they were supplemented by a growing number of small colliers from Swansea, Neath and Llanelly; and all these vessels occasionally laded corn in small harbours of Dorset or Hampshire. They brought back wool for the West Country cloth industries, and Bilbao iron. Little is known about these small craft; some were possibly engaged in pilchard fishing during the season, others in coastal or cross-Channel traffic or the trade with Ireland, and there were certainly a few which voyaged to the Biscay coast all the year round.[3] Small ships belonging to the Biscay ports themselves also engaged in the wool and iron trades — almost the only Spanish ships ever to appear in English harbours in peacetime.

The south Spain and Portugal trades, despite some differences between them, may be considered together. They were served by several streams of English ships. In the first place there were numbers of regular traders, always particularly important in the Portuguese traffic and growing considerably during the eighteenth century; ships making two or three annual voyages to Lisbon, Malaga or Cadiz. Such a vessel was the *Ceres*, which two or three times every year from her building in 1751 to some time after 1768 came into London from Oporto; a ship of about 120 tons, quite typical of the regular Portugal and Andalusia traders of her

---

[1] HCA 15–11, 24–123.
[2] *House of Commons Journals, 1705–8*, p. 143; *1714–18*, p. 185.
[3] A ship of 120 tons was too big for the Bilbao trade in 1714; 'We arrived theair in about Ten days, but with difficulty to get over theair bar, drawing so much watter' (J. Cremer, *Ramblin' Jack* (ed. R. R. Bellamy, 1936), p. 66).

time and long before.[1] In the second quarter of the seventeenth century, when the corsair danger was at its peak, much larger ships were commonly used, but as this danger faded the regular carrier of 80–120 tons was found to be most economical. These ships carried cloth out all the year round, usually finding sufficient return cargoes, if not in the staples (oil, wine, fruit) then in such minor commodities as shumack or cork; even at a pinch filling up with salt, though this was rather unprofitable because freight had to be pared to the bone for so cheap a cargo. There was no question of the 'regular' trader lying up for the winter, for the main branches of the Iberian trade, as we have seen, had a winter peak.

Secondly, additional ships were sent out in the autumn and early winter by London and Bristol merchants to their Spanish factors or partners. Sometimes these were ships managed by the merchants themselves (at times with part-owners drawn from their English friends in Lisbon or Malaga); very often they were chartered. On the whole they were larger than the regular traders. In all the major Portuguese and Spanish ports there were well-established English firms; the substantial merchant in England had regular relations with one or more of them and had indeed often served some years in Spain after completing his own apprenticeship. Outward cargoes were consigned to them; they prepared return cargoes in advance, arranged for ladings on freight and for the remittance of money, and sent a continuous stream of information on local commercial conditions and prices. Paul Dent in Malaga wrote a typical factor's letter to his London principal in February 1702:

Sr

My last to you was the 7th crrt, and your post came to hand Yours of the 5th with Bill of Lading for 40 bayes laden on the Resolution Capt Darby whoe as yet appeares not. When God willing he does shall have a quick dispatch his cargo, being all provided and your 10 tonns also in ½ fruit and ½ oyles and no peece fruit, being very badd and decae this yeare which made me forbeare buying any for you, and as soone as you advised me said ship comeing out I made provision for her which I could not doe had I stayed until she was assured, by reason that fruit and oyle requires time to have it brought from the Counttry and had any freight offered since the vintage ships went

[1] From the London records of Seamen's Sixpences, Adm. 68–194 *et seq.*

away I had certainly shipped barrel fruit for you, but none offereing I think I have done well.[1]

The masters of these ships were very much in the hands of the owners' or charterers' agents. They were committed to taking the cargoes brought forward for their principals by the merchants in Spain, but this cargo, virtually guaranteed though it was, was rarely enough to fill the ship; the merchants and agents, or the master himself, had to go out and seek further cargo. In good years the ships committed in this way were likely to be the first to complete their ladings; in bad years when there was sharp competition for cargo they might be the ones to suffer. Having a certain part-cargo of seasonal commodities, they could not go far afield in the Mediterranean in search of further ladings, or wait indefinitely to be filled up, for merchants had to be encouraged to use these ships by the expectation that their cargoes would arrive in the forefront of the market rather than straggle in at its tail. Difficulties were sometimes overcome by joint chartering of a ship by several merchants who had small cargoes in prospect. In the early part of the seventeenth century charter-parties arc often found in which the ship's capacity is divided into lots of 10, 15 or 20 tons, each lot taken up by one of the contracting merchants; but this practice quickly died out after the Restoration; presumably because the trade was becoming better organised and difficulties in getting cargo were less extreme.[2]

The third group of ships was made up of those bringing fish from Newfoundland. Fishing boats and the first of the sack ships sailed from English ports in March or April; they were followed during the summer by other sack ships, whose owners and charterers had made arrangements with earlier departures to buy fish on their behalf. Many of them called at French Biscay ports (or later on, at Setubal in Portugal) to load some salt for the fishery; some were ballasted with lead which would ultimately be sold in Spain or the Mediterranean; as the Newfoundland settlements grew, so did the practice of taking out provisions to them from Ireland. Late in August all the ships were leaving the Banks, and by the end of September they were beginning to arrive in

[1] HCA 24–129.
[2] For the same reasons time charters, which were not uncommon in these trades up to 1640, disappeared thereafter. They, too, reflected uncertainty as to the possibilities of getting cargoes without long delay or resort to several ports.

Cadiz and Malaga, or more rarely in Bilbao, Lisbon, Alicante or
Barcelona. There the fish was sold; the proceeds might be used
to buy a cargo of fruit or wine, but usually a part of it was remitted
direct to England, and some cargo on freight was sought from the
English factors. These sack ships, which were of every size up
to 200 tons — mostly coming from London or Bristol and many
of them chartered by London merchants — in normal years lifted
a great part of the seasonal peak cargo of Malaga wine and raisins.
When ships were chartered for this triangular trading voyage,
freight was calculated for the whole voyage at a rate per ton of
fish delivered at the discharging port, whatever the final homeward
cargo.[1] The instructions given to the master of an early sack ship
illustrate the structure and problems of the trade:

A Memorandum for Master Thomas Breadcake, master of the Ship
called the Faith of London of about 240 tonnes whome God preserve.
1. You are to make all haste possible you cann to be att the Newfoundland att or before the five and twentieth day of Julie next,
according to Charter Partie the copie whereof I give you; pray have a
spetiall care that you lose no tyme for it doth much concerne me to be
first at markett, in the saille of my fishe.
2. Att your arrival att Newfoundland you are to receive there of the
Ship called the Eagle of Dartmouth of about 300 Tonns John Talier
Master, the quantity of two thousand quintalls of good merchantable
drie Newfoundland fishe of 112 lbs. weight to the quintall, which I
bought of Master Richard Lane at 11/– per quintall to paie in London
at 47 daies sight, for the which you are to give him bills of exchange
upon me.
3. More you are to receive att the Newfoundland of the Ship called
the Ollive of Dartmouth of about 120 tonnes, Nicholas Webber
Master, the quantitie of one thousand quintalls of good merchantable
drie Newfoundland fishe of 112 lbs. to the quintall, which I bought
of Master Richard Lane at 11/– per quintall, to paie in London at
47 daies sight, for the which you are to give him bills of exchange
upon me.
4. You are to receave also att the Newfoundland of the Ship called
the Desire of Dartmouth of 250 tonnes John Haley Master the
quantitie of one thousand quintalls of good merchantable drie fishe of
112 lbs. to the quintall, which I also bought of Master Richard Lane
at 11/– per quintall to paie in London att 47 daies sight, for the which

[1] Before the Civil War there were very few sack ships; those that are found
were usually on time charter, though it was not unknown for them to pay a
freight calculated on the tonnage of wine shipped home.

you are to give him bills of exchange upon me, The copies of the said three Covenants have given you for your better instructions.

Alsoe I have given you three letters of Master Richard Lane to the said Masters, for the delivery of the said fishe; if you should want any fishe Master Lane hath written to the Masters to furnish you of such quantities as you should want, as you may see in the letters I have given you.

5. If you doe not receave content, in the receit of your fishe, or otherwise, from the said Masters, then be sure that you cause a Protest to be made in good forme; and be sure that you lie the fishe close.

6. Haveing receaved your full loading of the fishe, then pray loose no time, but saile directly, and to be there one of the first, to Cartagena, there to deliver my letter to the Procurator of John & Irigo Romenos, of whome you shall take directions if you shall unload there parte, or all your fishe, or if you shall proceed for Alicant, Tarragona and Barcelona, to unload the rest of your fishe; if you unload any of your fishe at Cartagena, then within 10 daies after your arrival my factor is to give you an answer, if he will have your Ship to reload for London; if he will have her, then you must load such goods as he shall appointe you at Majorca and Allicant, and to receave no outward freight for the fishe only primage and average; you must tell them that in all the portes you are to staie for you unloadinge of your fishe but twenty daies, and if they reload you that then you are to staie thirty daies more, in both portes for your reloading.

7. If within 20 daies after your arrival my factor saieth that he will not reload you, then you must receave of him your outward freight for your fishe, the sum of four thousand pieces of eight which is thirty two thousand single reals, as I have advised him. By noe means lett not my factor know that I have your ship absolutely out and home, and if they reload you, then you must tell them that I am to pay you at your retorne £5 10s. a tonn for 240 tonnes. To this purpose I give you alsoe an open letter to my factor, that in case he should refuse to pay you the outward freight, that then you may by virtue of my said letter, recover there your outward freight, if they give you not under there hands that they will reload you. If you take in 4000 quintalls of fishe, then your outward freight is just eight single reals for each quintall; howsoever if you take in less fishe they must pay you inall for your outward freight eight [sic] thousand pieces of eight.

8. If my factor reload you not then I would have you bring me home the eight thousand pieces of eight and to goe first for Allicant, there to take in such goods for the Downes and London as you can gett, and to agree for the freight the best you cann for my advantage, not but that you will get above three pounds a tonne freight. And if you

should want of your full loading att Allicant, then you may touche at Malaga, there to take in the rest of your full loading and to gett as much freight as you cann, being at Allicant you must appoint some brooker to go from house to house. If at Allicant you shall want but 40/50 or 60 tonnes of goods then you may buy Allamatta salt, for my account as you will loade your ship, because you should lose no time, to staie or touche at Malaga. Desiring you have a spetiall care that I runn in no daies of demurrage, and to be a good steward to me for your paines I shall not be ungrateful to you.

9. I desire that noe man should know that I have any interest in the fishe onlie my factor.

10. And lastly pray lett me continually hear from you from time to time and from all partes and at your retorne to the Downes send me an express if you be reloading for me, that I may accordingly give order if there you shall unload any part of my goodes, and to send my letters. Master Pieter Maes of Sandwich is my factor there, and he will send me an express with my letters, thus wishing you a good voiage and safe return

Your loveing friend
John della Barre[1]

These were the main shippers to England. Much less important, except in years of very heavy corn export from England, were the ships which came out without settled arrangements for their return cargoes, to pick up what they could. Such vessels played a large role in the carrying of oranges and lemons from Lisbon and Seville; these 'pipiners', as they were called, were often drawn from the smaller vessels of the Newcastle coal trade, making a single southward trip on charter in September or October before lying up for the rest of the winter. The English and other merchants in Spanish ports, though they had their English correspondents, were eager to act as brokers to the various ships arriving with no established connections. One of these firms wrote sourly from Cadiz in 1697 that Captain Smallwood of the *Mercy*, who had just arrived 'thinks he may do his business himself, thereby saving the expenses of commission, and insists that the owners think it too much to allow commission'; but after twenty-four hours he thought better of it and applied to them for help.[2]

Freight rates in these trades were high in the early part of the seventeenth century, when danger from Moorish corsairs was

[1] Charterer's instructions to master of the *Faith*, 1634 (HCA 15–5).
[2] Norris MSS., Liverpool Public Library.

great; they rose sharply from levels of 45s. to 50s. a ton, homeward from Malaga or Cadiz, the level settled immediately after the peace with Spain in 1604, to £3 10s., £4 or even £4 5s. for wine from Malaga in the thirties and forties. As the danger abated and ships could carry smaller crews, the peacetime rate came down and settled at £3 to £3 10s. in the sixties, and this rate was generally maintained until increasing efficiency caused further reductions half a century later.[1] The Lisbon rate, in the sixties £2 10s. to £3 a ton, had declined to £2 by 1720, and fixings can later be found as low as £1 10s. a ton.[2] The charter rate for the round voyage England–Newfoundland–Spain–England, a voyage likely to last seven or eight months and to constitute a year's utilisation of the ship, had settled at £5 a ton by the end of the 1630's, and for the rest of the century varied very little from that rate in peacetime.[3]

There were, of course, short-term fluctuations in freight rates; week-to-week changes reflecting unbalance between the cargoes coming forward and the tonnage of ships actually in the harbour or definitely expected, and those due to war and alarms of war. The former are illustrated by the course of the freights paid by John Aylward's agents in Malaga in the winters of 1684–5 and 1685–6. In September 1684 the rate, first fixed at £3 7s. 6d., rose quickly to £3 15s., falling away to £3 10s. in October and remaining stable at that level until, with the main cargoes shipped, a new irregularity set in during March, with rates of £4 and £3 succeeding one another. The following crop year, freights started very high, at £4 10s. and £4 7s. 6d., creeping down to £4 in November and £3 10s. in early December. Possibly the early high rates attracted excess tonnage to the port, for later in December the rate collapsed to £2 10s., recovering to £3 5s. and £3 in January; in the following month, at the tail-end of the season, one shipment was fixed at £2.[4] Such data on changes within a

---

[1] From the 1690's onward the rate per ton of raisins in barrel rose sharply above the rate for wine. From the rises in tobacco and sugar freights (pp. 287–9, below) it may be inferred that the size or the density of packing of the raisin barrel were increased. A ton was conventionally eleven barrels of raisins.

[2] The Oporto rate in the peace years after 1783 was normally £2. Society of Shipowners of Great Britain, *Collection of Interesting and Important Reports* (1806), pp. cxv–cxvii.

[3] No eighteenth-century evidence is available; this form of Newfoundland charter was apparently becoming uncommon.

[4] Aylward MSS., Institute of Chartered Shipbrokers.

season are hard to come by, and it would be unwise to draw firm conclusions from such a small set of Bills of Lading (there are twenty-five of them) as that quoted. It might be expected, however, that even in a trade which, like this one, had good connections between the producing area and the market, and which used loading ports where information was available on freight opportunities in the Mediterranean, there would be short-term fluctuations in rates. Downswings might have been easily corrected by the departure of ships to seek alternative cargoes, but for two complicating factors; the constant arrival, during September, October and November, of ships from Newfoundland whose market information was three months out of date — ships, moreover, which had to discharge their outward cargo before it perished — and the sending of ships by London firms which were committed to local merchants to pick up cargoes from them.

In the Iberian trades as in others, wartime freights soared to two or three times the peacetime level, reaching as much as £6 for cargoes from Lisbon and £8 for Malaga wine shipments.

During the seventeenth century there was an important trade with the (Spanish) Canary Islands. Originally suppliers of sugar, they were driven by the competition of the Brazilian sugar plantations to become wine producers on a large scale. A small English demand for Canary wine appeared after the peace with Spain in 1604, grew very fast for nearly a century, and then collapsed suddenly around 1700. Canary prices were rising in the latter part of the seventeenth century, but the death blow was apparently given when port acquired a privileged position after the Methuen Treaty of 1704.

The Canaries are isolated, on the way to nowhere in Europe. There were some English merchants on the islands,[1] but they were not served by regular trading ships. Ships were chartered each year for the Canary wine trade, nearly all of them coming direct from England. Very rarely a sack ship from Newfoundland appeared in the Canaries harbours; occasionally when freights were low at Malaga or Lisbon a handful of ships was diverted from those ports; English Mediterranean traders sometimes

---

[1] An account of one of them will be found in *The Life of Marmaduke Rawdon of York* (Camden Society, 1863). See also C. A. J. Skeel, 'The Canary Company', *Eng. Hist. Rev.*, Vol. XXXI, 1916.

brought cargoes of corn from Sicily. There was little outward cargo from England; exports to the Spanish mainland paid for some of the wine, but it was necessary to ship quantities of bullion, legally or illegally, from England.[1] The trade was altogether more specialised than that with Spain; there was virtually only one commodity, wine, and its shipment was restricted to a very brief season.

Ships entering London from the Canaries

	1664	*1686*
January	10	8
February	1	2
March	4	4
April	2	2
May	—	—
June	1	—
July	—	—
August	1	—
September	—	—
October	—	—
November	2	1
December	23	7

Ships were often consigned to members of the considerable English merchant settlement, but a large proportion of ships went out speculatively, sent by owners or charterers to get such cargo as they could. Freight rates probably varied more than did those from Spain and Portugal, and were certainly much higher; peacetime rates in the late seventeenth century were normally £4 10s. to £4 15s. per ton.[2] These high rates reflect not only the longer distance, the absence of outward cargoes and the uncertainty of homeward ones, but also the peculiarly dangerous conditions of the Canaries harbours. There were no safe anchorages; all ships lay in an open roadstead, and when bad weather blew up had to stand out to sea until it abated. This had its reflection in the conditions of charter-parties. Not merely were long laydays allowed for loading — usually forty to forty-five working days — but these laydays specifically excluded days when the ship was driven off by bad weather. The *Mary Bonaventure*, arriving at Oratavo, the principal loading place for wine, on 1st February 1701, anchored in fifty fathoms; she was driven from

---

[1] J. Child, *A New Discourse of Trade* (4th ed., 1740), p. 170.

[2] No regular rates can be quoted for the small trade which remained in the eighteenth century, but there were shipments in 1729 and 1736 at £3 per ton from Teneriffe.

the roadstead by gales from 8th–14th February, 1st–6th March
and 14th–24th March, finally getting away on 27th March. She
was particularly unfortunate, but most ships could expect one or
two spells of bad weather during their winter stay in the islands.[1]

Madeira and the Azores attracted few ships from England until
Madeira wine began to be popular in the middle of the eighteenth
century,[2] though Madeira had long before this become a popular
port of call for ships bound to America. Since Madeira was
outside Europe, the Navigation Acts did not prohibit the direct
export of its products to British possessions outside Europe, and
for a long time it was the principal source of wine for the West
Indies and the southern colonies of the American continent.

English trade by sea with the Mediterranean,[3] which was on a
very small scale during most of the sixteenth century, re-emerged
when English ships appeared at Leghorn about 1570 and at
Venice and Turkish ports in the following decade. The last years
of the Anglo-Spanish war, around 1600, saw English trade with
the Mediterranean firmly established and rapidly growing.

Apart from Mediterranean Spain, which has already been dealt
with, the trades fall into two distinct but interconnected groups;
with the central Mediterranean (Italy and the Greek islands under
Venetian rule) and the Turkish eastern Mediterranean. The
authority of a monopolistic chartered company, the Levant
Company, extended to Venice and its possessions, but for most
practical purposes these were separate from the true Levant trade.
English trade with the Mediterranean was carried on almost
entirely by English ships; by 1600 it was unusual for a merchant
ship of any Mediterranean state to appear in the English Channel,
and the possibility of the Dutch taking part in the import of goods
was ended by an Order-in-Council of 1615 which, anticipating
the later Navigation Acts, prohibited import from the Mediterranean except in ships of England or of certain Mediterranean
ports.[4] All the most valuable part of the trade was carried on from

[1] BM Sloane MSS. 3237. Next year she got away in twenty-seven days.
[2] An excellent picture of the small earlier Madeira trade is given by A. L.
Simon (ed.), *The Bolton Letters; Letters of an English Merchant in Madeira,
1695–1714* (1928).
[3] There are two studies of the East Mediterranean trade; Epstein, *The Early
History of the Levant Company* (1908) and A. C. Wood, *History of the Levant
Company* (Oxford, 1935).
[4] See pp. 302–3, below.

SPAIN AND PORTUGAL

Statistics:

1. TONNAGE OF ENTRIES AND CLEARANCES (000 TONS)

	1686		1715–17	1771–3	
	e	c	c	e	c
Spain	19·9 (0·6)	12·5 (0·3)	18·3 (1·2)	26·8 (1·7)	12·1 (1·7)
Portugal	10·0	8·0	16·8	27·1 (0·9)	17·8 (1·7)
Islands	3·2	3·7	9·0	in S. and P.	

2. VALUE OF TRADE (£000)

	1699–1701		1771–3	
	I	E	I	E
Spain	516	517	514	956
Portugal	219	334	350	624
Islands	99	55	13	46

3. CHIEF ENGLISH PORTS IN SOUTHERN TRADES

	1686		1715–17	
	Number of ships		Ships out	
	In	Out	No.	tons
London	247	182	244	20·8
Exeter	53	26	30	1·6
Bristol	49	33	48	3·1
Plymouth	31	42	19	0·9
Liverpool	4	1	23	1·5
Falmouth, Looe and minor Cornish	7	3	149	6·9

4. CHIEF ENGLISH PORTS, 1715–17, TRADING TO DIFFERENT COUNTRIES

	Total		N. Sp.	S. Sp.	Port.	Islands
	No.	tons				
London	244	20·9	0·9	5·2	9·5	5·3
Exeter	30	1·6	0·2	0·2	1·0	0·2
Bristol	48	3·1	0·6	1·0	0·6	0·9
Plymouth	19	0·9	0·5	0·1	0·1	0·2
Liverpool	23	1·5	0·1	—	0·2	1·2
Falmouth, etc.	149	6·9	1·9	3·6	0·8	0·6

5. AVERAGE TONNAGE OF INDIVIDUAL ENGLISH SHIPS

		1686	1715–17 c.	1726 e.	1766 e.	1771–3 e. c.
Spain	L	126	88	83	108 ⎱	
	O	68	50		⎰	92
Portugal	L	102	85	74	117 ⎱	
	O	80	67		⎰	95
Islands	L	129	96	61	71	
	O	40	71			

London; but the bulkier export trade in fish, and some of the bulk imports, were handled at provincial ports.

Seaborne trade with Italy was revolutionised in scale and character in the course of the seventeenth century. At the beginning it was very small, consisting in the main of some exchange of fish and lead for currants; more valuable articles of trade came overland to Hamburg or Middelberg and by sea from those places to England. Soon after 1610, however, the East India Company's agents began to sell large quantities of pepper and other Eastern goods for shipment through the Straits of Gibraltar, and these found their chief Mediterranean market in the free port of Leghorn, whence they were widely distributed. Leghorn was by this time becoming a common port of call for ships going to and from the Levant, and a place where cargoes were often transshipped and warehoused. From the mid-twenties, when the Thirty Years War closed the overland routes from Italy to North-west Europe, Anglo-Italian trade became almost entirely seaborne and largely centred upon Leghorn. Once the English connection with Leghorn was firmly established, about 1630, a number of ships began to trade regularly between Italy and England.

It was difficult, however, to find homeward cargoes in any quantity from Leghorn itself. The bulk cargoes homeward from the central Mediterranean were first currants from the islands of Zante and Cephalonia, the shipments of which grew very fast to a peak in the middle of the seventeenth century, when they began to meet some competition from Turkish currants; and secondly olive oil from Apulia, which began to be imported in quantity after 1630. These were the staple homeward cargoes; most ships taking English goods out to Genoa, Leghorn or Venice found cargoes to bring home in Zante or Apulia. The establishment of a free port at Trieste in 1719 led to the gradual rise of a new traffic, but it was on a very small scale for the first half-century. In the eighteenth century the value of imports from Italy rose precipitately, reflecting the growth of an enormous import of raw silk and silk yarn. Great though the value of this trade was, it involved the transport of only a few hundred tons a year; but this was sufficient to bring a small but increasing number of ships home directly from Leghorn instead of going south to collect cargo.

Outward cargoes in English ships were at first of a very mixed character; pepper, lead, tin and small but increasing quantities of cloth. They were soon supplemented, however, by one substantial bulk cargo — red herrings from Yarmouth. In the early decades of the seventeenth century Dutch ships were generally used for the cheap transport of this cheap commodity, in spite of a stream of protests from the shipping interest,[1] for the freight charges to Mediterranean ports formed a material part of its selling price. From the time the Dutch became involved in the Thirty Years War, their competition ceased. The herring trade continued to grow, employing large ships to transport the cargoes, and contributed much to the astonishing prosperity of Yarmouth in the first half of the eighteenth century.[2] The ships were usually Yarmouth or London owned, and were chartered for the Mediterranean voyage. The cargoes were purchased by London merchants for sale in Italy, generally under the single control of an individual or small syndicate, the usual method of handling cheap commodities. Often the ship put into the Thames or to Dover to add a small amount of cloth to its lading of fish; then it would go on to Genoa or Leghorn, or possibly Venice, to deliver its cargo. The proceeds of the sale were remitted home, and the ships went to find return cargo of oil in southern Italy, or more often currants at Zante or Cephalonia. The freight earned outward was often used to procure a part-cargo home for the owners' account, and the ship was filled up, if possible, with goods taken on freight. A smaller stream of vessels from south-western ports took pilchards (sometimes owned by London merchants) and returned usually with oil cargoes; Bristol and Exeter imported quite large quantities of oil.[3] Occasionally a Newfoundland trader would bring its cargo of dried cod to Leghorn or Naples; but on the whole cod was a Spanish and red herring an Italian delicacy.

The red herring carriers provided a growing proportion of English shipping tonnage going to the Mediterranean; but they could not fulfil all requirements because they operated within a short season, the herring all being shipped in October, November

---

[1] APC 11th October 1613, 7th August 1624, 30th August 1624, 19th November 1624, 9th November 1625, 28th September 1627; M. Oppenheim (ed.), *The Naval Tracts of Sir William Monson* (Navy Record Society, 1902–14), Vol. V, p. 235.
[2] See Yarmouth petitions. *House of Commons Journals, 1718–21*, p. 271; *1745–50*, pp. 336–45.
[3] W. B. Stephens, *Seventeenth Century Exeter* (Exeter, 1958), pp. 176–7; P. V. McGrath (ed.), *Merchants and Merchandise in Seventeenth Century Bristol* (Bristol Record Society, 1955), pp. 284–92.

or early December. There was a growing number of regular traders, however, carrying mixed cargoes; ships of 100–200 tons which went out part-laden, collecting further cargo from Cadiz and perhaps Alicante on the way and discharging some English cargo in those ports. Their cargoes for Genoa[1] and Leghorn — cloth, pepper, lead — were carried on freight for various merchants, including, usually, some part-owners of the ships. From Leghorn the ship was likely to go in ballast, or with the small cargo to be dropped at Naples or Messina, down to the Gulf of Taranto, first to lade empty barrels or pipestaves to make them and then, in the barrels, olive oil from a whole range of small ports stretching round southern Italy from Naples to Brindisi. Leghorn factors advised the master where oil was plentiful; often they arranged the cargoes through their agents in the south. Captain John Payne wrote to his owners in London in September 1679:

Sr

From Gallipoly[2] I then wrote you what was needful, Now have to Acquaint you of my Arrival heare where have laine 7 daies and done nothing of Business more then the Landing of the Empty Cask which I brought from Gallipoly to put my Loding of Oyle in and they are now a-fitting for my Loding and I hope in two daies more may make a begining, here being 200 Salmes in readiness, and the Person whoe is to lode 600 Salmes more, not to be heard of, soe feare shall be forced to stay longer than I did expect to have done, but Mr Davies have given Orders heare that in case that Party comply not in 20 daies that a second Person shall comply for him. But that is not all the loss that I am like to have neither; for Mr Davies promised me Salmes 1000 but I find hath only Salmes 800 soe must goe hence ded freighted about one third of my loding, by Reason of the Sicklyness of the Place and Scarcitye of Oyles, that Commodities being worth 16 per Salme which is very deare. Colde he have complied with my Salmes 1000 then I should not have feared to have got my full Loding at Liverno but nowe have some feares maye not attaine it theare, however I question not but in toucheing at Malhago I may gitt full and have as good a freighte as this one would have bine. It is in vaine for me to acquainte you how lowe freightes are abrode and yet how scarce to gitt Imployment, I suppose you dayly heare the same

[1] Genoa, which was usually avoided by English ships before 1660 owing to its Spanish connections, thereafter became a regular port of discharge, though always less important than Leghorn.
[2] This is Gallipoly in southern Italy, not the more famous Turkish place.

Coments by others, so you are not allone in this case, however I could wish times were better for everybody. I shall hasten for Liverno when I cann hopeing to gitt the Company of the Scandrone convoy home . . [1]

More rarely some of these regular traders went to Zante for currants; a minority returned straight home from Leghorn and Genoa with such cargo as could be obtained there, picking up more at Spanish ports on the way.

The regular traders of London, and the fish carriers of Yarmouth and the south-west, were the main suppliers of tonnage for the direct in-and-out trade between England and the central Mediterranean. Levant ships took some cargo to Leghorn, and in the mid-seventeenth century frequently collected part of their homeward cargo there; indeed, the private ships in the Levant trade came to be as much concerned in Italy as in Turkey. Many ships, however, came into the Mediterranean freight market speculatively; because freights were unattractive at Lisbon, Cadiz or Malaga, or because they had been chartered at Lisbon to take some of the large sugar and tobacco cargoes which were sent from there to Italy, or at Cadiz to carry wool; or because they had taken out government stores to Tangier, Port Mahon or Gibraltar; or simply because they had secured outward cargo for the Mediterranean. All relied on the chances, not only of good homeward cargoes, but also of taking part in the internal Mediterranean carrying trade. English shipping found in the Mediterranean the first region in which it could play a significant part in the carriage of goods between foreign harbours. This was largely because in the seventeenth century English ships were among the safest for the carriage of goods in that sea. They were often neutral in Mediterranean wars, well armed and capable of some defence against the Moorish corsairs (and after 1655 usually protected from them by treaty), and immune from the attentions of Tuscan and Maltese privateers which preyed on Turkish shipping. Consequently their services were in demand from both Christian and Turkish merchants. In the early seventeenth century the great Levant Company ships were able to secure high freights for the carriage of valuable foreign goods through dangerous waters; but by the thirties the main basis of the English carrying trade was being altered to the ultimately more remunerative task of helping

[1] Lloyds, Bowrey MSS., 933.

to shift the great bulk cargoes that moved within the Mediterranean basin. The most important of these was grain, and the main granaries were the Greek Archipelago and Sicily. From the islands, from Palermo and from Cagliari in Sardinia, ladings were available in plenty in most years for Genoa and Leghorn, Alicante and Lisbon and the Canary Islands. This was possibly the greatest of all the Mediterranean trades in volume. Sometimes English ships went to the Mediterranean deliberately with the intention of earning freights in this intra-Mediterranean traffic, but more often they came to take part in it because hoped-for opportunities of different kinds failed to materialise. The *Daniel & Thomas* was sent out from London in 1677 with some goods on freight for Genoa and Leghorn, as well as a cargo of lead and tar on the owners' account. The freight earned was paid at Leghorn and Venice, and the owners' cargo sold at Venice. All the freight collected at Leghorn was to be remitted to Venice to the owners' agent, Aloisio Morelli, who was also entrusted with the sale of their cargo. He was to hand over the whole proceeds of freight and cargo (advancing the expected proceeds of the latter if necessary) to the master in pieces of eight, in Venice; and with this cash the ship was to go on to Zante and the master would buy currants for the owners' account. Morelli was to arrange for further goods on freight to complete her lading. In fact it was a bad year for currants at Zante, and these careful arrangements were upset; so the ship went to Cagliari and without difficulty secured a freight of corn there for Leghorn. At Leghorn the ship was chartered for a further voyage to fill in time to the next currant crop — a voyage to Alexandria and back — but the crew, who had been engaged for a direct out-and-home voyage, refused the further extension.[1] Or again, there was the *Harle Frigate*, which came into Leghorn from England in May 1722 expecting to find a return cargo there. Finding none, she took a small cargo to Alicante and laded salt for Villafrance and Nice, going on in ballast to Genoa. There was still no adequate homeward cargo, so this ship, too, went down in ballast to Cagliari and brought corn back to Genoa. There, in December, a homeward cargo was secured.[2]

The corn exporting ports, in the Mediterranean as elsewhere, had no significant bulk imports, and ships had usually to go to

[1] HCA 15-11; HCA 13-131.   [2] HCA 15-35.

them in ballast or with trivial cargoes; and the principal destinations of corn import were the north Italian cities where bulk cargoes were hard to secure. Perhaps, therefore, this traffic was not very profitable, but it postponed the day when a ship would have to find a homeward cargo, and a series of such postponements until a new oil or currant season began might make a vital difference to the success of the voyage as a whole.

There were other cargoes to be had in the Mediterranean; rice from Venice round Italy to Genoa or Leghorn or to Lisbon; salt from Trapani in Sicily or from Alicante to Italy or Mediterranean France; flax and rice from Alexandria to Constantinople or Leghorn; large miscellaneous cargoes of Turkish and Syrian wares to be taken to Leghorn all through the year. By 1720, large salt cargoes from Sicily were being taken in English ships right out of the Mediterranean to the northern ports of Riga and St Petersburg. The character and destinations of the intra-Mediterranean cargoes changed gradually — old cargoes such as corn from the Archipelago faded out as Turkish needs expanded; new ones like corn from Ancona and Tunis appeared. The one constant factor, from a little after 1620, was the standing of Leghorn and Genoa as the foci of a great part of Mediterranean trade, drawing in bulk foodstuffs for the massed population of the north Italian cities and sending out in return a small but immensely valuable stream of manufactures and raw materials; and because of their central role, acting also as warehousing and trans-shipment centres for all kinds of Mediterranean commodities. As a last example we may look at the *St Quinton* which went from London to the Mediterranean in 1727 with small cargoes for Lisbon, Alicante and Leghorn. From Leghorn it got a small freight for Palermo, and a short journey in ballast took the ship to Jurgento, where a corn cargo for Lisbon awaited it. It went back in ballast to Jurgento and took another corn cargo to Lisbon. Bringing cocoa from Lisbon to Cadiz, it found little business there, and went on to Genoa. Here, too, nothing was offered, so the *St Quinton* went off in ballast to the Gulf of Negroponte to collect a corn cargo for Genoa. There was no return lading at Genoa and the ship had to sail in ballast again, this time to Leizat in Sicily, where a cargo of salt for Ostend was found to bring her home.[1]

[1] HCA 13–88.

Possibly the English ships which relied for their main earnings on outward cargoes and on freights from Cadiz into the Mediterranean, and on the homeward earnings of oil or currants, were able to cut rates when they entered the intra-Mediterranean traffic in order to fill in time until good homeward cargoes were available. Many ships, however, engaged their crews for voyages of uncertain duration and extent beyond Leghorn or Cadiz, undertaking to pay wages on account at fixed intervals or in successive discharging ports; clearly, from the outset, the owners were contemplating that their ships should make prolonged stays in the Mediterranean, and it was not uncommon for vessels to spend two or three years there. The early advantages of English vessels in their superior defence against corsairs were weakening before the end of the seventeenth century as local shipping changed its character; but under the protection of English naval power which menaced the corsair ports English merchant ships were able to reduce the size of their crews and operate increasingly cheaply, particularly when the new ship types developed in the eighteenth century made their appearance in the Mediterranean. These English 'port-to-port' or 'trading' voyages, as contemporaries called them, continued to be a feature of the eighteenth as of the seventeenth century. In their successful execution much depended on the quality of the master; while his owners or charterers directed him to their agents in the principal Mediterranean ports, these in turn would often send him through a succession of minor ports where he had to rely on English or foreign brokers or his own diplomacy to find further cargoes.

Freight rates for bulk cargoes from the Mediterranean reflected the fact that the London–Leghorn–Zante/Ancona–London voyage was likely to take seven, eight or nine months and be regarded as a year's employment for the ship; the homeward rate for currants from Zante and oil from southern Italy in peacetime, between 1650 and 1720, varied between £5 and £5 10s. per ton. At this rate the ship which had a good outward cargo of herrings or pilchards or other goods should have made profitable voyages, but vessels more dependent on their homeward freight were in a less happy position. Most of them, however, did have some outward earnings, including those on the part of the voyage between Cadiz and Italy. With falling costs, and the growing corn trade from England to Lisbon and Cadiz to provide outward cargoes part of the way, shipping bound for the Mediterranean should have had increasingly good prospects in the eighteenth century; unfortunately, a dearth of information after 1720 obscures knowledge of how far this was counterbalanced by declining freight rates.

The trade with Asia Minor and Syria was a monopoly of the Levant Company, and an exclusively London trade, until 1750. Its essence was the exchange of English woollen cloth for Turkish or Persian raw silk. The valuable silk cargoes were supplemented by cheaper bulk cargoes of cotton, mohair, galls (a dyestuff) and later currants; and in the eighteenth century, sometimes, by the even cheaper potash. The highly valued cloth exports were similarly carried in ships weighed down with larger tonnages of lead, tin and hides, which added little to the value of the trade. Aleppo (with its port of Alexandretta, at that time known as Iskanderun or Scanderoon), Smyrna and Constantinople were the chief places where the English had their permanent settlements of factors, though cotton, galls and some minor commodities were laden in Cyprus.

The Levant shipping was usually handled by the Company itself. From 1625 until 1744, except during a few short periods (1649–60, 1683–6, and some odd years between 1687 and 1718)[1] the Company itself chartered ships in peacetime — one or two at a time in the early seventeenth century, five, six or more after the Restoration — and let space in them to those of its members who wished to trade with the ports to which they were directed.[2] Usually when these 'general' ships were operating on the Company's behalf, other ships were forbidden to go from England to the Turkish ports, or penal duties were imposed on goods carried in them; but it was impossible to prevent English goods being forwarded from Leghorn to Turkey, and difficult to prevent the import of Turkish goods through Leghorn. At the end of the sixteenth century the Levant ships were the largest of English merchantmen; constantly carrying immensely valuable cargoes to and fro, they had to be ready, during the first seventy years of the trade, to fight Moorish corsairs and sometimes Spanish men-of-

[1] Wood, op. cit., p. 136.
[2] In the very beginning of the trade, before 1600, the Levant Company had owned the ships it sent out.

war. They were usually ships of 300–450 tons, though some carried as much as 600 tons, and were powerfully armed. As the Mediterranean became safer the Levant Company used smaller ships, particularly in its eighteenth-century decline; but still, at around 300 tons, they were among the more substantial under English ownership, and they continued to be well-armed and fairly well-manned. The separate ships which the Company at times (usually in war) allowed its members to send to its territories were usually much smaller, at 150–200 tons, and smaller vessels still began to sail from England to the Levant ports after 1744, the year in which the Company finally abandoned the practice of chartering ships.

So long as the Company was using large and heavily-armed ships, of little use for other purposes except East India trade, it recognised an obligation to continue employing those which had been built to meet its needs, and the same ships with the same masters appear as the Company's general ships year after year. The masters, because they handled very large ships with valuable cargoes, and because their duty was primarily to their owners and the Company rather than to the individual merchants whose goods they laded and whose agents they dealt with in Scanderoon or Smyrna, were men of high standing. Though under tight regulation and entirely excluded from any active part in the commercial operations of their employers, they were given valuable privileges for personal trade which could quickly make their fortunes. Many of them rose in time to be Levant merchants themselves, trading from London; often a name which has once appeared in the Company's records as a ship's master employed by it will turn up again, a decade or two later, in the list of the members of the Court of Governors.

Nevertheless, employment was irregular during the first half of the seventeenth century, when sailings were often only made in alternate years. Sailings from London were made, if possible, in the early autumn; the ship was put at the charterers' disposal three or four months earlier for the Company's members to lade their goods. A two months' voyage each way, usually including a call at Leghorn and long stays in the Turkish ports, kept the ship away from home at least until the following midsummer.[1]

---

[1] Charter-parties of the 1630's allow for 90 working days at Scanderoon and Cyprus; 130 at Smyrna and Constantinople.

The homeward freight rate of raw silk paid by the Company's members is the best indicator of movements in the charge of this voyage. In the 1630's it was £6 or occasionally £5 10s. per ton;[1] it rose to £7 after the Restoration, and was generally at that level in peacetime for the next hundred years, though there were individual fixings as low as £6. In wartime the rate for this voyage through dangerous waters rose very steeply, reaching peaks of £21 in 1746 and in 1761–3. The principal cheap commodity, galls, paid the much lower rate of £4 per ton after 1660; and potash, carried home as ballast in many ships during the eighteenth century, went for as little as £2. On cloths taken out the usual charge by the Company was one piece of eight[2] per cloth, often increased by 12½ per cent; while it is difficult to assess this in terms of tonnage, it may be noted that the same rate was fixed for a hundredweight of pepper in the odd years when this commodity went to Turkey. The general ships were usually fully laden outward, and the company could expect fully to cover the costs of its chartering, which appears to have been based on a rate per ton of the ship's previously agreed carrying capacity.[3]

The Levant trade was not, of course, wholly separate from other English Mediterranean shipping interests. Its ships took some goods to and from Italian ports; at times, particularly in the early part of the seventeenth century, they were active in carrying goods for foreigners between Mediterranean ports. When the carrying trade was left open by the Company, Turkish ports offered opportunities to English ships of all kinds in the Mediterranean.[4] We may conclude with an illustration of the great flexibility of English shipping operations in the Mediterranean; the orders given to the supercargo of the *Rainbow*, which went out during a brief period of peace after the First Dutch War, and while the Levant Company was not operating its general ships.

3 September 1655

Mr Thos Baker
    Herewith wee deliver you factory and bill of Lading of the Ship Rainebow Cargason Consigned to your selfe in Tituan Algeire and

---

[1] A notional ton of 12 cwts (Levant Company Court Minutes 7th March 1632, 20th December 1633, 2nd June 1636).
[2] Its value fluctuated round 4s. 6d.
[3] £11 10s. per ton during much of the seventeenth century.
[4] Indeed, it complained in 1636 that Englishmen were losing trade because of 'the great trade driven by strangers in English shipping' (Court Minutes, 19th December 1636).

Tunis. When you come to Tituan make what dispach you can possible for you know the danger in that open Road. Take good Monyes and advance the most you can for our Comodityes. Having ended there you must proceede for Algeire at which two places wee hope you may dispose of all our goods. If you meete with any prize goods there, and to be had on reasonable termes, you may buy them and having with you a Bill of prices, If you thinke such goods most proper for England you may send them hither, If proper for Italy thether you may goe. Some Imployment or other you must have for the Shipp, to that end wee will order your Correspondants in Italy to send you advise to Algeire or Tunis, to which latter place you must goe if Algeire shall leave any considerable matter of goods in your hands, and thence lade corne for Italy if you finde encouragement. If you reserve any goods for Tunis be mindfull to keep Iron for the markett. And our desire is that you make use of Consul Woodhouse but leave no effects ashore behinde you. Be very cautious there how you land any estate, unless you are well assured of their good Complyance. For your Correspondents in any other Places, Wee leave it to your Discrecon and because you will have more Stock than will Employ your Ship, If any other Vessels shall present for Italy you may Invest the Rests of our Stocke in Corne or any other Goods that you conceave may turn best to Account. And when you are in Italy and find incouradgment for a trading voyage take as much effects as will Imploy the Shipp and leave the Rest of the effects at our Disposall. If you cannot at any time sell your Goods yourselfe rather than our Shipp should spend much time in port leave the Goods with your Correspondents to sell for our Account and take Monyes aboard or Goods for another Tripp. Now if trading Voyages should not turn well to Account then we leave it to you either to lade Oyles from Italy, currants from Zante, or goe down to Scanderoon with all your Stock, and invest the same in Cyprus Cottons, Gaull and Burmi Legge and Cleanest Ardas[1] you to touch at Cyprus in your way. If Cottons bee not at 50 or 60 per kyntall cleare aboard medle not with them but downe for Scanderoon and doe your owne business before you oblige to take in goods for any other.

If you medle with Prize Goods either for England or Italy be sure to put oute the marke that they may not be knowne and if at Algeire you can lade either for Italy or hither with hopes of considerable profitt doe, els from Tunis for Leghorn, invest your stock in corne waxe and greate hides and the overplus carry over in money; and betwixt Barbary and Italy you may find good business; and at Laghorne if you make use of any lett it bee of Mr Mays & Forster,

---

[1] Two grades of raw silk.

who have an interest in the Ship Cargason; and if the Acorne shall overtake you at Tituan or bee there with you, shee being to goe to Algeire you may chance to have the starne of her at Tunis proceed thither directly without touching Algeire without letting any take any notice of it. In Italy are in good request all sortes of hides but sugars are a drug. Aniseed and such other comodityes as you shall think fitt but if you can trade betwixt Barbary Leghorne or Genoa which wee doubt not of wee recomend that to you as a very good buiseness. But above all be sure to spend noe time in porte but make as quick dispach in all places as you cann possible. When you have any overplus of stock and occason offering for Turkey send it to Smyrna to Sam: Pentilo and Robert Nelson and to Scanderoon to Mr Gamalial Nightingall with order to have it invested in superfine Legee or Ardas to be consigned as per convenance, and what you may afterwards want for to complete the Stock for Imployment of the Shipp that the Shipp may not want good Imployment which pray be very carefull of. You may vallew upon us by exchange to make up the stock 10000 which Mr Mans will supply you or if at Leghorne you finde good Imployment for Lisborne and back to Imploy the stock at Cambio pray doe. And in all things seek our uttmost advantage as wee doe noe wise question but you will in which confidence wee reste.[1]

[1] Bodleian Library, Rawlinson Letters 60, p. 18.

MEDITERRANEAN

Statistics:

1. TONNAGE OF ENTRIES AND CLEARANCES (000 TONS)

	1686		1715–17	1771–3	
	e	c	c	e	c
Marseilles, Italy					
and Greece	13·9 (0·1)	6·6	16·5 (0·2)	11·3 (0·1)	22·2 (0·3)
Turkey	6·8	3·9	1·6	1·6	1·5
'Straights'	4·8	8·2	12·0	0·7	5·4
Barbary	0·2	0·1	0·2		

('Straights' is a description of the Mediterranean, not specifying any particular places.)

2. VALUE OF TRADE (£000)

	1699–1701		1771–3	
	I	E	I	E
Italy	355	114	762	821
Venice	50	35	84	84
Turkey	316	233	139	79
Straights		420	6	119

3. CHIEF ENGLISH PORTS

	1686		1715–17	
	Number		Out	
	in	out	no.	tons
London	118	79	95	16·1
Yarmouth		15	35	4·4
Falmouth, Looe,				
etc.	1	4	47	5·6 (0·1)

4. CHIEF ENGLISH PORTS, 1715–17, TRADING TO DIFFERENT COUNTRIES

	Total		Genoa, Leghorn, Marseilles	S. Italy	tons Venice	Turkey	Straits and Barbary
	No.	tons					
London	95	15·9	1·8	0·1	0·4	1·6	12·0
Yarmouth	35	4·4	2·6	0·3	1·5		
Falmouth							
and Looe	47	5·6	3·1	0·5	2·0		

5. AVERAGE TONNAGE OF INDIVIDUAL ENGLISH SHIPS

		1686	1715–17 c	1726 e	1766 e
Italy and Greece	L	189	183	147	148
	O	95	105		
Turkey	L	271	282	199	165
Straits	L	233	165		

XII

The East Indian Trade

Though a good deal has been written on the shipping affairs of the East India Company, nearly all of it relates to the last years of the eighteenth and to the nineteenth century, and impressions derived from this period will mislead if they are incautiously applied to earlier times.[1]

The English East India trade was opened by the voyage of the *Red Dragon*, *Hector*, *Ascension* and *Susan*, which sailed for Java and Sumatra in 1601. The import trade in pepper and spices from the Indonesian Archipelago, which they inaugurated, was savagely contested by the Dutch, who by 1623 had driven the English out of all this area except a weak foothold at Bantam in Java. A more secure start was made on the Indian coast, at Surat in the territory of the Mogul Emperor, in 1607, and English trade with India was gradually expanded during the seventeenth century despite Portuguese, Dutch and later French competition. New trading stations were established, notably those of Madras (1639), Bombay (1662) and Calcutta (1686). Trade was soon developed, too, with ports of the Persian Gulf and the southern part of the Red Sea.[2]

From the early trading bases two principal bulk commodities were drawn; pepper from the East Indies and the Malabar Coast, and saltpetre from northern India. A wide variety of other goods of much greater total value came in — silk and cotton fabrics, indigo, drugs of all kinds — but pepper and saltpetre constituted most of the *volume* of every ship's cargo. When the *Berkeley Castle* sailed for home in 1681 'reputed for Cargo the richest Ship which ever went out of Madras Road', its cargo was worth some £80,000, but well over half the tonnage aboard consisted of

---

[1] This warning is particularly necessary because there are two excellent works on East India shipping after 1783, neither of which is altogether reliable in its comments on the earlier history. These are C. Northcote Parkinson, *Trade in the Eastern Seas, 1793–1813* (Cambridge, 1937); E. Cotton, *East Indiamen* (1949).

[2] The most useful studies of this trade are W. Hunter, *History of British India* (1899–1900) and Bal Krishna, *Commercial Relations between India and England, 1601–1757* (1924).

saltpetre, which contributed only a negligible amount to this great value.[1] Exports were very limited; some cloth, a good deal of lead and iron ballast (much of it coming all the way home again), a little iron- and brass-ware, beer and a vast wealth of bullion.

A number of efforts were made to penetrate further east, but despite the presence of an English trading settlement in Japan from 1611 to 1623 they were of little significance until the flowering of the China tea trade at the end of the seventeenth century. After 1713 the Company's efforts were increasingly directed towards China, for tea had found an apparently limitless market in Europe, and could be carried home in great quantities accompanied by more valuable Chinese silks and porcelain.

With the important exception of this China tea trade, English trade in Asia was not markedly seasonal. The length of the voyage out to India could vary by a long period from the normal of five or six months, and the time spent in collecting cargoes and trading between Indian ports might be extended almost indefinitely. It was desirable to avoid going round the Cape of Good Hope in the midwinter gales; but the one absolute fixed point was the need to get away from the Indian coast before the end of January 'to save the monsoon for that year'. Failure to do so meant a delay in sailing until June or July, and under the terms of the Company's charter-parties involved the Company automatically in payment of four months' demurrage. The China tea trade was seasonal, requiring the arrival of ships in August or September; since foreign competition was intense in Chinese ports the ship which arrived very late was likely to have some difficulty in securing a good tea cargo.

Seasonality was therefore important only in a limited sphere. The volume of goods coming forward for shipment each year was not very irregular, for Europe made only marginal demands on Asia's production. Variations in imports generally reflected the amount of shipping which the Company decided to send out; a slackening of the trade meant that these highly specialised ships lay idle in the Thames or followed alternative employments to which they were not well suited, rather than that they made voyages with part-empty holds or at lowered freights.

For the long, difficult and imperfectly known voyage to the East, the Company at first found it necessary to use its own ships,

[1] BM Sloane MSS., 3668.

buying the first large ones from the Levant merchants. Its needs
were to some extent contradictory. On the one hand, it was
engaged at the beginning in a fighting trade; large well-armed
vessels were needed to deal with Dutch and Portuguese anta-
gonism, and to make an impression on the Mogul powers whose
benevolence was essential to the holding of the Company's position
in India. On the other, it was not easy to find cargoes to fill very
large ships without making up unduly high values which it would
be preferable to spread over many ships in order to reduce the
risks from loss at sea. The objection to the introduction of large
ships into the Bay of Bengal trade, as late as 1773, was that a
large ship fully laden with the products of the Ganges valley —
mostly textiles — would bear too much wealth in a single bottom.
The Company had an early lesson in the risks of excessive size.
In 1607, becoming dissatisfied with the ships available for purchase, it began to build its own ships at Deptford; the first and
largest ship launched there was the *Trade's Increase* (1609), of
nearly 1000 tons burden.[1] She was wrecked off Java during her
first voyage. Other ships approaching her in size were built in
the next two decades — the *Royal James*, *Royal Charles* and
Palsgrave; but the Company settled down to a general use of ships
of 300–500 tons. Company building continued at Deptford, and
for a few years in Ireland. Ownership of its own vessels was
satisfactory while the trade was being expanded, but when a
period of recession set in in the mid-twenties the grave drawbacks
to the system became apparent. The Company owned a full
complement of large ships appropriate to a high level of trade,
and these could not easily be diverted to other uses when trade
declined. From 1629 onward there was an attempt to reduce the
burden by hiring ships to meet some part of requirements instead
of owning them all, and the collapse of the trade in the Civil War
and its aftermath led to a near-cessation of new building. The
Blackwall yard was sold in 1654 (to Henry Johnson, who was to
be for thirty years the largest builder of East Indiamen) and only
a part of the Deptford yard was kept as a store and repair depot.
Reorganised with a charter from the Protectorate government in
1657, the Company began to flourish once more, but from this
time onward it depended on the hire of privately owned ships for

---

[1] The tonnage usually quoted for this ship — 1293 — is measured tonnage;
for such a ship at that date it would correspond to 950–1000 tons burden.

almost all its trading activities. It was not easy to get large ships built, of a kind suited to the Company's requirements, unless those who were invited to finance their ownership had some assurance that the Company would make regular use of them. The Court Books of the East India Company show that these ships were built only after the prospective managing owners had approached the Company and received promises that their vessels would be admitted to its service; and continuing use was to some extent secured by associating the leading figures of the Company in the owning groups. Such prominent members of the Company's Court as Sir Josiah Child, Sir Jeremy Sambrooke, Richard Hutchinson and Charles Duncombe figure time after time in lists of part-owners of Company ships in the post-Restoration decades. At this date, a ship which was maintained in good condition was normally employed for sixteen years, after which it was considered to be unfit for long tropical voyages. The system quickly crystallised into a rigid one of formal, saleable rights; the right of the owners to have their ship employed in strict rotation with others of the same standing; of its owners to be allowed to replace it by putting another vessel into the Company's service when it was worn out; of its master to be continued as a master in the Company's service, in his original ship or another, until he chose to retire; and so on. When the system became fully-fledged in the pattern so clearly described in Miss L. S. Sutherland's book *A London Merchant*[1] is not clear, but it was probably after the ending of the inter-company struggles for East India trade and of the war with France in 1713.

The effect of the obligations which the Company assumed was to re-create much of the rigidity of a century before, when it had owned its own vessels. Certainly it was free to vary the number of ships it sent out as trade required, and the ships that lay idle when trade was bad were not a direct charge on it. In the eighteenth century, however, when regular East Indiamen were hardly ever switched to other uses in peacetime, and when freight rates were settled by a ring of managing owners who formed a powerful group within the councils of the Company itself, the costs of idleness — and of idleness, apparently, on an increasing scale — were passed on to the Company in high freight rates for

---

[1] Oxford, 1933. This book provides an excellent account of the activities of a ship's husband in the East India trade in the mid-eighteenth century.

the ships that were operating. A political storm broke around the East India shipping interest in the 1770's, largely because of the enormous over-expansion of the East India fleet in the previous thirty years, which had made it necessary for ships to lie in the Thames for very long periods between voyages even when the trade was flourishing, and for owners to compensate themselves by maintaining high and even increasing freight rates in a world where shipping costs and charges were generally dropping.[1]

Throughout the life of the East India Company, the ships it employed were the largest in the English merchant service. Though the early experiments with ships approaching a thousand tons were abandoned, and the majority of the ships during the rest of the seventeenth century were in the range 300–500 tons, even these were hardly matched in other trades. With the resumption after 1657 of building specially for the Company's service there was a new growth in maximum size until a peak was reached with ships of over 800 tons burden in the early nineties; but the group of very large vessels was only one component of a mixed fleet. For the early, tentative China trade after 1680 a number of small ships of 150–200 tons were employed; the average size was gradually increased, being assimilated to that of the main part of the Company fleet by about 1730[2]; and later in the century the China trade employed the largest of all in the Company's service. During the period from 1698 to 1709 when the Company's monopoly of East India trade was temporarily suspended and it had to meet the competition of private traders, its shipping policy changed, probably as a result of lessons taught by those competitors. The Company had for too long been haunted by the ancient needs of defence against hostile Dutch and Portuguese; it was now reminded that the time had come for defence to take second place to commercial considerations. Moreover, the proportion of high-value goods — above all cotton and

[1] The four voyages a ship made in the Company's service were spread over some fourteen to fifteen years, although the voyage itself rarely took more than two years. Mr Snodgrass, a surveyor of East India ships, said in 1772 that ships lay idle for one year in three ('Fifth Report from the Committee of Secrecy on the State of the East India Company', in *Reports of Committees of the House of Commons*, Vol. IV, 1772–3, p. 260). This report is a mine of information on East India shipping in the middle decades of the eighteenth century. It was followed by legislation (12 Geo. III, c. 54) which put a limit on the total tonnage of shipping which might be employed in the East India trade.

[2] H. B. Morse, *The East India Company Trading to China* (Oxford, 1926), pp. 307–13.

silk textiles — in the trade was growing fast, and it was becoming more and more difficult to keep the value of cargoes in large ships down to tolerable levels. The great ships of 700–800 tons were replaced as they wore out by much smaller ones; the size of East Indiamen became more standardised. Most ships of the first half of the eighteenth century were in the range 400–600 tons;[1] the smaller ones carrying the most valuable cargoes (with a high proportion of silk and cotton manufactures) from the Bay of Bengal, and the largest coming from China once this branch of trade was firmly established. As in most other trades, a new and rapidly accelerating growth in ship sizes came after the middle of the century; in 1769 the peak size of the 1690's was passed by the *Princess Royal* of nearly 900 tons, and in 1787, when the first thousand-ton English merchant ship, the *Ceres*, came into service, the old *Trade's Increase* was at last definitely surpassed.

These ships were chartered by the Company, using its own form of charter party, which from the 1680's was becoming highly standardised. From the beginning, two rates of freight were specified, one for 'gross' or 'gruff' goods, goods which were cheap in relation to their bulk, such as saltpetre, sugar, pepper, cowries, turmeric; and one for 'fine' goods — the high-value silks, calicoes, indigo, drugs and spices; and there was a specially low rate for 'ballast goods' such as iron, lead and copper. The rates varied, though within quite narrow limits, according to the territory for which the ship was bound; surprisingly, the rates for the China trade were lower than those for India.[2]

The rate from all the west coast stations of India, during peacetime in the thirty years after 1657, was usually £17 for gross and £20 or £21 per ton for fine goods, and this rate also applied

---

[1] The true tonnage of East India ships becomes obscure from about the end of the seventeenth century. The Company then began to charter definitely a tonnage of 499 tons in every ship not smaller than this (see p. 264, below). The practice has led some writers to assume that the size of the ships was standardised at this level, and even to attempt explanations of this supposed fact. In 1768–72, for instance, 136 ships were chartered:

chartered at 499 tons	67,864
measured tonnage	93,617
goods brought home	85,110

(Report, op. cit., p. 278). The beginning of this practice does undoubtedly coincide, however, with the abandonment by the Company of the very large ships it had favoured in the eighties; though many were still well over 500 tons, and the tonnage was slowly tending to rise again in the first three-quarters of the eighteenth century while the 'chartered' figure remained at 499 tons.

[2] Probably because ships from China had a very high proportion of their cargo in a moderately priced product, tea.

to Bantam in Java.[1] The wartime rise in rates was smaller than in other trades, for during much of the voyage the dangers the ships encountered were no greater in war than in peace, and in European waters they were capable of defending themselves against most privateers; whilst their crews included an unusually high proportion of specialists, whose pay was not so sharply advanced as that of seamen. The rates from 1702 onward can be listed in detail:[2]

Freight rates per ton, 1702–72

	China		Malabar Coast and Bay of Bengal		Bombay and Surat	
	g	f	g	f	g	f
1702			30	30	30	30
1703			33	36	33	36
1704			33½	36	33½	36½
1705			31	35	32	34
1706			30	33		
1707			31	36	33	34
1708–11			30½	37	34	33½
1712			24	29½	26	27
1713			22	27¼	24¼	25
1714–17			21	26	23	24
1718			23	28	25	26
1719–20			24	29	26	27
1721			22½	29	25½	26
1722–34			22	27	24	25
1735–9			21	26	23	24
1740			30	35	32	33
1741			31	36	33	34
1742			30	35	32	33
1743			29	34	31	32
1744–7			32	37	34	35
1748			26	31	28	29
1749			25	30	27	28
1750			24½	29½	26½	27½
1751–2			24	27	27	27
1753–4			24	27	27	30
1755			25	28	28	31
1756			31½	34	34½	37
1757			33	36	36	39
1758			34	37	37	40
1759			35	38	38	41
1760–2			37	40	40	43
1763–4	31	34	31	34	34	37
1765	30	33	30	33	33	36
1766–70	29	32	31	34	34	37
1771	30	33	32	35	35	38
1772	29	32	34	37¼	37⅜	40⅜

[1] Freight rates from HCA sources are supplemented by those in Bal Krishna, *Commercial Relations between England and India, 1603–1757* (1924), pp. 321–3.
[2] 1702–62 from R. Wissett, *A Compendium of East Indian Affairs* (1802); 1763 onward from the Report, op. cit., p. 258.

s

This table is not, unfortunately, an accurate guide to the real movements of freights paid by the Company. The reason is a complicated one. In the seventeenth century ships were hired on their tons burden; that is, the Company undertook to fill them up with a tonnage closely approximating their capacity as defined in the charter-party, and to pay for the whole of the tonnage at the two fixed rates for gross and fine goods. From soon after 1700, however, the standard charter-party provided that the Company should pay for only 404 tons at the rates set out in the charter-party. A further 80 tons of iron kintledge or ballast, to be taken out and home, was to be paid for at a very low rate; these two items together made up the 484 tons which the Company guaranteed to pay for;[1] and an allowance of 15 tons for the ships' officers made up the charter tonnage of 499 tons. Most ships could carry more than this — perhaps 50 or 60 tons more in 1710, 300 or 400 tons more in 1770 — and the Company had the right, but not the obligation, to fill the ship up, paying for most of the cargo over 499 tons at half the charter-party rate.[2] The average rate paid to the shipowner was therefore less than the charter-party rate, and was tending to become a declining percentage of that rate as the size of the ships employed increased in the course of the century — particularly after 1749. In the years 1770–2, for example, of a total of £1,629,399 paid by the Company to shipowners, 75 per cent was for freight at charter-party rates, 16 per cent was freight at the lower rates on extra tonnage, and 9 per cent demurrage;[3] the average rate per ton was five-sixths of the charter-party rate. This may partly account for the apparent steep rise in freight rates between 1753 and 1772. Except in the China trade, where for a few years the lading of tonnage above 499 tons was restricted by agreement,[4] the use of larger ships meant that a higher proportion of total tonnage was paid for at half price — or less.

When all this complication has been allowed for, however, it may be doubted whether the average rates paid from India in 1770–2 or 1753–5 were as low as those paid on the same voyage

---

[1] Except, of course, in ships of less than 499 tons.
[2] A small part at double the rate for kintledge; and the remainder at half-freight. In addition, it became customary after 1760 to pay £5 per ton for any outward cargo in excess of 333 tons (Report, op. cit., p. 257).
[3] ibid, p. 278.
[4] ibid., p. 279.

in the 1730's or even half a century earlier still. It seems to be true that in this trade as in no other, freight rates failed to decline under the impact of technical improvements in ships, and that the critics of the East India shipping interest were in the main justified in the complaints which were aired before the Parliamentary Committee of 1772.

Save for its extremely detailed character, there was little in the standard East India charter-party that was unusual.[1] It regulated the quantity and kinds of goods which could be carried on behalf of the officers and crew — on a generous scale, as we have seen. It fixed the rates of demurrage, and in the case of ships chartered for India provided that a ship not despatched before a date towards the end of January should be paid four months' demurrage from that date; it promised an advance payment, originally of two months' freight but in the later charter-parties four months', and for payment of the balance a few weeks after discharge. Early charter-parties defined 'gross' and 'fine' goods and contained lists of tare for various commodities, but these details were later embodied in the Company's general regulations, to which all shipping arrangements were understood to conform.

The charter-party put the ship completely under the control of the Company's agents — its supercargoes aboard the ship, its officers and factors in the eastern ports — from the beginning to the end of the voyage. Neither master nor owners were in any way concerned with the handling of the Company's commercial affairs. The master was a seaman, who took the ship where he was directed and did no more; during the long-drawn-out business of gathering cargo in the sweat and stench of Calcutta or Canton he could devote himself to his own profit-making concerns. He was, however, a highly privileged seaman, appointed with the Company's approbation, usually paying very heavily for his command, and entrusted with bringing home safely a cargo worth tens of thousands of pounds. Though his range of duties was much narrower than that of many a ship's master in the Spanish or West Indies trade, he was for these reasons far superior to them in status and income. Similarly, his owners were likely to be drawn from the highest ranks of commercial society, and to secure gains from their operations which provoked the envy of

---

[1] A late form of the charter-party is reproduced in the Report, op. cit., pp. 264–77.

every merchant and shipowner excluded from their circle — gains
which became in time so inordinate as to lead to the overthrow
of their privileged position by the action of parliament.

EAST INDIA

Statistics:

This is entirely a London trade, though entries at south-western ports are
occasionally recorded.

1. TONNAGE OF ENTRIES AND CLEARANCES (000 TONS)

	entries	clearances
1686	5·8	8·4
1715–17 av.		4·3
1771–3 av.	14·1	13·9

2. VALUE OF TRADE (£000)

	imports	exports
1699–1701	756	136
1771–3	2096	990

3. AVERAGE TONNAGE OF SHIPS

1686	365
1715–17 av.	361

XIII

The American and West Indian Trades

The English colonies in America divide economically into two groups. On the one hand are the plantation colonies — the tropical islands and the warm middle colonies of the mainland; the West Indies, Florida and Georgia, the Carolinas, Virginia and Maryland. These were very largely dependent on the production of staple export crops for Europe. On the other, there are the colonies from Pennsylvania northward, places of small farming and lumbering settlements, which always had difficulty in procuring suitable goods to send to England in exchange for the manufactures they required. Of all the areas which demanded the services of English shipping during the seventeenth and eighteenth centuries, the plantation colonies of America grew most consistently and most rapidly in importance, and by 1775 the traders with them were by far the biggest customers of the English shipping industry. They must provide the main theme of this chapter. The northern colonies traded with England in quite small volume, and to an increasing extent in ships owned in the ports of New England; they will be dealt with briefly at the end.[1]

Permanent English settlement in America began on the shores of Chesapeake Bay in 1607, was extended to New England in the next decade and to the West Indian islands in the twenties; by 1632 Barbados, Nevis, Monserrat, Antigua and part of St Kitts were occupied. On the American mainland settlement spread steadily inland and along the coast; the islands were taken in leaps, Jamaica in 1655 and St Vincent, Dominica, St Lucia and Tobago

[1] The best accounts of these trades are A. P. Middleton, *Tobacco Coast* (Newport News, Va., 1953); L. C. Gray, *History of Agriculture in the Southern United States to 1860* (Washington, 1933); M. S. Morriss, *The Colonial Trade of Maryland, 1689–1715* (Baltimore, 1915); R. G. Albion, *Forests and Sea Power* (Cambridge, Mass., 1926); F. W. Pitman, *The Development of the British West Indies, 1700–1763* (New Haven, Conn., 1917); R. Pares, *A West India Fortune* (1950); K. G. Davies, *The Royal African Company* (1957); R. B. Sheridan, 'The Sugar Trade of the British West Indies, 1660–1756' (unpublished London Ph.D. thesis, 1951).

267

at various dates before 1763, when they were formally annexed. The early colonies all grew food crops for their own support, but within a few years Virginia found its export staple in tobacco; the West Indian settlers quickly followed suit, and fast-growing tobacco production caused a collapse of tobacco prices in the twenties and thirties. After some years of uncertainty and experiment with such crops as ginger, cotton and indigo, the West Indies found their true fortune when Barbados planters, influenced by Dutch expelled from Brazil, began about 1640 the cultivation of sugar cane. Other islands followed, though slowly and less wholeheartedly, and by 1660 sugar was the principal crop throughout the West Indies, and was everywhere encroaching on the lands formerly devoted to other products.

From this time onward, the main task for English transatlantic shipping was the carriage to Europe of sugar from the West Indies, and tobacco from Virginia and Maryland. Almost the whole of this trade was carried in English-owned ships; the large New England shipping which grew up devoted itself to trade along the coasts of the continent, and between the mainland and the islands. Other commodities, such as indigo and cotton, retained a minor importance; but new ones rose to prominence in the eighteenth century. There was rice from South Carolina, its export enormously developed after 1700; pitch and tar from all the mainland colonies, stimulated by English bounties after 1705, and above all, from the middle decades of the century, timber[1] — particularly the tropical hardwoods which became fashionable for the furnishing of English drawing-rooms. Even so, sugar and tobacco still accounted for more than half the volume of shipments from the plantation colonies in the mid-eighteenth century.

The Navigation Acts prohibited the colonies from bringing in European goods, unless from England, and from sending their basic products out except to England;[2] high discriminatory duties and the prohibition of tobacco growing in England gave colonial sugar and tobacco a virtual monopoly of the English market after 1660. These plantation colonies developed few manufactures, and

---

[1] New Hampshire in the far north had even in the seventeenth century sent large supplies of mast timber to England.
[2] After 1739 the direct export of sugar to Europe was permitted (12 Geo. II, c. 30); but re-export had long since ceased, except to Ireland, and this measure did little to recover the old Continental markets.

were almost entirely dependent on England for woollen, cotton, linen and silk goods, hats and leather, beer, metalwork of all kinds. The supply of these needs with English manufactures, or with Continental goods handled by English merchants, went far to balance in value the sugar and tobacco imports to England. But in volume these export cargoes were much too small to fill the ships that lifted the tobacco and sugar crops, and they were supplemented in a number of ways.

One was the supply of foodstuffs. All the colonies were nearly self-sufficient in their early days, and the mainland colonies remained so. With the turn to sugar planting in the islands, however, the area of land reserved for food crops was gradually cut down to make room for more canes, and a demand for foodstuffs grew up and eventually reached vast proportions. England itself met only a small fraction of this demand, with a few thousand barrels of fish, and in the mid-eighteenth century some thousands of quarters of oats and wheat. The great supplier of provisions for the West Indies from about 1670 to 1720 was Ireland;[1] and it was convenient for the westbound English ships to call in south Irish harbours — Cork or Kinsale — and fill their holds with barrels of beef, pork, butter and cheese for sale at their destinations. Ireland remained, perhaps, the chief source of outward cargoes from the British Isles though the competition of the North American colonies reduced its share of the West Indies provision trade in the course of the eighteenth century. Other ships from England touched at Madeira and loaded wine for America; yet others went down the coast of Africa to the Isle of May in the Cape Verde Islands, and on the deserted beaches their crews made salt to take across the Atlantic. Both these trades were necessarily of very limited size.

The shipment of people provided another balance for the transatlantic trades. Most westbound ships carried a few returning planters, merchants, artificers; and they took to the mainland colonies a larger number of indentured servants going to try their luck in the New World. The passage money made a small but useful supplement to the ship's earnings. Much more important was the trade in African slaves, which began in the mid-seventeenth century and grew to great proportions as the plantation

---

[1] Encouraged by the acts of 1663, 1667 and 1680 which made it impossible to export Irish provisions to England.

system triumphed in all the sugar islands. Small cargoes of guns, brassware, spirits and textiles were shipped to the West African coast and bartered there for slaves; the slaves were transported across the Atlantic and sold, and the ships stood ready to lade cargoes for England.

The colonial trades were dominated from the beginning by London, with Bristol as a minor participant. London retained its hold on the sugar trade — in the mid-eighteenth century it still handled almost three-quarters of the imported sugar[1] — but the tobacco trade was rapidly passing out of its hands before 1700, and with the Act of Union with Scotland (1707) bringing Glasgow within the circle of privileged trade London's share fell further; in mid-century Scotland had taken over half the tobacco trade, and London held only half of the remainder. For a time southern ports such as Plymouth, Exeter, Bideford and Cowes carried on a tobacco trade which was largely one of formal customs entry at an English port before final shipment to a Continental destination; but they faded out in the early eighteenth century. The long series of French wars which began in 1689 encouraged the convenient habit of discharging transatlantic ships in ports of the north-west, well removed from the privateer bases; this brought Liverpool and Glasgow to the forefront of the tobacco trade, and even such minor places as Whitehaven, Lancaster and Beaumaris showed great activity for a time. The hold of Liverpool and Glasgow on the trade was retained in peacetime for reasons considered below.

In the very first years of colonial trade the ships which visited the colonies were those sent by the organisers of colonisation. As export crops were developed, however, casual traders appeared, travelling merchants or supercargoes who bought the planters' crops on the spot. Many trading ships of this kind continued to come throughout the seventeenth century, though increasingly the master shouldered the trading functions. The instructions one group of outport owners gave to their ship's master illustrate the duties and problems of a great many of them:

Bideford, November
27th 1684

Mr Nicholas Bear

We desire you to take the first opportunity of a faire wind and tide that god shall vouchsafe, and sayle out over the Bar with our shipe

[1] Sheridan, op. cit. p. 76.

Vineyard, and if possible, to stop in the Road of Cloveley so long as to take in twenty-three barrels of Herrings from Mr. Benjamin Coker, from thence directly for Waterford in the Kingdom of Ireland, There to address yourself to Mr. Richard Mabanke Merchant, whome we desire to provide for you such provisions as amount to one hundred poundes or thereabouts, the perticulers of which, goes with you to him unsealed you are to take care that Itt be all very good If freight present to the place you are bound you may Imbrace it and when you have gotten all on Board which we hope you will doe with all Expedition, that then you sayle directly for Mountserrat in the West Indies, there to dispose of all such Goods, Wares and Merchandises as you carry Along with you on our Account to the Best Advantage,[1] and if Posable to leave no Debts, and to demand and receive of Mr. Thomas Attwood and Mr James Linch (who were ordered by Mr William Andrewes to do our business in his absence) All such Debts as are dew to us in that Place, and be sure to see that the Goods be all well condicioned, and if you stand in needs of their Assistance in the disposeing of the Goods you carry with you, or Receiving the Effects of the same, You may if you think fitt make use of them but that we leave to your Discrecion Together with all other of our Conferens with you If you have any Rome to spare you may take in some Freight if it offers, for this place and when your Business is over to come directly home for Bideford We hope that your Care, Prudence and Dilligence will be such (in the Management of all our Affairs) that may make much for your Credit and Honer, and have the continuance of the favour and respects of

Your loveing friends
John Darracott
Edward Wren
Robert Wren

Mr. Bear if you are
Disapoynted in
Anything above saide
that then you may have
the Lyberty to doe with our Ship
and goods as you think fitt for
our Best Advantage.[2]

Still more vessels appeared to take home on freight the cargoes collected by merchants and factors settled in the colonies. Later in the seventeenth century the organisation of the London part

---

[1] This means sell in exchange for sugar and other goods; it was rarely possible to obtain money in the islands.
[2] HCA 24–122.

of the colonial trade began to change; the substantial planters who were emerging acquired London agents and, instead of selling their crops locally, sent their sugar or tobacco to these London houses for sale on a commission basis.[1] The agents soon undertook many other functions for the planters, including, to an increasing extent, the supply of transport. By the beginning of the eighteenth century many planters regarded it as an obligation of their English correspondents to send ships — whether their own or chartered — to lift the crops. John Molineux wrote in 1723 from Barbados to his Bristol agent, 'I assure you that you miss a hundred hogsheads yearly, consignments for want of a vessel that your friends may depend upon.'[2] Increasingly the agents found it necessary to become managing owners of ships or even of small fleets, frequently with planters among the part-owners; the London sugar agent Richard Lascelles owned shares in twenty-one ships in 1753 (though it is not clear that they were all engaged in the sugar trade, and it is most unlikely that he managed them all).[3] In 1723 a broker in Barbados wrote,

'The planters are so ingaged to Londoners who constantly use this trade that it is no easy matter to procure a stranger a freight. . . . We expect freight will be plenty in a little time, the Londoners being very near loaden.'[4]

The master of an independent ship, the *John*, wrote to his owners from Jamaica in 1728:

'I am sorry to tell you that I have got but 79 hogs. of Sugar aboard and 24 tons of logwood. The reason that we are so far behind, that those Gentlemen who gave us those words to ship on board us depart from those Words by reason that all the great Londoners has owners here and are upon Charterparty.'[5]

Increasingly in the eighteenth century, therefore, the ships from London were tied to giving priority to the cargoes of particular

[1] On the development of the commission system, see K. G. Davies, 'The Origins of the Commission System in the West India Trade', *TRHS*, 5th ser., Vol. II, 1951; Sheridan, op. cit., pp. 227–44; Middleton, op. cit., pp. 104–10. It can be found operating at the other old centre of colonial trade; see R. Pares, *A West India Fortune* (1950).
[2] W. E. Minchinton, *The Trade of Bristol in the Eighteenth Century* (Bristol Record Society, 1957), p. 92.
[3] Sheridan, op. cit., p. 76. He owned $\frac{32}{16}$ in all. Dr Sheridan asserts that 'most of the London ships were owned and controlled by planters and agents by the middle years of the 18th century', but the evidence he uses seems too scanty to bear such a generalisation.
[4] Minchinton, op. cit., pp. 98–9.   [5] HCA 24–136.

planters, from whom the masters in their turn expected preference in loading. The whole structure of transport showed a growing tendency to inflexibility; but the strength of this must not be exaggerated. There always remained numbers of ships which had been sent out speculatively by owners or charterers with few or no fixed commitments, to pick up most of their cargo by negotiation on the river banks and in the planters' houses. Even in the sugar trade, which London commission agents dominated most completely, the extensive arrangements between agents and planters for the supply of shipping were only growing in the eighteenth century and were far from universally adopted as late as 1775. The Commissioners of Trade and Plantations, receiving evidence in 1784 on West Indies trading a decade earlier, were told:

'The course of the trade is as follows; the principal British Merchants are concerned with Houses in the West Indies to whom they send their ships, which carry out goods from hence and who provide cargoes of the West India produce to load them home; these ships are called Stationed Ships and seldom or ever vary their Course; but there are many others who go to the West Indies to look for Freight and are called Seekers in contradistinction to the Stationed Ships. When we exported Grain to Portugal and the Southern parts of Europe, Madeira and the African Islands many of the ships which carried the same, when they had left their cargoes of grain went on to the West Indies to look for Freight. The ships also which arrived there from the coast of Africa with Negroes wanted Freight home.'[1]

As to the tobacco trade, here the growth of the commission system was itself to some extent responsible for the turn away from London connections.

The most important groups of independent carriers in the eighteenth century were, in the tobacco trade, the ships of Liverpool and Glasgow; and in the sugar trade, the slave traders.

Dr A. P. Middleton has suggested one reason for the relative decline of London and the rise of the north-western ports in the tobacco trade.[2] The commission agency system developed very early in this trade, possibly owing to the important part played by London merchants in financing the colonies' first difficult decades. But Virginia and Maryland were not, like the West Indian islands, tropical dependencies quickly losing their white

[1] BM Add.MSS. 38388–10.   [2] op. cit., pp. 104–10.

population as slavery grew, places the well-to-do aimed to abandon
for mansions in England; they were comfortably situated colonies
which became permanent homes for a rapidly growing white
population of planters, large and small. As wealth accumulated
it was not sent to England to establish county families and
peerages; it was spent on the spot, creating a large demand for a
variety of imported goods and scope for intensive merchant
activity. English merchant firms found it worth while to establish
branch establishments to retail English goods and in return to
buy the colonists' tobacco outright. Some of the wealthier
planters, too, took a hand in trading, buying up the crops of their
smaller neighbours to sell along with their own. By 1731 it was
said that almost all the tobacco made by the 'common people' —
i.e. the smaller planters in Virginia — was sold 'to the merchants
in this country and the factors from the outports' against goods
from their stores.[1] The tendency was strengthened as, in the
eighteenth century, settlement and tobacco planting spread
further inland, creating producing areas fairly remote from navigable water, whose settlers could not deal directly with the shipmasters and had to have local intermediaries. Because the London
merchants connected with these colonies were heavily involved in
the commission system, these new kinds of trading were developed
particularly by merchants of the outports; and the north-western
ports had, in Scottish and Irish linens, Lancashire cottons, and
the metalwares of the Birmingham area, saleable lines for stocking
their American warehouses. The high demand for certain kinds of
English goods, and the marketing relations established to sell
these goods, were chiefly responsible for the binding together of
Liverpool, Glasgow and the Chesapeake Bay settlements by commercial ties. In a year of bad crops (1732) therefore it was possible
for a writer from Virginia to report,

> It is indeed probable that some of the Factors[2] may object to the
> disappointment they have this year mett with in the lading of their
> ships; but there is an answer ready at hand; the merchants who
> adventure goods hither to purchase tobacco in the country, have mett
> with no such accident; their ships are gone home full, and so far are
> they from being sufferers, that tis very demonstrable they will be
> this year great gainers by their purchase.'[3]

[1] *CSPAWI 1731*, No. 67.
[2] Meaning in this case the commission agents.   [3] *CSPAWI 1732*, No. 406.

There is a less polite explanation of the development of the north-western ports — smuggling. Tobacco was imported in casks of varying sizes, and compressed to various densities. In Lancashire and in the Scottish ports soon after 1700, when the art of compression of tobacco was being perfected, it was not a difficult matter to get the customs officials to weigh the lightest cask of a shipload, and then charge duty on all the casks on the basis of that one's weight. There was a great scandal over this practice at Liverpool in 1702–5, and at Glasgow in 1722;[1] serious fraud was probably stamped out then, but while it was having its run some tobacco trade fortunes had been made and firm connections had been created between the outports and the colonies.

The slave traders' numbers grew very fast in the West Indies, and they began to appear in the Chesapeake after 1713. It was apparently unusual for these to be tied to the needs of particular planters' homeward shipments, for two reasons.[2] The triangular voyage and the indefinite period of chaffering on the African coast made the time of their arrival in the West Indies unpredictable. Moreover, their masters or supercargoes had to buy large cargoes of sugar for the account of their owners.[3] The slaves they brought could not be sold in the West Indies for cash, since there was little money circulating in the islands; they had to be exchanged either for bills on London (the supply of which was increasingly limited as planters became more dependent on their London agents and more in debt to them) or for local commodities. A slave cargo acquired on the African coast and not suffering unusually heavy mortality on the voyage was worth at least twice as much as the sugar which could be stowed in its place,[4] so that far from being

[1] C. Northcote Parkinson, *The Rise of the Port of Liverpool* (Liverpool, 1952), pp. 72–6. T. C. Barker, 'Smuggling in the Eighteenth Century; the Evidence of the Scottish Tobacco Trade', *Virginia Mag. Hist. Biog.*, Vol. LXII, 1954; J. M. Price, 'The Rise of Glasgow in the Chesapeake Tobacco Trade, 1707–1775', *William & Mary Quarterly*, 1954.
[2] The slave trade with Virginia and Maryland was not large until late in the eighteenth century. Moreover, there was some prejudice against the carriage of tobacco in slave ships, so they made only a small contribution to its transport (Middleton, op. cit., p. 141).
[3] As explained in Chapter V, slave cargoes after the days of company trading were nearly always owned by the ships' owners.
[4] The prices of both slaves and sugar were rising (with many short-term fluctuations) throughout the century after 1689, so this generalisation is broadly true though the exact relationship between the two sets of prices varies.

free to take great quantities of sugar home on freight, the slaver's master was sometimes compelled to hire space in other ships to take home sugar he had acquired in excess of his own carrying capacity. This may go far to explain the rapid disappearance of London interests from the slave trade after the eclipse of the Royal Africa Company; for the sugar commission agents who dominated London's West India trade could not easily reconcile their obligation to lift their clients' cargoes with the necessity of bringing home the sugar of those planters who happened to have exchanged some for slaves. On the other hand, the slave trade must have provided an increasing proportion of the shipping bringing sugar into Bristol and Liverpool.

The experience of the Royal Africa Company, which handled a great part of the slave trade between 1673 and 1713, is of some interest.[1] From 1673 to 1689, its most profitable years, the Company usually chartered ships for the outward voyage to Africa and the West Indies (using the same ships and masters year after year if they proved satisfactory), making payment per head of negroes delivered alive in the West Indies. In spite of every effort to remit the proceeds home in bills on London, the Company's West Indian agents were always left with large cargoes of sugar and other goods taken in exchange for slaves, to be shipped for England. They hired cargo space in whatever ships were available; and among the ships seeking cargo were, of course, those that the Company had employed for its outward voyage with slaves. Moreover, the Company insisted that the shipowners should take part of their freight (after 1678, two-thirds of it) not in cash but in slaves;[2] the shipowners' agent or the master had to find means of remitting home the proceeds of the sale of these slaves, and therefore he also had to find space to ship goods on owners' account. Though the organisation of the slave trade was changing fast after 1702, these problems remained. The large and growing volume of sugar lifted by the slave traders came from those planters who preferred — or who were for financial reasons compelled — to sell their crops locally rather than to send them home for sale on a commission basis by agents in London.

[1] K. G. Davies, op. cit., Ch. V.
[2] Like all charter-parties, those of the Royal Africa Company provided for payment at the end of the voyage; and the voyage for which the Company hired these ships ended in the West Indies.

The presence of a large number of uncommitted ships ensured that there was a single freight market in the Leeward Islands, in Jamaica, and on the Chesapeake, and (within narrow limits) a single level of freights in each of these markets during the peak loading period of every season. Though attempts were occasionally made to settle freight rates before the ships went out from England, they always foundered on the competition for freight and cargo space in the islands themselves. 'The freight must always be settled abroad and not at home', wrote the London sugar merchants and shipowners, Wilkinson and Gavillier, in 1747, 'We attempted to settle it at home last year for Barbadoes and thought to have fixed it at Nine shillings per cwt., but the Gentlemen would not allow more than 7/6d, and at that rate the ships loaded, and indeed high and low freights must always depend upon the plenty and scarcity of shipping.'[1] The ship's master had to take his part in the making of this local freight market; once the rate was settled he had to accept the prevailing level or be abandoned by his connections — though on the other hand he might lose future business simply by demanding the current rate from them when this was a high one, if they felt they were entitled to special consideration from him. The complexities of the relations between these tied shipmasters and the planters are well illustrated by the letters of Robert Carter, a large Virginia planter, to his English connections.[2] In 1720, a year of large crops, he wrote:

'This accompanies the *Carter*.[3] She is loaded at £10 per ton, which I hope will in some measure retrieve the great, great losses upon her late voyages. Captain Kent is threatened mightily to be remembered when a scarce year comes, but that humor will go near soon to blow over. There is no reason that we who venture our money should be losers by it. . . .You make a proposal about selling the *Carter*. I have no reason to fall into it, I'm sure. I can hardly believe you are in earnest; when that time comes you'll be the greatest sufferer; unless another ship supplies her place, your business will soon droop here.'[4]

[1] R. Pares, 'A London West India Merchant House' in R. Pares and A. J. P. Taylor (eds.), *Essays in Honour of Sir Lewis Namier* (1957); he gives other examples of attempts to fix freight rates at home.
[2] L. B. Wright (ed.), *Letters of Robert Carter 1720–27* (San Marino, Cal., 1940).
[3] The writer was a part-owner of this ship, along with his London agent and others.
[4] To Wm. Dawkins, 13th July 1720.

The following year saw a reversal of fortunes:

> 'Its said most of the York ships will want of their loading and that
> there is some thousands of hogsheads short of what there is ships to
> carry. I almost think the circumstances of our river are much the
> same. Kent is in great doubt whether he shall get full or no, although
> I did lade upon him more tobacco than ever I did. His old friends, in
> revenge for his £10 per ton last year, have all left him, and do him
> all the prejudice they can.'[1]

The sugar and tobacco crops were liable to violent year to year
fluctuations which could rarely be foreseen long in advance.
Letters home from colonial governors are full of crop forecasts, but
the information was not always soundly based, and in any case late
disasters could heavily reduce the crop after most of the shipping
for the season had been committed; news in England was several
months behind colonial events. A report by the Customs Commissioners in 1681 revealed a sceptical view of crop forecasts:

> 'Mr. Spencer says . . . there are now on the ground the greatest crops
> ever known, which, when added to the stock still in the country, will
> be as much as, if not more than, the ships can carry off in two years.
> But we are informed that there have been the like reports of great
> crops in former years, and that our shipping has rather wanted
> freight than crops a sale.'[2]

More than any other trades, these were speculative ones for the
shipowner; his ships might arrive in the expectation of good crops
and high freights and find that the crops had been ruined and
there was little to carry home. This was a temptation towards the
tied ship system; though the master could not improve on market
rates for freight, it might at least secure him from the horror of
low freight rates on cargo in an almost empty ship. The salvation
of the shipowners, however, came with the development of
alternative cargoes in the eighteenth century — pitch and tar in
America soon after 1700, timber from all the transatlantic regions
twenty years later, and eventually grain from Virginia. The value
of these to the shipping interest was clearly recognised; the writer
of *A Letter To a Member of Parliament Concerning the Naval Store
Bill* in 1721, for example, declared that

---

[1] To Messrs. Perry, 2nd June 1721.
[2] *CSPAWI 1681–5*, No. 3. In 1724 an unusually large crop was expected in
Virginia; it was largely destroyed by a violent storm on 12th August (*CSPAWI
1724–5*, No. 487).

'In the Navigation we now carry on to our Plantations, it often happens that the Crops of Tobacco and Sugar etc. fall short; so that many of the Ships are forced to come home dead-freighted, and some lie a whole season for the next Crop, which (if Encouragement was given for bringing Timber, etc. from our Plantations) would, upon such disappointments, be sure of a Loading'.[1]

Sugar cane was cut during the summer; it was partly processed in the islands to produce a rough brown substance, muscovado, for export. The by-products of the refining process, molasses and its derivative rum, went mostly to the North American colonies, though by the middle of the eighteenth century rum shipments were reaching England in some quantity. The processing of the cane occupied the last months of the year, when the island paths were swamped by the rains and hogsheads could not be moved to the wharves. Shipment began early in the new year and continued until July[2] when the onset of the hurricane season and of the most dangerous period for fever drove most ships' masters away even if their vessels were not filled up. In any ordinary year, this gave ample time to get all the crop laden and carried away; when Henry Bibby's ship reached Nevis after various delays on 1st September 1712 'sugars were very scarce and the ship could not be laden until new Canes were ripe and new Sugars gotten'.[3] The ships arrived back in England, therefore, in the summer and autumn, sailing again for the direct trade with the West Indies in December and January. If there was some all the year round traffic, this must be attributed largely to the difficulty slave traders had in timing their operations precisely to arrive in the islands at the best time; direct traders came early to have the peak of the season in the islands between February and May, and hurry home. Nevertheless, a ship's stay in its West Indian harbour was usually a long one. Every ship going out carried some cargo, small perhaps but valuable. While much of it was sent out by London agents and charged up to the planter's running account with them, a great deal was sold to the island's merchants, shopkeepers and independent planters. It was every exporter's dream to sell for cash or goods and leave no debts behind him; the island

[1] Similar views were expressed by Joshua Gee in 1718; *CSPAWI 1717-18*, No. 819.
[2] In the late eighteenth century insurance rates were doubled on ships which remained in the islands after 31st July. BT 6-189 (1788).
[3] E. 134 1 Geo. I, Easter 21.

T

courts gave few favours to far-off English creditors. But it was a dream, for debt always remained, to be collected by the agent or the master on the next voyage, or the next, or the next . . . but the attempt slowed up movement.

Arrivals from the West Indies

	London 1686	Bristol 1687	London 1736	London 1766
January	16	7	13	10
February	7	1	8	8
March	11	2	4	13
April	14	2	2	6
May	18	6	3	9
June	25	4	16	16
July	29	4	26	59
August	21	8	38	53
September	27	3	29	62
October	25	3	28	29
November	19	1	10	26
December	13	1	18	20[1]

Except when crops were unusually abundant, it was a slow process to secure full cargo from a number of plantations, possibly in different harbours[2] or even in different islands. The well-known delays in the islands were reflected in charter-party conditions. All the early ones were time charters, throwing the costs and uncertainties of delay on the hirer, and the time charter continued to be fairly common in this trade for some years after the Restoration, when it was rarely found elsewhere outside the Mediterranean. As the tonnage charter gradually superseded it, the terms of this again reflected the expectations of delay, in the long laydays allowed, usually 70–80 working days.[3]

Again, the difficulties and slowness of getting cargo were reflected in the smallness of the ships undertaking this long voyage. From the mid-seventeenth until the mid-eighteenth century, the typical London ship sailing to the West Indies was of 150–200 tons, while the outport trader was more commonly 100 tons or less; the few larger ships were seen only at Barbados

---

[1] The very marked increase in London's seasonal concentration in the eighteenth century is probably associated with the port's exit from the slave trade.

[2] At one time local craft brought the Jamaica sugar to Kingston or Port Royal for lading in the ships; but by about 1730 the practice had grown up of the ships themselves calling in various harbours all round the island (*CSPAWI 1732*, No. 327).

[3] See *CSPAWI 1696–7*, Nos. 247, 254, 267.

and Jamaica, and were for a long time rarities there. In the early eighteenth century ships of 300–400 tons became much more evident in the Jamaica trade, probably because of the dangers from Spanish *guarda-costas*. Only in mid-century did average tonnage begin to rise sharply and the 300-ton ship to appear in considerable numbers in the West Indian harbours. This change arose from the sharp expansion in the sugar trade itself, which reduced the risks of under-capacity loading, and from the appearance of considerable timber shipments which provided alternative cargoes to fall back on, specially suited to large ships. Right up to the end, however, small vessels of 30 or 40 tons could be found trading between the West Indies and English provincial ports. A large and rapidly growing proportion of all these ships came from the shipyards of the North American colonies, many of them sailing direct from Salem or Newburyport to the islands, lading sugar for England, and being sold to English owners on arriving in the English outports. Few American-*owned* ships, however, played any regular part in the trade between England and the West Indies; the American ships seen in great numbers in the islands were engaged in traffic with their own home colonies and with Southern Europe.

This was, therefore, a trade in which ships normally made a single voyage each year. For the slaver this was a very full year, and even the direct trader sailing in January was lucky to get home before August, too late for the owner to trouble to find temporary employment for the ship in the interval before she had to be prepared for the Caribbean again. In a year of good harvest, an early ship which was loaded and despatched quickly and was fortunate in her voyages might be home in May, and with a certain amount of risk could just get in another voyage; but this was a rare achievement. The Bristol firm of Pinney made attempts to operate their ships on a two-voyage a year basis, but never had much success until the nineteenth century; in 1791 it confessed this was 'a matter which we have constantly intended, but in which we have hitherto been always disappointed'.[1]

Because of the slowness with which reliable crop information reached England — almost the sole importer of British West Indies sugar — short-term fluctuations in crops were reflected not so much by the number of ships which were engaged in importing

[1] R. Pares, op. cit., p. 227.

them, as by the difficulties which these ships encountered in
getting cargo: measured by half-empty holds, low freights and
long loading delays when crops were poor, and by high freights
for quickly laden full cargoes when the crop had been a good one.
The situation was gradually modified, during the eighteenth
century; on the one hand by the growth of American merchant
shipping and its connections with the West Indies, providing a
limited alternative market for sugar and a reserve of transport
capacity which in an exceptionally good year could be quickly
turned to the carriage of sugar to England; on the other by the
development of alternative cargoes, especially timber from the
Central American mainland and Jamaica. The rigidity of the supply
of shipping within any crop season for sugar relaxed to some
extent after 1713, but it remained high.

Freight rates in this trade, therefore, showed considerable
fluctuations even in peacetime. This is most clearly seen in the
long series of rates in the records of the Royal Africa Company,
covering the years 1678–1717. (See table opposite). Even within
individual years rates changed rapidly, as fresh ships arrived
unexpectedly, or those expected failed to appear.[1]

These violent fluctuations make generalisation about freight
rates difficult. It does appear, however, that there was a downward
trend in peacetime rates; the minimum rate between 1650 and
1670, frequently encountered, was £3 15s. to £4 per ton, while
just a century later it was £3 to £3 10s. per ton net. Moreover, by
the latter period the very wide upswings in freight rates which
characterised the years of good crops in the seventeenth century
had almost disappeared; in the years 1763–7, for example, John
Okill of Liverpool was regularly paying for shipments of sugar
within the range of £3 to £3 2s. 6d. per ton.[2]

There is a special difficulty over sugar freight rates. Sugar (like
tobacco) grew up with a trade convention of charging freight on a
ton of four hogsheads. These hogsheads in fact varied in size
from place to place; and in the course of time they grew far beyond
the five hundredweight on which the standard was originally
based, commonly reaching ten to twelve hundredweight — at
Nevis 14 cwt. casks are recorded in 1730.[3] There was some early

---

[1] Freight Books: T 70 — 962 et seq.
[2] Okill MSS., Liverpool Public Library.
[3] E. F. Gay, op. cit., p. 166. The average Barbados hogshead was said to
weigh eleven hundredweight in 1764 (BM Add.MSS. 38373–160).

dissatisfaction with this method of charging — for instance, a
Barbados contract of 1655 gives alternative rates of £4 per ton
net or £3 15s. per ton 'in casks as customary' — but it had not
been generally broken down before the war of 1689–97. Probably

*Freight rates per ton paid by the Royal Africa
Company for homeward shipments of sugar*

| | Annual Averages, £'s | |
	Barbados	Jamaica
1678	5·2	6·5
1679	4·0	6·6
1680	3·5	5·8
1681	3·5	6·1
1682	4·0	6·1
1683	3·6	5·0
1684	3·5	5·1
1685	4·8	4·6
1686	5·2	4·2
1687	4·4	4·0
1688	4·2	4·0
1689	6·1	5·6
1690	10·1	7·8
1691	7·5	14·0
1692	7·8	16·9
1693	7·7	12·0
1694	7·2	12·0
1695	9·5	17·5
1696	11·2	18·0
1697	12·5	25·9
1698	6·4	16·2
1699	3·1	9·9
1700	3·2	6·7
1701	2·8	6·9
1702	2·5	8·0
1703	3·6	13·6
1704	9·6	16·0
1705	10·1	18·0
1706	8·4	20·5
1707	7·6	16·8
1708	7·5	17·2
1709	9·6	18·6
1710	7·5	—
1711	6·0	—
1712	5·3	—
1713	5·4	—
1714	4·0	9·6
1715	3·5	8·9
1716	3·3	—
1717	3·4	10·0

it was already being replaced, for when peace came in 1697 freight (except in the Jamaica trade) was being charged per ton of sugar, net, weighed in England and expressed in such terms as 'Ten shillings a hundred for every hundred of sugar weighed at the Queen's Beam in Liverpool'.[1] Naturally this change caused a sharp reduction in the apparent freight rate. The Jamaica rate, still on the conventional standard though the 'ton' of four hogsheads probably weighed more nearly two tons than one by this time, was left much higher than the others. Average rates paid in peacetime by the Royal Africa Company make this clear:[2]

	Barbados	Jamaica
1678–82	£3 19s.	£6 4s.
1683–8	£4 11s.	£5 4s.
1698–1702	£3 1s.	£8 1s.
1714–17	£3 12s.	£9 6s.

By the 1760's the Jamaica custom had been assimilated to the general one of payment per net ton, and the whole West India trade had settled down to rates of £3 to £3 10s. per ton, with the Jamaica rate commonly 7s. 6d. to 10s. higher than the others. This was less than the true rate of a century before, but it had changed little from the levels prevalent about 1700; the economies of larger and cheaper ships do not appear to have been passed on to the sugar planters, perhaps because the demand for shipping in this trade was rising very fast in the middle decades of the eighteenth century.

In wartime the trade showed exceptionally violent movements in freight rates, for the islands, intermixed with French and Dutch possessions and close to the Spanish Main, were infested with enemy privateers and even endangered by regular naval forces. Sugar was shipped at rates as high as £25 per ton in wartime, and freights remained at £10 to £12 for year after year. The Bristol and Liverpool rates in wartime were markedly lower than those for London and much traffic was diverted to these ports, returning to London after the wars were over. The island assemblies tried at times to limit freight rates by law (as, for

---

[1] Slowness of adjustment in Jamaica trade may be because the Jamaica hogshead was smaller. In 1702 it was said that Barbados hogsheads weighed 10–12 cwt., the Jamaica hogshead 7 cwt. (*CSPAWI 1702*, No. 97).

[2] The Jamaica voyage was genuinely more costly than others; it was slightly longer and more difficult, and involved greater danger from the Spaniards; moreover, its serious development began little before 1680.

example, by the Barbados act of 1690 which limited freights to £7, an act which was eventually disallowed by the Privy Council in 1695).[1] But planters were anxious not to drive away the carriers of their crops, on whom they were totally dependent.[2]

Tobacco was a seasonal crop, but stripping and packing for shipment went on over several months. While loose tobacco might be available in August, the first packed hogsheads came forward in October and the bulk of the crop during the next two or three months, while smaller quantities were sometimes being packed right through till May and June. The ships therefore sailed from England in the early autumn, and because of the long loading delays in the creeks of the Chesapeake did not sail for home before the late spring. The pattern was slowly changing in the second quarter of the eighteenth century; sailings were later, and shipment reached its peak in the late spring and early summer rather than the early winter.[3]

Arrivals from Virginia and Maryland

	London 1686	Bristol 1687	London 1736	London 1751	London 1766
January	2	2	5	16	10
February	—	1	6	5	8
March	9	4	1	4	9
April	7	3	2	1	5
May	12	3	3	2	1
June	3	4	—	2	2
July	23	4	6	1	4
August	10	3	5	3	6
September	8	1	3	5	8
October	5	1	13	9	4
November	1	1	19	6	17
December	1	—	21	20	11

There are a number of possible explanations of this change.[4] One is the gradual shifting back of tobacco planting into the areas beyond tidewater; in the freshes where the teredo worm did not menace ships' timbers, masters were in less hurry to get away before the

[1] *CSPAWI 1693–6*, Nos. 692–3, 893, 917, 978.
[2] 'Had not the merchants engaged to pay more than the limited price, not a ship would have left London for Barbadoes this season' (ibid., No. 893).
[3] The pattern is confirmed by the dates of fixtures of freight rates in Maryland, recorded by J. M. Hemphill, II, 'Freight Rates in the Maryland Tobacco Trade, 1705–62, *Maryland Hist. Mag.*, Vol. 54, 1959, pp. 154–87.
[4] I wish to acknowledge the assistance given by Mr J. M. Price and Mr J. M. Hemphill, II, on this point.

hot weather brought the worms.[1] The local Tobacco Inspection
Acts of 1730 in Virginia and 1747 in Maryland had their influence
in delaying shipments. Finally, the growth of merchant intermediaries in the colonies, dealing frequently with planters far from
navigable water, led to a certain amount of local stockholding of
a kind which few planters had been willing or able to undertake.

Large ships were always quite common in this trade. The
lightness of the commodity gave a special advantage to the Dutch
flyboat, designed to give high stowage in relation to tons burden;
and the Dutch made heavy incursions just before 1650.[2] After
the Dutch wars English shipowners used large numbers of Dutch
prizes until the supply was exhausted, and for some decades after
1690 Virginia and Maryland shipping appears to have been
operated rather less efficiently than in the flyboat era. Ships of
400 tons were seen on the Chesapeake before 1640, and continued
to sail from London right up to the Revolution; even the more
typical London trader of 200–250 tons, was a good deal larger
than ships in most other trades. With the rapid growth of outport
participation in the trade from the late seventeenth century,
however, much smaller vessels came into use as tobacco carriers.

Though the Atlantic crossing was not a long one — eight weeks,
more or less, on the east-bound voyage and a little longer on the
westbound — those ships which took part regularly in the Virginia
and Maryland trade rarely made more than one voyage in a year.
Despite the earmarking of cargoes for particular ships before they
were even chartered in England, the masters had to wait the
planters' pleasure for loading, except when crops were abnormally
heavy. Moreover, they had to present themselves for lading at
various points up and down the chosen river, and until after the
passing of the colonial Inspection Acts (Virginia in 1730 and
Maryland in 1747) they normally provided boats and seamen for
fetching the cargo from the shore; indeed, the seamen sometimes
had to roll the hogsheads down to the shore from miles inland.[3]

---

[1] The *Charles* was on the Patuxent River from 8th May to 27th July 1674;
she sailed though the master knew she was worm-eaten and sank off the Virginia
coast (HCA 13–131).
[2] G. L. Beer, *Origins of the British Colonial System, 1578–1660* (New York,
1922), Ch. XI.
[3] If it was necessary to hire boats locally to speed the lading, this could add
5s. or 10s. a ton to the ship's costs (HCA 15–8, *Postillion*, 1696; HCA 15–35,
Hill Galley, 1720).

Finally, except in years of very heavy crops, most of the masters had to tout for business to complete their lading — and sometimes to seek, in the end, for cargo of some other commodity. All this involved long waiting, which is reflected in the laydays customarily allowed for in Virginia and Maryland charter-parties — 80 to 100 working days. A French observer wrote: 'Un vaisseau est ordinairement trois à quatre mois, et souvent six mois, dans la pays à rassembler une cargaison qui ne l'y retiendroit pas quinze jours si on emanagasinoit le tabac dans les portes marqúes'.[1] Eighty working days was over three months; with the voyage out and home and lading and discharge in London, eight or nine months was a normal time from charter or the beginning of lading until final discharge. Preparations for the following year's voyage, and refitting and repairs, allowed little margin for other operations; the only ones undertaken — and those not frequently — were the onward carriage of tobacco from the outport where it had been entered to comply with the Navigation Acts to its foreign destinations, and the collection of some cargo of Dutch or German goods towards the next outward voyage.

The homeward freight of tobacco, therefore, represented nearly the whole of a ship's earnings for the year. Outward freight was rarely considerable, since it was usual to carry goods freight free for charterers and for others who promised return cargo. Most vessels in this trade carried some passengers — merchants or returning planters or officials paying full fares and accommodated with the captain, and indentured servants or redemptioners going to seek fortunes in a new land — and these augmented the earnings of owners to some small extent, and gave the masters considerable opportunities for gain.

In this as in the West India trade, comparison of freight rates over time is made difficult by the changing size of the unit on which freight was calculated. Freight was charged, throughout the period when tobacco was a major commodity of commerce,[2] on the ton reckoned as four hogsheads. The equation of the hogshead with the quarter-ton may initially have been a real one; in

[1] G. M. Butel-Dumont, *Histoire et Commerce des Colonies Angloises dans l'Amerique Septentrionale* (Paris, 1755), p. 260.

[2] In the earliest days tobacco was shipped loose in rolls which took up a lot of space and paid a high freight per ton. Later, some rolls were carried along with the hogsheads, because they could be pushed into the spaces between the barrels. The practice was considered to give too much scope for smuggling, and was banned in 1700 (10 and 11 Wm. III, c. 21).

1669 it was said that the normal contents of a hogshead were 350 lb. of tobacco,[1] which with the hogshead's own weight would give about the right total. However, two changes began to be effected, first in the density of the packing and second in the size of the hogshead itself.

Tobacco as originally barrelled was a very light commodity, taking up a great deal of space in relation to its weight. But it was compressible, and tigher packing was an advantage to the planter paying freight by the number of barrels, and no detriment to the ship, which was merely saved the trouble of ballasting too light a cargo. Planters paid much attention to improving the process of 'steving' or compressing tobacco in the barrels to reduce the burden of freight — sometimes, it was alleged, carrying the process so far as to damage the leaf.

The other measure, increasing the size of the hogshead, was very much at the shipowners' expense, and colonial legislatures, under pressure from the home government, passed a number of acts in the late seventeenth century to limit it.[2] Nevertheless the Virginia and Maryland hogshead of 1716 was very much bigger than that of half a century earlier.[3]

Neither of these processes had gone very far before 1689, but both were widely exploited in the next two decades, under the stimuli of high wartime freight rates and new possibilities of profit seen in customs evasion. Though the size of the hogshead reached its maximum in 1716, improvements in tobacco compressing continued to increase the contents of the hogshead throughout the colonial period, and the weight of its contents was at least trebled between 1660 and 1774. The logical conclusion was probably reached with the mid-century casks into which 1100–1400 lb. were pressed; with a load of the heaviest of these, a ship's load-carrying capacity would be almost fully taxed when the holds were full.

With the increased size of the hogshead, of course, the shipowner could carry a significantly smaller number of conventional 'tons' (of four hogsheads each) in a hold of given size in 1720

---

[1] Gray, op. cit., Vol. I, p. 220.
[2] Middleton, op. cit., p. 117; Gray, op. cit., Vol. I, p. 221.
[3] In Virginia, the dimensions rose from 43 in. × 26 in. to 48 in. × 30 in.; in Maryland from 43 in. × 27 in. to 48 in. × 32 in. (Gray, op. cit., Vol. I, p. 221). Hogsheads of 700–900 lb. were well known as early as 1702 (*CSPAWI 1702*, No. 391).

than he had done in 1670 — it was claimed to be one-fifth less.[1] The freight rate per conventional ton was bound to rise if only for this reason. Moreover, the burden of freight rates on the planter was being progressively eased by the tighter packing of hogsheads, and this again may have tended to help the shipowners to resist long-term decline in the general level of freights.

Once the Virginia–Maryland trade had become firmly established in the 1630's, freight rates of tobacco in hogsheads settled down to a level of between £5 and £6 per ton, rising to £10 at the peak of the First Dutch War, and fluctuating between £5 10s. and £7 during the Spanish War of 1655–60. With the coming of peace the normal rate settled down at £5 to £5 10s., occasionally dropping as low as £4 15s. and rising sharply in years of bumper crops, such as 1687, to £7 or more.[2] In the wars after 1689 rates as high as £12 or £13 were normal for long periods, with peaks of £14 in 1691 and £16 in 1709. The return of peace brought some degree of stability, but not at the old levels, for it was during the wars that hogsheads had swelled and grown heavier. The new rates fluctuated round £7 per ton for Maryland[3] and £7 10s. to £8 for Virginia, with a very slow tendency to decline up to the end of the colonial period. These new rates fully reflected the increased size of the hogshead; the general lowering of the costs of ship operation were reflected only very slowly in lowered freights.[4] However, from the planter's point of view there was a vast saving. The freight rates of the eighteenth century offered large and continuing reductions in the effective freight rate per hundredweight of tobacco; a rate of £7 per 'ton' for four hogsheads in 1770 gave a real cost of about 3s. 6d. per net hundredweight of tobacco, as compared with 7s. per net hundredweight represented by £5 per 'ton' a century before. The cost of transport to England dropped (allowing for the change in the long-term

---

[1] See *CSPAWI 1706–8*, Nos. 1024, 1059, 1149, 1216, 1259 for discussion on the carrying capacity of ships in tobacco trade.

[2] 'Intended to have consigned to you 20 or 30 hogsheads Tobacco, but there was this year such plenty of tobacco and scarcity of Ships, that freight was hardly to be procured on any terms' (*Virg. Mag. Hist. Biog.*, Vol. I, 1893, Fitzhugh's letter of 18th April 1687). Most freights that year were at £7, with odd ones at £7 5s.

[3] J. M. Hemphill, op. cit.

[4] Since the tobacco trade began to use considerable numbers of captured flyboats in the middle of the seventeenth century (though conventional English ships were used alongside them) the scope for reducing operating costs later on was less than in other long-distance trades.

average price of tobacco) from some 60–80 per cent of the planter's selling price to 10–20 per cent of it. The significance of this for demand in the *English* market was obscured by the enormous taxation of tobacco, from William III's time, beside which original cost and transport made up only a small percentage of the final price.

A word must be said on the shipment of the other products of the southern colonies. None was of any importance in the seventeenth century, but there were a number of important developments around 1700. Rice growing in South Carolina began an extraordinarily rapid expansion in the last few years of the seventeenth century, finding markets in England and in Southern Europe, to which direct export was permitted except in the years 1704–30.[1] The most rapid growth of the export to England took place after 1720, and before mid-century rice had become, in volume, one of England's principal imports. Unlike tobacco, sent out from innumerable wharves along the tidewater creeks, rice export was concentrated in the port of Charleston, which at the time of the Revolution had become the fourth city of America.

A second important product of Virginia, Maryland and South Carolina was pitch and tar. Its production and export from America were encouraged by English bounties which more than covered the excess of freight costs from America over those from the Baltic, and within a few years after the introduction of the bounties in 1705[2] it had driven the Swedish product from the English market. This, too, found an important outlet at Charleston, and helped to attract very large ships to the port.

Other developing exports of some importance to shipping were iron and timber. The iron producing industry was growing fast in all the American colonies during the eighteenth century, though most of their demands were still met from England. The southern colonies were able to export their iron to England in some quantity, for packed among the tobacco or rice barrels iron occupied space which would otherwise be wasted, and it was consequently accepted at very low freight rates — 7s. 6d. or 10s. a ton.[3] New England iron, on the other hand, could not easily be

---

[1] In 1704 rice was put into the list of 'enumerated commodities' which had to be shipped to England (3 and 4 Anne, c. 5) but colonial agitation led to the repeal of this measure in 1730 (3 Geo. II, c. 28).

[2] 3 and 4 Anne, c. 9.

[3] K. Johnson, 'The Baltimore Iron Company seeks English Markets: A Study of the Anglo-American Iron Trade, 1731–55', *William & Mary Quarterly*, Vol. XVI, 1959, p. 44.

shipped to England, for in the absence of large cargoes of loosely packed light goods shipowners expected iron to pay a rate per ton more comparable with that of other goods — up to 40s. a ton[1] — and at this rate the trade was not profitable.

Finally, before the mid-eighteenth century the southern colonies had joined, if on a moderate scale, in the supply of timber to England; probably heavy shipments depended on the spasmodic appearance of surplus shipping tonnage in the major trades of the region, ready to turn to timber-carrying at moderate charges.

By contrast with those already discussed, most of the more northerly colonies created farming settlements, grew their own food and eventually more than they needed, and developed towns and merchant communities and even industry in endeavouring to achieve self-sufficiency. They had little to export to Europe — furs from the backwoods, fish from the Newfoundland banks, timber from the northern coastal fringes of settlement in New Hampshire, Maine and Canada. They developed a large fishing industry, quickly took over most of the coastal trade of the continent from the West Indies to the Canadian frontier, and by the early years of the eighteenth century were beginning to be the principal suppliers of food, timber and horses to the West Indian colonies of England and other powers. They derived some benefit from the pitch and tar bounties in England in the eighteenth century, but the volume of their trade with England remained on a small scale, though their import requirements became very great in value as prosperity and the demand for English manufactures grew among them. The permanent adverse balance of payments with England was eventually brought within bounds by transferring to England some of the earnings of West India trade.[2]

New England was the home of the American shipbuilding industry, and American ships soon began to carry a considerable part of the limited volume of trade that was available. The real importance of New England to this study lies not in the subject dealt with here — the demands of trade on the English shipping industry — but in its role (though a surprisingly small one) as a

---

[1] *House of Commons Journals, 1737–42*, p. 109.
[2] A useful discussion of the trade of the northern colonies is C. P. Nettels, 'England's Trade with New England and New York, 1685–1720' in *Transactions of the Colonial Society of Massachusetts*, Vol. XXVIII, 1930–3, pp. 322–50.

competitor in other branches of transatlantic traffic, and its important place in the eighteenth century as supplier of a substantial proportion of the new ships bought and built for English owners.

Only on the fringes, in New Hampshire and Maine, in Nova Scotia and after 1759 along the St Lawrence, was there much work for English ships. These sparsely populated territories were recognised early in the seventeenth century to be possible sources of masts for the English navy; the first shipments from Penobscot Bay are said to date from 1634, and there was a regular supply to England from the time of the First Dutch War.[1] The area ultimately became England's principal source of masts,[2] and the cutting off of the supply in the War of Independence produced a crisis in the English naval dockyards.[3] The mast trade with England was almost all to meet government, rather than private, requirements. The great contractors who dealt with the navy chartered very large ships — commonly of 400–500 tons, and after 1750 of as much as 700–800 tons — to meet its needs, directing the ships' masters to the government agents in the colonies who ordered the cutting of the timber.

The principal function of the English-operated slave trade before the American Revolution was the supply of slaves to the West Indies. The plantation colonies of North America had few slaves before 1713, and when they did begin to import slaves on a considerable scale much of the traffic was handled by American ships sailing from American ports.

Negro slaves appeared in the West Indies in small numbers before 1640, but the large trade awaited the development of the large sugar plantation. From early days, some of the products of the trade were sent on from Jamaica to Spanish America, and to the French West Indies. Because the slave trade required the maintenance of fortified trading stations on the West African coast, and involved diplomatic upsets with the Portuguese and the Dutch, it was for the forty years before 1702 monopolised, in theory, by companies operating under royal charter, though in fact English interlopers continued to be very active. The last of

---

[1] W. H. Rowe, *The Maritime History of Maine* (New York, 1948), p. 34.
[2] H. S. K. Kent, 'The Anglo-Norwegian Timber Trade in the Eighteenth Century', *Econ. Hist. Rev.*, n.s., Vol. VIII, 1955, p. 64.
[3] R. G. Albion, op. cit., Ch. VII.

these companies retained control of the forts, and the right to levy a duty on all English participants in the trade, until 1713, and subsequently until 1750 received a state subsidy for the upkeep of the forts. Nearly all the trade, whether of the companies or interlopers, was carried on from London until well after 1700. The Royal Africa Company's loss of its monopoly in 1702 was soon followed by rapid growth in Bristol's share in the trade, but only in the twenties and thirties did the Bristol interest overtake that of London, whilst Liverpool was only just beginning to compete.[1] In the early forties, there were said to be some 55 Liverpool, 40 Bristol and 10 London ships annually engaged in the trade, and numbers were rising fast.[2]

There are few branches of maritime activity in which London showed absolute decline during the eighteenth century, and it would be interesting to know why the slave trade was one. Mr Northcote Parkinson's explanation that the Londoners were attached to their Companies — the Royal Africa Company and after 1711 the South Sea Company,[3] can hardly stand, for in this as in other company trades most of the interlopers as well as the legal traders were, in the seventeenth century, Londoners. The decline is possibly connected (as suggested earlier) with the increasing rigidity of ties between sugar planters and London commission houses which dominated the London sugar market. The commission houses were experts on sugar and on plantation finance, and had no wish to put their capital into so different a trade as slaving; they committed a large proportion of the London West India fleet to the direct voyage out and home. The outport merchants trading to the West Indies were less specialised and were less closely concerned with the supply of shipping to particular individuals. Liverpool's rise to take the leading place in the slave trade after mid-century may be associated, further, with the growth of Lancashire industry producing the cotton fabrics wanted both in Africa and the West Indies, and importing the cotton of which the West Indies had become the principal supplier.

Small cargoes of light textiles, metalwares, beer and spirits and other miscellanea were taken by the slave ships from England to the African coast — generally the Gulf of Guinea. In the trading

[1] CO 390–7.   [2] CO 388–43.
[3] C. Northcote Parkinson, op. cit., pp. 91–2. The number of trading ships in 1710 was: London 24, Bristol 20, Liverpool 2 (*CSPAWI 1710–11*, No. 544).

stations of the coast the captains and supercargoes, or the Company's permanent agents, chaffered with the African traders, bartering their wares for slaves.[1] A full cargo could usually be secured in time (unless quarrels with the Dutch or Portuguese caused ships to move off); some of this cargo would be lost on the transatlantic passage. The *Constant Ruth* in 1652 lost 90 slaves out of 207;[2] the *Fortune* (in the Royal Africa Company's service) 132 out of 320 in 1678.[3] Such losses may not have been exceptional in the early years of the trade, but as experience was accumulated they became rare. The destination until about 1680 was usually Barbados; after that date Jamaica rapidly overtook it as the chief market, for it became a slave trading centre for the whole Caribbean, as well as a great employer of labour in its own plantations.

The ideal timing of the voyage was clearly understood:

'I am of opinion that the properest season to render the Guinea Voyages most prosperous and safe, is to depart from Europe about the latter end of September, to enjoy the longer there on that coast, and to have a sufficient time to carry on the trade there, so as to reach the Leeward Islands of America by the latter end of April following, which is the time when they make the sugar there, and sail thence to Europe again before the season of hurricanes there, and arrive here before the boisterous weather, which usually reigns on our coasts about the beginning of October'.[4]

This programme, however, required a reasonable success in slaving on the African coast, and a very quick despatch in the West Indies, which was hardly possible if the destination was the great eighteenth-century slave market of Kingston, Jamaica, rather than one of the more accessible Leeward Islands. Such a programme could not be maintained year after year by any ship, and in fact though autumn was a favoured time for departing for the West African coast, slavers could be found departing at all times of the year.

Under the developed organisation of the Royal Africa Company in its prime, large chartered ships were used, generally of 200–300

---

[1] The importance of local knowledge and experience of this trade is clearly brought out in Nathaniel Uring's account of his difficulties as a slaver in 1701 (A. C. Dewar (ed.), *The Voyages and Travels of Captain Nathaniel Uring* (1928), pp. 22–48).
[2] HCA 15–6.
[3] HCA 13–131.
[4] Churchill's *Collection of Voyages and Travels* (1732), Vol. V, p. 523.

tons. The independent traders which at times competed illegally and which ultimately took over the trade were of a variety of sizes, on the whole smaller; the use of large ships did not become general again until after 1750, by which time ships specially designed for the slave trade were in use. Almost invariably ships not in the Company's service traded on behalf of the ships' owning groups; the part-owners of the ships shared the costs of cargo from England and from Africa, and the proceeds of the cargo, in the same proportions as their share in the ships. The master or, very often, a supercargo was the manager of affairs; the business required a close knowledge of the West African coast and trading conditions, and a capacity to get cash and goods in return for slaves in the West Indies — selling the slaves was easy enough. Some idea of the nature of the commercial operations may be derived from one of the earliest sets of instructions given a Liverpool master and supercargo in the slave trade:

16 August 1700

Mr. Thos. Brownbell, Leverpoole
Mr. John Murray

You being Captain and Supercargo of the good ship the Blessing by Gods grace bound for Guinea our Orders for you are as Follows: Wee order you with the first fair Wind and Weather that presents to make the best of your way to King-Sail in the Kingdom of Ireland where apply yr self to Mr Arthur Kreise Mercht. there who will ship on board you such provisions and other necessaryes as you shall want for yr intended Voyage, and if you find wee have omitted Anything in our Orders to him you may take anything that may be necessary for the Voyage.

Make all the despatch there ye well can and then with the first fair wind and weather make the best of yr way to the Coast of Guinea, where make to the Winder most part of the Gold Coast so ye will have an opportunity of the whole Coast to trade in, where dispose of what of the cargo is proper to purchase what slaves ye can. If ye find no Encouragement on ye Gold Coast go directly for Wida where if ye find Encouragement dispose of all yr cargo slave yr ship to her full Reach if you can and if any remainder be left lay it out in Teeth and Dust as ye have opportunity. Ye will quickly find whether ye can do yr business on the Gold Coast and Wida, if you find you can't sell only such Goods of the cargo as will be improper for Angola and make what haste ye can down to Angola where the Doctor is well acquainted and who will inform you what goods most propper for that place.   When you arrive at Angola dispose of the remains

u

of yr cargo there and slave the ship to her full Reach as she will conveniently carry I hope there you will slave yr ship easy and what shall remain over and above slaving the ship lay out in Teeth which are there reasonable. When you have disposed of yr cargo and slaved yr ship make the best of yr way to the West Indies if you slave at the Gold Coast and Wida touch at Barbadoes where if you find the marketts reasonable good sell there if Dull go down Leeward to which Island you shall see convenient where dispose of your Negroes to our best Advantage and with the Produce load the Ship with sugar cotton ginger if to be had. What all remains over and above loading yr own Ship invest in the same commodities take freight for England to London or this place and wherever you sell the slaves and load sugar despatch yr own ship as soon as possible and make the best of yr way home and what effects of ours you can't stay to be freighted home leave in the hand of some honest man on the Island where ye load if at Bardadoes apply yourself to Mr Moor at Antigua Mr , at Monserratt Mr Chaney, at Nevis Solomon Issarell, but if you go down to Angola when you are there laden make the best of yr way directly to Jamaica, where what slaves ye purchased on the Gold Coast will sell well and the Angola slaves will turn to good use at Cartagena where if you see convenient send Mr Murray and the Doctor down with a parcel thither where there never fails of a good price. When have disposed of all the slaves relade the Ship with Sugar Cotton Ginger and Indigo and what you have over and above the loading bring home in weighty Pieces of Eight for at Cartagena what negroes you dispose on will be for good ps. 8 So that whatever is over in yr loading bring home in the specie. If you should have occasion for any assistance to leave any concern behind you in Jamaica apply yr self to Mr Holstead mercht there. When you have loaded the Ship make the best of yr way homeward but call at Kingsaile for orders. The concern wee here intrust you with, is very considerable and will require all yr care and dilligence to make itt to the best advantage. Both of you consult together with the Doctor who is the only Man you have to trust to to assist you in the tradeing part of the Country and yr Management there I doubt not but will doe good service, read over ye Invoyce frequently and ye may be better acquainted with the Goods. Wee have not limitted you to any Place only if you can't do business on the Gold Coast and Wida, to go to Angola, the ship wee think not proper to goe into the Byte. Wee leave the whole management of the concern to you and hope the Lord will direct you for the best. Be very cautious of speaking with any ships at Sea for the seas are dangerous. Endeavour to keep all the Men sober for Intemperance in the hot Country may

destroy yr Men and so ruin yr Voyage.   Lett everything be
managed to our best Advantage pray be good husbands, lett nothing
be Embezzled. Wee cannot pretend to give you particular direction
about the management of our affairs in Guinea but refer it to you
and the Doctor who have been there before and shipt on purpose for
the Design. Pray be dilligent careful and prudent in all our affairs and
be assured yr dilligence shall not go unrewarded.   Wee committ
you to the care and protection of the Almighty who we hope will
preserve you from all Dangers and Crown all our Endeavours with
success and bring you home with safety which shall be the constant
prayer of
Gents yr Loveing friends

Be sure to make all the despatch ye can through the course of the
whole voyage. Take such particular notice of all the method of
management of the trade on the Coast that you may be able to inform
us truely in all things Matterial in the trade which will be yr own
profitt as well as our advantage and write from all places where you
can have convenience of sending[1]

[1] Norris MSS., Liverpool Public Libraries.

WEST INDIES

Statistics:

1. TONNAGE OF ENTRIES AND CLEARANCES (000 TONS)

	1686		1715–17	1771–3	
	e	*c*	*c*	*e*	*c*
Barbados	20·5	18·2	12·6 ⎫		
Jamaica	15·0	6·2	7·6 ⎬	90·4	84·1
Other W.I.	8·2	6·3	12·2 ⎭		
Africa	0·7	3·3	3·3	5·4	20·4

2. VALUE OF TRADE (£000)

	1699–1701		1771–3	
	I	*E*	*I*	*E*
West Indies	743	344	2968	1274
Africa	22	129	86	791

3. CHIEF ENGLISH PORTS IN WEST INDIES TRADE

	1686		1715–17	
	Number of ships		*Ships out*	
	in	*out*	*No.*	*tons*
London	225	161	164	23·8
Bristol	42	56	81	7·1
Liverpool	8	2	20	1·6

4. CHIEF ENGLISH PORTS, 1715–17, TRADING TO DIFFERENT COUNTRIES

	Total				*Other*	
	No.	*Tons*	*Barbados*	*Jamaica*	*W.I.*	*Africa*
London	164	23·8	6·2	4·7	9·6	3·3
Bristol	81	7·1	3·3	2·6	0·9	0·3
Liverpool	20	1·6	0·9	0·3	0·4	—

5. AVERAGE TONNAGE OF INDIVIDUAL ENGLISH SHIPS

		1686–7	*1715–17 c*	*1726 e*	*1766 e*
Barbados	L	179	169	148	236
	O	110	81		
Jamaica	L	214	178	168	225
	O	100	106		
Other W.I.	L	144	132	137	170
	O	91	69		
West Africa	L	119	118		101
	O		96		

NORTH AMERICA

Statistics:

1. TONNAGE OF ENTRIES AND CLEARANCES (000 TONS)

	1686		1715–17	1771–3	
	e	c	c	e	c
Northerns[1]	3·3	5·6	10·2		
Newfoundland	3·0	5·8	5·8		
V., M. and C.	29·3	21·8	24·3		
total	35·6	33·1	40·3	96·9	99·0

(While none of these ships were technically foreign, some belonged to the colonies themselves.)

2. VALUE OF TRADE (£000)

	1699–1701		1771–3	
	I	E	I	E
Northerns	59	159	306	2212
Newfoundland	18	17	62	92
V., M. and C.	265	202	1086	1214

3. CHIEF ENGLISH PORTS

	1686		1715–17	
	Number of ships		Ships out	
	in	out	No.	tons
London	110	114	130	18·8
Bristol	31	17	69	6·9
Liverpool	13	13	28	2·8
Whitehaven	8	—	20	2·4

4. CHIEF ENGLISH PORTS, 1715–17, TRADING TO DIFFERENT COUNTRIES

	Total		Northerns	Newfoundland	V., M. and C.
	No.	tons			
London	130	18·8	4·5	0·7	13·6
Bristol	69	6·9	1·8	0·8	4·3
Liverpool	28	2·8	0·4		2·4
Whitehaven	20	2·4	0·1		2·3

5. AVERAGE TONNAGE OF INDIVIDUAL ENGLISH SHIPS

		1686	1715–17 c	1726 e	1766 e
Northerns	L	120	102	104	133
	O	—	74		
Newfoundland	O	68	70		
Virginia, Maryland,	L	209	192 ⎫	142	176
Carolina	O	116	106 ⎭		

[1] New England colonies, New York, New Jersey and Pennsylvania.

XIV

The Government and the Shipping Industry

Whatever view may be taken of the long-continued arguments among historians and economists over the consistency and self-consciousness of mercantilist policy, it is evident that most English governments in modern times took some interest in the maintenance of the English merchant shipping industry. At the very least, they were anxious to keep the supply of trained seamen at the highest level possible, since the navy could only be manned in wartime by taking great numbers from the merchant service. Until the end of the seventeenth century they also wished to see large reserves of merchant ships to act as auxiliaries to the royal fleet, and especially of large ships which could take part in fighting alongside it. Recognition that the merchant service was the support of the navy provided the continuing thread in maritime policy. In the seventeenth century a growing consciousness of the economic problems associated with the balance of trade, and the enlargement by colonial development of the area over which English commercial legislation could be effective, wove new strands into the motivation of policy. The view became explicit that it was desirable to keep down foreign participation in the carriage of goods in English trade, not only in order to boost English shipping for the benefit of the navy, but also to evade the burden on the balance of payments of freight charges due to foreigners. So there were renewed and more care-fully thought out efforts to eliminate foreign ships from trades where they could be replaced by English. In the Navigation Acts from 1651 onward, the second approach is clearly embodied along with the first, and during the rest of the seventeenth century there was further legislation against the foreigner and in support of English trade and shipping. But the Navigation Acts were only the precursors of a great wave of discriminatory legislation in all economic fields, which was set in motion when the authority of Parliament was extended after 1688. This found its expression in a whole range of subsidies to individual industries, bounties for exports, prohibitions of imports, protective tariffs and so on, as parliament warmed to the task of aiding English industry and its raw material suppliers, incidentally giving some further privileges to English shipping.

The origins of policies to promote English at the expense of foreign merchant shipping are to be found in a series of fourteenth-century acts, which must be discussed here because their authority was still being cited to support administrative measures in the reign of James I. These acts first directed all English merchants to freight English, not foreign ships — if English ships were available in the merchants' ports and if their owners would take reasonable gains for freight.[1] To this rather vague admonition was added a peremptory one concerning the most important of bulk trades of the day; that wine from Gascony was to be brought only in English or in Gascon ships.[2] The laws stood almost unchanged for a century, but it is not possible to judge their effectiveness. The coming of the first Tudor, who had learned from his own experiences the vulnerability of his realm to invaders from across the sea, brought a new body of law which has the appearance of serious intent. Acts of 1485 and 1489 required that Gascon and Guienne wine and Toulouse woad should be imported only in English ships; and again an aspiration was expressed in the enactment that Englishmen would not lade their goods in foreign ships if English ones were available.[3] The effectiveness of some part of these measures is attested by an act of 1516 which, reciting that many licences had been granted by the crown to permit disregard of the provisions of these laws, declared all such licences void.[4] In 1532 and 1541 new acts declared these measures to be still in operation, and even underlined the injunction on Englishmen to lade their goods in English vessels when these could be had.[5] To make this more palatable, a schedule of maximum freight rates to be charged by English shipowners for goods in various trades was attached to the act of 1541.

In the first year of Elizabeth I, 1558, all the effective parts of the navigation laws were abolished, and Englishmen were free

[1] 5 Richard II, c. 3 (1382); 6 Richard II, c. 8 (1383); 14 Richard II, c. 6 (1391).
[2] 42 Edw. III, c. 8 (1370). Gascony at this time was a part of the dominions of the English crown.
[3] 1 Henry VII, c. 8; 4 Henry VII, c. 10.
[4] 7 Henry VIII, c. 2.
[5] 23 Henry VIII, c. 7; 32 Henry VIII, c. 7.

to have their goods carried in any ship, paying small extra customs duties for using foreign ships.[1] The term of this act, however, was limited to five years, and when it expired in 1563 the obligation to import French wine and Toulouse woad only in English-owned ships was re-imposed. In 1563, moreover, the English coasting trade was closed to foreign ships — a restriction which lasted, with small gaps, for nearly three hundred years.[2] It is not clear whether in law, the expiry of the repeal provisions of the 1558 act brought back into force the older legislation which it had repealed, but it was taken for granted by the authorities that it did. Elizabeth's Privy Council, for example, sent a letter to the Customs Commissioners in 1588 commanding that no English goods might be laden in foreign ships, but only in English ships, English manned.

The situation as it was left by the expiry of the 1558 act and the new enactment of 1563 was not further changed by statute until 1650, but in the new century royal proclamations were issued to restrict the use of foreign ships. As the flyboat, backed by Dutch capital and Dutch trading connections, began to appear in every ocean, the intensified lamentations of the English shipping interest penetrated to the chambers of the Privy Council and produced new remedies for the English shipowner — if new restrictions for the English trader. The first response was in two proclamations of 1615, reminding citizens of the state of the law. First, that the act of 1563 was still in force; it was, in fact, still being observed. Then, that the acts of 1386, 1489 and 1541 were in force as well — the acts which provided, among other things, that goods were not to be shipped into or out of England except in English ships.[3] The legality of this view was dubious, but nobody argued about it; and in any case the proclamations were not really aimed at such wide objectives. Their real purport was to control the handling of particular trades, and in the first place the Mediterranean. No goods, it was ordered, were to be imported from the Mediterranean except in English ships. Under pressure from Venice, the government agreed that Mediterranean states could send their own goods in their own ships; but this was a

---

[1] I Eliz., c. 13.

[2] 5 Eliz., c. 5. This act had a wider scope than that dealt with here, embracing the development of the fishing industry and the encouragement of the use of large ships. It may be noted that, despite this act, Elizabeth allowed the import of wine in French ships at times; e.g. in 1565 (*CSPD 1547–80*, pp. 241–2).

[3] R. Steele, *Tudor and Stuart Proclamations, 1485–1714* (Oxford, 1910), 17th April 1615, 12th October 1615: APC 2nd October 1615.

concession of little practical importance. The proclamations were aimed, like so many other measures in succeeding decades, against the Dutch. The following year the Privy Council acknowledged the hardship which general regulations involved:

> 'Divers marchantes have since their tyme ben put to harde exigente for want of English shippinge in forraine partes to bring home the same in straingers' bottomes, to the hazarde and forfeiture of the said goods without his Majesty's gracious favour; and on the other side, that the owners and masters of Shipps do complayne of the small prize of fraightment offered and given unto them by the marchantes.'[1]

The Northern traders, who apparently disregarded the more general terms of the injunction placed upon merchants, were in 1622 required — again in the name of the old legislation — to ship their imports, other than corn, in English ships.[2] In 1626 there were complaints that traders to France employed ten foreign ships to one English 'contrary to divers proclamations' and they too were ordered to obey the ancient laws.[3] Meanwhile, the prospects for the expansion of English shipping in the new-born colonial trades had been recognised, and in 1624 it was ordered that 'no person whatever, either stranger, denizen or naturall born subject, presume to import any Tobacco whatsoever in any forraine bottom'.[4]

In the years when their Twelve Years' Truce with Spain (1609–21) enabled the Dutch to exert the full force of competition in shipping, the English government made a determined effort to turn the medieval navigation laws into operative instruments, by making specific regulations deriving authority from them in relation, at least, to the major middle-distance trades — the Mediterranean and the Baltic — and to the new colonial trade. Meanwhile England's status in the long-distance trade with the Indian Ocean was being asserted in local armed struggles with the Dutch. After 1621 the Dutch gradually became immersed in new war which lessened the force of their competition; before their war had ended, the authority of King and Privy Council in England had been overthrown and the Long Parliament had become the ruling power, though overshadowed by the army.

---

[1] APC 3rd April 1616.   [2] APC 11th July 1622; proclamation 21st July 1622.
[3] APC 8th August 1626.
[4] Proclamation 29th September 1624. Tobacco was at this time the only significant import from the colonies.

It would be a mistake, therefore, to see the Commonwealth Navigation Ordinance of 1651 as a new departure reflecting the newly raised voice of commercial interests in government. Those interests had been pressing their claims to assistance on the government for nearly four decades. They had been able to do so because of the ever-present government concern with maritime power, and because the shipping interest had become — perhaps for the first time — of real importance within the English economy; and they had been driven to do so by the emerging menace of Dutch competition. All the reasons for protecting English shipping had become stronger in the first decades of the seventeenth century, and would have gained yet more force if Dutch pressure had not been temporarily halted by war. The provisions of the Ordinance of 1651 were foreshadowed by James I's proclamations, and it may well be thought that only the entry of the Dutch into the Thirty Years' War prevented the comprehensive system of the Navigation Acts from being developed gradually instead of springing suddenly, as it did, from the conditions of 1651. The general principles of the later Navigation Acts had been enunciated already in 1624:

> 'The Native Commodityes of every countrye may be imported into this Realme, by the native Subjects, of the same Realme in theire owne Shiping, and all other Nacons to be prohibited the importation thereof, except in English Shiping.'[1]

It was the emergence of the Dutch from their war in 1648, at a time when English royal proclamations had ceased to have binding force, and when English shipping was troubled by Royalist and other privateers, that brought back, suddenly, the free competition of thirty years before, and precipitated action.

It has been shown that in putting forward their requests for government support for English shipping, merchants were able to play on the continuing interest in maintaining the supply of merchant ships and seamen for naval purposes. No progress was made towards expanding the royal core of the navy into a force of ships capable of fighting without merchant ship support, until the Commonwealth began to create a new fleet in the First Dutch War. One expression of government interest in merchant ships,

---

[1] 'Consideracons for the Imployment of Shipping and Men for the Increase of Mariners' (SP 15–43–45).

therefore, was in subsidies paid for the building of large ships. These can be traced back to the reign of Henry VII; it is not certain whether he and his son allowed shipowners to claim these subsidies as of right, but by the second half of Elizabeth's reign any group of persons that built a ship measuring more than 100 tons was clearly entitled to, and was paid, a bounty of five shillings a ton.[1] The payment of this bounty ceased in 1619 in the extreme financial stringency of James I's last years, but it was revived again in wartime, in 1625, though as a bounty, now, for ships over 200 tons — men's ideas of 'large' ships were changing fast.[2] Moreover, attempts were made at this time to prevent the sale overseas of large English ships. Though these sales had been prohibited as early as 1604,[3] when it appears that privateers were being sold with the coming of peace, the practice had not died out and it came into the limelight again in the trade depression after 1620, when certain specific sales were banned.[4] In 1626 the Privy Council reported that 'by colorable devises many ships of great burthen and good service are bought and sould and so transported into forreiners' hands', and it ordered that no ship of over fifty tons, capable of bearing ordnance, should sail on any voyage until her owners had given security in the High Court of Admiralty that she would not be sold abroad.[5] In 1629 the prohibition on the sale of ships to foreigners was again asserted by proclamation.[6]

The Navigation Acts from 1650 onwards have perhaps attracted more discussion than any other subject in the economic history of the seventeenth century. They have evoked one substantial monograph,[7] many articles[8] and long discussions in other works on the period.[9] In this work, the general situation of the shipping

---

[1] M. Oppenheim, *History of the Administration of the Royal Navy and of Merchant Shipping in relation to the Royal Navy* (1896), pp. 37–8, 88–9, 107, 167–9.
[2] APC 13th May 1625.   [3] Proclamation 15th October 1604.
[4] APC 19th June 1622, 7th August 1624, 8th January 1625.
[5] APC 15th February 1626.
[6] Proclamation 12th July 1629.
[7] L. A. Harper, *The English Navigation Laws* (New York, 1939).
[8] e.g. G. N. Clark, 'The Navigation Act of 1651', *History*, Vol. VII, 1923, pp. 282–6; O. A. Johnsen, 'The Navigation Act of 1651', *History*, Vol. XXXIV, 1929, pp. 89–96; C. M. Andrews, 'The Acts of Trade' in *Cambridge History of the British Empire*, Vol. I (1929), pp. 268–99.
[9] e.g. G. L. Beer, *The Old Colonial System* (New York, 1913); *The Origins of the British Colonial System* (New York, 1922); E. Lipson, *Economic History*

industry in the seventeenth century has been explained in Chapters I and III; the remoter background of the laws has just been discussed; now the details of the new legislation, which provided a framework within which the shipping industry had to work until the Navigation Acts were gradually modified and ultimately repealed in the nineteenth century, must be dealt with.

The Council of Trade which the Commonwealth parliament set up in 1650 was faced by a growing activity of Dutch merchants and Dutch ships in trade with the English colonies in America,[1] and by a heavy decline in the numbers of English ships trading to the Baltic, partly due to their replacement by Dutch vessels.[2] Complaints were appearing, too, of foreign competition in other trades, and over all English ships hung the menace of Royalist privateers and their French coadjutors. Under various pressures, and after limited temporary measures,[3] the Commons enacted in 1651 that goods imported should be brought to England direct from the country of production or the first port where they were usually shipped, in English ships or in ships of the country of origin or first shipment; and that all goods from outside Europe were to be brought to England in English ships.[4] This was the famous Commonwealth Navigation Ordinance, instigator of the First Dutch War and foundation of all subsequent legislation on the subject.[5]

Along with all other legislation of the Commonwealth, the Navigation Ordinance lapsed with the Restoration of Charles II in 1660. Once again, therefore, the collapse of an authority threatened to expose the shipping industry to the blasts of competition; and the industry, at the last ebb of the war with Spain, was in a very weak state. Within a few months of the king's return, therefore, a new and even more comprehensive (and better drafted) Navigation Act was passed, and this one retained much

of England (1930); D. Ogg, *England in the Reign of Charles II* (Oxford, 1934); M. P. Ashley, *Financial and Commercial Policy Under the Cromwellian Protectorate* (Oxford, 1934); D. Marshall, *English People in the Eighteenth Century* (1956).

[1] G. L. Beer, *Origins*, op. cit., Ch. XI.

[2] N. E. Bang, op. cit. *The Advocate* (1651) presents an extreme view of Dutch incursions.

[3] In 1647 and 1650. C. H. Firth and R. Rait (eds.), *Acts & Ordinances of the Interregnum* (1911), Vol. I, pp. 912–13; Vol. II, pp. 425–9.

[4] ibid., pp. 559–62.

[5] There are excellent accounts of the discussion on this measure in Harper, op. cit., 39–48; R. W. K. Hinton, *The Eastland Company and the Common Weal* (Cambridge, 1959), pp. 89–94.

of its force for 189 years. Its provisions, so far as they directly concerned shipping were:

(*a*) No goods were to be imported from or exported to the king's possessions outside Europe, or imported from other places outside Europe, except in ships belonging to people of England, Wales or Ireland, or in ships built by and belonging to people in the overseas possession themselves; ships, moreover, with English masters and crews three-quarters English.

(*b*) No tobacco, sugar, corn, indigo, ginger, fustick or other dyewood produced in English possessions outside Europe was to be exported to any place other than England or Ireland or an English possession. (These are the so-called 'enumerated commodities', the list of which was extended from time to time.)

(*c*) A wide range of goods, including nearly all the principal products of the Mediterranean and the Baltic,[1] and all produce of the Russian and Turkish empires, was to be imported into England, Ireland or Wales only in English ships, with masters and three-quarters of the crews English, or in ships of the producing country or of the place of first shipment.

(*d*) Foreign goods imported by English-built and English-manned ships were to be brought only from their places of origin or usual first shipment.[2]

(*e*) The coasting trade was completely reserved for English-owned ships, with master and three-quarters of the crew English.[3]

What scope did this leave to foreign ships to take part in carrying trade with England? They could export English or Irish goods to any place except the English colonies outside Europe. They could bring their own native produce to England. They could, in fact, bring most kinds of product of any country to England, but the list of exceptions included nearly all the European commodities which were carried in large quantities. The Dutch could no longer bring in the main products of Norway and the Baltic — but Danes, Norwegians, Swedes and Hanseatics

---

[1] Masts, timber, boards, salt, pitch, tar, resin, hemp, flax, raisins, figs, prunes, olive oil, corn, sugar, potash, wine, vinegar, brandy. Note that iron is not listed.

[2] English ships could bring the goods of Spanish and Portuguese colonies from Spain or Portugal; African and Levant goods from usual ports of shipment in the Levant; and East India goods from any port east of the Cape of Good Hope.

[3] 12 Charles II, c. 18. The more important sections of the act are printed in A. Browning (ed.), *English Historical Documents, 1660–1714* (1953), pp. 533–7.

could. The Dutch could not bring the products of the Mediterranean. They could not even take such things to their own ports and have them collected, for the short voyage to England, by English ships. Nor could they take any part in English colonial trade, or in the importation of goods from outside Europe. Insofar as the Navigation Act was enforced, the role of the Dutch as general carriers for England — limited though that role had been in practice — was ended. They were confined to sharing the carriage of Anglo-Dutch trade in their own and English products (though preferences given to English ships in the corn and coal export trades excluded them from most of this),[1] to the carriage of some minor commodities of trade in European waters and, if they wished, to the export of English goods to other foreign countries.

Other measures succeeded this Navigation Act, ironing out uncertainties and filling in details. The whole body of legislation became immensely complicated, and only the main outlines can be indicated here.[2] Two years after the great act, a measure 'For Preventing Frauds and regulating Abuses in His Majesties Customs' incidentally tightened up the provisions of the Navigation Act and elucidated some minor points. The 'three-quarters English' crews, it was declared, could include colonial subjects; and the three-quarters must be maintained throughout the voyage. The important new provisions were:

(*a*) No ship not built in England, Ireland or the colonies was to be treated, for the purpose of the Navigation Act, as belonging to England, although it was English-owned, unless it had been bought before 1st October 1662 and was at once registered accordingly, or was a condemned prize of war.

(*b*) Because of the ambiguities in the term 'port where the said goods and commodities can only or are or usually have been first shipped for transportation' the import of a list of commodities clearly not of Dutch or West German production[3] from Dutch or German ports was totally prohibited.[4]

An act of 1663 required that European goods for the English colonies outside Europe should be laden in England or Wales and

---

[1] See pp. 311–2, below.
[2] L. A. Harper, op. cit., pp. 387–414 summarises the whole of the legislation.
[3] Wine (other than Rhenish), spicery, grocery, tobacco, potash, pitch, tar, salt, rosin, deal, boards, fir timber, olive oil.
[4] 14 Charles II, c. 11.

carried directly to the colonies, with the exception of salt for the Newfoundland fisheries, Madeira and Azores wine, and horses and provisions from Scotland and Ireland.[1] Doubts which existed over the status of prize ships were cleared up in 1668, when it was declared that they stood in the same position as foreign-built ships bought before 1662 — that is, they could trade as freely as English-built ships.[2] An act of 1670 dealt with some minor points of colonial trade,[3] and in 1674 duties were placed on goods sent from one colony to another; some colonial merchants had claimed that, having made one such journey within the king's dominions, the goods could then be shipped direct to a foreign country.[4] A prohibitive duty was placed in 1685 on all foreign-built ships which might be acquired in the future that took part in the coasting trade, i.e. for the purpose of this trade even prize ships were placed in an inferior position to English-built.[5] Finally, William III's parliament in 1696 reiterated that goods were not to be carried between the extra-European colonies or to or from England except in ships English-owned, English-built (unless prizes) with master and crew three-quarters English; and it provided that ships which were intended to take part in trade with the colonies were to be registered, making a declaration in the following form:

Jurat A.B.   That the ship the
of   whereof   is at present Master being a
              Kind or Built of   Tunns built att
              in the Yeare   and that
              of   etc. are at present
Owners thereof and no   Foreigner directly or
indirectly hath any Share or part or Interest therein.[6]

This was the first Register of Shipping; a partial one, for of course a great many owners had no intention of putting their ships into the colonial trades. The register was kept in London and has long since disappeared; but four volumes of the local Liverpool register, for the years 1739 to 1774, may still be seen at the Customs House Library.[7]

[1] 15 Charles II, c. 7.   [2] 19 and 20 Charles II, c. 3.
[3] 22 and 23 Charles II, c. 26.   [4] 25 Charles II, c. 7.   [5] 1 James II, c. 18.
[6] 7 and 8 William III, c. 22.
[7] Independently of this, a register was kept up, derived from customs records, of all ships entering and clearing English ports. This has long since been lost. G. N. Clark, *Guide to English Commercial Statistics, 1696–1782* (1938), pp. 47–50.

The acts of 1660 to 1696 which have been described created the main structure of the English Navigation Laws, and it is plain that the act of 1660 remained the basis of the whole system. There were many amendments of a minor character during the eighteenth century — changing the list of enumerated commodities, permitting indirect shipments of a few classes of goods. The one really important change came incidentally, from the Act of Union with Scotland in 1707. Scotland had been treated as a foreign country, right outside the privileged circle of England and her colonies; now it was merged with England into Great Britain, and Scottish merchants and Scottish ships acquired identical rights with English — and quickly took advantage of them to secure a firm grip on a part of North American trade.

The laws were enforced with as much vigour as the administration could muster, which means that few infringements escaped penalty in England, but many did in the colonies and probably in Ireland. Confiscation of goods and confiscation of ship or (more normally) a heavy fine in lieu of confiscation, awaited merchants and shipowners who disregarded the law, or whose employees infringed it without their knowledge.

This was the legal framework within which English and foreign ships had to carry on the trade of England and her colonies until the American Revolution tore away the greater part of the colonial Empire and forced a gradual change in and an ultimate abandonment of these regulations. There were, however, some further protections given to English shipping — some of them of great importance — which must be noticed.

Customs statutes had long provided that goods carried into or out of England in foreign-built ships should bear a small extra customs duty — the 'Aliens Duty' — which was stabilised in 1660 at $1\frac{1}{4}$ per cent of the official value of the goods concerned.[1] (In 1673 the Aliens Duty was removed from all exports except coal.)[2] This was a very trivial burden, and it remained unaltered throughout the general steep increase of customs duties during the next century. A Customs statute of 1690 imposed many extra duties, and in the case of iron, and iron only, differentiated against the foreigner by adding ten shillings a ton to the duty if the iron were brought in foreign-owned ships.[3]

---

[1] 12 Charles II, c. 4.   [2] 25 Charles II, c. 6.
[3] 2 William and Mary (II), c. 4. Iron, alone among the major bulk commodities imported from the Baltic, was not included in the list in the 1660

It has been shown that the bulk of English exports was made up of coal and, after 1700, corn. Acting on the old principle that if the foreigner really could not do without any English commodity, advantage should be taken of the fact to squeeze something out of him, coal exports were heavily taxed; and from 1620 onward they were more heavily taxed when they were laden in foreign- than in English-owned ships. Changes in the rates of tax steadily increased the differentiation:[1]

Export tax on coal, per Newcastle chaldron

	In English ships	In foreign ships
1620	6s. 8d.	8s. 4d.
1660	8s.	16s.
1694	3s.	10s.
1710	3s.	12s.
1714	6s.	17s.
1757	10s.	21s.
1765	14s.	25s.

The extra duty on coal carried in foreign ships was, after 1660, an almost prohibitive one, adding a third or more to the cost delivered in a Dutch or French Channel-port; foreign ships almost disappeared from the trade after the Restoration.

A similar advantage was given to English vessels shipping corn. The great corn export of the first sixty years of the eighteenth century was carried on under the stimulus of an export bounty of five shillings a quarter for wheat, and rather smaller amounts for other grains. This bounty was paid only if the corn was shipped in British vessels, and the advantage it gave them made it impossible for foreign ships to compete in this trade.[2]

These two financial regulations,[3] affecting the great short-distance export trades, have attracted only a fraction of the attention which has been given to the Navigation Acts; but by effectively excluding the competition of Dutch ships which were so well suited to the carriage of corn and coal from England they

act of goods to be imported only in English ships or ships of the country of origin. Possibly the differential duty was intended as a remedy for this omission.

[1] J. U. Nef, *The Rise of the British Coal Industry* (1932), Vol. II, pp. 218–38; 6 and 7 Wm. III, c. 18; 9 Anne, c. 6; 12 Anne (II), c. 9; 30 Geo. II, c. 19; 5 Geo. III, c. 35.

[2] 1 William and Mary, c. 12.

[3] Similar preferences were given to English shipping in connection with other bounties.

x

had an influence on the development of the shipping industry comparable to that of the Navigation Acts themselves.[1]

Late seventeenth-century legislation contains one clear survival of government's direct interest in merchant ships for warlike purposes — the continuing payment of bounties for the building of large ships. Payment of the bounty for ships over 200 tons[2] presumably ceased after the Civil War broke out in 1642, if no earlier. When bounties were revived in 1662, the concept of the 'large ship' had again changed. Any persons who caused to be built 'within His Majesty's Dominions any Ship or Vessel of Three Decks and a Half with a Forecastle and five foot between each Deck mounted with Thirty Pieces of Ordnance at least and other Ammunition proportionable' were to have as bounty one-third of the customs duties on the goods it carried on its first two voyages.[3] The conditions were such that only East India and Levant traders were likely to qualify, and on their valuable cargoes the calculated bounty was a very large one. The expiry of this act in 1672 led to a revision of the terms. Two classes of ships were to receive bounties. Three-decked ships were to have one-tenth of the customs duties on the first two voyages; two-decked ships of over 300 tons were to have a bounty at half this rate. In both cases it was prescribed that the ship must carry 30 guns — which may be interpreted as being capable of carrying 30 guns, rather than normally carrying them.[4] Finally, an act of 1694 'For building Good and Defensible Ships' gave to ships of 450 tons or more, with three decks each six feet high, carrying 32 guns, a bounty of one-tenth of that part of the customs duties which had not been imposed additionally during the war, for the first three voyages.[5] This measure, which put the bounty out of reach of almost all ships but East Indiamen, remained in force for ten years; thereafter the interest of the crown in maintaining a supply of auxiliary fighting ships never rose to the point of subsidising them. The navy was at last, so far as its warships were concerned, fully professionalised.

In the eighteenth century, parliamentary intervention in shipping affairs was greatly extended. In part, this was simply because

[1] I have excluded from this discussion the mass of legislation on fisheries and whaling, though it had great importance for the shipping industry as a whole.
[2] See p. 305, above.
[3] 14 Charles II, c. 11.
[4] 22 and 23 Charles II, c. 11.   [5] 5 William and Mary, c. 24.

it gathered to itself the authority and many of the powers once wielded by the King in Council, and relatively trivial matters once settled by Order-in-Council and royal proclamation were now dealt with by the machinery of parliament. The occasional acts which assisted seaport towns to rebuild their quays and piers and authorised the levying of dues on ships for the purpose, grew into a flood after 1700; they included the authority for the first Liverpool docks in 1709 and 1739 and the first Hull dock in 1774.[1] Lighthouses, the provision and dumping of ballast, pilotage, quarantine, the powers of the various Trinity Houses, the relief of shipwrecked mariners, all formerly the subject of royal charters or grants, were now the subject of legislation. After half a century of collection of a tax on merchant seamen's wages to provide benefits for seamen injured in naval service, a small part of the collections was after 1747 allowed to go towards merchant seamen's hospitals and pensions.[2]

Beyond this, however, parliament was courted and cajoled by interests of one kind or another, to encourage it to initiate action which would positively aid particular sections of the community. The eighteenth century is an era of bounties, subsidies and special preferences to many kinds of industry in England, Scotland, Ireland and the American colonies; industry began to get, piecemeal, the state assistance and protection long before given to shipping and to the merchants in colonial trade. The shipping interest itself obtained some small fresh crumbs from the new activity of parliament. Merchant shipping ultimately profited from the government rewards offered for the development of precise methods of measuring longitude at sea, which helped to initiate the research that attained success with Harrison's chronometer in 1759. Some weaknesses in the shipowners' position were cleared up by legislation. The death penalty was imposed on masters who deliberately cast away or burnt their ships.[3] An attempt was made in 1730 to regulate the employment of merchant seamen and end squabbles over their wages and conditions of service;[4] and in the following year the legislature tried to bring to heel the shipmasters in the coal trade, who had for long been accustomed to

[1] 8 Anne, c. 12; 11 George II, c. 32; 14 Geo. III, c. 56. These were, with the exception of the not altogether comparable Howland Wet Dock in London, the first public docks in England.
[2] 20 George II, c. 39.   [3] 4 George I, c. 12; 11 George I, c. 29.
[4] 2 George II, c. 36; 2 George III, c. 5.

acting independently and even in defiance of their owners.[1] The liability of shipowners for embezzlement of cargo by their crews, formerly unlimited, was after 1735 restricted (if the owners themselves were innocent parties) to the value of ship and freight.[2]

[1] 3 George II, c. 26.   [2] 7 George II, c. 15.

XV

War and the Shipping Industry

War caused loss; to shipowners, to seamen, to the nation. Loss of ships; loss of life and limb and of seachests with their clothing and valuables; loss of trade owing to the slowing of the movement of shipping. By far the most spectacular wartime calamities were the capture of ships and their cargoes by enemy privateers and warships. From the national point of view these losses were usually compensated by captures from the enemy, since destruction for its own sake had not yet been extended to merchant shipping; though this was no comfort to the shipowner whose ship was taken, insurance might spread his losses. It is far from certain, however, that captures, numerous as they were, inflicted as much damage on the shipowning community as other, less dramatic, features of war.

The extent of merchant ship losses in wartime is not easy to ascertain; there was no reason for official recording of it in England, and it was obscured in later wars by the practice of ransom. The Admiralty estimate of losses by the war of 1689–97, for example, was 4000 ships — a figure almost incredible at first sight. When it is remembered, however, that a great many of these were ransomed — that is, set free at once in return for guarantees of a money payment to the capturer — and that some may have been repeatedly seized, the figure appears a possible one, though not necessarily true. Propagandist exaggeration does appear in some of the figures, but there were a number of attempts to make reliable estimates.

For the war with Spain and France between 1624 and 1629 a vague and incomplete account suggests that losses to the enemy may have exceeded 300 ships, including well over a hundred 'large' ships of over one hundred tons apiece.[1] This was a considerable loss for the quite small merchant fleet of the time, and it is unlikely that it was counterbalanced by prizes captured. There were losses, of unknown extent, to French privateers and

[1] BM Sloane MSS., 826–130.

to Royalists operating from foreign bases, in the late forties. In the three Dutch wars of 1652–4, 1664–7 and 1672–4 losses were very small, totalling according to Pepys no more than 500 ships in all three wars together,[1] and captures from the Dutch were enormous; these were the wars which reconstituted the English merchant fleet with Dutch flyboats. The Spanish War of 1655–60, it is generally agreed, caused extremely heavy losses which were the subject of an unusual amount of discussion and comment; estimates vary between 1000 and 1800 ships.[2] Captures from the Spaniards were in much smaller numbers, and shipbuilding at a low ebb; England emerged from this war with her merchant shipping depleted.

The Admiralty estimate of losses in the War of the League of Augsburg, 1689–97, was 4000 ships; it was put forward some years later as part of an argument that the protection provided was being improved, and merchants claimed that it was too high.[3] If Pepys is to be believed, all the losses of this war, beyond about 500 vessels, were sustained during its last four years, when the French abandoned fleet actions and turned their maritime effort to war on commerce.[4] The greatest commercial disaster of the war, the loss of the Smyrna convoy in 1693 owing to faulty naval intelligence, was followed by an outcry which compelled a searching enquiry into the working of the convoy system.[5] While French privateering became increasingly dangerous after 1693, it is noteworthy that the Levant Company, which had suffered so severely in this episode, stated in 1695 that in the previous two years it had no losses at all, thanks to the excellence of convoys.[6]

---

[1] J. R. Tanner (ed.), *Sam. Pepys Naval Minutes* (Navy Record Society, 1925), p. 270. R. Coke, *Discourse of Trade* (1670), p. 27, says the prizes of the first and second Dutch wars were four times as great as English losses.

[2] *CSPV 1657–8*, p. 245; *CSPV 30 May 59*; *CSPAWI 1675–6*, No. 475; Rawlinson MSS., A. 271, p. 278; J. Bland, *Trade Revived* (1659); R. Baker, *The World's Mistake in Oliver Cromwell* (1661); BM Harleian MSS. 6287.

[3] *HMC House of Lords MSS. 1706–8*, p. 190.

[4] *Pepys Naval Minutes*, op. cit., p. 270. See also C. Davenant, *Works* (ed. C. Whitworth, 1776), Vol. I, pp. 263, 406.

[5] This was a very large and well-escorted convoy, which encountered the French navy in force too great for the escort to combat. The papers of the enquiry are in *HMC House of Lords MSS. 1693–5*, pp. 93–294. The best accounts of the affair are H. Richmond, *The Navy as an Instrument of Policy, 1558–1727* (Cambridge, 1953), pp. 237–46, and C. de la Roncière, *Histoire de la Marine Française*, Vol. VI (1932), pp. 139–48.

[6] *HMC House of Lords MSS. 1695–97*, pp. 77–8. The valuable Levant ships were exceptionally well convoyed.

The convoy system again came under attack in 1707, the merchants declaring that they

'have of late years been such great sufferers by the ill-timing of convoys and want of cruisers, that they dare no longer engage the remainder of their estates to carry on their several trades'.[1]

The Admiralty, in replying, estimated that 1146 merchant ships had been lost, but this figure was regarded by some merchants as an under-statement.[2] After the enquiry there was a marked improvement in protection, complaints ceased and it may be assumed that captures declined in the last five years of war. Nevertheless, the total loss in this war of 1702-12 must have reached 2000 ships, and may well have been far greater.

Losses were not large in the first three years of the war of 1739-48, for the Spaniards were the only enemies engaged in maritime war. Nevertheless, the merchants complained of their losses in January 1742, pointing out that better protection against Spain should be well within England's naval capacity.[3] When France became fully engaged against England the following year the captures rose sharply in numbers, and in the last years of the war averaged over 500 ships a year; it seems likely that in the whole course of the war well over 3000 ships were taken.[4] The total burden, in relation to the size of the English merchant fleet, may have been no greater than in the war of 1702-12, especially since an increasing proportion of captured 'English' ships were, by this date, colonial-owned ships engaged in inter-colonial trade.

In the Seven Years War (1756-63) merchant ship losses aroused little comment. With a much enlarged navy and an efficient administration, England had made the seas safer for her merchant shipping. It need not be assumed that losses were trivial,[5] but they were probably less severe than they had been in the past.

[1] *HMC House of Lords MSS. 1706-8*, p. 99. The report on the enquiry into the convoy system occupies pp. 99-226.
[2] ibid., pp. 114, 183.
[3] *Gentleman's Magazine*, Vol. XII (1742), pp. 150-2. They declared that up to December 1741 301 ships had been taken. Another estimate, made shortly afterwards on behalf of insurance interests, was of a loss of 337 ships (BM Add. MSS. 19034, f. 57).
[4] *The Gentleman's Magazine* published monthly lists of losses from the latter part of 1743 to the end of the war. The lists are ambiguous in some respects, but figures derived from them should be reasonably accurate.
[5] For example, Liverpool lost 103 ships between 1739 and 1748, and 97 between 1756 and 1763. C. Northcote Parkinson, *The Rise of the Port of Liverpool* (Liverpool, 1952), pp. 105, 111. Between the two wars Liverpool's shipping activity had increased by nearly 50 per cent.

Finally, the losses in the American War of Independence, 1776–83, were estimated at 3,386 ships;[1] much the same as those in the time of William III, when the merchant fleet was only half the size.

Despite all complaints, the risks of capture were not extraordinarily high. In 1693 and 1694, when losses were perhaps greater in relation to the volume of shipping leaving English ports than ever before or afterwards until the present century, French privateers were accounting for no more than seven or eight hundred ships a year. This compares with several thousand sailings from English ports, and it is certain that losses were least among the most valuable, and therefore best protected, ships. This view is confirmed by an examination of insurance rates.

The early history of marine assurance in England, which predates by at least a century and a half the foundation of Lloyd's Coffee House, still awaits a historian; but it seems likely that, during most of the seventeenth century, the practice of insuring goods carried by sea was very widespread while insurance of the ships themselves was uncommon. The wars around the end of the century gave the decisive impetus to marine insurance, and the habit of insuring ships, especially in wartime, acquired a firmer hold as the organisation of the insurance market became more clearly defined, with its chief centre at Lloyd's.[2]

Wartime insurance rates were high; yet their level makes it clear that the great majority of ships could be expected to accomplish their voyages in safety.[3] Henry Johnson insured his parts in East India ships regularly at 6 guineas per cent in the 1680's; from the outbreak of war in 1689 the rate went up to 14 per cent and stayed at that level.[4] Charles Peers was paying 8 to 10 guineas per cent for the homeward voyage from Malaga in 1691–93 (reduced to 6 guineas per cent if the ship were sailing in convoy); the peacetime rate for the voyage *out and home* was 3 per cent.[5] From Scanderoon (Alexandretta) to London, the firm of Radcliffe paid 2 per cent insurance premiums on its cargoes in the years 1714–16; during the preceding war years, 1710–12, and the later

[1] C. Wright and C. E. Fayle, *History of Lloyd's* (1928), p. 156.
[2] C. Wright and C. E. Fayle, op. cit., gives much information on marine insurance in the eighteenth century.
[3] Possibly the rates were not high enough; there were many failures among underwriters in wartime.
[4] BM Add.MSS., 22184.
[5] Peers MSS., Guildhall Library, London.

war year of 1741, it paid, with equal regularity, 5 per cent.[1] A century before, incidentally, John de la Barre was paying the same premium of 4–4½ per cent for Leghorn voyages in peace and war between 1620 and 1629; the corsair danger far overshadowed, at that time, all the risks of seizure by European privateers.[2] The London–Leghorn rate in the 1730's was 1½ per cent, but in the war of 1739–48 6 to 8 guineas per cent was paid.[3] The wine importing firm of James Gordon paid regular premiums of 25s. per cent for shipments from London to Madeira between 1763 and 1776; in the war years of the early sixties it had on occasion paid 6 per cent without convoy, or 3 per cent with convoy for the whole length of the voyage.[4]

These are examples of normal wartime rates; in exceptional circumstances, whether because enemy ships were especially active or because the English merchantman was in particular difficulties, the rates were pushed very much higher. The *William & Mary* was insured at 35 per cent on her voyage from Scanderoon to London in July 1704.[5] William Stout wrote in his journal for 1707 that in the Virginia trade, 'Though at the height of the war, no insurance was then made, which if it had, would have exceeded the profit'.[6] Insurance rates did run high, and might swallow up the normal profit on goods if prices could not be pushed up above peacetime levels. It would be a mistake, however, to suppose that they seriously checked the operation of ships, the 'prices' of which — that is, the freight rates — were raised enormously in wartime; though of course, in Northern trades where wartime freight rates were large in relation to the cost of the goods carried, it became impossible for English ships to compete with any neutrals whom the Navigation Acts permitted to trade. Consider for example, a 200-ton ship making the Barbados voyage in 1704. Her peacetime earnings at £4 a ton (rather a good rate) would have been £800; at the not specially high freight rate for 1704 of £10 a ton, the owners would have received extra war pay of £1200. Against this, an insurance rate which had trebled from

---

[1] Radcliffe MSS., Guildhall Library, London.
[2] HCA 30–635.
[3] DuCane MSS., Essex County Record Office, Chelmsford.
[4] Lloyd's MSS., Add. Docs. 50–52. Several of the rates quoted here are for goods, which tended to differ a little from the rates on ships; but the relations between wartime and peacetime rates are the same for ship and goods.
[5] SP 110–69.
[6] *The Autobiography of William Stout* (1851), p. 75.

its peacetime level, to 15 guineas per cent, would cost them no more than £210 in additional premiums even if the ship were new and expensively fitted. Of course, there were reasons other than financial ones why owners might not wish to lose their ships; but these can hardly be priced. Insurance was not such a complete and satisfactory safeguard as it is nowadays; if the ship were lost, at any time before about 1720 the owners would have to meet between 10 per cent and 20 per cent of the loss themselves;[1] they were quite likely to find the underwriters, when faced with a loss, dilatory, obstructive and even at times fraudulent;[2] while even among the most honest and punctilious of underwriters there was some bankruptcy in every war.[3] Taking all this into account, however, it seems evident that the wartime rise in freight rates, coupled with the probability that those ships that did venture to sea would secure fuller cargoes in war than in peace, far more than covered all the possible risks and costs which arose out of the danger of losing a ship to the enemy. Indeed, there were bitter complaints in Parliament in 1692 that merchants were too ready to take risks with ships that were insured; 'the Insurers have brought these Losses upon you, by making the Ships ready to go without Convoys . . . As for the Merchants, they are hasty to make their Profit, and this, it is said, comes from the Insurance'.[4]

Where, then, did the extra costs of wartime lie, if not in the covering of risks?

Much the most important factor was the soaring of wages, partly due to the seaman's unwillingness to risk capture by an enemy, but even more to his terror of impressment for the English navy. The navy had a very small regular peacetime establishment; some 3,000 to 5,000 officers and men in the second half of the

---

[1] A. H. John, 'The London Assurance Company and the Marine Assurance Market of the Eighteenth Century', *Economica*, n.s., Vol. XXV, 1958, p. 140.

[2] V. Barbour, 'Marine Risks and Insurance in the Seventeenth Century', *Journal of Economic and Business History*, Vol. I, 1929–30, pp. 580–8.

[3] See, for example, the abortive 'Merchant Insurers (War with France)' Bill of 1694, which was to relieve the insurers of one third of their liabilities (*HMC House of Lords MSS. 1693–5*, p. 358); and the situation in the American War eighty years later, of which it was said that among Lloyd's underwriters 'There were some considerable failures at that time, and others who were in better circumstances, and conceived themselves competent to their engagements, quitted the Coffee House from the great losses they had sustained, to give them time to look into their affairs and wind up their account' (*Report of Committee on Marine Insurance* (1810), p. 47).

[4] See the debate on convoys in *HMC House of Lords MSS. 1693–5*, pp. 93–294.

seventeenth century,[1] with a slow tendency to rise; the number
was still no more than 7,000 or 8,000 in some quiet years of the
1730's,[2] and was maintained at around 16,000 after the Seven
Years' War.[3] These numbers were trivial in relation to wartime
needs. In the Second and Third Dutch Wars, peak (nominal)
complements of 35,000 were reached in 1666 and 1674 — increases
of over 30,000 on the peacetime establishments.[4] In the 1690's
and after 1702 the number of officers and men soared to well over
40,000;[5] the war of 1739–48 employed much the same numbers,
but at its climax in October 1747, 51,999 men were mustered in
the fleet;[6] and all these figures were quite eclipsed in the tremendous effort of the Seven Years' War, when 84,770 men were
mustered aboard the ships in September 1762.[7]

The navy held out various baits in an attempt to attract
volunteers, but those who responded were generally seamen
already and so could be ill spared by the merchant service.[8]
Impressment was, through the seventeenth and eighteenth centuries, almost the sole means of augmenting numbers considerably
and rapidly in time of war. Though the power to impress seamen
was not defined by statute, and in retrospect appears to have had
a rather dubious legal standing, it had long been exercised and
the occasional attempts to question it were not taken seriously.[9]
Impressment was, in spite of the romantic literature of the
subject, almost entirely confined to seamen and shipyard workers
in our period; indeed the chief hunting grounds of the press gangs
were not the streets of towns but the sea approaches to the great
ports, where crews could be taken from incoming ships. Evidence
given by a Liverpool pilot in 1744 vividly reveals the general
attitude to impressment and the press gangs:

[1] J. R. Tanner (ed.), *Further Correspondence of Samuel Pepys, 1662–1697*
(1929), pp. 226, 228; *Calendar of Pepysian Manuscripts* (Navy Record Society,
1903–22), Vol. II, p. 7.
[2] *House of Commons Journals, 1737–41*, pp. 19, 221.
[3] *House of Commons Journals, 1766–8*, pp. 24, 451.
[4] Pepys, *Further Correspondence*, pp. 93, 125; *Calendar of Pepysian MSS.*,
Vol. II, 170.
[5] *House of Commons Journals, 1702–4*, p. 425; J. Ehrman, *The Navy in the
War of William III* (Cambridge, 1952), p. 110.
[6] *House of Commons Journals, 1745–50*, p. 501.
[7] *House of Commons Journals, 1761–4*, p. 441.
[8] see e.g. 7 and 8 William III, c. 31; 8 and 9 William III, c. 23.
[9] Ehrman, op. cit., pp. 115–16; W. S. Holdsworth, *History of English Law*
(1904–52), Vol. IV, pp. 330–1. For a detailed contemporary argument against
the legality of impressment, see W. Horsley, *A Treatise of Maritime Affairs*
(1744), pp. 12–16.

'Soon after his boarding the *Tarleton* the ship's crew asked him if there was not a hott press at Liverpoole and he told them that there had been a hott press but that it was not so at that time only that seamen were pressed on the water from foreigners. . . . James Berry the Ship's Carpenter proposed to the other crew aboard to defend themselves from being impressed to which they all agreed and brought up on the said Vessel's deck small arms blunderbusses pistols and cutlasses and he heard one of the saylors say that one of the said ship's gunns was laden with grapeshott and all the saylors swore they would fire upon the King's Boats before they would be impressed. . . . When the King's ship of warr called the *Winchelsea's* boats came nigh unto the said *Tarleton* and then the crew bid the said boat keep off or that they would fire upon them at the same time pointing Musketts at them whereupon Lieutenant Gideon who was in the *Winchelsea's* barge called out to the crew on board the *Tarleton* and told them that if they would suffer him to come alongside and board the said vessel neither the first and second mates Boatswain and Carpenter should be pressed but the ship's crew told him that he should not come aboard and severall musketts were then fired at the boat by the Ship's crew and some fires were returned by the boat . . . during the whole time of this resistance Captain Thompson at the request of his people went into the said Ship's Cabbin but was neither compelled so to do nor confined therein, and then the said James Berry the Carpenter assumed upon himself as Captain during that time . . . the said Captain Thompson never used any Means Threats or Persuasions to prevent his crew from taking the Ship's arms and firing at the Boat but left them wholly to themselves only that he would frequently call out to this deponent from the Vessel's round house to take care of the ship'.[1]

No doubt the navy did take some landsmen — volunteers for glory and prize money as well as mistakes in the press; foreign seamen and English landsmen brought into merchants' ships in the early stages of war were likely to be swept up later by the press gangs; some craftsmen were recruited ashore, though the fleet had to contend with the shipyards for them; such dubious seamen as the Thames watermen were forced into the service,

---

[1] HCA 15–48. The ship ran into the dock and the crew all escaped ashore. The pilot disclaimed knowledge of any of the crew but the master and carpenter. The master was proceeded against, not for resisting the press gang, but for not lowering his topsail or striking his colours to the *Winchelsea*! In a long and detailed allegation and description of the affair compiled from naval witnesses, there is not a word about the purpose for which the *Winchelsea's* barge came alongside. The Admiralty was never anxious to have the legality of impressment argued in the courts.

and soldiers were often put aboard. When all this has been taken into account, however, it is evident that many tens of thousands of seamen had to be taken from the merchant service.[1]

The number of merchant seamen and fishermen was no more than 50,000 before the outbreak of war in 1689; out of this, over 30,000 men had to be taken for the navy. On the eve of the Seven Years' War, the much larger merchant fleet, with its ships more lightly manned, may have had, along with the fisheries, 70,000 or 80,000 seamen; war demanded some 60,000 of these. When it is remembered that war casualties and the heavy drain through sickness had to be replaced; that ships' masters and their first mates were not liable to impressment; that impressment from the east coast colliers (in which, during most of our period, at least a quarter of English seamen were serving) was always restricted and at times completely prohibited;[2] that in the depths of war some merchant ships stayed away from home ports for years at a time; then it seems as if almost every foreign-going seaman who could be found, along with the non-exempt coastal seamen and fishermen, must have been dragged into the navy's net in each of these wars. This view of the almost complete stripping of the merchant fleet of its seamen is, indeed, confirmed by the reading of day-to-day reports of the progress of impressment. It was mitigated in the earlier wars by the seasonal character of naval demands; until well into the eighteenth century the greatest ships of the line were laid up from October to April, for they could not be risked in the gales of winter. Throughout the seventeenth century the control of merchant ships' activities in wartime was operated with this in mind; in November 1666, for example, the Farmers of the Customs were ordered 'to hasten away all Ships outward bound and to take bond of the Masters for them to return by next Spring . . . to the end the Seamen and Mariners may be back against the next Spring for the manning of His Majesty's Fleets'.[3] There was a growing tendency, however, for

[1] A detailed study of naval recruitment in 1689–97 is made by J. Ehrman, op. cit. pp. 110–20.

[2] e.g. proclamations of 26th April 1665 (freeing Newcastle and Sunderland colliers); 3rd May 1672 (freeing all colliers); 6 and 7 William and Mary, c. 18 (1695) gives a scale of minimum crews which must be left to colliers, not very far short of their full complement. Acts of 1708 and 1737 prohibited impressment from ships in America and the British West Indies (6 Anne, c. 19; George II, c. 30).

[3] APC (Col.) 14th November 1666. Cf. the City of London letter to the Privy Council on 7th March 1691, 'The use of foreign seamen is only designed

the winter establishment in wartime to be maintained at a level near to the summer strength.[1]

Impressment was, of course, bitterly unpopular among the seamen. At times it encountered violent resistance from ships' crews; press gangs were said to have left many fingers behind on the bulwarks of Hull whalers, sliced off by the flensing knives of crews who were hardier, and who had more to lose, than most. Nevertheless, avoidance was always preferred to resistance. In the English Channel in particular, crews would desert to avoid the press;[2] 'The Merchant is sometimes at an extraordinary Charge to get Men to bring his Ship up the River, since his own Company often forsake it, in time of War, at the first Port they come to, in order to skreen themselves from the Press'.[3] It was said in 1693 that there were twenty-five ships laid up in Virginia harbours because, to avoid impressment when they came home, their crews had deserted them there and gone into privateering or colonial ships.[4] Even more important, and more effective, was the mass withdrawal from the seaport towns of those men who were fortunate enough to be ashore when war needs loomed up. 'Many seamen', declares a royal proclamation of 1672, 'have left their abodes and moved to obscure places in inland counties . . . to avoid the press;' the justices are enjoined to hunt them out.[5] Henry Maydman wrote in 1691, 'Many Men, when War is, do betake themselves to live with their Friends in the Inlands, and follow their Occupations, and at the end of the Wars, do return to their Maritime Lives, or wait to make slips into Merchantmen.'[6]

The offer of high wages to merchant seamen in time of war was not, therefore, simply a compensation for the risk of capture by the enemy, which might if the ship were not ransomed involve

until the great ships are laid up at the end of the summer and Englishmen may be had' (*HMC Lindsey MSS.*, p. 159).

[1] Maximum and minimum numbers mustered for navy:

		Max.		Min.
1704	(June)	41,613	(January)	37,607
1747	(October)	51,999	(January)	45,870
1762	(September)	84,770	(January)	78,984

(*House of Commons Journals, 1702–4*, p. 425; *1745–50*, p. 501; *1761–4*, p. 441.)

[2] Until after 1730, a man deserting his ship did not inevitably lose his wages.

[3] Philanthropus, *The Encouragement and Increase of Seamen* (1728), p. 9.

[4] *CSPAWI 1693–6*, pp. 2, 198.

[5] *CSPD 1671–2*, p. 253. There are many such proclamations in the state papers.

[6] *Naval Speculations and Maritime Politics*, p. 263. The standard account of impressment is J. R. Hutchinson, *The Press-Gang Afloat and Ashore* (1913).

loss of liberty and wages. It was also a lure to induce them to run the risks of impressment; and an attraction, too, for landsmen who could in wartime take to the sea on terms more favourable, financially, than most of them could ever expect to secure in shore occupations. In 1693, high wages in the Newcastle coal trade were 'not to be attributed to the Want of Men (for its Apparent to the Contrary) But its the Fear the Men are in of being Prest when they come into the River . . . no sooner was the Grand Fleet out but the wages in the Newcastle trade sunk 30/–'.[1] The high wartime wages, of course, made naval service at 26s. per (calendar) month, paid long after the due date, still less attractive to seamen.

The shipowner therefore had great difficulty in getting seamen in wartime, though officers were more easily come by. The seamen he did secure expected enormously inflated wages, and were quick to desert if the ship — in search, perhaps, of more men to fill up the crew — delayed her sailing long enough for those on board to imagine the hot breath of the press gang on their necks. Wages contract books during the wars of 1739–48 and 1756–63 are full of entries of seamen, marked 'run' before the ship sailed, and occasionally a ship would go through two or three entire crews before a complete one was mustered together and the voyage could be begun.[2]

Protections, guaranteeing individual men and even whole crews from impressment, might be secured at a price; Edward Lloyd of the Coffee House was one of the people who apparently had channels for securing them.[3] They were not always easy to obtain, however; they were sometimes cancelled wholesale by Orders-in-Council;[4] and naval officers at sea did not always treat them with respect.[5]

Impressment could cause further expense and loss to the shipowner. The Channel and the approaches to the western ports were the favourite lurking places of the press gangs, which secured

[1] R. Crosfield, *England's Navy Revived* (1693).
[2] e.g. *London* in 1740 (SP 15–42).
[3] The owners of the *Rising Sun* had a bill from Lloyd in 1703 which included 'To a protection for a Mate and Boatswain 10/–, To a Protection for all the Men £3. 5. 6d' (Lloyd's Bowrey MSS. 913).
[4] As they were on 10th April 1672, in the Third Dutch War (R. Steele, *Tudor and Stuart Proclamations, 1485–1714* (Oxford, 1910)).
[5] The *Jonathan & Abigail*, bound for Russia in 1665, secured protections from the Navy officials, but her owners failed to apply for confirmation of them to the Duke of Albemarle, in command of the fleet at the Nore, and his officers seized the crew when the ship came down the river (HCA 13–75).

their prey most easily from the crews of incoming ships, leaving the ships defenceless and with crews barely adequate to handle them. In 1728 the owners, masters and freighters of ships trading from London presented a petition to the House of Commons declaring that

'Petitioners have for many years past struggled with very great Losses and Hardships, by the Impressing Seamen from on Board Merchants' Ships, by the total decay of the Cargo, if loaded with Perishable Commodities; which is not only a loss to the Freightor, and to the Commerce of the said City, but to the Nation in General, by giving Foreigners an Opportunity to supply the Markets; that the Impressing Seamen, and the long Time they are continued in the Service, unpaid their Wages, must expose their Families to great Necessities, and be a Discouragement to the Seamen, and occasions them to leave the Service of their Native Country, and consequently lays the Merchant under the Necessity of raising their Wages; which is a great Clog to the Employment of our Freight Ships, the great Nursery of our Seamen, and, if not timely prevented, may prove the Ruin of the best part of our Navigation'.[1]

Had the clauses of the Navigation Acts, which required that ships which claimed to be treated as English should have crews which were three-quarters English, been vigorously enforced in wartime, few English ships could have continued to operate. In fact these clauses were suspended in wartime before 1688 by Orders-in-Council and thereafter by acts of parliament. In the two Dutch wars of 1664–7 and 1672–4, wrote James Houblon, 'Merchants ships were manned then with old men boys and a great many foreigners.'[2] A petition of 1664 from owners of a number of east coast traders asked for an allowance of two able seamen to each ship; all the seamen from the ships had been taken for the navy, and the owners thought it unsafe for the ships to sail manned entirely with foreigners.[3] The proclamation of 10th April 1672, which revoked all protections for English seamen, provided that English ships might engage foreign sailors, who should be free from impressment; this was one of many such orders.[4] During

[1] *House of Commons Journals, 1727–32*, p. 85. This was during a brief war with Spain.
[2] Rawlinson MSS. A. 171–278.
[3] SP 29–107–85.
[4] For further examples see the references in J. Reeves, *The Law of Shipping and Navigation* (Dublin, 1792), pp. 214–51, 257–8; L. A. Harper, *The English Navigation Laws* (New York, 1939), p. 68, n. 18.

the war of 1689–97 there appear to have been no formal arrangements for permitting the peacetime quota of foreign seamen to be
exceeded; there was an attempt to organise a system of rationed
allowances of English seamen for various trades which may have
acted as some substitute,[1] and in any case the activity of English
shipping declined to an extraordinary degree during this war.
From Anne's reign onward parliamentary authority was resorted
to; in 1704 permitting ships to be manned to the extent of one-half,
and in 1708 to the extent of three-quarters, by foreigners in
wartime;[2] the latter measure was repeated in 1741, when the king
was empowered to make this concession by proclamation in future
wars.[3]

For protection in wartime merchant ships depended on cruisers
patrolling the coast and the approaches to the English Channel,
and on convoys. Cruisers were always too few to be fully effective,
though their work was greatly valued and the demand for increased
numbers of them was constantly voiced. An adequate supply of
them might have solved all the problems of wartime shipping,
but it was far beyond the resources that could be mustered for
maritime war. Convoy was the more general form of protection;
more economical of warships, quite effective in defending those
ships which came into convoys, but involving special kinds of loss
and delay which drove many shipmasters to attempt to operate
independently of convoy.

The first and most important of the disadvantages of convoy was
the great delay which convoy involved; necessary delay while all the
ships were assembled, waiting for the last of the latecomers, and the
not always excusable wait for the convoying warships to arrive.[4]

'Amongst the many and almost insupportable dead losses the
merchants sustain may be ranked the vast disappointments all ships
meet with by long detention waiting for convoy, as the Barbados,
Virginia and Maryland fleets outward last year, and tedious lying
in ports of almost all ships homewards.'[5]

[1] An attempt to secure parliamentary sanction for employing foreign seamen
failed in 1692; *HMC House of Lords MSS. 1692–3*, 72.
[2] 2 and 3 Anne, c. 19; 6 Anne, c. 37.
[3] 13 Geo. II, c. 3. Nevertheless further legislation was resorted to in 1745
and 1757; 17 Geo. II, c. 36, 29 Geo. II, c. 34.
[4] The Mediterranean convoy which was involved in the disaster of 1693 is
an extreme example of this; it had been assembled awaiting convoy for nearly
a year before it sailed (*HMC House of Lords MSS. 1693–5*, p. 104).
[5] *CSPD 1700–2*, p. 586.

Y

During these delays the high wages of wartime, as well as other operating costs of the ships, continued to accumulate.

Secondly, the arrival of a whole season's supply of sugar from the West Indies, tobacco from Virginia and Maryland or wine from Andalusia in one great convoy put a serious strain on the market and on merchant finances, as did the appearance all at once in Cadiz, Lisbon or Boston of a year or more's exports of English cloth and other goods. 'So many Manufactories and so much Fish would come to forrain parts to the Market at once, that our Manufactories would be disesteemed, and have very great abatements of their Prices, and the one half of the Fish would be lost.'[1] A long discussion of 'The Inconveniences and Danger of Convoy in a War against France' in 1695[2] declares that 'Buying Goods all at a time here makes them very dear, and coming together in a Glut to the Markets abroad, causes them to be sold Cheap, whereby the Advantage that might be made by Trade is lost'. It also, of course, caused long delays in loading and unloading when ports were choked with great fleets of merchantmen all needing attention at once.

These general complaints, and the outcry against naval captains who expected the merchants to reward them for doing their duty to the ships under convoy,[3] died away in the eighteenth century after a last outburst of criticism in 1708.[4] Thereafter convoy was taken for granted, its value clearly indicated by the differences in insurance rates on convoyed and unconvoyed ships.[5] It remained true that convoy, while mitigating the risks of loss of ships and cargoes, imposed its own costly burdens in delay and the glutting of markets. Richard Stratton, an Aleppo merchant with many idiosyncracies, summed up and exaggerated the objections to convoy in a letter from the Levant in 1747:

'With pleasure I observe that the Insurers think the risk by Running Ships is little more than by Convoy, as it squares with my Opinion, for the time the latter are on their Voyage gives all the opportunity

[1] R. Baker, *The Merchants Humble Petition and Remonstrance to his Late Highness* (1659).
[2] In *Some Thoughts Concerning . . . Trade and Navigation*.
[3] See, for example, Sir Robert Clayton's speech in parliament on 13th November 1689. *Debates of the House of Commons, collected by Anchitell Grey* (1769).
[4] See the report of the enquiry of 1708 in *HMC House of Lords MSS., 1706–8*, pp. 99–226.
[5] See p. 318, above.

possible for the Enemy to fitt out Men of Warr to meet them and it is well known a Sixty Gun Ship might take the whole Convoy; but to the Trade, if you can Insure on running Ships at almost the same Premium, Sure the Trader has a great Advantage, he makes quick Voyages and Return, nay has his Silk home in time to pay for part of his Cloth, has all the Benefit that can be in buying his Goods both at home and abroad, as he is never pressed for time at the former, and buys at the latter by himself without Rivals and when the Market is not overloaded as by Convoys, and he brings a proper Assortment, as it is wanted, not Vaste Quantities together but just enough to supply the Market, he sells his Silk at home before the Glut comes at a good price and is not obliged to keep for a Market two or three Years together.'[1]

Shipping in wartime, therefore, could be very profitable — but not so profitable as a first impression of doubled and trebled freight rates would suggest. The counterpart of high freight rates was the high cost of unusually prolonged voyages; though monthly wage rates (considering the whole crew, officers and seamen) increased less than freight rates, this protraction of voyages inflated the total wage bill, as well as victualling costs. While repairs and other miscellaneous costs increased little, insurance premiums went up at least proportionately to freight rates. It is very likely that shipowners' profits were higher in war than in peace; they were undoubtedly much less certain, for the stability of wage and freight rates was broken and voyage times could not be at all closely estimated. Cargo carrying in wartime was, much more than in years of peace, a gamble in which the possibilities of great profits were balanced against those of substantial loss.

A number of courses of action were open in wartime to those who managed ships. The shipowner might accept the difficulties of manning, the delays of convoys, the risks of capture, and continue to provide his services to trade (though not necessarily to the trade in which his ship normally plied) and hope that the swollen freights of wartime would bring him his reward. He could withdraw from activity altogether, lay up his ship and wait for better times; though to lay up a ship through the whole of one of

---

[1] Radcliffe MSS., Guildhall Library, London. The Levant convoys were exceptionally vulnerable to French or Spanish attack, and offered an enormously rich prize to those who might capture them.

the long wars of the eighteenth century was commercial suicide, for no ship could survive seven or ten years 'by the walls' in good condition. Between trying to carry on the operations of trade, and abandonment of the struggle, there were two other possibilities of employment; in government service and in privateering.

In wartime the government needed not only seamen, but also merchant ships, in large numbers. During the wars of the seventeenth century the line of battle fleet was heavily supplemented from among the larger merchant vessels, and though the man-of-war outgrew this support a warlike function remained for merchantmen as convoy escorts and cruisers. Great numbers of smaller vessels were regularly needed as victuallers, water carriers, fire ships and hospital ships; and at times fleets had to be mustered for the transport of troops overseas — to the Isle of Ré in 1626-7, to Ireland in 1689-91, the attack on Brest in 1694 and the capture of Belleisle in 1761, or in smaller numbers across the Atlantic to garrison West Indian islands or to provide the stiffening which professional soldiers were convinced the colonial militias of North America needed.

There were solid advantages to hiring ships to the crown. The rates paid were reasonable; eight to ten shillings a month per measured ton for vessels employed as warships, and six shillings to seven and six for victuallers, transports, etc.[1] Out of these earnings the owners had to keep their ships in good repair (apart from war damage) and provide for their normal wear and tear. The problems of convoy and high wages ceased to be relevant, for the government (the navy or the transport department) paid the wages, and the ships were hired by the month. The earnings, therefore, were easily calculable, and compared quite favourably with those obtained in peacetime occupations. The shipowner putting his vessel into government service was opting for stability and certainty, rather than for the risks and the problematical profits of commercial operations in wartime. The special advantage of hiring a ship to the navy as a warship was that it eliminated, as far as the owners were concerned, the costs of loss by enemy action. A ship to be hired as a warship was appraised (by independent experts) and the crown recompensed the owners for war damage or loss, and even for some kinds of ordinary damage at

[1] Records of government hire can be found in great numbers in the State Papers, Domestic of the three Dutch wars; and in Adm. 49-29/34 for later wars.

sea, up to the extent of the appraisement.[1] Victuallers and other vessels of the same kind were not guaranteed against loss in this way, but they ran few risks, being usually employed under heavy escort.

Nevertheless, shipowners sometimes gave the appearance of being reluctant to hire their ships to the government. In 1665, for example, the navy encountered difficulties and had to secure from the Privy Council a reiteration of the view that it was entitled to use compulsory powers. The Lord High Admiral reported that he had ordered the principal officers of the navy

'To hire Divers Shipps, which they endeavouring to doe by Treaty with the Owners, found that the Rates and Prices of Shipps were dayly raised to His Majesty's disadvantage, according as the Owners found cause to believe the King's occasions most pressing, and they feared that inconvenience would increase, especially when the Embargo should be taken off; and it was further represented that only old Shipps and less serviceable were offered to the King's service by the Owners, and that when the Owners of the newest and best Shipps were invited to treat for their Shipps, they declined it, either by pretending their Shipps to be already lett to Freight upon Trading Voyages, or by demanding excessive Rates, or sometymes by absolutely denying to lett their Shipps'.[2]

This may have been a tactical resistance designed to secure the best possible bargain; but there was one real and important objection to dealing with the government; the difficulty of extracting from it the money it owed. At times — and 1665 was one of them — it was possible to have doubts whether money due from the government would ever be paid at all; and there was always long delay, though in this respect as in many others there was much improvement in the course of the eighteenth century. When in 1703, for example, the owners of six ships which had been hired for Newfoundland in 1697 petitioned the House of Commons to take some steps to get them their pay, the House went out of its way, in rejecting the petition, to brand it as frivolous![3] The shipowner, to get his money at all promptly, had to sell his paper claim on the government, and the discount, varying with the state of royal and parliamentary credit, might

---

[1] PC Register (PC 2–58), 2nd January 1665; *CSPD 1690–1*, pp. 103–4.
[2] ibid.
[3] *House of Commons Journals, 1702–4*, p. 152.

be a high one. The owners of the *Neptune*, which was in government service from 1706 until 1709, earned freights totalling £2,473 and received Transport Debentures for them quite promptly; these debentures were discounted at rates varying from 6 per cent to $21\frac{1}{4}$ per cent, and the discount and brokerage reduced the net amount the owners received in cash to £2,027.[1] Government finances were by this time far healthier than they had been half a century before; payment was certain, if likely to be long delayed. It is plain, though, that owners had to calculate for the reduction of their theoretical earnings in government service, by a cost of discounting or of interest lost which varied from time to time; and had at times to allow for the possibility that they would not be paid at all.

Nevertheless, it is doubtful whether the compulsory powers of taking ships into its service, which the government possessed, often had to be used. The owners of the *Neptune*, mentioned above, had bought the ship in 1706 solely for the purpose of putting her into government employ, and many examples can be found of small ships whose owners paid money to corruptible government officials for the privilege of being hired for the Ordnance Office or the Transport Service; as the *Blessing* in 1690 has recorded in its account book, 'Money laid out to get the ketch in the King's service, £6.'[2] For the shipowner whose regular trade had been cut off completely by the outbreak of hostilities, and whose ship was unsuited to privateering, government service was a way to avoid the difficulties of putting his ship to a new trade for the duration.

The other alternative to continuing commercial operation was privateering. Though it has superficially the appearance of an easy way to win wealth, the detailed studies which have been made of it do not confirm this view.[3] These studies cover one period of intense privateering activity, 1587–1604, and one when this activity was much smaller, 1689–97. In the war against Spain which ended in 1604 it seems there were times when most large ships were engaged either in government service or in privateering, and it is unlikely that privateering ever employed so large a

---

[1] C 6–357–85; *Johnson v. Colthurst.*   [2] HCA 15–16.
[3] K. R. Andrews, 'Economic Aspects of Elizabethan Privateering' (unpublished London Ph.D. thesis, 1951); G. N. Clark, *The Dutch Alliance and the War against French Trade* (1923), pp. 44–62; G. N. Clark, 'War Trade and Trade War', *Econ. Hist. Rev.*, Vol. I, 1927.

proportion of English merchant ships again.[1] In 1692 and the following years there were some fifty or sixty English privateers at sea;[2] judging from the number of prizes taken there were fewer in the Dutch wars. In the eighteenth century the scale of privateering was probably extended, though more by the use of larger and more powerful vessels than by increasing their numbers.

The privateer's crew was liable to impressment; the risks of damage in action and even of capture were considerable for any ship which did not modestly confine its attentions to the weakest enemy craft which would make the poorest prizes. The huge crew expected high wartime wage rates as well as a share in the prizes taken, and the Crown and the Lord High Admiral were entitled to one-sixth of the value of the prizes. The romantic view of the privateer is, alas, like the romantic view of so many other parts of our subject, a totally wrong one. It pictures the vessel careering across the high seas, each day picking up two or three ships laden with spices, silks and silver plate; dropping prize crews into them and turning up in port, eventually, to collect the vast fortune which is awaiting every member of the crew from the proceeds. Cold statistics tell us that two or three prizes a year was a more typical average; and most privateers which were lucky enough to capture two vessels in a day would have to return to port because no more men could be spared for prize crews in new hauls. Laden with hides, timber, sugar — any of the ordinary commodities of seaborne commerce — they would not go very far to repay the privateer's owners for their outlay. The attractiveness of privateering, for the larger privateers, lay in the *possibility*, though remote, of encountering a richly laden ship — with cochineal, cloth, silk or spices — which for some reason had become detached from convoy though too weak to fight effectively and too slow to run; the prize which would pay a dividend of hundreds per cent, and so justify all. Lotteries are run on the same principle; the near certainty of losing a little set against the remote chance of enormous gains. Such captures were indeed rare, and as defence by convoy or by building 'running' ships whose defence was their speed became more general, those who sought such prizes had to operate with large, specially built, costly ships.

---

[1] Indeed, many of the large ships of this period were built for privateering; this practice was not common again until after 1739.

[2] Clark, *Dutch Alliance*, op. cit., App. III.

In time of war, then, English trade had to contend with formidable problems of transportation; manning difficulties and the employment of ships by the government seriously reduced the tonnage available, wartime prolongation of voyages reduced the service which each ship could supply, and lowered supply and high costs caused great increases in the freight rates which merchants were obliged to pay. The volume of trade carried on was naturally reduced — perhaps very heavily reduced in the seventeenth-century wars, for which few statistics are available. It was maintained at a reasonably high level, however, by a great increase in the employment of foreign ships.

Tonnage of English and foreign ships in foreign trade, in peace and war (000 tons)

	Entries		Clearances		Per cent Foreign	
	Eng.	For.	Eng.	For.	Entries	Clearances
WAR 1692–4[1]	82	106	82	81	56	50
Peace 1699–1701[2]			294	44		8
WAR 1710–11[3]			255	63		20
Peace 1713–15[4]			421	27		6
Peace 1751[5]	421	59	648	46	12	7
WAR 1758	283	130	427	99	31	15
Peace 1772	652	128	815	73	18	8
WAR 1779	482	228	581	139	32	19

These figures, useful as they are, do not exactly reflect the changes which took place in wartime. In the first place, the only statistics before 1751 (except those of the war years 1693–4) are of clearances. Since most of the volume of English exports was in coal and corn, the former attracting an export duty and the latter losing an export bounty if carried in foreign ships, it is likely that the switch to the use of foreign ships was markedly greater in import than in export trade. This is plainly reflected in the figures which are available after 1751; in both the Seven Years' War and the American War a far higher proportion of entries than of clearances was foreign, and this difference almost certainly extends to the earlier wars of the eighteenth century.

[1] *HMC House of Lords MSS.*, 1695–7, pp. 419–21.
[2] G. Chalmers, *Estimate of the Comparative Strength of Great Britain* (1782), *passim.*
[3] CO 388–18.
[4] CO 388–18.   [5] From 1751 onward, BM Add.MSS. 11256.

The other source of misunderstanding points in the opposite direction. Englishmen, like the citizens of every other maritime state, turned their attention in wartime to devices for the 'colouring' of ships and goods, securing false papers for ships and their cargoes or carrying through bogus sales to citizens of neutral states, to be cancelled when the ships arrived safely at their home ports. William Slew, master of the *William & John* in 1673 'being homeward bound from Teneriffe, for his greater security against Dutch privateers made a formal sale of the ship to Carlo de Saldira, a Spaniard who put himself and twenty Spanish seamen on board'.[1] This did not save Slew's ship from capture by a Dutch privateer, for colouring could never completely eliminate risk. The build of ships showed national characteristics which were not easily disguised[2] and if suspicion was aroused the interrogation of the crew by a privateer's officer quickly produced the necessary damning information. However, all through the seventeenth century there is continuous evidence of the carrying on of these deceptions. As early as 1602, Monson advised warships seeking news at the Azores to 'ply into the roads of Villa France and St Michael, where you shall use your best endeavour to speak with the ships, there riding, that trade under the name and colour of Scots, but are properly English'.[3] The practice even received official recognition; in the Third Dutch War the Lords of the Treasury wrote to the Customs Commissioners:

'Considering the present state of affairs, we do think it very fit for the encouragement and security of the English merchants that they have liberty to take coquets in the name of strangers and accordingly we desire you to permit the same.'[4]

In the eighteenth century, with the growing efficiency of naval protection, Englishmen may have camouflaged their ships and goods in this way more rarely, but the possibility of it must be

---

[1] SP 29 334-142. See also, Edward Coxere's experiences in English ships trading with the Canaries during war with Spain in 1658 (*The Adventures by Sea of Edward Coxere* (ed. E. H. W. Meyerstein), Oxford, 1945), pp. 70-3.

[2] 'One great advantage the Hollanders have of us is in the build of their ships, there being little difference between the Hamburghers, or Easterlings, and them. This gives them a freedom of trade into all parts, as well friends as foes. As friends, they pass for Hollanders, as enemies, they take upon themselves the name of Easterlings' (M. Oppenheim (ed.), *The Naval Tracts of Sir William Monson* (Navy Record Society, 1902-14), Vol. V, p. 313).

[3] op. cit., Vol. II, p. 255.

[4] *Calendar of Treasury Books, 1669-72*, p. 1214.

taken into account when looking at statistics which show the employment of 'foreign' ships.

Until 1688, the turn to the use of foreign ships in wartime was facilitated by the issue of wartime Orders-in-Council which relaxed the requirements of the Navigation Acts. From 1665–8, for example, trade with America, Norway and the Baltic, Flanders, France and Spain was opened to all foreign shipping; similar concessions were made in the Third Dutch War, when foreign vessels were even allowed into the coasting trade from which they had been excluded for over a century.[1] After the Revolution such suspensions of the law required parliamentary authority, and were not made. Apart from reducing the requirements for the employment of English seamen, as already noticed, the Navigation Acts remained virtually in full effect in all the wars after 1688.[2] It may be supposed, therefore, that after that date the principal beneficiaries of the turn to foreign shipping in war were the Northern states — Denmark, Sweden, the Hanse towns — which were able to send their own goods in their own ships.[3]

Despite all this, the great sacrifices which merchant shipping had to make to meet the wartime needs of the navy involved the shutting down of much maritime activity, and at times the near-paralysis of the commercial metropolis, London. Merchant shipping bore its burdens, not that the navy might directly serve the special interests of shipowners, but in a wider national interest — for 'the wealth, strength, security and glory of Britain'.[4] That wider interest was interpreted, in part at least, as the extension of the English colonial empire. The English shipowner could expect his special reward in the days of peace, in the exclusive privileges he was given in the rapidly growing carrying trade of that empire. If, in the century after the First Dutch War, it was the English rather than the French or Dutch shipping industry which became the greatest transatlantic carrier, this was in large part the result of success in war, translated into the maintenance

---

[1] Proclamations of 22nd March 1665, 25th October 1665, 10th May 1672 (R. Steele, op. cit.).

[2] There were some very limited concessions. In 1747 the import of stores for the navy only, in neutral ships of all kinds, was permitted (19 Geo. II, c. 36). In 1745, permission was given for the import of many European commodities in foreign-owned, *British-built* ships (17 Geo. II, c. 36).

[3] Though Brewster wrote in 1695 that even the Portuguese were capturing English carrying trade (*Essays on Trade and Navigation*, 1695, p. 4).

[4] Lord Haversham in 1714 (*Cobbett's Parliamentary History* (1806), Vol. VI, 598).

and extension of an area within which Englishmen had a monopoly of trade and transport. The chief benefit to the shipowner of the navy's activities was not security and the protection of trade in wartime, but rather the extension of this monopoly; a benefit deferred indeed, and indirect, but none the less valuable in the long run.

XVI

Four Ships and their Fortunes

The greater part of this book has been devoted to discussing, separately and in some detail, the various aspects of the internal functioning of the shipping industry and its relations to the world outside. It may help to bring all this into focus if we now look at the realities of the working life of a few ships, the problems which their owners, charterers and masters faced in the course of earning livelihoods from them. The examples are not necessarily typical; they are simply the best documented. Nevertheless, they illustrate a wide range of ordinary maritime and commercial experiences at different periods of time.

Diamond, 1634–40[1]

The *Diamond*, 250 tons, was quite new in 1634 when her owners decided to dispose of her. She was sold to a new owning group whose leading figure was Thomas Soame, already a prosperous trader to the Mediterranean and presently to be alderman of London, Sheriff of Middlesex, and to attain to a knighthood. He was one of fourteen owners (including five of the former proprietors of the ship) and was evidently the director of its affairs. His own share was one-eighth, and the master, William Peers, owned one-sixteenth. The high price that was paid, £1,150, indicates that this was a specially strong and fast vessel suited to the conditions of the Mediterranean trade. There was much work to be done before the ship could be put to sea again; new sails to be made, new rigging to be erected, damaged woodwork to be made good, the carpenters' and boatswains' stores to be replenished. The owners laid out no less than £840 on all this. Moreover, the ship was bound for waters where the only defence against Moorish corsairs would be her own guns, manned by an ample crew; nine months' provisions for a crew of forty meant great

[1] HCA 30–635.

338

quantities of beef and biscuit, beer and cheese, and cost £340.
The ship's armament was inadequate for her protection in such
a voyage, and new guns with powder and shot were put in, adding
£247 to the owners' outlays. When, therefore, the owners came
down to the waterside in November to give the master his final
instructions, to hand him £15 towards his out-of-pocket expenses
abroad, and to bid him God-speed, they had set out nearly £2,600
on the vessel — some £10 for every ton of goods she was capable
of carrying.

For the time being they intended to treat the ship simply as an
investment, not despatched to carry her owners' goods or serve
their purposes, but hired out on time charter for the Mediterranean at the rate of £170 per month.[1] As was customary, the
charterers undertook to pay two-thirds of all port charges. The
charter party is not available so we cannot say who the charterers
were, but it is of course quite possible that they included some
of the ship's owners.

The crew was embarked at the last moment, receiving only four
or five days' 'river pay' at Gravesend. Their first duty was a
simple one; to take the ship up to Yarmouth where, since the
month was November and they were bound for the Mediterranean,
a cargo of red herrings was to be laden. This cargo was waiting
for them and quickly loaded, for they carried their pilot with
them all the way out of Gravesend past the shoals of the Thames
estuary and the Suffolk coast to Yarmouth, and back into the
Downs, dropping him there with his fee of £6, and turning into
the English Channel at the end of November. After this, nothing
more is heard of the *Diamond* for almost two months; she made
no calls in her passage down-Channel, passed by Cadiz where
nearly all English ships bound for the Mediterranean made a stop,
and ignored Leghorn, the principal centre of English trade in the
western Mediterranean. Her account book shows none of the port
dues, watering charges, guards' fees or other costs which marked
ships' calls in foreign ports, until on 25th January 1635 she drove
in past the sand-bars of the Lido to anchor in the port of Venice.
There her herrings were soon unloaded; 'the broakers that helped
to do our business' secured a quick turn-round, and in three

---

[1] The owners paying all running expenses.

weeks the ship was out again, though apparently in ballast. There
was a brief call at Ravenna — a place not otherwise mentioned
among the records of English shipping — and on 7th March they
entered the free port of Ancona, in Papal territory, where English
traders were beginning to become familiar as shippers of olive
oil. The *Diamond*, however, took in not oil but corn, 430 moyes
(about 270 tons) of it, to be carried to Lisbon at a freight of £3 a
ton. Though it was very late in the crop season, and all corn
available for shipment must have been already in store, it took a
long time to complete arrangements and get the corn aboard;
possibly the master wasted time seeking in vain for an oil cargo
for England, before accepting the corn as a second-best which
would at least see the vessel well filled for a part of her journey.[1]
Whatever the reason, it was not until the 6th June that the master
conned the ship beneath the fort of Sao Juliao into the mouth of
the Tagus. At Lisbon there was another sign that something had
gone wrong with the ship's plans at Ancona. When the freight
for the corn was received by the master on his charterers' behalf,
a part of it was at once used to pay three months' wages to the
crew. Such an advance, as we have seen, was required by crews
that were being asked to make longer and more complicated
voyages than they had originally contracted for. The master found
no cargo for home at this time of year, so he undertook a sub-
charter to carry salt to the Azores; and seeing a chance for
profitable trade he used some of his charterers' money to buy
sixty tons of salt on their account. The two dealings were incom-
patible; the salt the master bought kept out some of the salt he
had undertaken to carry for his Lisbon clients, and on arrival in
the Azores he had to compound with them for a reduced payment
of freight, 'not being able to accomplish our loading'. However,
he had the profit on the salt trade to counterbalance this. All that
now remained was to come home, and in the Azores in July there
was sugar to be had, readily saleable in an England whose West
Indian colonies were as yet little developed. The balance of
charterers' money in his hands was used to buy sugar (it was
not enough to make up a full lading) and the ship was quickly

---

[1] The master of a chartered ship was of course responsible for furthering the
charterers' interests. The search for cargo was of no concern to the owners,
secure in their monthly rate of hire.

despatched to arrive in England before the autumn gales broke;
she arrived in the Thames on 6th September 1635.

The story has too many gaps, and is too confused with the buying
and selling of goods, to make it possible to say how the charterers fared. Throughout the ship's rather leisurely meanderings
they had been paying a fixed monthly charge, and though she
had usually been well filled up it is likely that the whole voyage
had taken too long to be profitable to them on those terms. A
straight journey out to Venice with herrings, and home from
Ancona with a heavy cargo of oil, could hardly have failed to be
successful, and this is probably what had been contemplated when
the charter was signed. The results from the owners' point of
view, however, are fairly clear. For a little over ten months' hire
they received £1757, out of which the master's outlays (mostly
for payment of wages) swallowed £706. Here at first sight was a
very satisfactory balance; but of course a large part of the fitting
out and nearly all the victualling costs incurred at the beginning
must be charged against this voyage, and these had totalled
(excluding the artillery) £1180. The true profit, then, was not
substantial. The owners' criterion for dividend distribution,
however, was a simpler one. Out of the master's cash balance, the
cost of setting out the ship for the next voyage had to be met;
the remainder could be distributed to the owners.[1] On the basis
of this calculation they divided £378 13s., about 14½ per cent of
their original investment.

Refitting in London in the late autumn, the *Diamond* was well
situated to enter the race to bring home the Iberian wine and
fruit crops. Again, however, the owners did not employ her in
their own concerns. When the ship was ready to sail in mid-
December they again chartered her, this time for a defined voyage
to Lisbon and back; a tonnage charter at £4 per ton on 240 tons.
Since this freight was determined solely by the potential homeward cargo, it is impossible to say whether owners or charterers
took any cargo outward at all; but the quantity, if there was any,
was very small, for the master bought 129 tons of shingle ballast

[1] It need not be supposed that the owners naïvely thought this represented
the profit. There was no point in leaving cash idle; it was distributed when not
needed, just as a call would be made upon the owners when new fitting out
costs exceeded the balance in the master's hands.

at Tilbury at the usual rate of a shilling a ton. Then, on 28th December 1635 the *Diamond* sailed, dropping the pilot in the Downs and reaching Lisbon, after an unusually slow voyage, on 19th March. Here a quick despatch was obtained, and in June the ship was back in the Thames. This time the owners' receipts were £992 — the excess over the agreed freight of £960 having arisen from passenger fares and the sale of stores. The total outgoings of the voyage — fitting out and the wages and other outlays of the master — amounted to £1090, so there was an apparent loss of £98, which may be attributed to the slowness of the outward journey. However, the cash in hand was still surplus to the immediate needs for new stores and victuals, and a dividend of £169 1s. 9d. was distributed.

The owners determined on another Lisbon voyage, but this time not on charter, and with a significant variation. Six weeks after her departure from London, the ship is found in early October dumping her ballast in the harbour of Cork, and loading a great cargo of beef, pork and butter there. Many ships came empty to Cork and Kinsale to fill up for southern and transatlantic voyages; for so short a voyage as the one to Lisbon it was a rather big diversion from the direct route. However, this outward cargo, which earned the owners a freight of £430, was the salvation of the voyage, for arriving again at Lisbon on 9th December the master found there were no freights to be had. The obvious solution might have seemed to be to push on to Malaga or Cadiz for sherry and raisins, but instead Peers, possibly exploiting his earlier connections, negotiated a charter-party to take sugar from the Azores to England. His freight was £750, which we may suppose was for 250 tons of sugar at £3 a ton — a low rate appropriate to a time of cargo shortage in Portugal. Space was reserved for a few tons of sugar brought home by the master for the owners' account; after refunding the appropriate freight to the charterers a profit of £62 was earned on this sugar. The ship loaded at three islands in the Azores — Terceira, Fayal and St Michael's — during February 1637, and was home early in May. The outward lading had saved the voyage from disaster and made possible a reasonable profit. For this third voyage the owners distributed a dividend of £152 11s. 5d.

The ship was now back in London a little too early for the new southern wine season; the two Lisbon voyages of the previous year, which should have taken no more than nine or ten months, had begun late and had in fact occupied fourteen. Rather than rush into a different sphere of activity, however, the owners set about a leisurely refitting and provisioning; spring passed and early summer, and by the time the ship was ready for sea again August had come round once more, the time for the southern voyage. This time the Spanish port of Malaga was to be tried. It was the great lading place for sherry, and a ship which came early was almost certain to find a cargo. In fact the journey was quickly completed. The *Diamond* was in Malaga on 22nd October, and there the master no doubt went the rounds of the Malaga merchant houses; at any rate, the freight he earned, £866, came from five different merchants. She was back home at the end of January, and though this was not a specially fast voyage by the standards of the time, the ship's performance was better than it had been on past voyages. The avoidance of the heavy wages bill which delays had caused in earlier voyages enabled this one to earn a good profit. The owners found themselves with a large cash surplus, for they were able to share £352 13s.

At the end of February 1638, therefore, the *Diamond* was ready for new ventures. It was late in the season for another southern voyage, and while the essential refitting was carried out the owners contemplated possible alternatives. A whaling voyage to Spitzbergen? The ship was about the right size, but hardly of the appropriate build, and too expensive to be risked among the northern icefields. Preparations were put in hand, and then ceased. To Barbados? Barbados was not yet the great sugar plantation it was to become, but it already supported a dense population of small settlers and shipped large quantities of tobacco, cotton and indigo to England. Money was laid out to prepare for the voyage in March, April and May 1638; then the scheme fell through. We cannot tell the reasons; perhaps the owners feared the uncertainty of the freight market of this new and distant colony and contemplated again the relative certainties of the southern voyages they were accustomed to. In any case, the ship became involved in some kind of legal action during that spring which kept it idling in the river all summer and autumn; only when the issue was settled could a new voyage be determined, and by this time her condition had deteriorated and refitting had to be started again. It was not until March 1639, after more than a year's idleness,

z

that the ship put to sea. This time the owners did their best to wash their hands of all concern with the ship's earnings or her costs; they let her out on a time charter for a voyage to lade fish off Newfoundland, carry it to Spain and bring home a cargo from there, and agreed with the charterers that the latter were to bear the costs of victualling and to hire and pay the crew. Beyond putting the ship in good condition with adequate stores, therefore, the owners had little to pay. The *Diamond* was costing them nothing as she put out into the Channel in March, as she lay off the south coast of Newfoundland chaffering with the Newfoundland fishing vessels in June and July, and as she ran across the Atlantic to dispose of her cargo at Alicante in October. The factors, good or bad, which caused the ship to linger in the Mediterranean — at Barcelona and Majorca — as late as February, were of little concern to them. All that mattered was that when the ship returned in June 1640 the charterers paid their freight for every day of this long voyage, and a handsome profit was recorded — but one which had already been eaten away by the costs of preparation for the abortive Spitzbergen and Barbados voyages two years before.

For years, however, the owners had been running down their capital. Fitted out expensively in the first instance for a long and dangerous voyage, the *Diamond* had then gone on a succession of shorter voyages, requiring much smaller outlays on stores and provisions, and finally on one for which the owners did not have to supply the provisions at all. Moreover, though considerable repairs had been effected during her life, she was now after six years due for an extensive and costly overhaul to put her back into good shape. The last profit had pushed up the cash reserves, but these were now not adequate for extensive refitting and provisioning. For six years the owners had been distributing their cash surpluses as dividends. Though a profitable voyage had just been concluded they now had to forego a dividend. Indeed, as she was being fitted out for another Newfoundland voyage (this time, not on charter) the owners found to their dismay that they had to pay in £171 to meet an excess of fitting out costs. The *Diamond* was actually lying off Gravesend ready to sail with her ballast aboard when the quarrels about this heavy expenditure came to a head. The legal action that followed ended the master's job and his account book, and our story with it.

The *Diamond's* financial history can be summarised like this:

£	Earnings	Outgoings	Apparent Profit or Loss	Dividend
Mediterranean voyage, November 1634–September 1635	1757	1886[1]	−129	379
Lisbon voyage, December 1635–June 1636	992	1090	− 98	169
Lisbon voyage, August 1636–May 1637	1242[2]	1100	+142	153
Malaga voyage, August 1637–January 1638	880	784	+ 96	353
laid out for abortive voyages, 1638		162	−162	
Newfoundland/Spain voyage, March 1639–June 1640	846	519	+327	nil
laid out for Newfoundland voyage, 1640		956		

A genuine apportionment of the profits over the various voyages is impossible, though it is clear which were the really good ones. It is evident, however, that over a period of six years total income was only £176 more than outlay — that is outlay other than on the original structure of the ship and her armament. Out of this £1054 was paid in dividends. Yet even these dividends, unearned as they were, amounted to less than 7 per cent per annum on the original investment. They would not even have met a proper depreciation charge and insurance for the voyages in corsair-infested waters which the *Diamond* so often travelled into; they left no margin for the prudent owner, even if he believed, wrongly, that his ship had earned them. And at the end the owners had to re-invest capital and incur a large debt in addition, in order to prepare the ship for sea again in 1640.

What was wrong with the *Diamond's* management? Principally, I think, that she was constantly turned to new kinds of enterprise, so that the master and owners never had an opportunity to build up the local relations which could do much to ensure a good share of available cargoes and a quick turn-round. Yet on the two voyages which the ship undertook on time charter, when it was hardly possible to lose money, the returns were not very high. It certainly seems that the whole enterprise was over-capitalised; the price of the ship herself, at about £4 5s. per ton of tons burden,

[1] Including original fitting out costs.
[2] Outward £430, homeward £750, profit on sugar £62.

is a high one for a second-hand ship at that date; the original fitting out was on generous and costly lines, and the repair costs incurred from time to time were on the high side. At some 30s. per ton per annum, repair and re-equipment was costing more than twice as much as in a typical ship of her day; yet major repairs were not included in this, for they were carried out only in preparation for the final Newfoundland voyage. Her crew, varying from 34 in the second Lisbon voyage to 40 in the earliest Mediterranean voyage, was a normal one, normally paid; but their victualling, at some 24s. per man per month, was again very much more costly than the 15–17s. which normal experience would lead us to expect. All in all we may say that, the dignity of the future Alderman Sir Thomas Soame notwithstanding, the ship was inefficiently run; or alternatively that the master was making for himself the profit that eluded his owners. Either way, the situation says very little for the supervision which the owners exercised over an employee whom they retained in their service for more than six years.

Cadiz Merchant, 1675–84[1]

Edward Barlow, the writer of the journal, spent nearly twenty years of his life at sea before he rose from the forecastle to the dignity of second mate in a Jamaica trader in 1678. When he had completed two voyages in this capacity he took a rest ashore for some months, and then 'intending to go again for Jamaica, I shipped myself with one Captain Johnson, in a ship which was built at Newcastle, of the burden of 280 tons[2] carrying twenty-four guns, with two wooden ones to make a show, as though we had more'.[3] The ship was the *Cadiz Merchant*, and Barlow made two voyages in her, the first as second mate at 55s. a month, and the other as chief mate at 80s. a month.

A great deal can be learned about the *Cadiz Merchant*, for the ship was involved in a lawsuit in 1684, and when the commotion ebbed away Captain Johnson's account book for the years 1675–84 was left high and dry among the papers in the archives. The ship's story can be traced from this account book, and filled out

---

[1] HCA 30–664.
[2] A Bill of Sale gives the tonnage as 260; she was chartered as 270 tons.
[3] *Barlow's Journal* (ed. Basil Lubbock, 1934), p. 327.

with more information from the time Barlow first trod her decks in the spring of 1680.

Back, then, to 1675. The book opens with a voyage from Newcastle to London, which fits in with Barlow's statement that she was Newcastle built; though she carried coal on this voyage there seems to have been no intention of regularly employing the vessel as a collier, and indeed Barlow's illustration of her suggests a ship built for ocean trades. Nor, in spite of her name, was she well suited to the Andalusian trade, for she was much bigger than most ships which brought wine and raisins from Malaga and Cadiz.

The first cost and fitting out are not recorded. Newcastle-built, her price fresh from the shipwright's yard would have been between £1200 and £1500, while the further costs of setting her to sea including the master's 'stock' from which odd stores and provisions were purchased might be little less. It is not certain, though very probable, that the ship was in fact built for these owners rather than bought second-hand.

Her initial voyage brought the *Cadiz Merchant* to London in May 1675. This was a time of stress in European freight markets, for the Dutch were engaged in a closely-fought struggle with the recently emerged naval power of France, and while a mass of Dutch shipping lay idle, unable to put to sea, England as the chief maritime neutral was making heavy inroads into the vast European carrying trade with the Baltic countries. Great numbers of foreign ships came into English ownership, some genuinely, some fraudulently; but even these did not suffice to carry on the greatly enlarged English traffic with the Baltic, and many others — including the *Cadiz Merchant* — were attracted to it from their normal or intended occupations. When the ship reached London, therefore, her master resorted 'to the Broaker in London, when I took a Fright' [sic] for a Baltic voyage, at a cost of 30s. to the broker and 5s. for drafting the charter-party. Then he had to go to the Admiralty with 15s. 6d. to get a 'Sea Brief' to secure him from the attentions of armed ships of the warring nations. The sea brief is lost, but the form was a standard one, and it would have read like this:

> Charles the Second etc. Be it known unto all and singular unto whom these Letters of Safe Conduct shall be shown that Charles Johnson our Subject and Citizen of London hath humbly represented unto

us that the Ship called the Cadiz Merchant of the Burthen of Two
hundred and Seventy Tonns doth belong unto Him and Others our
Subjects and that they are Sole Owners and Proprietors thereof and
is now laden with the Goods which are contained in a Schedule
which she hath with her from the Officers of our Customs, and doe
wholly and truely and really belong to our Subjects and others in
Neutrality bound from the Port of London to such other Place or
Places where she may conveniently trade with the said Goods being
not prohibited nor belonging to either of the Parties in Hostility,
or else find a Freight which the aforesaid our Subject having attested
by a writing under his Hand and affirmed to be true by Oath under
Penalty of Confiscation of the said Goods; We have thought fit to
grant him these Our Letters of Safe Conduct. And therefore we do
hereby respectively pray and desire all Governors of Countries and
Sea, and Kings Princes Commonwealths and Free Cities, and more
especially the Parties now in Warr and their Commanders, Admiralls,
Generall Officers, Governors of Posts, Commanders of Ships, Captains, Freightors and all others whatsoever, having any Jurisdiction
by Sea or the Custody of any Port, whome, the Ship aforesaid shall
chance to meet, or amongst whose Fleet or Ships it shall happen to
fall or make stay in their Ports, that by virtue of the League and
Amity which we have with any King or State, they suffer the Master
with the said Ship the Cadiz Merchant persons things and all
Merchandize aboard her not only freely and without any molestation
detention or impediment to any place whatsoever to pursue this
Voyage but also to afford him all offices of Civility as to our Subject if
there shall be occasion, which upon the like or other Occasion We
and Ours shall be ready to return. Given at our Court at Whitehall.

Charles R   J. Williamson.[1]

Thus equipped, the *Cadiz Merchant* sailed on 16th May. She
was chartered to bring goods from Riga to Amsterdam, and was
therefore at her owners' disposal for the outward voyage. To
avoid a journey in ballast they sent her to Newcastle again to
take in a cargo of coal for sale on the owners' account at Copenhagen. Leaving Newcastle at the end of May, Johnson touched
at Helsingore[2] to pay his Sound Dues (ten rix dollars, about
£2 5s.) on 13th June, and two days later tied up at Copenhagen
to unload his coal. This was quickly done, for on 8th July the

---

[1] The example of a 'sea-brief' or ship's pass comes from the Register of
Passes issued, beginning in March 1676, in SP 44-49. These passes did not
give complete security; the French seized many ships in spite of them.

[2] Elsinore, where the Sound Dues were already being collected in Shake-
speare's day — but not in Hamlet's.

vessel passed the forts at the mouth of the Dvina and sailed on up-river to Riga to take in her main cargo. This was evidently waiting for her — Dutch trade with this area was very highly organised — for after a stay of only three weeks she was out in the Baltic again, passing Helsingore on 20th August and entering Amsterdam on 13th September. There the crew was paid off and a reckoning made, which showed an apparent profit (including that on the sale of coal) of £177. This was a good result for an operation taking little more than three months — it reflects the competition for ships which the Dutch withdrawal from the carrying trade had created.

To find a fresh occupation was easy; on 6th October Johnson records 'brokerage of a freight to Cales[1] and Malaga'; and since this was still, despite various treaties with the Moorish pirates, a rather more hazardous voyage than those in the North Sea and the Baltic, he bought four more guns, shot and twelve barrels of powder, and small arms. His last act in Amsterdam was to provide 'a great Feast to the Merchant, after our Contracts'; and then on 20th October the ship sailed for Hamburg, where most of the outward cargo for Spain was to be collected. Now began a series of delays, the reason for which is not apparent, for this was an ideal time of year for the Malaga voyage. The ship lay at Hamburg for two months and then crossed the North Sea with her cargo to the Humber; making her way slowly round the English coast with a call at Deal, she was in Plymouth as late as 26th February, having already spent three months on her voyage, with a large crew earning their full pay every day. Moreover, the result of these hold ups was to bring the ship to her Spanish destinations too late in the season to secure cargo easily for her charterers. She arrived at Cadiz on 22nd March and Malaga on 19th April, lying in these harbours all the summer until the new oil and wine harvests were in, and not finally clearing Cadiz homeward until 30th August. On 25th September the *Cadiz Merchant* anchored in the Downs, and a few days later was discharging her cargo of oil, wine and indigo in Hamburg. A year had been occupied in prosecuting a voyage which normally occupied no more than five months, and the owners had to bear the burden of cost. For this was a tonnage charter (at 103 marks per last of cargo brought back to Hamburg, about £3 17s. per ton), and although demurrage

[1] Cadiz.

was paid by the charterers for six days stayed beyond the laydays allowed in Spanish ports, the responsibility for the slowness of the outward voyage fell on the owners. When the crew was discharged at Hamburg, fifty-five weeks' wages were paid to them; the owners could only be thankful that the loss on the voyage was not a large one.

Again winter was near, and this time no southern voyage was attempted. The *Cadiz Merchant* was laid up at Hamburg throughout the winter, looked after by the master for nothing and the boatswain on half-pay; in March 1677 she slipped across to London with a useful freight filled out by a small cargo of pipestaves on the owners' account. At London another voyage was arranged of the kind which Dutch ships would have handled in normal times; to lade timber in Norway, take it to Portugal and return to Norway with salt, and then bring a timber cargo to London. The freight was settled at a lump sum of £900. Sailing from London on 4th May, the ship was taking in cargo at Drammen from 19th to 22nd, and made a slow journey back across the North Sea and down the Channel. On 9th July she was watering at Weymouth; on 12th August she left Lisbon for nearby Setubal (St Uves, as this great centre of the salt trade was known to all English seamen of the time), having unloaded her outward cargo and spent a little money on brokerage and 'a collation for the Merchant'. So far everything had been going smoothly, and sailing up-Channel in mid-September it must have seemed to the master that a quick and profitable trip would be achieved this time. But the season was far advanced, and in the North Sea they ran into continuous adverse winds and violent gales which drove Johnson to seek shelter, first at Harwich and then, on 9th November, in the Humber. At Hull the master searched out a notary to record in legal form a 'protest against the sea' — that is, to explain and disclaim liability for his delay in delivering the charterers' cargo. It was now getting late in the year to make a safe entry into Oslofiord, so Johnson discharged the crew and wintered at Hull, with the mate and one seaman on nominal wages. The *Cadiz Merchant* was out again on 12th March — the earliest possible moment of the new spring — quickly discharging her cargo at Oslo (Cristiania, as it then was) and laded a return cargo of deals for London, and was back in the Thames on 2nd June. Johnson's dismissal of the crew at Hull had done much to retrieve the situation; not delays themselves, but the wage and victualling bills which they usually involved, were the ruin of shipowners. There was no claim for damages for delay from the charterers; full costs had been borne for little more than the normal time for such a voyage, and consequently a small profit was secured — though of course it was not adequate to the use of the ship for a whole year on a voyage designed to take half as long.

Summer, 1678, had come; the plenipotentiaries were putting their seals to a European peace at Nijmwegen, and the Dutch merchantmen were emerging from their harbours. There was no room for such a ship as the *Cadiz Merchant*, with her crew of twenty-one, to continue operations in North European waters in competition with Dutch vessels bearing only two-thirds of this complement. After some fairly extensive repairs, which included graving and caulking, she was turned towards the south, on a tonnage charter to lade goods in Turkey and Greece at £6 10s. per ton.[1] Her armament was further strengthened by four more guns, and on 25th September Johnson cleared at Gravesend, and touching only in the Downs came into Cadiz to join other Mediterranean-bound ships on 15th November. There she came under convoy of the *Bristol* and *Portland* frigates, and followed the normal passage of east-bound English merchantmen to Port Mahon, Leghorn, Messina and Smyrna. At Leghorn, evidently, some cargo was discharged and little taken in, for fourteen boatloads of ballast had to be taken aboard. The extract from Captain Johnson's account will illustrate the kind of expense ships' masters incurred abroad; it shows his outlay at Leghorn in January 1679. The money is 'pieces of eight reals double plate of the mint of New Spain' — the big silver coins, worth 4s. 6d. at this time, which feature so prominently in the narratives of piracy. (See p. 352.)

Arriving in Smyrna on 20th February, the ship lay there for three months — a normal stay, allowed for in the calculation of freight rates for ships going to Turkey. Then began the long voyage home again in convoy; Athens, Zante, Messina, Leghorn, Alicante, Cadiz and at last, on 12th December, the Thames pilot's boat was alongside and the ship was home. She had had a

---

[1] The Levant Company records do not show that the *Cadiz Merchant* was in the company's employment; but these records are incomplete. It is probable, but not certain, that she was hired by a private group of the Company's members; the Company itself normally paid a freight for the round voyage rather than for homeward carriage alone.

	Pieces of eight	Reats
To Capt. James for convoy money	18	
two boats to help us into the Mould	3	
14 boates of ballast	36	6
men to help to deliver the ship and help us out of the Mould	6	
A barrell of Tar	6	
A small hawser and other ropes, 7 cwt. 2 qrs. at 6½	48	6
port charges 1/3[1]	8	6
A messenger sent to Florence at my arrival	3	
Beveridge wyne	6	
138 of oyle with charges	9	4
fresh meate	5	
60 pound of candles	4	4
Cabidges sallets and greene herbes	1	
	156	2

fifteen month voyage, but the freight and small earnings of demurrage were not inadequate. If the profit was again a poor one, this was due to initial repair costs which should strictly be applied against the profits of several voyages, though rather heavy damage to the cargo, which caused a deduction of £79 from the freight, played its part.

Now it was the spring of 1680 and the owners decided on an independent voyage, not chartering the ship but sending her out to Jamaica to pick up whatever cargo could be had from the sugar planters there. This was quite a new trade, for only in recent years had rapid development of the island begun, so there was scope for newcomers to get a share of the fast-growing cargo shipments. Johnson sought diligently and successfully for outward freights, posting bills on the Exchange and employing one Thomas Bell to collect the money.[2] Altogether £201 was earned for goods to be carried out, and in addition there were 69 passengers, paying £5 or £6 per head — 12 of them free and the others going out, at somebody else's expense, to serve four years as indentured servants in return for the passage money. It was no doubt to serve their needs that a chaplain — a very rare bird in ships' books — was engaged for the voyage, at 30s. per month.

[1] The charterers were responsible for the other two-thirds.
[2] Freight was normally paid when goods were delivered; the one exception was outward freight for the American and West Indian colonies, where currency was scarce; in these trades outward space was paid for in advance of sailing.

Edward Barlow was one of the crew that received their half pay at Gravesend on 20th April 1680; and he tells us that 'being at war with the Turks,[1] there were two fifth-rate ships in the Downs, that were to convoy us a hundred and fifty leagues from the Land's End'.[2] Staying in the Downs four days for an easterly wind, they sailed in a mixed company of ships for India, West Africa, the West Indies and New York, which began to disperse after passing through the Canary Islands, until only two remained to drop anchor at Nevis. Taking in water there, the *Cadiz Merchant* went on alone, arriving off Port Royal late in the evening of 25th June, and 'at daylight, making sail again, about ten of the clock in the forenoon, we came to an anchor in Port Royal harbour, saluting the great fort as we passed by, being arrived there having had a passage of seven weeks, and odd days from the Downs'.[3] Despite their quick passage the vessel had arrived very late in the season, and, to the master's dismay, he found the season had been a very bad one.

'There were several ships which were taking lading in for England, but sugars were very scarce, and other goods for loading, there having been such a dry season that all things were very scarce and the very cattle died for want of food. And them plantations which the year before had made a hundred hogsheads of sugar, had then but made twenty, all things being very dear and scarce.'[4]

They were saved from disaster, in the end, by another's misfortunes. A ship laden at Barbados with sugar, cotton and hides was driven into Port Royal, so badly damaged by a hurricane that she had to abandon the journey home, and the *Cadiz Merchant* took over her cargo. So on 12th November the ship at last got away from Jamaica, long after the end of the season when prudent men kept their ships in the Caribbean. She was revictualled with the Jamaica speciality — 2572 lb. of turtle meat at 2½d. per lb.[5] — and had a moderate cargo and two passengers. Johnson took the opportunity to buy two cheap guns (perhaps from the damaged ship) which would replace the two wooden guns 'to make a show'

---

[1] There was no treaty in force with the Moorish port of Sallee at this time.
[2] Barlow, op. cit., p. 328.
[3] ibid., p. 331.
[4] Barlow, op. cit., p. 331.
[5] These were caught in the Cayman Islands; ships waiting for cargo at Jamaica would often go to the Caymans and put their crews ashore to catch and salt down turtle there.

which Barlow had remarked on when he joined. The lowest freight rate paid by the Royal Africa Company for sugar from Jamaica in 1680 was £5 a ton, at the tail end of the season;[1] if it be assumed that Johnson secured some such rate for his cargo, then we must conclude that his ship sailed for home little more than half full.

They steered north-west from the Jamaican coast for Cuba, and east along the north Cuban coast past Havana;

> 'being past the Havanna and up with the highland of Matanzas, which lies ten or twelve leagues to the eastward of the Havanna, yet the masters of the two ships in our company, would have it to be the highland which lies ten leagues to the westward of the Havanna, and would scarce be persuaded; and none knew the land except myself and a Dutchman, who had on board as a passenger'.[2]

They got away safely, however, escaping the perils of the Bahamas shoals, running into adverse winds that so delayed their homeward passage that they had to go on short rations of bread and water until they were able to buy provisions from an outward-bound vessel; it was not until 14th February 1681, after a fourteen week voyage, that they dropped anchor in the Downs, a day on which they had 'boiled the last victuals we had on board'. They were paid off on 9th March, Barlow complaining bitterly that because some of the cargo had been damaged

> 'The poor seamen were forced to pay the most part of it, which is a thing against all reason, they being in no fault or occasion of it, but it came by reason of the leakiness of the ship and the bad weather we had, but it is a custom too long used in England to the oppression of poor seamen'.[3]

It is fair to point out, however, that £128 was stopped from the freight paid to the owners, and only £26 of this was passed on to the seamen in deductions from their wages.

It is tempting to say that this was another unlucky voyage. But the long delay, the small homeward cargo and the low freight rate, if partly attributable to small crops at Jamaica, must also be blamed on the late departure from London. Earlier that same season £6 and even £7 a ton had been paid for sugar from Jamaica,[4] and this clearly implies that cargo was then plentiful.

---

[1] Royal Africa Company Freight Books, T. 70–962.
[2] Barlow, op. cit., p. 333, 338.
[3] Barlow, op. cit., p. 341.
[4] Royal Africa Company Freight Books, T. 70–962.

The collection of passengers and outward freight produced a large income, but the time it occupied may well have caused the loss of a much greater sum in homeward freight. The final result of the voyage was a substantial loss.

The ship was quickly turned round for another Jamaica voyage, though it was evident that this must again bring her there very late in the season. Revictualled, refitted and newly sheathed for tropical waters, they sailed at the end of May 1681 with a good outward cargo and some fifty passengers. This time the *Cadiz Merchant* sailed alone, and at one point her crew feared they would have reason to regret this, for a few days out from the Lizard 'we espied a ship plying to the windward, which we took at first to be a Turk and prepared to fight her if she proved so'.[1] Fortunately it was only a small Dutch ship, and 'having a fair wind we continued our course, for we intended to pass to the westward of the Westward Isles [the Azores] to shun the way of meeting any Turks' ships'. Towards the end of July they touched Barbados, and then passed between St Lucia and Martinique into the Caribbean, reaching Port Royal on 1st August. This year there was plenty of cargo to be loaded, though the season was far advanced; sugar at £6 10s. a ton as well as logwood, hides, indigo, pimento, cotton and ginger, and 'in seven weeks time we were laden and as full as we could hold'.[2] Sailing from Jamaica on 4th October, they encountered heavy gales in the North Atlantic — not unexpected at that time of year — but reached home safely on 2nd January 1682. This was as good a Jamaica voyage as anyone could expect so late in the year — a quick journey (wages were paid for exactly eight months) with a good outward lading and a reasonable homeward one at a good rate.[3] A handsome profit was made, and the owners, feeling that they had at last broken into a worthwhile line of business, prepared for a third Jamaica voyage. Not, however, with Edward Barlow, who stayed at home throughout that year pulling strings — in vain — to get a command of his own.

[1] Barlow, op. cit., p. 343.
[2] ibid., p. 345.
[3] The freight earned homeward was £950, which at £6 10s. a ton represents 146 tons; yet Barlow says the ship was fully laden. The Jamaica hogshead was already coming to weigh more than the conventional 5 cwt. (see pp. 282–4, above) and each £6 10s. was therefore paid for four hogsheads weighing a good deal more than a ton; but not enough more, one would have thought, to account for this discrepancy with the ship's burden of 270 tons.

Once more, of course, the ship was late for the sugar season, but no attempt was made to hurry her away. The West India shipping was adjusted to a twelve-month routine, and though there were strong reasons for the *Cadiz Merchant's* owners to try and cut this down to ten or eleven months in order to get her to Jamaica by early summer, this was not done. She sailed at the beginning of May, reaching Port Royal on 23rd August — and found no cargo there at all. After five months of idleness, with a crew costing £60 a month in pay and provisions, Johnson adopted the desperate measure of taking a cargo of slaves to Porto Velho on the Spanish Main. Though this illegal trade was one regularly carried on from Jamaica, such large and valuable ships were seldom risked in it. However, the gamble succeeded; the *Cadiz Merchant* was brought back safely to Port Royal, and despite the high cost of the expedition (with a doubled crew at enhanced wages) the freight rate was ample to meet this and provide a surplus which overbalanced all the expense of the winter's stay in Jamaica. Charles Johnson did not enjoy his success, however, for on the return voyage, a few days out from Jamaica, he died. In circumstances which are obscure, his son of the same name took command, though he had been employed under his father in some quite humble capacity, at only £2 a month.

The 1683 sugar crop was a poor one, yet the *Cadiz Merchant*, returning from Porto Velho in April, should have had no difficulty in getting well laden for home so early in the season. But, as we have seen, planters and merchants had to have confidence in the master of the ship to whom they entrusted their valuable property; and it is very likely that they did not feel entirely assured of the competence and probity of this young man and inexperienced commander, accidentally elevated into his father's command. Ships' masters died often enough, but their chief mates were generally capable and experienced men; Charles Johnson, junior, had not been a chief mate and can hardly have had long experience. For whatever reason, the *Cadiz Merchant* came home with her holds only a quarter filled. A heavy loss was therefore incurred on the voyage, and in 1684 the whole enterprise broke up in lawsuits and the account book ceases.

The financial results of the *Cadiz Merchant's* operations, 1675–83, can be summed up as follows:

	£	Earnings	Outgoings[1]	Apparent profit or loss
1675 Newcastle–Riga–Amsterdam		469	292	+177
1675–6 Amsterdam–Cadiz–Hamburg		938	926	+ 12
1677 Hamburg–London		152	231	− 79
1677–8 London–Norway–Portugal–London		900	736	+164
1678–9 London–Smyrna–London		1769	1651	+118
1680–1 London–Jamaica–London		1160	1349	−189
1681–2 London–Jamaica–London		1385	1107	+278
1682–3 London–Jamaica–London		1413	2145	−732

Only one dividend was ever paid, £200 after the second Jamaica voyage; far from the master having cash surpluses in hand, he usually had to lay out some of his own money (or leave debts behind him) when he went to sea; at the beginning of his last voyage the owners owed him £261.

Omitting the last disastrous voyage, the record is still a poor one, nearly every voyage showing its bad luck in adverse weather, loading delays or shortage of cargo. Too much bad luck, however, must eventually lead to suspicions of bad judgment. Certainly the Jamaica voyages were badly timed. Yet the owners were evidently satisfied with Johnson for seven years; possibly the managing owner recognised his own responsibility for some of the loss. Only the death of the master under whom these sad results had been obtained precipitated crisis.

Diligence, 1728–42[2]

The next example, half a century later, must be dealt with more briefly. The *Diligence* of Whitehaven was bought at a public sale in January 1728 for a group of fourteen owners whose leading figure was Daniel Dixon, owner of $\frac{5}{18}$. The master, William Burton, owned no part of her at all. She was apparently a vessel of 80 tons — this was the tonnage carried in the Dublin coal trade, and on which she later paid dues in Maryland. The price paid, £525, suggests that the ship was quite new and in good condition, and well and recently equipped; and this is confirmed by the absence of repair expenditure in her early years under this management.

The *Diligence* was bought for the coal trade, and was soon plying between Whitehaven and Dublin. Little further capital outlay was needed, since the ship was already fitted out; few

[1] Excluding the cost of new guns. [2] HCA 30–655.

provisions had to be laid in for this short voyage; the coal —
carried on the owners' account — was bought cheaply; and £40
covered the whole of the extra expense incurred before the ship
discharged on the banks of the Liffey.

The ship's record gives the impression that the Irish coal trade
was not profitable at this time. Her master bought and sold coal
at the prevailing market rate; yet the first five coal voyages, over
a period of about six months in the spring and summer of 1728,
produced a dividend to the owners of only £16. True, the ship
was heavily manned (if we may judge her by the standards of the
east coast colliers) with a master and mate, five hands and two
apprentices to serve her eighty tons — all paid at a flat rate for
the voyage, the master £2 10s. and the crew £1 each. There was
no return cargo from Dublin: the receipts from coal cargoes were
only trivially supplemented by the occasional carriage of passengers,
who paid half a crown for the voyage either way.

The record of the *Diligence*, in fact, provides some confirmation
of the evidence produced a few years earlier (in 1721) by the
anonymous writer of *Some Calculations Relating to the Coal Trade*,
which purported to show that the coal trade had become unprofitable. The figures used to illustrate the thesis had to be
considerably stretched to produce the required result. The first
cost of the ships, the insurance rates on them and the speed of
their wearing out all seem greatly exaggerated. But the small
margin between the cost of loading coal at Whitehaven and the
proceeds of selling it at Dublin is plain enough, and suggests that
for a time the trade may have been one for philanthropists rather
than for business men. However, it was a growing trade; the
dolorous pamphleteer himself produces the figures which show
that Whitehaven coal exports rose from 35,756 tons in 1714 to
41,368 tons in 1719; if there was then a check it was only a
temporary one.

However this may be, the *Diligence* soon proved herself an
unprofitable ship in a temporarily depressed trade, and a way out
was sought.

It has never been easy to explain why Whitehaven became and
stayed for some time a major centre of the import of tobacco from
America.[1] Its hinterland was wild and thinly populated, and it

---

[1] Two writers have recently examined the facts; P. Ford, 'Tobacco and Coal'
a note on the Economic History of Whitehaven', *Economica*, Vol. IX, 1929;

was not conveniently placed to act as an entrepôt for exporting tobacco to continental Europe. On the other hand, it was the nearest considerable port to Scotland, and before Scotland became free to import tobacco legally from the colonies Whitehaven served it, and so established colonial connections which it was slow to break completely. Whitehaven, like Liverpool, carried on a large trade across the Irish Sea; like Liverpool it was able when the French wars began in 1689 to offer ships seaworthy enough for the Atlantic crossing which could pass out through the North Channel and avoid the privateers. A sufficient number of ship-owners were willing to try the new varied opportunities in colonial trade.

When the *Diligence* returned from her sixth Dublin voyage at the end of the 1728 season, therefore, she found the Whitehaven quayside piled high with hogsheads of the new crop tobacco which had been coming into the port in recent weeks. Nearly all this had to be re-exported by sea; and the *Diligence* was employed in taking 170 hogsheads to Holland at a freight of five guilders apiece (producing £77 in all) and returning with cargo for Belfast that brought the owners another £80. The whole voyage was only moderately profitable; but it provided a winter's occupation, and it introduced the ships' owners to the notion of the *Diligence* as a tobacco carrier. The ship's suitability for this having been demonstrated, she soon turned her back on her old trade.

In the spring of 1729 the ship passed out of sight of Whitehaven pier, bound, as in the previous spring, for Dublin with coal. But she did not return a month later to repeat the voyage; by that time she was far out in the Atlantic, with no cargo but a handful of passengers. Early in April she was standing into the mouth of the James River in Virginia — which of her company, one wonders, knew those difficult waters? She came home early in 1730 with 173 hogsheads of tobacco; not by any means a full cargo, and one that produced a profit on the year's voyaging of only £60. The result, though unspectacular, was nevertheless encouraging and could be improved upon as her master won the confidence of the Chesapeake planters.

Thereafter, for year after year, the *Diligence* plied the Virginia trade. On the first five voyages she dropped a coal cargo at

J. E. Williams, 'Whitehaven in the Eighteenth Century', *Econ. Hist. Rev.*, n.s., Vol. VIII, 1955-6.

Dublin on her way out, but as this added little to her now abundant profits she finally abandoned her old trade entirely, and sailed straight for Virginia. Here is the ship's financial record in the Virginia trade, 1729–42:

Date of completion of voyage and payment of final dividend		Cargo: hogs. tobacco	Freight per ton £ s. d.			Apparent profit £	Dividend £
March	1730	173	7	12	6	60	72
June	1731	202	7	15	0	107	118
April	1732					158	134
August	1733	201	7	15	0	135	143
June	1734	205	7	10	0	159	150
	1735	199½	7	10	0	106	102
	1736	197	7	10	0	99	104
	1737[1]	209	7	10	0	14	nil
March	1738	206½	7	10	0	127	101
November	1739	203	7	10	0	92	101
	1740	206	7	10	0	40	nil
July	1741	210	9	2	6	117	160
	1742	207½	9	2	6	115	nil

War came at the end of 1739, but it had not yet affected earnings seriously; seamen's wages rose rather more slowly than elsewhere in this remote corner of England and the rise in freights soon caught up with them, after one bad year, 1740. The shipping interest was not badly hit until France entered the war in 1744. Another kind of reckoning, however, was waiting for the owners of the *Diligence*. For many years they had been receiving handsome dividends, averaging, from the time the ship entered the Virginia/ Maryland trade until 1741, just under £100 a year, or 19 per cent on the original investment. This was enough to insure and amortise the vessel and leave a net return of 10 per cent. If the owners had distributed the profit of 1742 and sold the ship at what should have been her written down value of about £230, or even a good deal less, they would have been able to look back on a reasonably successful investment. The alternative — continued operation — was a costly one. The vessel had been fortunate in needing no major repair for some years; now the past accumulations had to be made up, and in the summer of 1742 £450 was spent on a complete overhaul. The owners had to advance nearly £400 to enable this to be done and to fit the ship out for another Virginia voyage; but soon afterwards the account book ceases, and

[1] £110 was spent on repairs in Maryland this year.

we cannot tell whether they recovered their money by continued profitable employment of the ship during the ensuing six years of war.

The experience of the *Diligence* shows that it was possible to make good money by regular journeys, with established connections to ensure cargo, and no undue delays. For, it must be admitted, she was far from being an ideal ship for the transatlantic trade. She was too small to be operated in the Atlantic at the most efficient manning levels — 80 tons, when the tobacco carriers were more typically of 150–200 tons and the London ships often much larger. The *Diligence's* crew varied, but it was normally ten men; a ship of four times her size in the Virginia trade would have only double her crew. Admittedly, her own crew was poorly paid,[1] but this was far from redressing the difference in the monthly cost per ton. There were advantages in smallness, of course; the small ship could more easily get a full cargo and get it quickly. But the general conclusion we must reach is that if the *Diligence* could operate profitably in this trade, any ship could, if — and the qualification is important — if the connections with shippers, necessary to secure something like full cargo in most years, had been established.

Caroline, 1754–66[2]

Only a bald summary is available of the life history of this vessel, a 150-ton Portugal trader; but this has its points of interest and example. She was managed by Captain John Clarke, who left the sea to become a merchant and shipowner when he inherited his father's estate in 1748. The *Caroline* was the third ship to come under his management; she cost £950 in 1752, probably as a new ship, and her owners then spent another £569 in setting her to sea. A false start was made with a voyage to fetch Carolina rice to Portugal; there are few details of it, but it seems to have been unsuccessful. Then the ship settled down to her regular occupation in life — the transportation of butts of port to satisfy the needs of the English squirearchy.

This vessel again illustrates the benefits of the steady pounding of a regular beat, where the master and his ship were well known

---

[1] In the Virginia voyages the master had £4 per month (and the right to carry a ton of goods freight free), the mate 35s. and the carpenter 48s.
[2] C 103–146.

and trusted and could get full cargoes with a minimum of difficulty. Despite the long wartime laying up, and the wartime delays which cut down the number of voyages to one in most years, the *Caroline* continued in war and peace to make profits. Only in wartime, however, did profits show signs of becoming really high, and then they would be partly offset by enhanced insurance rates.[1] The total earnings were not adequate, after allowing for insurance and depreciation, to give normal returns to the £1500 of capital originally invested in the ship. On the other hand, this was a trade in which a ship could be expected to make three voyages in a year not infrequently; something the *Caroline* never did. If returns to capital were low, they were earned in a series of operations carried on in a manner that was, perhaps, unduly leisurely.

	Cargo (pipes)[2]	Freight per ton (shillings)	Earnings	Outgoings	Profit or loss
1754	161	30			−62
1755	269½	30			4
1757	270	80	557	574	−17
	279	80	569	182	387
1758	283	80	567	307	260
1759	285	80	562	398	164
1760	287	70	509	214	295
1761	289	70	510	305	205
	288½	70	505	485	20
1764[3]	279½	40	283	666	−383
	285½	40	299	203	96
1765	284	40	297	215	82
	282½	30	212	171	41
1766	283	35	248	156	92
	256 and fruit	35	248	162	86

[1] Insurance of his part was a matter for the individual owner; it was not met by the ship's master or husband.

[2] Two pipes make one ton.

[3] The ship underwent a major refit at the end of the war, which inflated the charges of the first 1764 voyage.

XVII

Was it a profitable business?

The four examples in the previous chapter present a pattern; seventeenth century unprofitability, eighteenth century gains, in shipowning. It happens that the two early examples are of ships which had not firmly established themselves in particular trades, the two later ones of ships which quickly attached themselves to a single route and a single commodity and produced good results because they always secured full or nearly full cargoes without difficulty. The experiences of four ships cannot, by themselves, prove anything. However, I hope to indicate by the use of other sources — though the evidence is not sufficiently precise to justify a firm conclusion — that the trend accidentally illustrated may be a real one.[1]

It is first necessary to examine more carefully the whole make-up of the costs of operating ships, of which wages and the victualling of crews are only a part. The best evidence on costs — and indeed on earnings and profits — comes from account books kept by ships' masters, of which considerable numbers survive.[2] These are records of masters' financial relations with their owners; they show all the payments made by a master on his owners' account and his receipts on their behalf. The accounts may be misleading in minor respects — sometimes through deliberate falsification by

---

[1] It might be thought that the voluminous data on the tonnage of ships in such records as the Registers of Passes or Seamen's Sixpences, combined with the details of goods carried in ships shown in the Port Books, could be combined to produce the required evidence. It would no doubt reveal the ships which came in and went out half-empty. But these are the unusual cases; the real problem is whether ships were, at different times, 85 or 90 per cent, rather than 100 per cent, full; and the ambiguities in the tonnage figure for both ships and goods are so large that they cannot produce meaningful answers when such narrow margins are in question.

[2] A number of these account books are in the HCA Miscellaneous series (HCA 30) and the Public Record Office has a special index of ships' accounts contained in this series. Not all the items so indexed are, in fact, accounts. There is a much larger number of account books, or copies of or long extracts from them, scattered through the other HCA series, and particularly in the Instance Papers (HCA 15). I have encountered a few in the records of the Court of Chancery.

the master — but most of them are substantially accurate as records of receipts and payments.

The circumstances of their survival, however, indicate the chief difficulty in using them. Nearly all have been preserved in the records of the courts — particularly the High Court of Admiralty — after their production as evidence in legal actions. The most common reason for the kind of dispute which required the production of the ship's account book was a quarrel over finance between the master and his owners. Either the owners were querying some items of receipts or payments, suggesting that the accounts were fraudulent in specified ways; or they were expressing incredulity at the bad results of a voyage and imputing recklessness or negligence to the master. In either case, the results of the operations shown by the account book are likely to be untypical of the kind of activities which made it worth while to keep ships operating. If one simply aggregated the results of all voyages for which complete ships' accounts exist in the court records, the alleged total costs would certainly far exceed the alleged total earnings. Moreover, nearly all these account books cover only one voyage — the one in dispute — and they usually commence at the date of sailing, that is, they omit the initial expenditure on stores, repairs and victuals which formed a large part of the cost of any voyage. Therefore, while such accounts help to picture the kinds of expense incurred in foreign ports, give detailed evidence of wages paid, and often throw light on freight rates, they are of little value by themselves in establishing the total costs of voyages or the proportions of different kinds of expense to total cost or to earnings. There are account books, however — less than thirty out of some two hundred I have seen — which do show the results of several voyages, implying that for a time the master had satisfied the owners; and these should be of some value in the consideration of general questions of costs, earnings and profitability.[1]

Most of the data required for the study of costs and profits can be obtained from other sources in addition to ships' account books. The most important components of running costs were the crews' wages and victualling, and on these subjects there is an enormous

---

[1] Four of these are used in the previous chapter; a number of others are discussed in my article 'Earnings of Capital in the English Shipping Industry, 1670–1730', in *Journal of Economic History*, Vol. XVII, 1957. The majority of these thirty ships are coastal or short-sea traders.

mass of evidence, both as to rates of pay, scales of manning and length of voyages, which makes it possible for us to estimate these costs as accurately as the shipowners themselves did two or three hundred years ago. On the side of earnings, the considerable body of information on freight rates makes it possible to say what a fully-laden ship would have earned, in many trades, at most times between 1600 and 1775. It is possible, in fact, to perform with considerable accuracy, for many types of voyage, the calculation which is a commonplace one in shipbrokers' offices today — the preparation of voyage estimates. This done, the fixed charges of the industry — represented by depreciation of the ships, insurance and reasonable interest charges on the capital outlay — will have to be taken into consideration.

Running costs can conveniently be divided into four categories:

(a) Wages and victuals of the crew
(b) Repairs and stores
(c) Port charges, lighthouse dues, pilotage, etc.
(d) Normal miscellaneous expenses.

Wages and victuals were the only items which varied directly and almost precisely with the time spent on voyage between leaving the home port and returning to it. The experienced master could make small savings on victualling by buying some of his provisions in places where they were specially cheap abroad; this was one of the many ways in which, through minor gains and savings, his competence could decisively affect the ship's operating results. The character of the voyage partly determined the size of the crew, and so, within limits which were narrow but again might significantly alter profits, did the master's own decisions and even the accident of the number of men who turned up to be hired. The crews of ships usually show slight differences in size between succeeding voyages to the same destinations. The rates of wages paid — particularly of officers and specialists — varied a little from voyage to voyage. These differences from average in victualling costs, in crew size, in wage bargains, though marginal, could well add or take away half the normal net return to capital on a ship in an eighteenth-century long distance voyage.[1] The

[1] This is apart from the much greater variations caused by varying lengths of time taken for a particular voyage; again, something partly depending on the master's competence, but also partly on his owners' or their agents' arrange-

average costs — dependent on average wages, length of voyage[1], size of crew and victualling costs — are easily determined, however. Wage rates and crew sizes have been discussed in Chapters VI and VII, above. The other cost which depended on the size of the crew was victualling. This was conventionally estimated at twenty shillings per man per month (averaging the total costs over officers and seamen)[2]; but this seems to be the cost of providing victuals to take to sea, allowing an ample margin for delays in the voyage, rather than the cost of victuals actually consumed. Little of the food bought in bulk was perishable, and some of the surplus of a voyage could be sold to other ships encountered and the remainder carried over to the next voyage. The true costs of victualling in peacetime after the mid-seventeenth century are shown by ships' accounts to have been sixteen to eighteen shillings per month per man. The few cases where wide variations from this level are recorded probably represent on the one hand a period of short commons —

> 'Five and five to a Rat in every messe, and the ship-boy to the tayle, stopping their noses when they drunke stinking water that came out of the pumpe of the ship, and cutting a greasy buffe jerkin in tripes and broiling it for their dinners'[3]

and on the other hand either a wide margin of safety on a voyage performed very quickly, or fraud by the master. Most of the money was laid out before the voyage commenced on the standard rations of beef and pork, biscuit and flour, cheese and beer, butter and peas; but on a voyage of any length it was supplemented by the purchase of fresh food abroad.

The great cause of variation in apparent costs, for voyages of a similar kind, was the incidence of major repairs. These fell particularly heavily on the first voyage of a ship for new owners, for invariably there were fitting out costs of a character indistinguishable from repairs, though often including some alterations to

---

ments for supplying him with cargo, and partly on weather conditions. Calculations of time must have been based, however, on some sort of average; a longer or shorter voyage was simply one of the risks of ship operation, whereas the appointment of a competent master was, in principle, one of the chief functions of skilful entrepreneurship.

[1] Average length of voyage in different trades has been calculated from HCA records prior to 1660; from Port Books of 1662–3 and 1686–7, and from Seamen's Sixpences extracts described on p. 195, above.

[2] See, e.g. *Falcon* 1672 (HCA 13–77); SP 46 136–246/7.

[3] T. Nashe, *Lenten Stuffe*, 1599 (ed. A. B. Grosart), Vol. III, pp. 180–1.

the ship. The building of the ship by shipwright or carpenter meant building the hull and setting up masts and standing rigging. The ship was far from completed then; running rigging had to be set up, sails (including a spare suit) and anchors, blocks and cables, boats, guns, flags, compasses and a host of other accessories had to be provided, and a good deal of work remained to be done by craftsmen such as glaziers, joiners, smiths and bricklayers. Almost all these fittings and works, other than the ship's armament, wore out or were used up very quickly at sea, and needed frequent partial replacement or repair, and occasional complete replacement. In the regular refit after each voyage, the ropemaker's and sailmaker's bills always head the list, but the other tradesmens' bills make up a heavy total. The carpenters' and boatswains' stores were made up chiefly of the necessary materials for carrying out repairs at sea; that is why the categories of repairs and stores cannot be divided.

The incidence of these replacements and repairs varied from voyage to voyage. The main structure of the ship, the shipwright's work, also required considerable though intermittent expenditure to maintain it in a seaworthy state. Recaulking the seams was a regular process. The hull had to be cleaned of underwater barnacles or the ship's sailing qualities would in time be seriously impaired. Storm, collision and the ravages of worm compelled major repairs to the main timbers and the planking from time to time during the ship's life. For these structural repairs a ship was either careened — laid up on a beach — or, in a large port, taken into dry dock or graving dock.[1] Because major repairs took place at irregular intervals — sometimes when a particular voyage in contemplation required a specially high degree of seaworthiness, but more simply since they were done as necessity became apparent — and because, when necessary, their costs were heavy in relation to the total costs of any one voyage, repairs formed a violently fluctuating proportion of total costs.

A distinction must be made between, on the one hand, coasters and traders round the North Sea and Irish Sea, and on the other hand the ships that went farther afield to the south and west. The level of repair expenditure on the former was very much lower. These were cheaply built and cheaply repaired ships, on which the minimum of work was done, for a really large repair job might

[1] Graving is the process of cleaning the ship's bottom of barnacles, etc.

well cost more than buying another ship of the same quality. In the records of these ships, all the costs of routine upkeep are found; ropes and sails are renewed, timbers are occasionally replaced. Major repairs, however, are very rare. With ocean-going vessels more trouble was taken over decoration and appearance; and since they went on longer voyages, farther from any place where substantial repairs could be handled, they had to be more seaworthy when they were sent out, and better equipped with the materials for emergency repairs and replacements of all kinds. From a host of voyages it is possible to make a fair estimate of the general level of repair costs, though with the proviso that no individual ship on a particular voyage is likely to show costs agreeing exactly with the estimate. Over the whole life of an ocean-going ship, however, engaging regularly in transatlantic or Mediterranean voyages, having normal luck with weather and collision and not suffering from long intervals of unemployment, £1 per ton would be a rather high annual average for the cost of repairs and stores.[1] In the first years of the ship's life the average was very much lower, but the total increased as age made the struggle to keep the structure of the ship in reasonable condition more difficult. Repair costs averaged considerably less than half of this for ships in the coastal and short-sea trades; for many such ships, repairs did not rank as major items of expenditure. The very large vessels, East Indiamen and Levant traders, ran into the same kinds of extra costs for repairs that made their building expensive — the high cost of large timbers, for example — and their general standards of maintenance and appearance required a larger regular expenditure on repairs and stores.

Repairs constituted the great variable factor in ships' running costs. They might account for more than half the costs attributed to a voyage, though in such a case it would generally be equitable (if impracticable) to apportion them over the other voyages which contributed to the need for them. Moreover, few voyages would show 'average' repair costs, for it is characteristic that the average was made up by several voyages with moderate repairs followed by one voyage with very heavy ones. However, if we accept the rather unreal concept of the average, it may be said that repair costs for an ocean-going ship of the 1680's varied between something less than a quarter of total costs when she was fairly new and

---

[1] Before the middle of the seventeenth century it would be considerably lower.

something over a third in old age. This proportion was higher in the eighteenth century when wages and victualling costs had declined.

Port charges and other outlays of a similar nature were never a substantial part of total costs. They included fees for the use of wharves and equipment, payment for formal customs clearance and documents, health clearance and so on; for guards, sometimes for unloading or pilotage; and there are in addition such items as the fees collected for the maintenance of lighthouses on the English coast, and the dues which the Danish government collected from ships entering and leaving the Baltic.[1] These expenditures, of a kind that sometimes make up nearly half the operating costs of a modern ship, rarely amounted to as much as 5 per cent of the costs of an ocean-going ship in the seventeenth or the eighteenth century, though they were naturally more important to ships making short voyages.

Finally, every ship's master had a number of miscellaneous payments to make. There were his own personal expenses in entertaining freightors, officials and owners' agents, horse hire and odd gratuities round the English coast and in foreign ports, expenses in the tavern when a charter was signed and the owners' feast when the ship was set to sea. Other outlays included the cost of ballast — at Tilbury this cost a shilling a ton, while its shipping and discharge accounted for nearly as much again, so that it was quite a serious item of expense for short-sea traders. Casual labour was engaged from time to time for hauling the ship in and out of dock, and for night watchmen. Finally, there were fees of various kinds: to brokers for securing freights, collecting debts, getting money changed and remitting it home; to consuls for assistance abroad; to the commanders of men-of-war in convoy; to scriveners and notaries for odd legal services, especially the writing of documents. The master's personal expenses rarely amounted to more than 4 per cent of total costs; the other categories of miscellaneous expense varied from a negligible amount to perhaps 5 per cent of the total, or even more for coasters and short-sea traders.

Though there are many difficulties, it is therefore quite possible to make reasonably accurate voyage estimates for normal voyages

---

[1] When ships were chartered, it was almost invariably agreed that the charterers should pay two-thirds of all port charges and pilotage.

in many trades at different periods of time. I have produced elsewhere a set of such estimates to show typical profits in the 1680's,[1] and these suggest a fair degree of consistency in the annual gross rates of return. Here, to illustrate the long-term trends in profitability in our period, are two sets of voyage estimates, one for the Virginia and the other for the Malaga trade — the two trades which are best documented over the whole period. Each assumes a series of ships of unchanging size making their maiden voyages, fully laden, and without unusual events, at a series of different dates over a period of a century and a quarter.[2]

Voyage estimates for a ship of 250 tons in the Virginia trade

	1635	1680	1725	1770
Size of crew	30	25	19	15
Time of voyage (months)	9	8	7	7
Freight per ton £[3]	5¾	5¼	4	3½
Monthly costs:				
Wages	42	43	35	29
Victuals	25	21	16	13
TOTAL	67	64	51	42
Total of monthly costs for voyage	603	512	357	294
One year's repairs[4]	150	187	187	187
Port charges and miscellanea	50	50	50	50
TOTAL COSTS	803	749	594	531
FREIGHT	1437	1312	1000	875
Excess of earnings over total running costs	634	563	406	344

The story these figures tell is at first sight an unexpected one. Over a period when capital costs for building (in any particular port) and setting out a ship changed very little after an early rise, not only have running costs and earnings both fallen (as the

[1] See p. 364, n. 1, above.

[2] The cost of repairs, fairly stable from the time of the Civil War onwards, was rising in the early seventeenth century; for 1635, therefore, they are charged at rates slightly lower than those discussed above.

[3] The true freight earned per ton of ship's burden. The nominal freight rates per conventional ton of four hogsheads of tobacco have been adjusted as nearly as possible to true rates.

[4] At 12s. per ton for 1635, 15s. per ton for other years. These are low rates appropriate to the earliest years of a ship's life.

Voyage estimates for a ship of 120 tons in the Malaga trade

	1635	1680	1725	1770
Size of crew	18	15	12	9
Time of voyage (months)	5	4½	4	4
Freight per ton £	4	3¼	2½	2¼
Monthly costs:				
Wages	26	27	23	18
Victuals	15	13	10	8
TOTAL	41	40	33	26
Total of monthly costs for voyage	205	180	132	104
One year's repairs,[1] at two voyages per year, makes per voyage	36	45	45	45
Port charges and miscellanea	25	25	25	25
TOTAL COSTS	266	250	202	174
COSTS FOR TWO VOYAGES IN A YEAR	532	500	404	348
FREIGHT FOR TWO VOYAGES IN A YEAR	960	780	600	540
Excess of annual earnings over total running costs	428	280	196	192

reader of earlier chapters of this book will expect) but the profit margins have shrunk to an apparently disastrous extent. How can this be? The estimates, though subject to error at many points, are consistent in their general trend and conclusion. But more than this, they bring sharply before our eyes some things which on reflection are seen to be obviously true, whose truth is illustrated by, rather than dependent on, such estimates, but might pass unnoticed without this reminder. The first is that when (as here) both running costs and freight earnings are declining rapidly, then even if the ratio of running costs to freight remains (as it does) roughly the same, the *absolute* difference between them, that is the annual income, will be declining as well. The second is that, when running costs and freights are declining like this but capital outlays are approximately stable, the ratio of income to capital must decline heavily. The third is that, if such a tendency really exists, it should eventually drive investors away unless it

[1] At 12s. per ton for 1635, 15s. per ton for other years.

can be halted by an exceptionally sharp fall in running costs or by a halt in the decline of freights earned; or unless the annual fixed costs (which have not yet been considered) decline despite the stability of the capital to which they are related.

The slowing down of the rate of growth of the industry in the early decades of the eighteenth century which has already been noticed seems to indicate that this tendency did exist; that profits *were* in fact declining in relation to capital and so driving investors away. In spite of this, we cannot be sure that declining returns to capital really did emerge, for the loopholes of escape were substantial ones. Running costs *were* in fact reduced at a faster pace by the use of bigger ships; the fall in freights earned (as distinct from freight rates per ton) *was* checked by fuller utilisation of capacity, and capital charges *were* certainly falling.

To examine capital charges, it is necessary to look briefly at the cost of buying a new ship. This is less easy to determine than the reader might expect.[1] There are few surviving examples of contract prices (that is, prices for the shipwright's work of providing hull, masts and yards); the table on p. 373 lists them.

All shipwrights' prices are quoted per ton measured according to the custom of shipwrights.[2] This measured ton differed from the ton burden by which the owner reckoned his ship's capacity for all ordinary purposes, and the difference was by no means a regular one at any time, and changed fast during the eighteenth century. Probably in most English-built ships of the seventeenth century 'tons burden', deadweight tonnage, was not very far from three-quarters of measured tonnage. But this generalisation was becoming doubtful by 1700; the two figures were coming together, so that by 1700 many ships carried as much as they measured, and by 1775 most carried more than they measured. A price of £5 per measured ton in 1660, therefore, may indicate a ship quite as dear, from the point of view of the owners concerned with carrying capacity, as a price of £7 per measured ton in 1775.

---

[1] The extensive records of second-hand prices refer to ships in every condition; some stripped down to their decaying immovable fixtures, others almost new and fully equipped ready to sail on a long voyage. Little that is useful can be derived from these price series, beyond a reminder that it was not costly to become the owner of a ship to engage in trades where a very old and dilapidated one would serve. The maintenance of the shipping industry, however, required that there should be openings in which new ships could earn enough to justify their building.

[2] See p. 7, above.

ENGLISH MERCHANTMEN OFF GENOA, LATE SEVENTEENTH CENTURY

by W. Van der Velde the younger

AN EAST INDIAMAN, EARLY EIGHTEENTH CENTURY
by Peter Monamy

Shipwrights' contract prices

Date	Place of building	Tons	Price	£	s.	d.	Ref.
Ships of 60–99 tons							
1670	London	75		5	5	o[1]	
1704	Bristol	70	£180	2	11	5	HCA 15–29
1719	Southampton	74	£339	4	11	8	HCA 15–37
1731	Southampton	60	£261	4	6	10	HCA 15–42
1734	Selby	70	£195	2	15	10	HCA 15–40
1735	Hull	80	£360	4	10	o	HCA 15–39
Ships of 100–199 tons							
1607	London	155	£300	1	18	4	C. 2 Jas. I, L 4/19
1628	London	130		3	5	o	SP 16–94–85
1664	Newcastle	100	£240	2	8	o	HCA 15–8
1675	London	136	£688	5	1	o	HCA 15–14
1678	Yarmouth	170	£730	4	6	o	HCA 15–18
1704	London	141	£732	5	4	o[2]	
1704	London	155		4	17	o	C. 6 348–48
1714	Liverpool	120	£380	3	3	4	HCA 15–32
1715	London	100		5	o	o	HCA 15–33
1718	Yarmouth	140	£460	3	5	9	HCA 15–34
1727	Scarborough	150	£400	2	13	4	HCA 15–40
Ships of 200–299 tons							
1685	London	277	£1,895	6	17	o	HCA 24–124
1685	London	230	£1,200	5	2	o	HCA 24–124
1692	London	265	£1,400	5	5	9[3]	
1694	London	243		7	o	o	HCA 15–16
1700	Shoreham	240		5	5	o	C. 109–248
1707	Bristol	298	£1,131	3	15	11	HCA 15–35
1714	London	210	£1,161	5	11	o	HCA 15–37
1723	London	240		6	2	6[4]	
Ships of over 300 tons							
1676	London	423		6	10	o	BM Add.MSS. 22184–53
1683	London	816		8	5	o	HCA 15–16

It is impossible to say with certainty, therefore, how the price of building ships in England changed over two centuries. It may reasonably be supposed that shipbuilding was not immune from the rising trend of general prices in the first quarter of the seventeenth century. Moreover, it was asserted by post-Restoration pamphleteers that the price of English ships rose much further after the Navigation Act of 1651, which prevented the import of

[1] E. E. Rich, *The History of the Hudson's Bay Company* (1958), Vol. I, p. 66.
[2] R. C. Temple, *The Papers of Thomas Bowrey* (Hakluyt Society, 1925), pp. 128, 135.
[3] Corporation of Lloyd's; Bowrey MSS. 1250.
[4] Essex County Record Office, D/D Ne 83.

Baltic and Norwegian materials in cheap Dutch-owned ships and their supply from the great Dutch timber-yards and storehouses. 'The Dutch, French, Danes, Hamburghers etc. can have ship timber in Germany, France and Denmark for less than half the price of ours,' wrote one specially pessimistic author in 1680.[1] Timber prices were apparently going up,[2] and there was a continuing rise in shipwrights' wages until long after mid-century. From the last quarter of the century prices appear to have changed little, and it may reasonably be said that an ocean-going ship of 150–250 tons carrying capacity could be built in London or on the Thames estuary, at any time between 1675 and 1775 (except during wars) for £6 to £7 per ton of tons burden, i.e. at £5 per measured ton in 1675 and £8 to £9 per measured ton in 1775.

This does not imply, however, that the son, grandson and great-grandson of a shipowner of Charles II's reign had to pay the same price for their ships as he had done. One of the characteristics of the eighteenth century, we have noticed, was the turn away from the use of Thames-built ships; the growing willingness of owners — even London owners — to have their ships built on the north-east coast, in Scotland, or in America. The ships of Whitby, the Tyne and the Humber had advantages in their build, making them suitable for cheap operation in certain trades; but along with other provincial and colonial ships they shared the advantage of being more cheaply built than the products of Thames-side shipyards. It is true that this involved some sacrifice of quality; as late as 1784 the view could be widely held that

> 'None of the American-built ships were equally good with those built here; they could build ships cheaper in America, but I should suppose that a ship built in the River was in proportion to its quality, in the end as cheap as a ship built at Boston'.[3]

But the purchaser in London paid for more than quality. In the English provincial ports shipwrights' wages were much lower,[4]

---

[1] J. R. McCulloch (ed.), *Early Tracts on Commerce* (1856), p. 317. See also 'The Royal Fisheries Revived' (1670) in *Harleian Miscellany*, Vol. III, 410–11.
[2] Evidence of this is rather weak; see J. E. T. Rogers, *History of Agriculture and Prices in England* (Oxford, 1887), Vol. VI, pp. 494–506.
[3] BM Add.MSS. 38388–246; this was said in 1784 by Francis Anderson, a merchant who had lived in Massachusetts from 1753 until 1775. See also Lord Sheffield, *Observations on the Commerce of the American States* (1784), p. 139.
[4] During the century after 1660, the London rate was 3s. to 3s. 6d. a day, while in Liverpool and Hull 2s. to 2s. 6d. was normal. See H. E. Richardson,

and considerable supplies of timber could be brought from close at hand, until far into the eighteenth century.[1]

The special source of cheap ships in North America was the New England coast, where forests came down to navigable water, providing cheap timber, pitch and tar. The cheapness of these materials was to some extent counterbalanced by high wages[2] and the cost of importing sails, cordage and many iron fittings from England. Taking into account the generally poorer quality of the ships, the advantages of buying in America were not normally substantial, and until the middle and southern colonies began, in the mid-eighteenth century, to build good quality ships of live-oak, most buying of American-built ships took place in wartime.[3]

In 1784, at the conclusion of the American war, a number of informed persons were asked their views about the relative prices of ships. These were reported as follows:[4]

Price of a ship of 200 tons (measure) per ton

London	£8 8s. to £9 9s.
Outports	£7 5s. to £8 8s.
New York, Philadelphia	£6 8s. to £7 19s.
New England	£3 18s. to £5 9s.

So much for the cost of the ship. Next, what were the capital charges to be borne annually, in relation to the cost of the ship and her initial fitting out? An allowance had to be made for depreciation of the hull and body of the ship and the fixtures; the whole value of the ship with her stores and provisions as she was

'Wages of Shipwrights in H.M. Dockyards', *Mariners' Mirror*, Vol. XXXIII, 1947, pp. 271–3; W. S., *A Plea in Favour of the Shipwrights* (1770); Okill MSS. in Liverpool Public Library; W. J. Davies, 'The Town and Trade of Hull' (unpublished Cardiff M.A. thesis, 1937).

[1] Roger Fisher, *Hearts of Oak* (1763), pp. 32–4, 38–9.

[2] Shipwrights' pay in New England in the later eighteenth century was 4s. 6d. a day (Sheffield, op. cit., p. 86).

[3] W. B. Weeden, *Economic and Social History of New England, 1620–1789* (Boston, 1890), pp. 573–6, 613–14, 674–6, 765–6, gives a good account of the American industry. On the price of American-built ships, see V. S. Clark, *History of Manufactures in the United States, 1607–1860* (Washington, 1916), p. 591. Some indication of the quality of ships is given by Lloyd's Register ratings. In 1799, ships could remain in Lloyd's first class for a period of years varying according to the place of building: London or India 13 years, southern states of U.S.A. 12 years, Bristol, Liverpool, Quebec or Bermuda 10 years, Northern England, Wales, Scotland 8 years, other U.S. ports 6 years (*Annals of Lloyd's Register*, 1884, pp. 14–22).

[4] BM Add.MSS. 38388–349/352. See also Sheffield, op. cit., p. 139; he produces slightly different figures showing similar general relationships.

set to sea had to be insured, and the current rate of interest had to be earned on this whole cost. What was left — which economists would once have called profit — was the payment which the owners received for risking their money in this kind of investment rather than burying it safely and dully in a landed estate or the government funds.

Depreciation can be assumed to be stable; there is no reason to suppose that ships built in any given place wore out more quickly or more slowly in the 1750's than in the 1650's.[1] In contemplating the depreciation charge, of course, only the disappearance of the investment through wearing out of its value by age need be considered, for accidental loss must be assumed to be covered by insurance. The wooden ship, if well looked after, could have a very long life — so long, indeed, that one may suppose the majority of ships to have ended their days violently by wreck or tempest or fire, rather than to have rotted peacefully through old age as colliers and hulks. When the navy was taking up merchant ships as fireships for use against the Dutch in 1667, eight ships out of the twenty-six examined were over twenty years old, two were over thirty, one over forty and one was a veteran of sixty years' sea service![2] Similar evidence of the use of ships to a great age can be found in the Liverpool registration records of the mid-eighteenth century.[3] A very old ship, however, would have a restricted range of service or, if kept in ocean trades, a heavy repair bill; twenty or twenty-five years would probably see the end of its profitable and safe use in distant trades with cargoes of substantial value. Moreover, the saleable value of ships fell away sharply in the years after they were new, and the twenty-year-old, however well maintained, always fetched a very poor price. A depreciation charge of 4 per cent per annum seems the most reasonable one; the owner of a ship two centuries ago, like the owner of a piece of machinery today, sometimes got a bonus in the form of continued working and saleable value after its book value had been written down to nothing.

Insurance rates were falling. During the seventeenth century the oceans were practically cleared of pirates, and the Moorish

---

[1] The calculations below deal with ships built *in a given place*. When the possibilities, which emerged in the eighteenth century, of building more cheaply in Salem or Whitby, are considered, it may be necessary to set a higher annual depreciation rate against the lower capital outlay.

[2] SP-29-212-117.   [3] See p. 412, below.

corsairs were compelled to grant immunity to English ships, while during the next century insurers were getting the benefit of an insurance market which was becoming much more carefully organised and disciplined. Insurance rates for the early years of the seventeenth century are available only for Southern and Mediterranean trades where the corsair danger was greatest; in those trades they were halved between the early seventeenth and the early eighteenth century. The Virginia rate was falling during the latter part of this period, from the time rates become available.[1] During the eighteenth century rates showed, on the whole, a very slight falling tendency; but a vitally important change in insurance practice took place. It had been customary to pay out only a proportion, varying between 75 per cent and 90 per cent of the sum assured, when a loss occurred; in the 1720's and 1730's all insurers went over to payment of losses virtually in full — 98 per cent or 99 per cent.[2] The effect of this was much the same as the reduction of premiums by a fifth or a sixth; and working in the same direction was the decreasing frequency of default and bankruptcy among those who went in for marine underwriting.

Interest rates were falling as well. A maximum rate of interest was fixed by law, at 10 per cent until 1624, 8 per cent until 1652, 6 per cent until 1713 and 5 per cent from that time on. During at least the first three quarters of the seventeenth century, actual rates paid on good security — such as mortgages on land — pressed right up to the legal maximum; particularly before the Civil War, in nearly all contracts involving interest the maximum rate appears to have been charged. With the consolidation of the banking system at the end of the century and the emergence of a large government debt and a government borrowing rate which fell to 3 per cent in the thirties, private borrowing on security came to be undertaken at rates which fluctuated considerably and were usually below the legal maximum.[3] The fall in interest rates

[1] Premiums at Amsterdam. for ships trading to Southern Europe and the Mediterranean, fell by nearly half between 1650 and 1750. The fall in the North European trades (for which there is no substantial body of English data) was much smaller — 20 to 25 per cent (N. W. Posthumus, *An Enquiry into the History of Prices in the Netherlands* (1938), pp. lxiv–lxv.

[2] See, for example, the Insurance policies in Radcliffe MSS., Guildhall Library, London; C. Wright and C. E. Fayle, *History of Lloyds* (1928), pp. 40, 53, 144; A. H. John, 'The London Assurance Company and the 'Marine Assurance Market of the Eighteenth Century', *Economica*, n.s., Vol. XXV, 1958.

[3] On this falling tendency of interest rates, see H. J. Habakkuk, 'The Long-term Rate of Interest and the Price of Land in the Seventeenth Century',

down to 1713 was therefore taking place a little faster than the changes in the statutory regulation would suggest, and when the legal maximum stopped falling general interest rates continued to trend downwards. Before mid-century they had reached a minimum which was not substantially changed (except in short-term fluctuations) during our period.

Taking a London-built ship throughout, then it may be said that a 120-ton ship for the Malaga trade could be built at £6 a ton, and a 250-ton ship for the Virginia trade at £6 10s. a ton, at any time from 1660 onward.[1] To this must be added the costs of fitting out and victualling, tending to decline slightly as crews became smaller and voyages were accomplished a little more quickly, but otherwise showing no marked changing trend. These may be set, in 1680, at £5 a ton for the Virginia and £4 a ton for the Malaga voyage; a little higher than in 1635 when costs in general were lower, and than in later years when smaller crews reduced the necessary initial outlay on food and drink.

The calculations can now be carried a step further to take into account the capital charges.

Earnings of a 250-ton ship in the Virginia trade

		1635	1680	1725	1770
Capital costs:					
Ship	£	1300	1625	1625	1625
Fitting out		1150	1250	1225	1225
TOTAL		2450	2875	2850	2850
Percentage of capital:					
Net operational earnings		25·9	19·6	14·2	12·1
Depreciation, 4 per cent on cost of ship only		2·1	2·3	2·3	2·3
Insurance[2]		8·5	7·5	5·5	5·0
Interest		8·0	6·0	5·0	4·0
Total capital charges		18·6	15·8	12·8	11·3
Net margin		7·3	3·8	1·4	0·8

Econ. Hist. Rev., 2nd ser., Vol. V, 1951–2, pp. 26–45; T. S. Ashton, *The Industrial Revolution* (Oxford, 1948), pp. 9–10; Adam Smith, *The Wealth of Nations* (Everyman edition), Vol. I, p. 79; G. S. L. Tucker, *Progress and Profits in British Economic Thought, 1650–1850* (Cambridge, 1960), pp. 7–9, 30–2.

[1] See pp. 372–4, above.

[2] The rates current for 1635 and 1680 have been increased by one-fifth to allow for the fact that these rates failed to provide a complete cover in case of loss (see p. 377 above). The 1635 figure is estimated; since the Virginia

Earnings of a 120-ton ship in the Malaga trade

		1635	1680	1725	1770
Capital costs:					
Ship	£	580	720	720	720
Fitting out		440	480	470	460
TOTAL		1020	1200	1190	1180
Percentage of capital:					
Net operational earnings		42·0	23·3	16·5	16·3
Depreciation, 4 per cent on cost of ship only		2·3	2·4	2·4	2·5
Insurance[1]		12·0	9·5	5·5	5·0
Interest		8·0	6·0	5·0	4·0
Total capital charges		22·3	17·9	12·9	11·5
Net margin		19·7	5·4	3·6	4·8

The extraordinary net margin apparently earned by ships in Malaga trade in 1635 has two possible explanations. One is that there was much less certainty at that time of accomplishing two voyages a year regularly. The other is that the Moorish corsair danger was almost at its peak and insurance was not a full compensation for all that was involved in the loss of a ship in such circumstances, even if its cash value was fully covered.[2]

These estimates do not provide results which economists can use in developing estimates of changing general rates of profit; they have not sufficient precision. They are intended to demonstrate that a ship of given build and size which had regular employment, with full holds on homeward voyages, could be operated profitably; but that, despite a marked decline in capital charges, the rate of profit on such a ship declined considerably in the course of the seventeenth century, stabilising to some extent, after the ending of the war in 1713.

What of the other loopholes which mitigated, or which account for, the decline in profits? The ships in our example were assumed to have normally regular employment, with full holds on homeward voyages. How far was this in fact normal? It is impossible

trader did not face the corsair danger in 1635 so directly as the ship going to Spain, it may be supposed that the insurance rate for Virginia would not fall so sharply as that for Spain when the risk from corsairs had been reduced in 1680. I have seen no pre-Restoration insurances for Virginia.
[1] This of course includes two insurance premiums for the two inward and outward voyages.
[2] Most ships in 1635 were not in fact, insured; but some were and there is a clearly evident current rate in South European trades.

to say, for the records are too imprecise to show with certainty when ships were nine-tenths rather than ten-tenths full. It is worth recalling that of the four ships whose records were examined in the previous chapter, two which had no regular trade were on the whole unprofitable, while the two with regular runs made some profits after brief initial difficulties. Of the two latter, the *Caroline* never laded, after her first three voyages, less than 97 per cent of her maximum lading; the *Diligence*, after her first Virginia voyage, never less than 94 per cent of her maximum lading. Of course, these are odd examples, but they typify two differences; unlike the *Diamond* and *Cadiz Merchant*, the *Diligence* and *Caroline* had regular runs, and they were engaged in the carrying trade of the eighteenth rather than of the seventeenth century.

These things are in fact interconnected; and the connection lies in the increasing complexity and simultaneously growing security in commercial relations. This point has been touched on before, but it needs to be repeated here. Going back to the time when the *Diamond* made her voyages, the tonnage of goods carried (outside the coasting trade) by English ships was no more than a few scores of thousands — a quarter, a fifth, perhaps as little as an eighth, of the tonnage moved annually a hundred years later. In 1635 the English merchantman which pushed its bluff bows past the low shores of Cape Henry was entering a wilderness world, a world of Indian forest and swamp, with rare clearings in which a mere five thousand settlers were cultivating a tiny acreage of tobacco apiece, and raising corn to feed themselves. From the plantations among the silent woods a few hogsheads of tobacco would be ferried out, and the planters would search anxiously in the ship's outward cargo for the essential goods they needed from civilisation, for which they might wait another year if they were not to be had now. At that time the whole tobacco crop of Virginia and Maryland could easily have been laden in one large ship. A century later more than a quarter of a million people lived in the territories whose waters drained into Chesapeake Bay; the lower lands had all been settled and new settlement driven into the hills behind; rich planters, trading houses, factors and agents of all kinds were there; the tobacco trade had its firmly established routine for shipping seventy or eighty thousand tons a year to England and Scotland. No ship took away more than a tiny proportion of the whole crop. This situation, and the similar one in the West Indies, mark the extreme of change from pioneering to tight commercial organisation — but an extreme which by the middle of the eighteenth century was employing nearly half the tonnage of English foreign-going shipping. Nearly everywhere, moreover, change had tended in the same direction. Nearly everywhere trade with England had greatly expanded. In consequence there was now a wide range of European, as well as American harbours, where any single English ship made but a small impact on the total demand for shipping services; and this growth of trade had led to, or been accompanied by, the creation of a great network of English merchant houses and agencies abroad, closely linked with their homeland. Shipping had become less speculative because the demands made on it, and the industry itself had grown to an extent which reduced the significance of any single unit; in consequence the expectations of and from each unit could be more stable. The total impression one gets from the records of these two centuries is, indeed, of an industry slowly settling down to orderliness, regularity, an unromantic but gainful routine;[1] one in which by the early eighteenth century a normal rate of profit over the years could be expected, not with certainty, but subject to little more commercial risk than was presented by selling port in Cheapside.

This was the underlying cause of the decline in freight rates; and associated with it was the increasing use of larger ships as their economies ceased to be outweighed by the risks of under-lading. The use of increasingly large ships, which meant lower operating costs per ton of goods carried, was the other main factor in preventing decline in profits. It seems certain that a much larger proportion of ships in the eighteenth century than in the seventeenth had the opportunity to make regular runs. In each trade the hard core of regular traders was accompanied by a proportion of ships coming speculatively for the season; a proportion which grew smaller decade by decade. The great regularity of trading which was commented on in Chapter IX was only an accomplished fact for the eighteenth century; it was building up

---

[1] Notice for example, how until after the war of 1626–30 it was taken for granted that trading ships going beyond the English Channel would take out letters of marque, in wartime, and earn a little by privateering if they met small weak enemy ships; in later wars only a few of the larger ships did this, and privateering was generally left to specialists.

fast in the decades after the Restoration of 1660.[1] In the early seventeenth century there had been great uncertainty, much dissipation of effort between various trades, and frequent short lading, because the units — the ships — were large in relation to the total market for their services in each area; because, in fact, each uncertain ship, each unpredictable crop, each unreliable customer, was a big item in the total situation. So that the second consequence of settling down into stability was that ships — these bigger ships on more regular runs — could expect full or nearly full ladings with greater confidence in 1750 than they could in 1650. In postulating straightforward sailings and full ladings in the voyage estimates above, therefore, we were begging an important part of the question. Full voyages were the ideal. Returns on the full voyage declined over the years; but against this must be set off the increased chance of attaining them. The average income of the owner of a ship of given size in a given trade declined less over the years than the voyage estimates suggest, because he was approaching nearer all the time to the ideal of the full ship. Or perhaps we should say that he was approaching this ideal throughout the seventeenth century and had as nearly as possible attained it by the early decades of the eighteenth.

There remains one uncertain factor. The gradual abandonment of the London-built ship in nearly all but the Levant and East India trades, during the eighteenth century, must have been prompted by a belief that the cheapness of colonial and provincial building outweighed the deficiencies in quality, and particularly the shorter life. Here too, therefore, was a saving in capital costs — though its importance cannot be determined for the advantages cannot now be weighed against the disadvantages. I suspect the balance of advantage was small; but whatever view is taken, here is one more factor which complicates the general issue of the profitability of shipping.

The voyage estimates do not, therefore, lay bare the secrets of profitability before the Industrial Revolution. All this argument

[1] Only enormous labours on the seventeenth-century port books could establish this with absolute certainty; but the work I have done on the port books of 1664 and 1686-7 and on the Seamen's Sixpences records of the eighteenth century, along with the general impression left from examining thousands of cases in the High Court of Admiralty, leave me with no doubt on the matter.

has shown is that a variety of forces were working in different directions to keep shipping profits from moving far or fast; probably to keep them in line with those in similar fields of investment. But we shall see that they were not necessarily of precisely the same size as those obtainable elsewhere; shipowning had, for different groups of people, its own peculiar advantages.

There are other ways of approaching the question, 'was shipowning a profitable business?' We cannot say with precision what 'profitable' meant to the merchant or the investor of the seventeenth or eighteenth century. It is reasonable to suppose, however, that men would not have invested money in the shipping industry, on a scale that increased almost continuously through two centuries, if they had not been spurred on by the expectation of adequate gains and if on the whole and in the long run those expectations had not been realised. This has surely more importance than lack of evidence, or even than evidence which appears to point to a contrary view. It is easy to find complaints by or on behalf of the shipping interest in the seventeenth century, which suggest that such investments led only to ruin. About 1615, for example, 'All men in generall are so far from building anie new Shiping as they will hardlie repaire theire olde, for the freights that marchantes doe now geve is not able to repaire theire shipps in theire tackling and apparell'.[1] Or again, at the end of the same century,

> 'When you come to the Owners of Vessels, they give you a large Account of Many Thousands of Pounds ventured in their Bottoms, to no Advantage but to considerable Loss; if you should at any time accost the Masters of Ships, they are ready to make a doleful Complaint, that Freightage is now reduced to so low an Ebb, that they know not where to go, to get anything for themselves or Owners'.[2]

Such complaints died out in the eighteenth century,[3] though the compiler of the Board of Trade Navigation Accounts in 1788 notes that 'It is a general complaint among Merchants that they

---

[1] BM Lansdowne MSS. 142–306.
[2] C. Povey, *The Unhappiness of England as to its Trade* (1698), p. 2.
[3] There were complaints for a time by the coal shippers; they were facing a real situation of excess supply of shipping during the first half of the eighteenth century, but their condition was exceptional. See, e.g." *The Case of the Owners of Ships Employed in the Coal Trade* (early 1690's); *House of Commons Journals*, 1727–32, p. 373, 516, etc.

are Losers upon the Capital invested in Shipping which they find it necessary to Employ'.[1]

Business men of every kind are naturally more willing (except when facing the shareholders) to admit to depression and the prospect of ruin than to a prosperity and bounteous profits which may attract rivals to the trade; shipowners are and were not exceptional. Outsiders might counter them by talking of their large gains, though not necessarily with any authority; a disgruntled taxpayer of the 1690's, making *Proposals for Raising a Very Considerable Summe of Money on Shipps and other Vessels*, declared that 'Many Owners get Great Estates, only by the Freight of their Ships, that never Trade by way of Merchandise'. Pamphlet literature, often propagandist, sometimes ill-informed, and usually closely reflecting immediate short-term influences rather than long-term tendencies, is a dangerous guide to economic realities.

We may ask, nevertheless, whether the lure which brought the ever-expanding flow of fresh capital into shipowning, whether the 'expectation of adequate gains' which usually seems to have been present, was in fact an expectation that profits would be earned on capital invested at an average rate as good as or better than that encountered in other occupations open to investors. A number of reasons have already been suggested why people might be perfectly satisfied with a collection of benefits taken as a whole, though these benefits included direct monetary returns to their capital at rates lower than they would have accepted from other investments. The first case affected a limited but very important group of people, the shipmasters. The step from mate to master, it has been shown, was a great step both in status and in income; a step which, to modern ideas, was accompanied by an increase in rewards far greater than the heavier burden of duty or responsibility justified. It was a high step because it had usually to be paid for if there was no family influence to give a push; or it usually had to be paid for because it was a high step — the practice once developed, the causation becomes confused. The man who had to invest a few score or a few hundred pounds in a ship in order to secure the command was expecting to derive an additional income (and other incommensurable benefits) from his post, in relation to which one or two per cent more or less in

[1] Customs 17–10.

returns on his capital was an inconsiderable matter. If he was the sole, or a major or a very large part-owner — as he very often was in small ships in the coastal and short-sea trades — then his attitudes might determine whether a ship should be put into service, and should continue to be employed, though profit expectations were small. The attitudes of such masters may have coloured the whole level of earnings in parts of the coastal and short-sea trades; though not in others where substantial master-owners were rare.

The second applies to a great many of the more active ship-owners — the merchants. There were reasons, we have seen, why a merchant might, rightly or wrongly, value the control of a ship's activity; there were cases in which merchants had to control ships in order to keep or extend their trading business. It was humiliating and it was bad for business, for Thomas Hancock's London agent to be compelled to write to him in New York in 1750:

> 'We are sorry to be put to the disagreeable task of informing you that we have not been able to prevail upon Captain Spender to take in your Cambricks and Lawns etc., though they were quite ready (& we applied to him some time) before he was full, but his answer was, that what room he had, must be kept for his Owners' Goods; Tis crewell hard usage.'[1]

There were cases in which managing owners laded ships entirely with their own goods — in the timber trades, for example. Others who had considerable use of ships for their own business, and loaded or partly loaded ships of which they were managing owners, felt some convenience in this. If they felt this convenience, they were ready — though not necessarily consciously — to accept some abatement in normal rates of profit. Where shipowning and trading was entirely amalgamated, as in coal shipment and slaving, it was (and still is) difficult to disentangle the profits of the one from the other.[2]

The great majority of shipowners, however, were passive investors, whether London merchants taking in each others' shipping, or the wide variety of provincial men of some property who might be induced to put some money into the marine

---

[1] W. T. Baxter, *The House of Hancock* (Cambridge, Mass., 1945), p. 56.
[2] From this arises the popular view of the slave trade as a tremendously profitable one. When the cost of the slave goods bought in Liverpool is compared with the proceeds of the slaves in Jamaica, and all the cost of getting them there is ignored, the trade naturally looks like a gold mine.

activities of their own or a nearby port. The special attractiveness
of the ship as an avenue for profit-sharing investment offering
some limitation of risk, has been discussed. A price must have
been paid for this relative security.[1] The modest expectations of
such investors should have had a depressing effect on the general
level of earnings.

Finally, even when the industry had settled down to sober and
regular habits in the eighteenth century, a ship was an investment
which offered a fluctuating return, dependent on delays or
quickenings of voyages, on the rise and fall of freight rates in far
distant sub-tropical harbours, on the likelihood of storm, worm
or accident causing heavy repair costs. There was a substantial
element of chance in the returns to this investment — though it
was an element declining throughout our period, and one that in
any event was much smaller looked at from the point of view of
the whole life of the ship than it was in any single year. As they
so often do when a speculative element is present, investors may
have allowed the average return to be depressed in consideration
of the chances of occasional gains far above the average.

Must the whole growth of the shipping industry, then, be
brought down to these sordid calculations of profit and loss, of
the hunt for jobs and the reconciliation of security with gain?
Alas, this is a problem of money; people had to be attracted to the
building of ships, and to the manning of them, by adequate
financial rewards, and this is the way the world of money has to
go. The adventurous or enterprising poor might go to sea; they
could go only if other men, whose appetite for adventure or
enterprise found its outlet in business operations, set out the
ships. But perhaps, even among the monied men, there is a little
more to it than that; perhaps there were owners, as there must
have been seamen, who stepped on their own decks with prop-
rietorial pride; whose hearts swelled a little, with something more
than the legitimate satisfaction of seeing the physical embodiment
of a thousand-pound investment coming to temporary safety,
when the prow of the *Content* or the *Owners' Goodwill* was seen
nosing into the ruck of shipping in the Lower Pool, or emerging
from beneath the towering heights of Clifton Gorge, or creeping
past Paull Point, after six or eight months' absence. It is surely a
little easier to feel an affection for a ship than for a warehouseful,

[1] See pp. 101–5, above.

however valuable, of cowhides, smalts, and beads (crystal). Those who wish to feel there is some truth in this view may find comfort in words once set down by Jonas Hanway — though they contain a sad recognition of the winds of change:

'There was a time, *in my memory*, when merchants prided themselves in charming gallies they sent to sea; they saw and admired them with a lover's eye, and did not reckon on *much gain* on them, merely as a *ship-account;* but those days are gone.'[1]

[1] *Reasons for an Augmentation of at least Twelve Thousand Mariners, to be Employed in the Merchants' Service and Coasting Trade* (1759), p. 56.

XVIII

Conclusion

The English of the sixteenth century were a rural and an agricultural people, with no town of any size outside London, and no industry of more than local consequence except the making of woollen cloth. Though England was by no means self-sufficient, and its cloth industry depended heavily on foreign markets, its trade inward and outward was still mainly in valuable goods; the need had not appeared to bring in, and the opportunity had not arisen to export, large quantities of the cheap bulky goods which are the support of a great shipping industry. There was, it is true, a growing tendency to import corn; but this import trade was characterised by such violent fluctuations that it could provide no secure occupation for a specialised shipping, and most of it was handled by the Dutch and German ships which regularly distributed corn along all the western coasts of Europe. The shipping industry was, therefore, as yet of little significance in the English economy. It performed limited services (which foreigners would gladly have undertaken) and employed little capital and few men; it neither absorbed any important share of the nation's resources nor performed any very essential task. A good deal of such importance as it had was provided by the fishing fleets, which employed in the fishery and in the distribution of its product a large proportion of the total of English ships and seamen.

The growth of the industry in the following century has been described; it was based principally on a growing need to transport coastwise or overseas bulky goods of basic importance — coal and timber — and on colonial developments which so cheapened such goods as tobacco and sugar that a mass demand for them was created which made it profitable to bring great and increasing quantities of them three thousand miles across the Atlantic.

Between 1560 and 1689 shipping emerged from its earlier insignificance, becoming one of the fastest-growing of English industries. The statistics reveal that the tonnage of ships was

388

multiplied nearly seven-fold, during a period in which population was certainly no more than doubled, and in which it is hard to believe that national income showed anything like a seven-fold increase. The shipping industry's demands on the country's man-power were beginning to be considerable in the later decades of the seventeenth century. A rapidly rising need for seamen was outpacing the slow growth of population up to the very end of the century. Fifty thousand able bodied men had to be maintained in the merchant service, in a country which had in all only one-and-a-half million men, only a small minority of whom could be spared from the overriding needs of agriculture. When we consider the rapid turnover in seagoing personnel, this suggests that a very substantial proportion of the men who lived in the coastal counties and seaports must at some time during their lives have gone to sea. In terms of manpower, the industry may well by this time have been greater than any other except cloth making and building. Moreover, it was a heavily capitalised industry. A new ship set out for, say, Spain in 1688 employed nearly £100 of capital to each of the men who worked in her; over the whole English merchant fleet, large ships and small, new and old, built and captured, the capital per seaman can hardly have been less than £50. This was a great deal of money; four years of an able seaman's wages. The ratio was no doubt exceeded in some industries — iron making and coal mining, for example — but it was probably much higher than in the great cloth industry, in building and a host of others; and this in spite of the fact that the whole wages of a voyage taking many months were customarily paid out of the freight received at the end, and did not, as in many industries, have to be found out of capital before the product was sold. That is to say, the shipping industry was one of the country's chief users of capital; its demands on that part of the national capital not locked up in agricultural land and buildings were even greater proportionately than its demand for labour.

Finally, as to 'output'. The earnings of a normal ship in peace-time can be put at something over £5 per ton per annum; those of the whole shipping industry, therefore, at a figure approaching two million pounds a year in the 1680's. There are no figures for other industries with which a direct comparison can be made, although it seems possible that the output of the iron manufactur-ing industry was of much the same order of size, and evidently that of the cloth industry was several times as great. Some meaning can be given to the figure, however, by setting it beside other statistics. The import and export trades at this time ran at some five or six millions a year apiece. A hundred years later, after great economic expansion, MacPherson's estimate suggests that only three industries (woollen cloth, iron and leather) had a very much higher output than this one did in the 1680's.[1]

If we seek, again, to explain the growth of London — the trebling, quadrupling or quintupling of its population which took place between 1560 and 1689, it is surely necessary to look first to that great mass of persons who depended on the physical handling of seaborne trade; the seamen and warehousemen, all those concerned with the victualling and repairing and storing of ships, the river and quayside workers; many tens of thousands of people, requiring the services of many tens of thousands more to supply their needs and those of their families. Though today London remains one of the half-dozen leading ports of the world, only a quite small part of the population depends directly on the port. Around 1700 the proportion which so depended was very large — quite possibly more than a quarter of the total population — and taking into account all those who served the workers in these basic occupations it is plain that the greatness of London depended, before everything else, on the activity in the port of London.

From the time of the outbreak of the War of the League of Augsburg in 1689 the size of the merchant fleet grew much less rapidly, perhaps for some decades at a rate slower than the general advance of income. After the middle of the eighteenth century, the renewed rapid expansion of the shipping industry was a reflection of the accelerating pace of growth of the English economy — a growth which involved rising exports and rapidly growing home demands for industrial raw material and foodstuffs. There is no reason to suppose that, in this last period, the shipping industry was one of the pacemakers of advance. It seems possible, therefore, that in capital and output the industry reached a peak in relation to national wealth and national income, before the end of the seventeenth century, which was never exceeded. In the eighteenth century considerable economies of labour and capital were made; the shipping tonnage of 1775, double that of a hundred years before, employed only some 50 per cent more seamen; this

[1] D. MacPherson, *Annals of Commerce* (1805), Vol. IV, 15.

economised capital required for victualling, while the drift of shipbuilding towards the cheap north-east coast and to America was similarly saving capital.

The latter part of the seventeenth century was therefore the period in which economic problems relating to the shipping industry bulked largest in men's eyes and were most rapidly increasing in importance. The extensive literature on its problems, dying away from about 1680 and ceasing abruptly soon after 1700, was not merely a response to Dutch competition and the problems it posed; it also reflected the growing significance of the shipping industry to the whole English economy. The 'Act for the Encouragement of Shipping and Navigation' of 1660, the successor to the Commonwealth Ordinance of 1651 and the basis of all the Navigation Laws was, with its successors, watched critically for some decades with an eye mainly to its effect on shipping. In the eighteenth century, while of course the Acts remained fully effective, positive interest in and amendments to them were related much more to their influence on the direction and character of colonial trade. The English shipping industry of the eighteenth century could stand on its own feet. Taking the existing protection for granted, it no longer needed to call attention continually to its need for protection, and its affairs ceased to loom so large in the eyes of the nation as industrial expansion took the centre of the stage. The American Revolution was to bring men's thoughts back to the protection of English shipping interests by legislation.

What part did the shipping industry play in preparing for the greatest of all changes, the Industrial Revolution of the late eighteenth century? If we think only in terms of direct influence, then the answer must be, a very small part indeed. The first revolution at sea had taken place centuries before when the sail had been hoisted to supplement and eventually replace the oar; not until very late in the nineteenth century did the iron steamship finally triumph over the wooden sailing ship and again transform the industry.

There were, as we have seen, technical changes of some importance, that were labour saving without calling for additional capital; the typical ship of 1775 employed a good deal less labour and capital, per ton-mile, than that of a century or two centuries before, and the resulting economies brought down freight rates

2C

in several trades by a quarter or a third. This technical progress was made during a period in which few branches of the economy showed marked technical advances, and many showed none. The improvements in the ship probably did tend, on the whole, to reduce the proportion which transport costs bore to the cost of the goods transported. But the great bulk of goods carried by sea consisted — as it consists now — of foodstuffs and raw or partially processed materials; corn, coal, timber, sugar, iron and salt. Changes in the real cost of production of these goods did, no doubt, take place over time — though in ways it is most difficult to trace now — but their production was not susceptible to the revolutionary improvements in efficiency that eventually opened up for manufacturing industry. The violent fall in freight rates which took place in the century *after* 1775 — reducing the cost of trans-atlantic transit, for example, by five-sixths — had a real importance in stimulating the trade in goods of this kind; the reduction in transport costs in the century before 1775, which we are here concerned with, was too limited to have such an effect. Almost certainly it was of less importance to English industrial develop-ment than the eighteenth-century improvements in the inland waterway system which, when they made it possible to replace land carriage by water carriage, did effect sharp reductions in cost.

These genuine gains in the efficiency of the shipping industry, then, were useful; but they were not vital to English economic development. They sparked off no revolutionary changes. No decisive break-through in transport costs occurred, such, for example, as might have made it economically feasible to carry over long distances goods otherwise tied to their own places of production. Transport costs played too small a part in the total cost of most imports, and of most manufactures, for changes in them to be of the first importance. Most commodities were not affected in their delivered price to the extent of more than two to three per cent by the effect of falling peacetime freight rates, even over a whole century. There are exceptions. The greatest of them, timber, in the price of which transport was an important element, was simply carried in cheap Dutch and Scandinavian ships until the English were sufficiently improved to compete effectively; after which there was little further room for economies or freight cutting. As to coal, the normal price of its shipment is unfor-tunately lost among the general expenses of coal trading; but its historians make it plain that the improvement and enlargement of colliers was only one of many means by which the tendency to rising coal costs was fought.

No doubt the shipping industry helped to create the favourable background on which rapid industrialisation was built; through the capital accumulation which its profits facilitated, through its effect on the balance of payments, and by the example of its peculiar ownership structure. These effects, however, cannot easily be disentangled from those of trade, and it is unlikely that they were very great. The shipping industry was an important part of the English economy, both before and after the decisive decades of the Industrial Revolution, but it cannot be said to have made a contribution of a special character to the transition.

Yet its direct influence is not the whole or even the most important part of the story. If the shipping industry contributed little, colonial development contributed much; vast trades in sugar, rice, indigo, tobacco, cotton were the source of many of the fortunes, great and small, of the eighteenth century, and of huge contributions to the revenues of the state; while at the same time the colonies were the destinations of great exports of iron wares and later of cottons which played a vital part in the building of those industries to the point where technical change transformed their momentum of growth. The Navigation Acts, primarily intended to conserve and build up the English shipping industry as the reserve of ships and even more of seamen to give strength to the navy in time of war, incidentally secured a monopoly of English colonial trade and its profits for English merchants, and played a major part in protecting English industry's colonial markets from the effective competition of European manufactures. It is easy to argue the strict laissez-faire case, to point out the savings of cost which would have been made if the Dutch had been permitted, in the seventeenth century, to trade freely with the English colonies and to carry goods to and from them in their own ships. Perhaps the world would have been a better place; it would certainly have been a very different one. The indications of the mid-seventeenth century were that the Dutch had the capacity to take over all this colonial trade and transport and to maintain control over them for several decades. Would the colonies have remained English, would English industry have been built up, in those circumstances? From the end of the century England

was engaged intermittently in a savage struggle with the French
for colonial empire, emerging to an apparently decisive victory and
completely secure position only in 1763. It was an evenly balanced
struggle, which might well have ended differently had England
been markedly weaker at sea, poorer and less developed indus-
trially. If the normal sea links with the English colonies had been
in Dutch, not English hands, might not the balance of war have
tipped further against England? Both England and France
recruited their naval seamen, in wartime, mainly from their
merchant fleets; both merchant fleets included a very large
component engaged in colonial trade; but the French, significantly,
had allowed their traffic with the Baltic to fall into the hands of
the Dutch, as the English had not. If the English colonial and
North European trades had been largely in Dutch hands — and
the English shipping industry therefore less than half its actual
size — is it not at least a real possibility that the French navy
would have been the stronger at critical times, that the French
would have emerged from the wars with their colonial position
consolidated, that the transfers of West Indian islands would have
been from English to French hands rather than vice versa, the
ultimate settlement of North America one which left the English
colonies, if still English, a fringe on the east coast of a French
America? This is speculation; but it would take some hardihood
to deny it with any certainty. If colonial America had been lost
or whittled away; if during its lifetime it had been a Dutch
commercial province; where would have been the merchant
fortunes, the crown revenues, accumulated in England through
colonial trade? Where would the English industries have found
room for massive expansion? A much poorer, a much less indus-
trialised England in mid-century; would this have provided a firm
basis for the take-off into Industrial Revolution?

The needs of the state for naval power reinforced the demands
of the merchants and shipowners in securing legislation to preserve
the merchant marine, and so — for good or ill — preserved naval
power and the colonies; and colonial monopoly was one of the
bases — how important a one may be debated — for industrial
expansion. When colonial monopoly was broken after 1776 the
work was done; the wealth had been accumulated, and the
dependence of the American economy on England established too
firmly to be undone in less than another century.

Appendix A

A NOTE ON THE SHIPPING STATISTICS,
1686–1788

The pathway through the shipping statistics of the seventeenth and eighteenth centuries is a slippery and often misleading one. Several writers have attempted to follow it; in 1915 Walther Vogel, 'Zur Grosse der europaischen Handelsflotten im 15, 16 und 17 Jahrhundert'[1]; fourteen years later A. P. Usher, 'The Growth of English Shipping, 1572–1922'[2]; and in 1939 L. A. Harper, who devoted nearly a third of a large book to a most thorough investigation.[3] I myself spent much time gathering basic data and manipulating them; the results are in my unpublished London Ph.D. thesis.[4] The figures used here differ significantly from those developed in the above works (including the last). No doubt they will not escape revision in due time; but I hope future revisions will not be so drastic as to destroy the general picture of growth, slowing down and new growth which is presented here.

There are three potential sources of error in the preparation of comparative shipping statistics for this period.

(i) Errors in the original recording of or counting the number of ships. Nothing can be done about this; there is no reason to suppose it has much importance, though the existence of a smuggling fleet in the eighteenth century should be borne in mind.

(ii) Inconsistencies in contemporary recording of the tonnage of individual ships. This is much less important than many writers have supposed; almost invariably recorded tonnages are tons burden. Though, an individual ship may be put down at different times at several different tonnages, over a great mass of material these differences should be evened out; there is no reason to think that there were consistent errors in one direction followed at a later period by consistent errors in another. Two exceptions must be mentioned, however. One is the practice of recording the tonnage of East Indiamen, from the early years of the eighteenth century onward, at 499 tons or less, though many of them were far larger. This I shall remark again later. The other is the growth after 1773 of the practice of recording measured

---

[1] *Festschrift D. Schäfer zum 70 Geburtstag dargebracht* (Jena, 1915).
[2] *Quarterly Journal of Economics*, Vol. XLII, 1929, pp. 465–78.
[3] *The English Navigation Laws* (New York, 1939), pp. 239–364.
[4] 'The Organisation and Finance of the English Shipping Industry in the Later Seventeenth Century' (1955), pp. 34–83, 382–431.

395

tons rather than tons burden; of no importance in the period we are specifically concerned with, it makes comparisons with later dates very difficult — especially as measured tonnage came to be used invariably in records after general registration began in 1786.

(iii) The different methods by which lists of ships were compiled at various times. This is the most troublesome feature. The statistics of ships owned, from 1560 to 1629, are based on actual physical counts of the number of ships and their tonnage; and this procedure was followed to obtain a figure of outport ships in 1702. It is also, effectively, the basis for post-1786 figures; from that time onward it was necessary only to count the ships which had been registered.[1] However, for 1686 and years between 1709 and 1786 the fundamental data are in the Port Books. These are the records kept by customs officials of the names, destinations and cargoes (rarely the tonnages) of all ships entering and clearing English ports engaged in foreign trade. (Separate Port Books were kept for coastal trade, but a high proportion of these are lost.) From these it is possible to list, or to calculate in one way or another, the number and tonnage of English-owned ships. The process clearly requires adjustments and may introduce errors; it is less likely to produce a reliable result than a straight count. It remains, however, the only possible way of getting at shipping tonnage between the dates of the last count under Privy Council instructions (incomplete though this was) in 1629, and the first count under the new act for registration of ships, in 1788.

The sources of the counts in 1560–1629 and the adjustments made to them have been noted at the appropriate places in Chapter I. The way in which later figures have been compiled is now to be described, first for 1686, then for 1702 and finally for 1709–86.

1. *1686*

This year was selected for examination because it lies in the one long period of peace in the latter half of the seventeenth century, and is a year for which Port Books survive in some quantity. Attempts were made to produce comparable figures for the year 1663, but these proved to be too insecurely based to be put forward with the scholarly apparatus that implies pretensions to accuracy. Nevertheless, I have little doubt that in the first years of the sixties the tonnage of English-owned shipping was around 200 thousand tons — at or below this figure in 1660 and well above it when the Second Dutch War broke out late in 1664.

[1] An error quickly emerged in these totals derived from the registration records, because ships were often not removed from the register when they were broken up or lost. When the accumulated error was removed in 1827, the tonnage of ships on the register was reduced by 13 per cent.

The total tonnage owned in 1686 must be estimated in two parts — foreign-going shipping on the one hand, coastal shipping and inshore fisheries on the other. This will involve consideration of the overlap between the two.

For foreign-going shipping the primary data are in the Port Books, which are fairly complete for 1686; when the book for this year for a particular port is missing, the one for 1687 has been used instead.

Two alternative methods are available to produce from the Port Books a figure of the total tonnage of ships owned in England which engaged in foreign trade. One is to list the individual ships by name (counting each once only) and to allocate a tonnage to each. For many of them — particularly the larger ships — it is not difficult to find a record of tonnage;[1] to each of the others has been allocated the average tonnage of the typical ships engaged in the trade in 1715–17, distinguishing between London and outports.[2] The total tonnage arrived at in this way is 256 thousand; this is the tonnage of all the English-owned ships which at some time during 1686 took a part in foreign trade, though many of them engaged in coasting trade as well during the same year.

The second method is less direct. First, the number of entries and clearances in each branch of foreign trade at each port is listed.[3] To the numbers of ships so obtained are allocated average tonnages corresponding with the average tonnage of ships engaged in each foreign trade, at London and the outports, in the years 1715–17. This should give a quite accurate figure for total tonnage of entries and clearances in 1686. It is simple to discover from the Port Books the number of voyages a year made by a ship fully employed (but not making exceptionally rapid voyages) in each branch of trade, and to use this to calculate

---

[1] The principal source for tonnage was the Mediterranean passes issued by the Admiralty (Adm. 7–75/76). Other sources were the many incidental recordings of tonnage in High Court of Admiralty cases, the odd Port Books which recorded tonnage, references to ships hired by the government in the State Papers, Domestic, and various lists of East India ships, especially those in Bal Krishna, *Commercial Relations between India and England, 1601–1757* (1924), pp. 334–59.

[2] I had earlier attempted to estimate the average tonnage of ships in each trade from immediately contemporary data of the kind described in the previous note. This produced a total about 6 per cent higher than that obtained with the aid of the 1715–17 average. Since it seems unlikely that average tonnage of ships fell between 1686 and 1715 (though the effects of the Great Northern War make it just possible) it had been thought better, in the interests of comparisons with later years, to use the 1715-17 tonnages in calculating these totals. They are derived from CO 390-8. The average tonnage of *all* outport ships in 1715-17 has been applied to the numbers of *all* outport ships in 1686; to do this by individual ports would have led to distortion by accidental variations, since the numbers in each trade at each outport are small.

[3] The detailed figures will be found in my Ph.D. thesis, op. cit., pp. 383–403.

from the total tonnage of English entries and clearances[1] the total tonnage of ships needed to serve the trade. The grand total will be the size of the merchant fleet needed to serve all the English foreign trade carried on in English ships, assuming that every ship is fully occupied, and that every ship occupies itself in foreign trade to the total exclusion of coastal trade or inshore fishery. The following table sets out the calculation:

Foreign-going shipping in 1686 (000 tons) by calculation

TRADE:		Entries or Clearances London	outports	Number of voyages per year	Tons owned London	outports
Northern Europe	E	42	42	3	14	14
North-west Europe (except Holland with outports)	E	56	40	London 4 outports 5	14	8
Holland (outports)	C		66	5		13
British Isles:						
London	E					
outports	C	5	38	8	1	5
Southern Europe	E	21	11	2½	8	5
Mediterranean	E	23	3	1	23	3
East India	E	6		½	12	
North America	E	18	16	$1\frac{1}{10}$	16	14
West Indies	E	35	9	$1\frac{1}{10}$	31	9
				TOTAL	119	71[2]

i.e. GRAND TOTAL, 190 thousand tons

We now have two figures for shipping engaged in foreign trade:

Method A: 256,000 tons — a total known to be too large since it includes some tonnage of ships which spent a part of their time in coastal voyages.

[1] A ship was only 'entered' or 'cleared' and recorded as so doing if carrying some cargo — no matter how little. In most trades, ships invariably entered with cargo, though sometimes going out in ballast, so that for most trades entries provide the best guide to shipping activity. In a few trades, however, ships going out were always laden while ships coming in were often empty; in such cases, clearances rather than entries are the best indicators of shipping traffic. In the calculation, figures of entries have been used in all cases except those of outport trade with Holland and Ireland. These trades were dominated by the transport of coal, and clearances have been used as the basis of calculation.

[2] Entries and clearances include as English all the colonial, Irish and Channel Islands' ships; this follows the practice of the eighteenth century statistics. In calculating the tonnage of ships owned in English ports these must be removed. To arrive at the figure used above, entries and clearances were reduced by the following amounts (000 tons); British Isles trades: London 3, outports 20; North America trade: London 1, outports 1; West Indies trade: London 1. The basis for estimating the totals of non-English shipping of this kind is discussed on pp. 42–3 of my thesis, op. cit.

Method B: 190,000 tons — a total known to be too small because it represents a fully employed fleet; while a few ships did even better than the normally 'fully employed', variations the other way, in the inefficient use and under-utilisation, would certainly be larger.

Now coastal shipping (and the tiny inshore fisheries)[1] must be brought into the picture. Professor Harper has devised a method for calculating these which can hardly be improved upon, though it leaves room for considerable error.[2] The first part of this consists of taking the best possible estimates of coal shipments from north-east coast ports[3] and assuming each collier made a certain number of voyages a year. On the basis of Professor Nef's estimates, Professor Harper has taken eight voyages a year as a standard; but from the evidence of many account books of colliers, and taking into the account the fact that much coal was not shipped for such a long distance as that from Newcastle to London, I am inclined to suppose that ten voyages a year is a more reasonable figure. The result is a figure of 80,000 tons of colliers. The second part of the calculation is the assumption that the proportion of coasters, other than colliers, to all other shipping was the same in 1686 as in 1772–81, years for which figures are available in BM Add.MSS. 11256; a very dubious assumption, but the figures involved are not large.[4] The proportion of non-coal coasters to all English shipping in 1772–81 was $15\frac{1}{2}$ per cent; to arrive at the total of English shipping, therefore, it is necessary to multiply any total of foreign-going ships, colliers and inshore fishing-boats by $\frac{100}{84\frac{1}{2}}$.

It is evident that the basis used for arriving at the total of colliers is the same as that used in the second method of calculating tonnage in foreign trade; and the two totals arrived at by this method may be added together:

Foreign-going, method B	190
Colliers	80
Inshore fisheries, say	5[5]
	275

[1] Ships in the Newfoundland fishery would normally make an appearance among the entries for foreign trade.

[2] op. cit., pp. 330–8.

[3] From J. U. Nef, *The Rise of the British Coal Industry*, App. D, it appears that 800 thousand tons would approximately represent the coastal coal shipments; about half of them went to London.

[4] Some other coasters besides colliers were excluded — i.e. lime, chalk and manure carriers — but few of these would have been specialised to such a commodity as coal was. On the other hand, the impression received from T. S. Willan, *The English Coasting Trade, 1600–1750* (Manchester, 1938) is that during the eighteenth century, the non-coal coasting trade was growing in volume at a faster rate than foreign trade.

[5] See Harper, op. cit., p. 339.

Multiplying this by $\frac{100}{84\frac{1}{4}}$ to allow for the other coasters, we have a grand total of 325 thousand tons.

The first method for calculating foreign-going ships has the merit of directness; the difficulty arises in fitting it in with coastal tonnage. For the coastal (or at least the collier) tonnage is the calculated minimum necessary to carry the goods, assuming all the ships concerned engaged solely in coastal trade. The foreign-going tonnage, on the other hand, includes many vessels which in fact during some part of the year took a hand in coastal trade. There is some danger of double-counting here.

It may, however, be possible to eliminate this danger. Very few ships which took part in coasting trade ever went further afield than the Atlantic and North Sea coasts of Europe. Taking the known, named ships engaged in the Norway, Germany, Holland, Flanders, France, Portugal, Spain, Ireland and Channel Isles trade, we can make two totals:

(*a*) The actual tonnage of these ships.

(*b*) The total arrived at by dividing the tonnage of each ship by the proportion of the number of voyages it made in its particular foreign trade to the number of voyages made in that trade by a ship fully engaged in it throughout the year.[1] The difference between these two totals can be taken to represent that part of their tonnage devoted to coastal trade; the extent to which these ships were not 'foreign-going'.

The actual tonnage of ships which at some time during 1686 engaged in the trades specified was 98 thousand. The proportion, overall, of their tonnage which was not 'foreign-going' was $42\frac{1}{2}$ per cent, i.e. 41 thousand tons. Deducting this from the total of 256 thousand tons of 'foreign-going' ships previously listed, we can make the following calculation:

Foreign-going, by Method A,

$$256-41 = 215$$

Colliers   80

Inshore fisheries, say   5
                                                  ———
                                                  300
                                                  ———

Multiplying this by $\frac{100}{84\frac{1}{4}}$ to allow for the other coasters, a grand total is arrived at of 355 thousand tons. This compares with 325 thousand tons calculated by the other method.

There are some remaining difficulties about both methods. The first contains a small excess because in a period of twelve months some ships newly built and some ships lost or scrapped would have been listed,

---

[1] Some ships engaged in more than one branch of foreign trade; but the number is small and they are easily dealt with.

which would not have existed simultaneously at any given date during the year. The second method does not allow for ships laid up, requiring unusually lengthy repairs, or otherwise not fully utilised by the normal standards of the time. Neither method allows for ships which were absent throughout the year — of which there were over six thousand tons of East Indiamen alone.[1] On the whole therefore, the intermediate round figure of 340 thousand tons seems as near an approximation to the truth as we are likely to obtain.[2]

2. *1702*

The total tonnage for this year is arrived at by two separate calculations for the outports and for London.

The basic figure for the outports comes from the 'Returns made to the Commissioners of Customs in answer to their Circular Letter of 24th January 1701/2 from the severall outports underwritten'.[3] This list results from an actual enumeration of ships belonging to each port, made by the local Customs officers; the total is 2,721 ships of 176,340 tons. A few ports are omitted[4] and using the data for 1716 discussed

[1] From Bal Krishna, op. cit., pp. 334–59.

[2] There is a contemporary figure of 285,800 tons, which has been widely reproduced following G. Chalmers, *Estimate of the Comparative Strength of Great Britain* (1794), p. 206. This figure is without foundation; it is obtained in the following manner. The House of Lords in the 1670's ordered the preparation of some trade statistics for 1663 and 1669. In the 'Book of Tables' in which these are now recorded (BM Add.MSS. 36785) is a figure of 142,900 tons of shipping. The tables are of London trade only, and this undescribed 142,900 tons is probably the tonnage of clearances from London, average of the years 1663 and 1669. The compiler of the tables guessed that one-third of this tonnage was foreign-owned; he divided it precisely into two-thirds English, 95,266 tons, and one-third foreign, 47,634 tons. The 1668 figures are simply a doubling of all these; 190,533 tons English, 95,267 tons foreign, total 285,800. That is, the 1688 figures are simply a derivation from the commonly held view that English shipping doubled during the reigns of Charles II and James II; they are not in any way a confirmation of it. Even if the view were true, the basic figures (for 1663–9) are not and have never purported to be figures of the tonnage of English-owned shipping.

Professor L. A. Harper produces a figure of 161,619 tons for 1660 (op. cit., p. 339). This, however, is demonstrably calculated on an inadequate basis; if it is right, it is right by accident, but I think it is too low. His figures depend on the assumption that nearly all ships which engaged in foreign trade obtained Mediterranean passes. Comparison of the passes for 1662–64 which he uses, with the Port Books, shows that nearly three-quarters of the ships obtaining passes were engaged in trade with Southern Europe and the Mediterranean, and most of the remainder were in American trade. The Norway and Baltic, German, Dutch, French and Flemish trades, and those with Ireland and Scotland, are hardly represented. The passes are, by themselves, quite inadequate as sources for determining the total tonnage of shipping. Professor Harper briefly 'confirms' his figures by two other methods; the first ultimately based on these same passes, and the second on the statistics in BM Add.MSS. 36785 which have just been discussed.

[3] CO 388–9.

[4] Hastings, Lymington, Fowey, Preston, Southwold, Berwick, Neath, Cardiff, Llanelly, Cardigan, Aberdovey, Carmarthen.

below an allowance of seven thousand tons has been made for these, bringing the outport total up to 183 thousand tons.

The total for London is of a quite different character; it is of 'Ships belonging to the Port of London . . . which have been visited by the Surveyor of Navigation since the beginning of September 1700 in order to their getting passes securing them from the Algerines'.[1] 560 ships, of 84,882 tons, are so listed. But compiled on such a basis it excludes nearly all coasters, ships in the North Sea, Channel and Baltic trades, and many in North American trade, as well as those ships which did not happen to come into London during the period. The tonnage of London ships in Northern and North-western European trades in 1686 was 29 per cent of the whole London tonnage in overseas trade; the changes since then pulled in various directions, and may have left the proportion little altered. Making a small allowance for the America traders whose owners were ready to take a risk, we may suppose that at least one-third of London ships in overseas trade did not have passes. If the Surveyor's figures correctly represented the total tonnage of the ships in certain trades at some given date in 1701, it could be multiplied by $\frac{3}{2}$, producing a figure of 127,323 tons. In fact, figures collected in this way over a period of fifteen months would slightly exaggerate the total, by including both ships lost and scrapped, and ships newly built, which did not exist at the same time. Taking off 5 per cent to allow for this, a figure of 121 thousand tons is arrived at for London ships in foreign trade. To this must be added an allowance for ships which were overseas throughout this period, which might bring the figure back to around 130 thousand tons.

What of London-owned coasters? Most of the ships which carried on London's coastal trade were owned in the outports, but London's small share of the vast total made up a tonnage by no means negligible. Brand's *History of Newcastle*[2] reproduces some statistics, of uncertain meaning and derivation, which nevertheless say unambiguously that just under one-sixth of the tonnage of ships taking coal from Newcastle to London in 1702–04 was London-owned. If this was true of the Sunderland trade too, London's tonnage in the coal trade was about 9 thousand.[3] London's coastal intake of other goods from places beyond the bounds of the Thames estuary[4] was rather less in total; so it might be supposed that the total London tonnage in coasting trade would

[1] CO 388–9.   [2] (London, 1789), Vol. II, p. 677.
[3] London coal imports, 1702–4, averaged 458 thousand tons a year (Nef, op. cit., Vol. II, p. 381). Assuming eight voyages a year for each ship, this would require 57 thousand tons of shipping; one-sixth of this is 9 thousand tons.
[4] There was a considerable trade from Kent and Essex coasts of the Thames estuary into London, all of which appears from the Port Books to have been carried in craft owned in the various small ports.

be no more than 15–20 thousand tons. Again, the question of overlap with ships engaged in foreign trade as well arises, but the possible total is not large; 130 thousand tons in foreign, and 15–20 thousand tons in coastal trade, leads reasonably to a final London figure of 140 thousand tons.

In support of this rather cursory dismissal of London's coastal tonnage, we may cite the view of the compilers of later statistics of the eighteenth century, that 'no coasters belong to this port'.[1] This was not true at the time of registration in 1786; the records of Seamen's Sixpences show it was not true in the late twenties and early thirties, though in the mid-thirties the recorded number and tonnage of London-owned coasters entering London did fall away sharply. Even in the late twenties, however, these records show much the greatest part of the coastal tonnage entering London was owned elsewhere.[2] It seems most unlikely that London-owned coasters can have totalled more than a very few tens of thousands of tons at any time during the eighteenth century.

The total arrived at for 1702, therefore, is 323 thousand tons, i.e. London 140 thousand and outports 183 thousand. There are two checks on these figures, apart from the rather doubtful 1709–86 statistics shortly to be discussed. One is the 1686 calculation reproduced above, giving a total of 340 thousand tons, divided between London and the outports roughly in the proportion of 150 : 190. Reasons were put forward in Chapter II to suggest that tonnage in 1702 would have been no higher than in 1686, and might well have been lower. The other is W. Maitland's list of ships owned in London in 1732;[3] listed by name with their individual tonnages, they total 178,557 tons. While English-owned shipping had grown considerably in thirty years, it is surprising that the rise from the levels of 1702 should have been so much as from 140 to 179 thousand tons for London. I am inclined to suppose that the 1686 figure is more nearly accurate than that for 1702, and that the latter is too low. However, 323 thousand tons is the best total I can produce by rational calculation; the error may well be as much as 10 per cent.

3. *1709–86*

The 1702 figure fits in very well with those produced by the Customs authorities for various dates between 1709 and 1786. There are, unfortunately, very strong reasons for doubting these.

[1] BM Add.MSS. 11256.
[2] Adm. 68–194/196. Many of the coasters owned in outports did not pay in their Sixpences in London, and so do not appear in these records. It is therefore impossible to derive from them an estimate of the proportion of coasters entering London which were London-owned.
[3] *History of London* (1756), Vol. II, 1260–62.

These statistics, to be found in BM Add.MSS. 11256, are obtained by making 'An account of the Tonnage of all Ships and Vessels belonging to each respective Port of England that have traded to or from Foreign Parts or coastwise or have been employed as Fishing Vessels, distinguishing each Port and each Year and accounting each Vessel but once in the Year'. They are available for the outports for years 1709, 1716, 1723, 1730, 1737, and 1744; and for all ports every year from 1751 onward. The war years, however, must be ignored, for the laying up of ships, the entry of large numbers into government service,[1] and convoy delays which kept many ships overseas for more than a year, completely distort the wartime figures. The useful years, therefore, are 1716, 1723, 1730 and 1737; 1751–5 and 1764–75. For these years the figures are reproduced on p. 27, *supra*.

There are a number of reasons for suspecting the accuracy of these figures. In the first place, the London totals begin in 1751 at 119,350 tons, and the highest level they reach before 1775 is 149,694 tons in 1770. As we have already seen, Maitland's *History of London* has a list of London-owned ships, by name, for the year 1732, totalling 178,557 tons; whilst the calculation made here for 1702 gives a total of 140 thousand tons. Secondly, the provision for coasters seems insufficient. The totals are divided (for the outports) into foreign-going, coastal and fishing vessels. The total under coasting is hardly sufficient even to provide for the carrying on of the coastal coal trade,[2] making no allowance at all for other branches of coastal trade.

One explanation of the apparent deficiency, then, may be the refusal to consider the possibility that coasters belonged to London; it is in connection with these statistics that the dogmatic assertion noted above was made, that 'no coasters belong to this port'. Yet the registration returns of 1789 show 26,839 tons of coasters belonging to London.[3] If in fact ten or fifteen thousand tons or more of coasters belonged to London in mid-century or earlier this would go some way towards

[1] Ships carrying goods or men in government service were not recorded in Customs entries or clearances.
[2] According to Nef, op. cit., Vol. II, pp. 380–1, almost exactly a million tons of coal was shipped coastwise from Newcastle and Sunderland in the years 1732–33; to this must be added some 40 thousand tons from other north-eastern ports, and some scores of thousands from South Wales. Little more than half of this great total went to London, and much of the remainder was sent on shorter voyages. We may, then, assume as many as ten voyages per annum for a coaster in the coal trade, taking all branches of it into account. Then at least 110,000 tons of shipping would be required to carry it on. The tonnage of *all* coasters given in BM Add.MSS. 11255 is 109,810 in 1730 and 117,743 in 1737.
[3] B.T. 6–191. This record slightly exaggerates the total; by including some river craft which were registered so that they could go to sea if they wished, and by including all vessels registered up to 30th September 1789, some of which would no longer exist at that date.

DIVERSION OF SHIPPING ROUTES BY THE PRIVATEER MENACE:
A FRENCH VIEW

THE 'CADIZ MERCHANT' IN THE JAMAICA TRADE 1682
from Barlow's Journal

making up the deficiency in the London totals in relation to Maitland's figures, and in the coasting totals in relation to the probable demand for coasters.[1]

There are other sources of deficiency. Maitland's list includes East Indiamen totalling seventeen thousand tons. More than half of these would not have entered or cleared in the year 1732; it is unlikely that an adjustment was made in the totals for these and other ships which remained abroad throughout the year. Moreover, they would all (except those that were smaller) have been recorded at 499 tons; a deficiency of a few thousand tons would arise in this way.

Finally, the 1709–86 figures[2] must be set against those first available from the registration of ships; the total of English-owned ships on 30th September 1788.[3]

	Total		London		Outports	
	No.	Tons	No.	Tons	No.	Tons
1786	7,926	751,626	777	186,121	7,149	565,505
1788	9,375	1,055,299	1,523	315,346	7,852	739,953

Once more, some error in the older London figures is suggested. The number of London ships could not have doubled in two years; and there is no discrepancy in the outport figures which would suggest that registration caused a change in recorded ownerships between outports and London.[4] As to tonnage, the change from tons burden to measured tonnage should not, at this time, have produced any increase and in any case a great many ships were declaring measured tonnage rather than tons burden to the Customs officials in 1786.

There are, then, many reasons for doubting the accuracy of this, the most comprehensive series of shipping statistics available before registration. Nevertheless, they have considerable value; it is unlikely that there are major inconsistencies within the series itself at least before its last decade[5] so for comparisons of progress over the period 1751 to 1786 they may safely be used. When all the different sets of statistics are considered, even if they have to be considered in separate groups,

---

[1] The extent of the deficiency in coasters, if any, is obscure. Many of them would also have engaged in foreign trade during the year; unless there was a consistent policy of recording such ships which engaged in both foreign and coastal trade as coasters rather than foreign-going (and there is no reason why there should have been) the total listed as coasters is bound to be short of the theoretical requirements of coasters.

[2] BM Add.MSS. 11255 ceases to record the figures after 1781, but they can be found thereafter (recorded on the same basis) in Customs 17.

[3] Customs 17–10.

[4] There are great changes in apparent ownership between particular outports, especially on the north-east coast.

[5] The gradual change after 1773 from the recording of tons burden to that of measured tonnage would have begun to make some impact on the totals some years before 1786.

the general conclusions of the argument in the main text are supported; that the growth of the shipping industry was markedly slowed down between the outbreak of the War of the League of Augsburg in 1689 and the end of the War of the Austrian Succession in 1748, and that in mid-century a new growth began, which accelerated in the last years before the War of American Independence.

Appendix B

SOURCES FOR THE HISTORY OF THE
SHIPPING INDUSTRY

Scores of millions of words have been written about English ships and shipping; but serious attempts to account for the growth of the shipping industry and to explain its organisation are very few, and relate almost entirely to the nineteenth and twentieth centuries. C. E. Fayle's excellent little book *A Short History of the World's Shipping Industry* (London, 1933) covers, as its title suggests, all time and all space; its discussion of the English, or indeed the European, industry in our period is very brief, though it packs a great deal of valuable information into its short space. W. F. Lindsay's *History of Merchant Shipping and Ancient Commerce* (London, 4 vols., 1874–5) is very useful for the period of Lindsay's personal recollections, the first sixty years or so of the nineteenth century, but the earlier volumes are a valueless hotchpotch of largely inaccurate information about explorers and privateers. L. A. Harper's *The English Navigation Laws* (New York, 1939) incorporates a long and useful study of the industry the laws were made to protect. Beyond these three works, there is nothing that offers very substantial help. Nor is the industry seriously discussed by writers on trade, or even by the nautical archaeologists. The former, with a handful of exceptions, avoid shipping topics; the latter confine themselves to warships and East Indiamen. Much information about shipping can be picked up incidentally from these works, but they give no general guidance. The seventeenth century saw much discussion of the English and Dutch shipping industries, and there is a good deal to be learned from this largely propagandist literature, which died away soon after 1700. A number of seamen throughout the period wrote of their experiences, in diaries or in later memoirs which have since been published. Books in all these categories have been consulted, and this work owes much to them; they are referred to in the footnotes to the main text. It would be impossible, however, to build any history of the shipping industry on such sources, and there seems little point in producing a bibliography which, extending to many pages, would hardly touch on the sources upon which this book depends.

This book has necessarily been based upon manuscript sources, to which the printed material is merely supplementary. Because the history of the shipping industry will one day be written again, it seems worth while here to set out some comments on the principal classes

of manuscript sources which have been used. I have, I believe, over-
looked only one group of manuscript sources of the first importance —
the local records of the seaports. The next advance in the history of the
merchant marine may well come from the writing of substantial
histories of the ports; there are none now in print.[1]

The principal manuscript sources used can be divided into three
groups:

1. The legal records. Since there are no shipowning firms whose
history goes back to the years before the American Revolution, and
only a limited number of records of merchant houses which throw
light on shipping interests, legal records provide most of the information
on the internal organisation of the shipping industry and its relations
with its customers.

2. Business papers; those which have proved most helpful for the
study of the shipping industry are listed below. Incidental information
has come from others, which are noted in the text.

3. Statistical records. There are very extensive statistics, of great
variety, throwing light on the industry; these collected statistics, and
the sources from which other statistics may be built up, are listed.

These three groups do not exhaust the manuscript evidence used.
Information has come from the State Papers, Domestic; from Colonial
Office papers; from a great number of documents, generally listed
under the heading of naval affairs or trade, in the British Museum
and the Bodleian Library, Oxford. Reference is made to all these in
the text in appropriate places. But from a vast mass of such material,
little has come that is helpful. The structure of this book depends on
the three main groups of sources listed above, and described further
below.

1. *The legal records* (all in the Public Record Office)

In the sixteenth century and much of the seventeenth, nearly every
kind of maritime case came before the High Court of Admiralty. The
most valuable of its series of papers are:

Instance Papers (HCA 15). Running from about 1630, these bundles
contain the documents put into court as evidence and not reclaimed;
thousands of bills of lading, hundreds of bills of sale of ships and
charter parties, a very great number of business letters of every kind
(including many between owners and masters), nearly two hundred
ships' accounts, and a miscellany of other useful documents. From

---

[1] Mr R. C. Jarvis has produced two valuable articles in the *Journal of Transport History*, III, 1957–58; 'Sources for the History of Ports' and 'Sources for
the History of Ships and Shipping'.

1730 onward there are very large numbers of seamen's wages contracts.

Libels and answers (HCA 24). These are the detailed accusations made and the defendants' replies to them, containing long circumstantial descriptions of events leading up to the causes of actions, and often long extracts from contracts and letters. Many documents which should have gone to the Instance papers lodged here; these are the bundles where documentary exhibits before 1630 are usually found.

Examinations (HCA 13) and Interrogatories (HCA 23). These present the evidence brought forward on behalf of plaintiffs and defendants, and amplify, from several different viewpoints, the statements made in Libels and Answers. They are full of entertainment as well as information. In these series, too, documents are occasionally found.[1]

Miscellanea (HCA 30) contains an extremely valuable series of ships' account books and log books.

In the reign of Charles I the opposition of the common law courts to the prerogative courts — of which the High Court of Admiralty was one — came to a head. The Admiralty Court was defended less vigorously than others by the king, who let it be shorn of much of its jurisdiction; on the other hand, since it was clearly not just one of the instruments of royal oppression, the Long Parliament allowed it to survive. From the third decade of the seventeenth century, however, much of its business of a commercial nature — relating to chartering, freight contracts, ownership — was drifting away to other courts. By the end of the century the amount of this work left to it was very limited, and in the eighteenth century it came to spend most of its time on wage claims and collision cases.[2] The commercial quarrels of the shipping industry, and all the information they convey, have to be sought in the eighteenth century in other courts.

It has been possible to examine all the records in the most useful High Court of Admiralty series (those listed above) for the seventeenth and eighteenth centuries down to 1775. The same course cannot be followed with the much vaster Chancery records in which most of the later shipping material would be found, or with the other common law courts. In their tens of thousands of bundles, shipping cases are scattered lightly, and there are few adequate indexes. They have been used when indexes which describe the subject-matter of cases are available, that is:

[1] D. O. Shilton and R. Holworthy have abstracted some examples from this series, in *High Court of Admiralty Examinations, 1637–38* (1932).

[2] On these legal developments, see W. S. Holdsworth, *History of English Law* (1904), Vol. I, pp. 556–8; R. G. Marsden, *Select Pleas in the Court of Admiralty* (Selden Society, 1897), Vol. II, pp. lxxxix–xcviii.

Chancery; the reign of James I and part of that of Charles I (C.2) and a small proportion of the cases of 1660–1714 (C.6) for which the new index to Collins Division (Appendix) is useful.

Court of Exchequer. There is an admirable index of the depositions made in this court (T.134) which include a small number of shipping cases.

Most valuable of all these later records is the great series of documents known as Chancery Masters' Exhibits (C.103 to 114). This corresponds to the Instance Papers of the High Court of Admiralty; it is the collection of documents put into court as evidence and never taken away by its owners, and contains great masses of business correspondence, contracts, account books, etc. It is, in fact, the greatest collection of English business records of the seventeenth, eighteenth and early nineteenth centuries, and naturally contains much shipping material. There is an adequate index to it.

2. *Business papers*

British Museum; Haddock MSS. (Egerton 2521 to 2524) and Johnson MSS. (Add. 22183 to 22189)

Guildhall Library, London. Radcliffe, Bowrey and Peers MSS.

Lloyds, London. This has the bulk of the Bowrey MSS. relating to shipping affairs, and several other collections which are very useful, including excellent sets of bills of lading.

Institute of Chartered Shipbrokers, London. Aylward MSS.

Essex County Record Office, Chelmsford. Braund[1] and Ducane MSS.

Liverpool Public Library. Norris and Okill MSS.

In addition, the records of the great trading companies contain much shipping material; those of the Royal Africa Company and the Levant Company in the Public Record Office (T.70 and S.P.105); of the South Sea Company in the British Museum (Add.MSS. 25567). East India Company records in the Library of the Commonwealth Relations Office contain a mass of shipping data, but I have not used them.

3. *Statistics.* (a) In the Public Record Office:

Lists of ships made by order of the Privy Council at various dates between 1560 and 1629; detailed references to these lists in the State Papers, Domestic are given on pp. 1, 7 and 10, above.

Lists of large ships whose builders received a bounty from the crown, until 1618, in the *Calendars of State Papers, Domestic, passim*; the details for the reign of James I are in SP 38–7/10 and SP 39–1/10.

---

[1] The Braund MSS. are the basis of Miss L. S. Sutherland's book, *A London Merchant, 1695,–1774* (Oxford, 1933).

Trinity House certificates for the supply of ordnance, giving dimensions and tonnage of the ships; these are summarised at the end of each year's proceedings in the *Calendar of State Papers, Domestic,* from 1625 to 1638; details are in SP 16–16/17.

The Port Books (E.190). These list all entries and clearances of ships and goods from the mid-sixteenth century until various dates in the 1780's. There are many gaps; in particular, the London books from 1696 onwards have all been destroyed.

Registers of Mediterranean and other passes issued by the Admiralty. These list, with tonnage, guns and size of crew (and in the later registers with destination) all ships whose owners applied for passes. With the exception of SP 44–49 which refers to ships going into the Baltic between 1676 and 1678, they deal with ships going to southern Europe and across the Atlantic; those for 1662–68 are in Adm. 7–630, and from 1682 onward in Adm. 7–75/103.

Seamen's Sixpences records. The annual summaries (Adm. 68–1 and Adm. 68–89 *et seq.*) provide statistics of the relative development of the various English ports throughout the eighteenth century;[1] the detailed record of collections, available for London only from 1725 (Adm. 68–194/218) gives much information about the ships themselves; a fairly complete record of London shipping could, with much labour, be derived from this.

Colonial Naval Officers' returns. These correspond to the English Port Books; there are many of them scattered through the State Papers, Colonial, of the late seventeenth and early eighteenth century. The chief groups are CO 5–508/11 (South Carolina); 749/50 (Maryland); 848/51 (Massachusetts); 1441/50 (Virginia).

Letters of Marque. The declarations made and bonds given by masters and owners of ships to which these were granted give details of a large number of vessels and their ownership. HCA 25 and HCA 26 contain a fairly complete record of these from 1689, and some earlier data.

Lists of prizes taken in war. The various sources for these are given on pp. 51 and 68, above.

Documents relating to government hire of ships in wartime. These are particularly useful because they often give the dimensions of ships. There are great numbers of them in the State Papers, Domestic, during the periods of the three Dutch wars; and in Adm. 106–3068/72 and Adm. 49–29/34.

High Court of Admiralty, Sales and Appraisements (HCA 4), from which a detailed study of developments in the equipment of ships can be made.

[1] See my article 'Seamen's Sixpences; an Index of Commercial Activity, 6916–1828', *Economica,* n.s., Vol. XXIII, 1956.

Colonial Office papers. The series CO 388 and CO 390 are particularly important, containing many sets of statistics, including those of clearances 1710–14 (CO 388–18), 1715–17 (CO 390–8) and 1718 (CO 390–5).

Board of Trade papers. BT 6 contains many sets of statistics, including, in BT 6–185, tonnage of entries and clearances 1771–3.

Customs Ledgers (Customs 3) give the volume, as well as the value, of trade in each commodity with each country, in English and foreign ships, for every year from 1696 onward. Customs 17 includes the official navigation returns from 1771 onward.

Statistics. (b) Outside the Public Record Office

British Museum Add.MSS. 11255–11256. These two volumes are devoted to statistics of the tonnage of entries and clearances, and of ships owned, at English ports.

Board of Customs and Excise Library; the Liverpool Plantation Registers, 1739–74. These provide, within their limited field, a foretaste of the mass of information on ownership which the General Registry of Shipping has for years after 1786.

INDEX

Radcliffe, 318–19

Ragusa, 2

raisins, 97, 228, 230, 231, 307, 342, 347

Rait, R., 306

Ramsay, G. D., 175

ransom, 69

Ravenna, 340

Rawdon, Marmaduke, 240

Reading, D. K., 211, 218

Reddaway, T. F., 18

Red Sea, 257

Reeves, J., 326

registration of ships, 35, 62, 70, 79, 80, 100, 108, 309

regularity, 195–6, 361–2, 363, 380–2, 386

repairs, 55, 73, 160, 194, 330, 338–9, 344, 346, 352 355, 360, 362, 365, 366–9, 370–1, 376, 386

resin, 307

Rhode Island, 68, 73

rhubarb, 148

rice, 18, 23, 24, 31, 40, 95, 177, 183, 184, 188, 190, 249, 268, 290, 361, 393

Rich, E. E., 132, 373

Richardson, H. E., 374

Richmond, H., 316

Rider, Sir William, 87

rig, *see* sails

Riga, 19, 30, 42, 71, 73, 195, 213, 219, 220–1, 225, 249, 348–9, 357

risk, 48, 87–9, 90, 102–3, 194, 195, 209, 258–9, 318–19, 328, 330–1, 333, 376–7, 382, 386

Robinson, E. F., 163

Rochelle, 210

Rogers, J. E. Thorold, 152, 374

Romano, R., 5

Romenos, John & Irigo, 237

ropemaker, 81, 97

rosin, 19, 308

Rotherhithe, 55

Rotterdam, 202, 207, 20

Rouen, 202, 203

Rowe, W. H., 292

Rowntree, A. S., 64

Royal Exchange, 91, 128, 162–3

Royal Exchange Assurance, 88

Royal Hospital School, Greenwich, 125

rum, 279

Russia, 17, 30–1, 40, 42, 60, 72, 78, 133, 166, 180, 211, 212, 218, 219–222, 223, 225, 226–7, 307

Rutter, 123

Rycaut, Sir Paul, 54

sack ships, 230, 235–8, 239, 240

sailmaker, 81, 112, 113

sails, 44, 46, 49, 75–8, 160

St. Kitts, 172, 267

St. Lawrence River, 292

St. Lucia, 267, 355

St. Petersburg, 31, 42, 71, 73, 219, 220, 221–2, 223, 225, 249

St. Vincent, 267

sale, bill of, 94, 100, 103, 108, 109, 122, 346

Salem, 281, 376

Salisbury, W., 7

Sallee, 96, 353

salt, 28, 38, 48, 185, 187, 204, 219, 224, 225, 229, 234–5, 238, 248–9, 307–9, 340, 350, 392

saltpetre, 186, 257–8, 262

Sambrooke, Sir Jeremy, 260

San Lucar, 228

Santa Cruz, 172

Sardinia, 248

Saunders, Peter, 169

Scammell, G. V., 2

Scanderoon, 247, 251, 252, 254–5, 318–19

Scandinavia, 17, 30, 60, 96

Scarborough, 33, 35, 62, 63, 64–5, 78, 93, 106, 373

schooner, 66, 80

Schreiner, J., 83, 213, 223

Schumpeter, E. B., 175

Scotland, 23, 28, 31, 86, 200, 205, 210, 270, 309–10, 339, 375

Scott, W. R., 102

sea brief, 347–8

seamen, 110–58, 205, 324–6, 389, 390
  conditions of, 113–14, 115 16, 120–121, 126–8, 145–6, 151, 152, 154, 156–8, 205, 313
  earnings of, 133–50, 151–2, 166
  foreign, in English ships, 136, 307–309, 322–4, 326–7, 335–6
  irregularity of employment, 116–17, 128–9, 134, 151, 389
  recruitment and training, 4, 113–21, 151, 153, 203, 322, 325
  wartime, 115, 154, 320–7
  see cargo, crews, master, mate

seasonality, *see* cargo

Seine, 69

Selby, 373

servants, indentured, 149, 150

Setubal (St. Uves), 225, 325, 350

Severn, 80

Seville, 2, 228, 229, 23

Shadwell, 55, 153

shallop, 46, 111

shares, *see* parts

Shaw, Sir John, 52

sheathing, 160

Sheffield, Lord, 21, 374, 375